CORPORATE FINANCE

Mohamed Amine Hamdani

Toronto Academic Press

Table of Contents

3 INTEREST RATES 67

4 DISCOUNTED CASH FLOW (DCF) ANALYSIS 109

8 RISK AND THE COST OF CAPITAL 263

9 CORPORATE CAPITAL STRUCTURE 307

List of Figures

List of Tables

PREFACE

Financial markets around the world have become more accessible than ever before, allowing investors and corporations to engage in cross-border transactions with unprecedented ease. However, despite this increased accessibility, each country operates within its unique framework of financial, accounting, legal, and fiscal systems, and adheres to its own cultural norms. This diversity raises an important question: can we apply the same corporate finance concepts universally when we cross borders?

This book aims to address this question by introducing students to the intricacies of corporate financial decision-making within an international context. It focuses on the most critical financial decisions that corporations make, including capital structure, risk management, capital raising, and mergers and acquisitions. Each of these decisions is explored through the lens of global challenges such as political and exchange rate risks, and the varying standards of corporate governance across different countries.

Throughout the book, students will gain a comprehensive understanding of the legal frameworks that govern firms in different jurisdictions, as well as technical skills in valuation and risk management techniques. These topics are essential for navigating the complexities of international finance, where financial decisions are influenced by a multitude of external factors that do not exist in a purely domestic setting.

The overarching aim of this book is to equip students with the key concepts in international corporate finance, enabling them to develop and implement effective strategies in global finance and investment. Corporate finance is a vital discipline as it empowers corporations to manage their financial risks. For instance, by hedging against fluctuations in the stock market or interest rates, companies can stabilize their financial performance. Additionally, enterprises can mitigate their exposure to currency risk, safeguarding their operations from adverse exchange rate movements.

In the long run, mastering corporate finance provides businesses with the necessary tools to make sound financial decisions that foster growth and ensure long-term success. By understanding how to apply these principles in an international context, students will be better prepared to navigate the global financial landscape, make informed decisions, and contribute to the financial stability and prosperity of the corporations they serve.

Content/Structure of the Book

This book offers a comprehensive exploration of corporate finance, meticulously structured into 10 chapters that cover the fundamental concepts and advanced topics essential for understanding and applying financial principles in a corporate setting. Each chapter is designed to build on the previous one, ensuring a cohesive and thorough learning experience.

Chapter 1 provides a foundational overview of corporate finance. It discusses the role and objectives of corporate finance, emphasizing the importance of financial management in achieving corporate goals. Key topics include the financial environment, the functions of financial markets, and the relationship between corporate finance and other business disciplines.

Chapter 2 introduces the critical concept of the time value of money (TVM), which is fundamental to all areas of finance. It explains why money today is worth more than money in the future and covers essential calculations, including present and future value, annuities, and perpetuities. Practical applications in investment and financing decisions are also explored.

Chapter 3 is focused on the nature and determinants of interest rates. It examines the various types of interest rates, including nominal, real, and effective rates, and explains how they are influenced by factors such as inflation, monetary policy, and economic conditions. The chapter also covers the term structure of interest rates and yield curves.

In Chapter 4, students learn about Discounted Cash Flow (DCF) analysis, a core valuation method in corporate finance. It explains how to forecast cash flows and discount them to their present value to assess the value of an investment. The chapter includes detailed examples and case studies to illustrate the application of DCF in real-world scenarios.

Chapter 5 focuses on measuring and evaluating the return on investment (ROI). It covers various metrics used to assess the profitability of investments, including net present value (NPV), internal rate of return (IRR), and profitability index (PI). The chapter also discusses the importance of comparing ROI across different projects and investments.

Chapter 6 provides an in-depth analysis of fixed income securities, including bonds and other debt instruments. It covers the characteristics of fixed income securities, valuation techniques, and the factors that influence bond prices and yields. The chapter also explores credit risk and the role of rating agencies.

Chapter 7 examines the methods used to value equity securities. It covers dividend discount models (DDM), free cash flow to equity (FCFE) models, and price multiples. The chapter provides practical insights into how investors and analysts determine the intrinsic value of stocks and make informed investment decisions.

Chapter 8 addresses the concepts of risk and return, and their implications for the cost of capital. It explores the different types of risks faced by investors and companies, including systematic and unsystematic risk. The chapter also discusses how to estimate the cost of equity and the weighted average cost of capital (WACC).

Chapter 9 focuses on corporate capital structure, examining how companies finance their operations through a mix of debt and equity. It discusses the theories of capital structure, including the Modigliani-Miller theorem, trade-off theory, and pecking order theory. The chapter also explores the impact of leverage on a company's risk and return.

The final chapter focuses on the strategies and tools used in risk management. It covers the identification, assessment, and mitigation of financial risks, including market risk, credit risk, and operational risk. The chapter also discusses the use of financial derivatives, such as options, futures, and swaps, in managing risk.

Together, these 10 chapters provide a robust framework for understanding and applying corporate finance principles. The book is designed to equip students and professionals with the knowledge and skills necessary to make informed financial decisions, manage corporate resources effectively, and achieve long-term business success.

Audience

This book is an essential read for a diverse audience ranging from students and academics to professionals in the financial sector. It serves as a comprehensive guide for undergraduate and graduate students pursuing degrees in finance, business administration, and economics, providing them with foundational concepts and advanced theories necessary for mastering corporate finance. Additionally, it is an invaluable resource for academics and researchers seeking to deepen their understanding of financial management principles and practices.

Professionals in the field of finance, including financial analysts, corporate managers, investment bankers, and consultants, will find this book a practical tool for enhancing their decision-making skills and strategic financial planning. The book's thorough exploration of financial concepts such as capital budgeting, risk management, mergers and acquisitions, and corporate governance makes it a must-have reference for those involved in financial decision-making and policy formulation.

Furthermore, the book is beneficial for policy makers and regulatory bodies who need to stay informed about the latest trends and developments in corporate finance to craft effective financial regulations and policies. Overall, this book is tailored to meet the needs of anyone interested in gaining a comprehensive understanding of corporate finance and its applications in the real world.

Learning Features

- Start-of-chapter learning objectives
- Key terms in each chapter
- Summary Points at the end of each chapter
- Review Questions at the end of each chapter
- Case Studies and Activities in each chapter for solving real problems
- References at the end of each chapter

CHAPTER

1 Introduction to Corporate Finance

LEARNING OBJECTIVES

After studying this chapter, you will be able to:

- Understand the overview of corporate finance;
- Discus elements of corporate finance; and
- Explain the types of corporate finance.

KEY TERMS FROM THIS CHAPTER

- Capital budgeting
- Cash flow analysis
- Corporate restructuring
- Corporate valuation
- Debt financing
- Equity financing
- Financial leverage
- Financial reporting
- Capital structure
- Corporate governance
- Corporate strategy
- Cost of capital
- Dividend policy
- Financial analysis
- Financial markets
- Initial public offering (IPO)

INTRODUCTION

Corporate finance is a fundamental aspect of business that deals with the financial activities related to running a corporation. It encompasses a broad range of decisions, processes, and strategies designed to enhance the value of a company to its shareholders while ensuring the firm's long-term sustainability. The primary objective of corporate finance is to maximize shareholder value through strategic financial planning, investment decisions, and the efficient management of financial resources. This field involves analyzing and managing financial risks, securing funding for business operations and growth, and making informed decisions on capital expenditures, mergers, acquisitions, and other strategic initiatives. A critical component of corporate finance is capital budgeting, which involves evaluating potential investment opportunities and deciding which projects or assets the company should invest in. This process requires a thorough analysis of potential returns and risks, using techniques such as net present value (NPV), internal rate of return (IRR), and payback period calculations. Additionally, corporate finance professionals must manage the company's capital structure, balancing debt and equity to optimize the cost of capital and ensure financial stability. This involves making decisions about issuing new equity, taking on debt, repurchasing shares, and managing dividends.

Another essential area within corporate finance is working capital management, which focuses on managing the company's short-term assets and liabilities to ensure sufficient liquidity for day-to-day operations. This includes optimizing cash flow, managing receivables and payables, and maintaining an adequate level of inventory. Effective working capital management helps prevent liquidity crises and supports smooth business operations. Corporate finance also involves strategic financial planning, where long-term financial goals are set and strategies are developed to achieve these goals. This includes forecasting future financial performance, conducting financial analysis, and making strategic decisions about resource allocation. By integrating financial planning with overall business strategy, companies can better navigate economic challenges, capitalize on opportunities, and achieve sustainable growth.

1.1. OVERVIEW OF CORPORATE FINANCE

Corporate finance plays a vital role in every business. Irrespective of the size or type of business operations, every company seeks to streamline its corporate financing arm for optimal wealth distribution and return generation. Considering these factors, this extends to an array of financing and investment decisions that cover four primary aspects:

- Planning finances
- Raising funds
- Investing
- Monitoring

Corporate finance is a field that focuses on managing financial resources and investments within a corporation. It involves making strategic decisions to maximize shareholder value while balancing risks and returns. Key areas of corporate finance include capital budgeting, which involves analyzing investment opportunities; capital structure, which determines the mix of debt and equity financing; and dividend policy, which determines how profits are distributed to shareholders. Corporate finance professionals also evaluate mergers and acquisitions, manage working capital, and assess the financial health of the organization. Overall, corporate finance plays a crucial role in driving business growth, profitability, and sustainability. (Roberts Richard, 2008).

1.1.1. How Does Corporate Finance Work

Corporate finance operates by employing various financial principles and techniques to manage a company's financial activities. It involves assessing investment opportunities, estimating their potential returns, and conducting financial analysis to guide decision-making. Corporate finance professionals determine the optimal mix of debt and equity financing to fund operations and projects, taking into account factors such as risk, cost of capital, and financial leverage.

They also engage in financial planning, forecasting, and budgeting to ensure effective resource allocation. Additionally, corporate finance involves evaluating and managing financial risks through strategies like hedging and insurance. Ultimately, the goal of corporate finance is to maximize shareholder value by making informed financial decisions that align with the company's strategic objectives.

- **Examples of Corporate Finance:** Corporate finance has many arms, each requiring different input to control how businesses, markets, assets, investors, and financial institutions interact. Examples of corporate finance activities include:
    - o **Growth Planning Strategies:** Businesses must create a plan for future growth. That involves expanding into new markets, increasing capacity,

or launching new products.

- o **Risk Management:** This involves identifying and addressing the operational and financial opportunities available, as well as market risks.
- o **Finance Management:** A company must implement measures to manage its financial resources efficiently and effectively. As such, it must create financial plans, make wise investment decisions, and monitor cash flow.

1.1.2. Corporate Finance Principles

Corporate finance is a critical area of finance dealing with the financial decisions that businesses make and the tools and analysis used to make these decisions. Below are the key principles of corporate finance:

1. **Time Value of Money (TVM):** The time value of money is the concept that money available today is worth more than the same amount in the future due to its earning potential. This principle underlies various financial decisions, including investment analysis, loan structuring, and retirement planning.
2. **Risk and Return:** Investors expect to be compensated for the risk they take. The greater the risk of an investment, the higher the expected return. This principle helps in making decisions regarding investment opportunities, portfolio management, and capital budgeting.
3. **Cash Flow is King:** Cash flow, not accounting profit, is the primary focus. Financial decisions should be evaluated based on the projected cash flows they generate. Positive cash flows are essential for maintaining operations and financing growth.
4. **Market Efficiency:** The market efficiency principle suggests that financial markets are "informationally efficient," meaning that asset prices reflect all available information. This impacts corporate strategies, such as timing of stock issues or repurchases and mergers and acquisitions.
5. **Agency Problem:** The agency problem arises when there's a conflict of interest between the management (agents) and the shareholders (principals). Solutions include aligning incentives, implementing performance-based compensation, and improving corporate governance.
6. **Capital Structure:** The mix of debt and equity financing affects a company's risk and value. The optimal capital structure minimizes the cost of capital and maximizes the firm's value. This involves trade-offs between the tax benefits of debt and the increased bankruptcy risk.
7. **Dividend Policy:** Decisions about whether to return cash to shareholders through dividends or share buybacks versus retaining and reinvesting in the business. This depends on the company's growth opportunities, liquidity needs, and shareholder preferences.
8. **Valuation Principle:** The value of an asset is determined by the present

value of its expected future cash flows, discounted at an appropriate rate reflecting the risk of those cash flows. This principle is crucial in valuation methods such as Net Present Value (NPV), Internal Rate of Return (IRR), and Discounted Cash Flow (DCF) analysis.

9. **Cost of Capital:** The cost of capital is the return required by those who provide capital, such as equity investors and debt holders. It serves as a benchmark for evaluating investment projects. The weighted average cost of capital (WACC) is often used to assess the attractiveness of potential investments.

1.1.3. Benefits of Corporate Finance

Here are some of the major benefits of corporate financing.

1. **Efficient Business Operations:** Well-planned corporate finance ensures that your business' finances are in top shape and capital allocation is streamlined effectively.

   This means that your loans are cleared on time, you are able to buy raw materials as required, employee salaries are paid on time, new product launches go as planned, and marketing efforts for said new products, as well as the existing ones, are well-budgeted.

2. **Research and Development:** Market and product research requires considerable funding resources, both material and human, to be conducted effectively. Running out of funding at any point during the process would mean a lot of work and work hours going to waste. Well-planned corporate finance would help ensure steady financial support for research efforts that ultimately help your business succeed.

3. **Keeps Expansion Plans on Track:** Modern techniques and equipment are necessary for the diversification and expansion of an enterprise. Planning your corporate finance in advance will ensure that you have a steady flow of funds to acquire future-forward technology and equipment for your business.

4. **Operation Management:** Corporate finance plays a vital role in the coordination and control of various activities in an enterprise. For instance, your production will drop if the finance department does not offer sufficient finance to buy raw materials and meet other daily financial needs for running the production unit smoothly. This would further make sales suffer, and eventually, affect your profits.

5. **Timely Payment of Fees & Taxes:** Your organization needs to pay taxes to the government, which includes Goods and Service Tax (GST) and Income Tax. You may also be required to pay fees to the Registrar of Companies. Accounting for these while planning your corporate finance helps pay these fees and taxes.

6. **Risk Management:** Your company needs to manage several risks like a loss because of natural calamity, sudden drop in sales, loss due to strikes, etc. Provisioning for these while planning your corporate finance proves to help manage such risks.

7. **Streamlined Asset Allocation:** Well-planned corporate finance helps you keep funds handy for the replacement of fixed assets that get worn out over the years.
8. **Interest and Dividend Payments:** The right amount and timely arranged corporate finance help companies pay interest to banks or creditors as well as dividends to shareholders in a timely and efficient manner.
9. **Improves Decision-Making:** A majority of the vital business decisions in organizations are determined by considering fund availability. Performing any function independently without finance is challenging in an enterprise.

1.2. ELEMENTS OF CORPORATE FINANCE

Indeed, capital budgeting, capital structure, working capital management, and dividend distribution are central elements of corporate finance. Here's a brief explanation of each:

1.2.1. Capital Budgeting

Capital budgeting refers to the process by which businesses make decisions about long-term investments in projects, machinery, equipment, and other assets. These decisions are crucial as they involve substantial financial commitments and impact the company's future profitability and growth. Capital budgeting aims to answer questions such as whether to invest in new equipment, expand operations, develop new products, or acquire another company (Cassis Youssef, 2006).

Key Steps in Capital Budgeting:

1. Identification of Investment Opportunities:
   - Businesses first identify potential projects or investments that align with their strategic objectives. These opportunities may arise from research and development, market demand, technological advancements, or competitive pressures.
2. Estimation of Cash Flows:
   - Once potential investments are identified, the next step is to estimate the cash flows associated with each project over its lifespan. Cash flows include initial investment outlay, operating cash inflows, and terminal cash flows from asset disposal.
3. Risk Assessment:
   - Assessing the risk associated with each investment is critical. Factors such as economic conditions, market demand volatility, technological obsolescence, and competitive pressures need to be considered. Techniques like sensitivity analysis, scenario analysis, and simulation can help quantify and manage risk.
4. Selection of Evaluation Techniques:
   - Various evaluation techniques are used to assess the attractiveness of investments. These include:
     - **Net Present Value (NPV):** Calculates the present value of expected cash flows minus the initial investment.

- o **Internal Rate of Return (IRR):** Determines the discount rate that makes the present value of cash inflows equal to the initial investment.
- o **Payback Period:** Measures the time it takes to recover the initial investment.
- o **Profitability Index (PI):** Compares the present value of future cash flows to the initial investment.
- o **Accounting Rate of Return (ARR):** Calculates average accounting profit as a percentage of the average investment.

5. Decision Making:
    - Based on the results from the evaluation techniques and risk assessment, management makes a decision whether to accept or reject the investment proposal. Investments with positive NPV or IRR greater than the cost of capital are generally accepted, while those with negative NPV or insufficient IRR may be rejected.

1.2.1.1. Challenges in Capital Budgeting

Capital budgeting faces several challenges, including:

- **Forecasting Cash Flows:** Estimating future cash flows accurately can be difficult, especially for long-term projects or in uncertain economic conditions.
- **Risk Assessment:** Quantifying and incorporating risk into decision-making can be subjective and challenging.
- **Selection of Discount Rate:** Choosing an appropriate discount rate (cost of capital) that reflects the project's risk and opportunity cost can impact the evaluation results.
- **Intangible Benefits and Costs:** Some benefits (e.g., brand enhancement) and costs (e.g., environmental impact) are difficult to quantify and incorporate into traditional financial metrics.

1.2.1.2. Real-World Applications and Examples

Capital budgeting is applied across various industries and scenarios:

- **Manufacturing:** Deciding whether to invest in new production equipment to increase efficiency and reduce costs.
- **Technology:** Evaluating the development of a new software product based on market demand and technological feasibility.
- **Retail:** Assessing the profitability of opening new stores in different geographic regions based on demographic trends and competitive landscape.
- **Infrastructure:** Determining whether to invest in upgrading transportation networks or utilities to meet growing demand.

1.2.2. Capital Structure

Capital structure refers to the composition of a company's total financing in terms of debt and equity. It is a critical decision for firms because it affects their risk profile, cost of capital, and ultimately their valuation and ability to grow. This essay explores various aspects of capital structure, including theories, factors influencing decisions, empirical evidence, and practical considerations.

1.2.2.1. Theoretical Perspectives on Capital Structure

1. **Modigliani-Miller Theorem:** The Modigliani-Miller (MM) theorem, proposed by Franco Modigliani and Merton Miller in 1958, provides a foundational theoretical framework for understanding capital structure. It posits that, under ideal conditions (perfect markets without taxes, transaction costs, or information asymmetries), the value of a firm is independent of its capital structure. This theorem comes in two propositions:
   1. Proposition I (without taxes): The total market value of a firm is equal to the value of its assets, regardless of the mix of debt and equity used to finance those assets.
   2. Proposition II (with taxes): Introducing corporate taxes, MM argue that the value of a levered firm (with debt) exceeds that of an unlevered firm (without debt) by the present value of the tax shield on debt.
2. **Trade-Off Theory:** The trade-off theory of capital structure suggests that firms weigh the benefits of debt (interest tax shields, financial flexibility) against the costs (bankruptcy risk, agency costs, financial distress). The optimal capital structure, according to this theory, balances these costs and benefits to maximize the firm's value.
3. **Pecking Order Theory:** Proposed by Myers and Majluf in 1984, the pecking order theory asserts that firms prefer internal financing (retained earnings) over external financing (debt and equity). When external financing is necessary, firms prefer debt over equity to avoid signaling adverse information to investors.
4. **Agency Costs and Capital Structure:** Agency costs arise from conflicts of interest between shareholders (principals) and managers (agents). Debt can help align these interests by imposing discipline on managers (through debt covenants) and reducing free cash flows that managers might misallocate.
5. Factors Influencing Capital Structure Decisions
   1. **Financial Flexibility:** Financial flexibility refers to a firm's ability to raise funds quickly and at a reasonable cost when opportunities arise. Companies with more stable cash flows and access to diverse funding sources can afford higher leverage.
   2. **Industry Characteristics:** Industries with stable cash flows (like utilities) can support higher debt levels compared to those with volatile earnings (like technology startups). Regulatory constraints and industry norms also influence capital structure choices.
   3. **Growth Opportunities:** Firms with growth opportunities may use more equity financing

to preserve financial flexibility and avoid excessive debt that could constrain future investment.

iv. **Tax Considerations:** Interest payments on debt are tax-deductible, making debt financing attractive for firms in high-tax jurisdictions. This tax shield lowers the effective cost of debt and influences firms' capital structure decisions.

v. **Market Conditions:** Access to debt and equity markets, as well as prevailing interest rates, affect a firm's cost of capital and its optimal capital structure. Economic cycles and market sentiment also impact financing decisions.

6. **Empirical Evidence on Capital Structure:** Empirical studies provide insights into how real-world firms determine their capital structures:

   i. **Pecking Order vs. Trade-Off Theory:** Empirical research generally supports the pecking order theory, showing that firms prefer internal funds first, followed by debt and then equity issuance.

   ii. **Influence of Taxes:** Firms in high-tax jurisdictions tend to have higher leverage ratios, reflecting the tax advantages of debt financing.

   iii. **Industry Variations:** Capital structures vary significantly across industries, with capital-intensive sectors (like utilities and telecom) relying more on debt.

   iv. **Market Conditions:** During economic downturns, firms may reduce leverage to strengthen their balance sheets and improve financial stability.

7. Practical Considerations in Capital Structure Management

   i. **Risk Management:** Balancing debt and equity to manage financial risk is crucial. Techniques include stress testing, scenario analysis, and maintaining liquidity buffers to withstand economic shocks.

   ii. **Cost of Capital:** The cost of capital reflects the overall cost of financing a firm's operations. It comprises the cost of equity and the after-tax cost of debt, weighted by their respective proportions in the capital structure.

   iii. **Capital Structure Ratios:** Key ratios such as debt-to-equity ratio, debt-to-capital ratio, and interest coverage ratio provide insights into a firm's leverage and ability to meet its financial obligations.

   iv. **Capital Structure and Firm Valuation:** Optimal capital structure enhances firm value by minimizing the cost of capital and maximizing shareholder returns. Valuation methods such as discounted cash flow (DCF) analysis incorporate the effects of capital structure decisions on future cash flows.

1.2.3. Working Capital

Working capital estimates are derived from the array of assets and liabilities on a corporate balance sheet. By only looking at immediate debts and offsetting them with the most liquid of assets, a company can better understand what sort of liquidity it has in the near future.

Working capital is also a measure of a company's operational efficiency and short-term financial health. If a company has substantial positive NWC, then it could have the potential to invest in expansion and grow the company. If a company's current assets do not exceed its current liabilities, then it may have trouble growing or paying back creditors. It might even go bankrupt.

1. Components of Working Capital
   i. **Current Assets:** Detail the types of current assets (cash, accounts receivable, inventory, etc.), their liquidity, and how they contribute to working capital.
   ii. **Current Liabilities:** Explain various types of current liabilities (accounts payable, short-term loans, accrued expenses, etc.) and their impact on working capital.
2. Importance of Working Capital
   i. **Liquidity and Solvency:** Discuss how adequate working capital ensures a company can meet its short-term financial obligations.
   ii. **Operational Efficiency:** Explore how efficient working capital management enhances operational capabilities and reduces financial risks.
   iii. **Investor Confidence:** Explain how investors and stakeholders perceive a company with strong working capital management practices.
3. Management of Working Capital
   i. **Strategies for Working Capital Management:** Discuss various approaches (conservative, aggressive, moderate) and their implications on liquidity and profitability.
   ii. **Tools and Techniques:** Detail specific tools like cash flow forecasting, inventory management systems, and receivables management strategies.
   iii. **Challenges and Risks:** Address common challenges in working capital management (cash flow fluctuations, seasonal demand changes, etc.) and how to mitigate associated risks.
4 Impact of Working Capital on Business Operations
   i. **Industry-Specific Considerations:** Analyze how working capital requirements vary across industries (e.g., manufacturing vs. service sectors).
   ii. **Case Studies:** Provide examples of companies with effective or ineffective working capital management and their outcomes.
5. Financial Analysis and Metrics
   i. **Key Performance Indicators (KPIs):** Discuss metrics such as current ratio, quick ratio, and days sales outstanding (DSO) in evaluating working capital efficiency.
   ii. **Benchmarking:** Compare industry standards and best practices for working capital management.

6. Strategic Considerations
   i. **Long-Term vs. Short-Term Financing:** Evaluate the balance between using short-term loans versus long-term debt for financing working capital needs.
   ii. **Capital Structure:** Discuss how working capital decisions impact a company's overall capital structure and financial flexibility.
7. Global Perspectives and Trends
   i. **International Business:** Consider how multinational corporations manage working capital across diverse markets and currencies.
   ii. **Technological Innovations:** Explore the role of fintech and automation in optimizing working capital processes.

1.2.4. Dividend Distribution

Dividends represent a portion of a company's earnings that is distributed to its shareholders as a return on their investment. This distribution can be in the form of cash, additional shares of stock, or other assets. Dividends are typically paid regularly, often quarterly, and are a key factor in determining the total return on investment for shareholders.

1. Types of Dividends
   i. **Cash Dividends:** The most common form, where shareholders receive cash payments directly into their accounts.
   ii. **Stock Dividends:** Instead of cash, shareholders receive additional shares of the company's stock. This is typically expressed as a percentage increase in the number of shares owned.
   iii. **Property Dividends:** Shareholders receive assets other than cash or stock, such as products manufactured by the company.
2. Reasons for Distributing Dividends
   i. **Return of Profits:** Companies distribute dividends as a way to share their profits directly with shareholders.
   ii. **Signal of Financial Health:** Regular dividend payments signal financial stability and confidence in future earnings.
   iii. **Attracting Investors:** Dividends can attract income-focused investors who seek a steady stream of income.
   iv. **Tax Efficiency:** In some jurisdictions, dividends may be taxed at a lower rate than other forms of income, making them attractive to investors.
3. Methods of Dividend Distribution
   i. **Declaration Date:** The date on which the company's board of directors announces the upcoming dividend payment.
   ii. **Ex-Dividend Date:** Investors must own the stock by this date to receive the dividend. If purchased after this date, the dividend goes to the seller.
   iii. **Record Date:** The date on which the company determines which shareholders are entitled to receive the dividend.
   iv. **Payment Date:** The actual date on which dividend payments are made to eligible shareholders.

4. Dividend Policy
   i. **Residual Dividend Policy:** Companies pay dividends from residual earnings after covering all capital expenditures and other obligations.
   ii. **Stable Dividend Policy:** Companies aim to pay a steady dividend amount regardless of fluctuations in earnings.
   iii. **Constant Payout Ratio Policy:** Companies pay out a fixed percentage of earnings as dividends, resulting in fluctuating dividend payments.
5. Factors Influencing Dividend Policy
   i. **Profitability: Companies** with stable and predictable earnings are more likely to adopt a consistent dividend policy.
   ii. **Investment Opportunities:** Companies may retain earnings instead of paying dividends if they have profitable investment opportunities.
   iii. **Legal Constraints:** Some countries have regulations limiting the amount of dividends that can be paid out.
   iv. **Shareholder Preferences:** Companies may consider shareholder expectations and desires for income when formulating dividend policies.
6. **Dividend Yield:** Dividend yield is a financial ratio that shows how much a company pays out in dividends each year relative to its share price. It is calculated as:

$$\text{Dividend Yield} = \frac{\text{Annual Dividends per Share}}{\text{Stock Price per Share}} \times 100\%$$

7. **Dividend Reinvestment Plans (DRIPs):** DRIPs allow shareholders to reinvest their dividends into additional shares of the company's stock, often at a discounted price. This can compound investment returns over time.
8. **Taxation of Dividends:** Dividends are typically taxed differently from ordinary income. In many jurisdictions, they benefit from preferential tax treatment, either at a reduced rate or with certain exemptions.
9. Dividend Payment Issues
   i. **Cash Flow Concerns:** Companies may face liquidity issues that prevent them from paying dividends as planned.
   ii. **Legal and Regulatory Issues:** Companies must comply with various legal and regulatory requirements when declaring and paying dividends.
   iii. **Shareholder Expectations:** Failure to meet expected dividend payments can lead to dissatisfaction among shareholders and impact stock price.
10. Dividend Policy and Stock Valuation
    i. **Dividend Discount Model (DDM):** A method for valuing a stock based on the present value of its expected future dividend payments.
    ii. **Impact on Stock Price:** Changes in dividend policy can influence investor perceptions of a company's stability and growth potential, thereby affecting stock price.

1.3. TYPES OF CORPORATE FINANCE

Here are the types of corporate financing.

1.3.1. Equity Financing

Equity financing is the process of raising capital through the sale of shares in a company. Companies can secure funding by offering ownership stakes to investors, who in return expect future returns on their investment through dividends and capital gains. This form of financing is particularly crucial for startups and growing businesses that might find it challenging to secure traditional debt financing due to a lack of credit history or collateral (Jensen Michael & Smith Clifford, 2000).

1. **Mechanisms of Equity Financing:** The mechanisms of equity financing involve several key steps:
   - i. **Issuance of Shares:** Companies issue shares to investors, which represent ownership in the company. These shares can be common or preferred stock.
   - ii. **Pricing of Shares:** The price at which shares are sold is determined through various methods, such as book building, fixed pricing, or auctions.
   - iii. **Regulatory Compliance:** Companies must comply with regulatory requirements, including those set by the Securities and Exchange Commission (SEC) in the United States, which govern the issuance and sale of securities.
   - iv. **Investor Relations:** Maintaining transparent and effective communication with investors is crucial to build trust and attract further investment.
2. Types of Equity Financing
   - i. **Seed Capital**: Initial funding used to start a business, often sourced from the founders, friends, and family.
   - ii. **Angel Investment**: Early-stage funding from affluent individuals who support startups with high growth potential.
   - iii. **Venture Capital**: Funding provided by venture capital firms to startups and small businesses with long-term growth potential.
   - iv. **Initial Public Offering (IPO)**: The process through which a private company becomes publicly traded by offering shares to the public.
   - v. **Secondary Offerings**: Additional shares sold by a company that is already publicly traded.
3. **Advantages of Equity Financing:** Equity financing offers several advantages:

i. **No Repayment Obligation:** Unlike debt financing, equity does not require regular repayments. This alleviates pressure on cash flow and allows companies to invest more freely in growth opportunities.

ii. **Risk Sharing:** Investors share the business risks, as their returns are tied to the company's performance. This can be particularly beneficial for startups and high-risk ventures.

iii. **Improved Creditworthiness:** Equity financing can improve a company's balance sheet by reducing leverage, making it easier to obtain debt financing in the future.

iv. **Access to Expertise:** Equity investors, particularly venture capitalists and angel investors, often bring valuable expertise, networks, and mentorship to the companies they invest in.

4. **Disadvantages of Equity Financing:** Despite its benefits, equity financing has some drawbacks:

i. **Dilution of Ownership:** Issuing new shares dilutes the ownership stake of existing shareholders, which can lead to a loss of control for original owners.

ii. **Cost:** Equity financing can be more expensive than debt due to the need to share future profits and the higher returns expected by equity investors.

iii. **Regulatory Scrutiny:** Public companies face stringent regulatory requirements, including financial reporting and disclosure obligations, which can be costly and time-consuming.

iv. **Investor Pressure:** Investors may exert significant influence over business decisions, potentially leading to conflicts with the company's management or founders.

1.3.2. Debt Financing

Debt financing refers to the method of raising funds through borrowing. Unlike equity financing, where funds are raised in exchange for ownership shares, debt financing involves the commitment to repay the borrowed amount over time, along with interest. This repayment is often structured in regular installments, although the specifics can vary significantly depending on the type of debt instrument used.

1.3.2.1. Types of Debt Financing

- **Short-Term Debt:** Short-term debt typically refers to financial obligations that are due within one year. Examples include:
  - o **Commercial Paper:** Unsecured, short-term promissory notes issued by companies.
  - o **Lines of Credit:** Flexible borrowing facilities provided by banks or financial institutions.
  - o **Trade Credit:** Deferred payment terms extended by suppliers.
- **Long-Term Debt:** Long-term debt comprises obligations that extend beyond one year. Examples include:
  - o **Term Loans:** Loans from banks

or financial institutions with a set repayment schedule.

- o **Bonds:** Debt securities issued by corporations or governments to investors.
- o **Mortgages:** Loans secured by real estate, typically repaid over 15–30 years.

- Secured vs. Unsecured Debt
  - o Secured Debt: Loans backed by collateral, reducing the lender's risk (e.g., mortgages, auto loans).
  - o Unsecured Debt: Loans without collateral, carrying higher risk for the lender and typically higher interest rates (e.g., credit card debt, personal loans).

1.3.2.2. Mechanisms of Debt Financing

- **Loans:** Loans are the most straightforward form of debt financing, where a lender provides a borrower with a specified amount of money under agreed terms of repayment, including interest rates and maturity dates.
- **Bonds:** Bonds are debt securities that entities (such as corporations or governments) issue to investors. Bondholders receive periodic interest payments and the principal amount at maturity. Bonds can be classified into various types, such as:
  - o **Government Bonds:** Issued by national governments.
  - o **Corporate Bonds:** Issued by companies.
  - o **Municipal Bonds:** Issued by local governments.
- **Lines of Credit:** A line of credit provides flexible access to funds up to a pre-approved limit, allowing borrowers to draw and repay as needed within the agreed terms. It is particularly useful for managing short-term liquidity needs.
- **Trade Credit:** Trade credit is an arrangement where suppliers allow buyers to purchase goods or services on account, deferring payment to a later date. This form of financing is commonly used in business-to-business transactions.

1.3.2.3. The Role of Interest Rates

Interest rates are a crucial element of debt financing, representing the cost of borrowing. They can be fixed or variable:

- **Fixed Interest Rates:** Remain constant throughout the life of the loan, providing predictability.
- **Variable Interest Rates:** Fluctuate based on market conditions, potentially leading to higher or lower costs over time.

Central banks influence interest rates through monetary policy, impacting the cost and availability of debt financing.

1.3.2.4. Advantages of Debt Financing

- **Retained Ownership:** Debt financing allows businesses to raise capital without diluting ownership. Shareholders maintain control and share in future profits without giving up equity.
- **Tax Benefits:** Interest payments on debt are typically tax-deductible, reducing the overall tax burden for businesses and making debt a tax-efficient way to raise capital.

- **Predictability:** Debt agreements specify repayment schedules, making cash flow planning easier. This predictability helps businesses manage their finances effectively.

1.3.2.5. Disadvantages of Debt Financing

- **Repayment Obligation:** Debt must be repaid regardless of the business's financial performance. Failure to meet repayment terms can lead to default and potential bankruptcy.
- **Impact on Cash Flow:** Regular interest and principal payments can strain cash flow, especially for businesses with inconsistent revenue streams.
- **Credit Risk:** High levels of debt increase the risk of financial distress. Lenders assess credit risk, and high leverage can lead to higher interest rates or difficulty obtaining additional financing.

1.3.3. Venture Capital

Venture capital firms pool funds from various sources, including institutional investors and high-net-worth individuals, to invest in high-risk, high-reward startups. These firms provide capital in exchange for equity, or an ownership stake, in the companies they invest in. The goal of VC is to generate substantial returns through the growth and eventual exit of the invested companies, typically via an initial public offering (IPO) or acquisition.

1. **Types of Venture Capital**

- Seed Capital:
  - o This is the earliest stage of venture funding. It is typically a small amount of capital provided to an entrepreneur to prove a concept. Seed funding supports initial market research and product development.
- Startup Capital:
  - o Startup capital is used to fund companies that have completed the seed stage but need more funds to develop and market their products. This stage focuses on scaling the business model and expanding the team.
- Early-Stage Capital:
  - o Early-stage capital is for companies that have a developed product and a business model but require further funding to increase their market share. This stage includes Series A and Series B funding rounds.
- Expansion Capital (Growth Capital):
  - o This is for more mature companies looking to expand or enter new markets. It helps in scaling operations, entering new geographical areas, or developing new products. This stage typically includes Series C and beyond funding rounds.
- Late-Stage Capital:
  - o Late-stage capital is provided to companies that have achieved significant milestones and revenue growth. This funding is often used to prepare for an IPO or acquisition.

2. **The Venture Capital Process**

- Sourcing Deals:
  - o VC firms source deals through various channels, including

networking events, referrals, pitch events, and direct outreach from entrepreneurs.

- Due Diligence:
  - Once a potential investment is identified, VC firms conduct extensive due diligence. This includes evaluating the business model, market opportunity, financial projections, competitive landscape, and the capabilities of the management team.
- Investment Decision:
  - Based on due diligence, the VC firm decides whether to invest. If they proceed, terms are negotiated, including the amount of funding, the equity stake, and governance terms.
- Post-Investment Support:
  - After investing, VC firms often take an active role in guiding the company. This can include strategic advice, networking opportunities, and sometimes even operational support. They often hold seats on the company's board of directors.
- Exit:
  - The final stage is the exit, where the VC firm sells its stake in the company. Common exit strategies include IPOs, acquisitions, or secondary sales to other investors.

3. Benefits of Venture Capital

- Access to Capital:
  - VC provides significant funding that may not be available through other sources, especially for high-risk startups.
- Expertise and Mentorship:
  - VC firms bring industry expertise, strategic guidance, and mentorship to startups, helping them navigate complex growth challenges.
- Networking Opportunities:
  - Startups gain access to the VC firm's network, including potential partners, customers, and future funding sources.
- Validation and Credibility:
  - Receiving venture funding can validate a startup's business model and increase its credibility in the eyes of customers, partners, and other investors.

4. Drawbacks of Venture Capital

- Dilution of Ownership:
  - Entrepreneurs must give up a portion of their ownership in exchange for VC funding, which can lead to significant dilution of their stake.
- Loss of Control:
  - VC firms often require significant influence over business decisions, including board seats and veto rights on key decisions.
- Pressure to Exit:
  - VC firms typically seek high returns within a specific timeframe, which can pressure startups to focus on rapid growth and eventual exit rather than sustainable long-term strategies.
- Intensive Due Diligence:
  - The due diligence process can be lengthy and intrusive,

requiring extensive disclosures and scrutiny of the startup's operations and financials.

1.3.4. Private Equity Financing

Private equity (PE) financing plays a crucial role in the global economy by facilitating investment in businesses that may not have access to public markets or traditional bank loans. PE firms manage funds pooled from institutional investors, endowments, pension funds, and wealthy individuals. These funds are deployed across various investment strategies aimed at generating returns through capital appreciation and operational improvements in portfolio companies (Ederington & Lee, 1996).

1. **Stages of Private Equity Investment**

- Venture Capital (VC):
    - o **Definition:** Early-stage financing provided to startups and emerging companies with high growth potential.
    - o **Focus:** Technology, biotechnology, and other innovative sectors.
    - o **Investment Structure:** Often involves higher risk but potentially higher returns if the company succeeds.
- **Growth Capital:**
    - o **Definition:** Financing for established companies seeking capital to expand operations, enter new markets, or finance a major acquisition.
    - o **Focus:** Companies with proven business models and revenue streams.
    - o **Investment Structure:** Lower risk compared to venture capital but still involves significant growth expectations.
- **Buyouts:**
    - o **Definition:** Acquisition of a controlling stake in a mature company, often with the goal of restructuring and improving operational efficiency.
    - o **Types:** Management buyouts (MBOs) where existing management buys out the company, and leveraged buyouts (LBOs) where debt financing plays a significant role.
    - o **Investment Structure:** Focus on cash flow generation and operational improvements to enhance value.
- **Special Situations:**
    - o Definition: Investments in distressed companies, turnaround situations, or special opportunities.
    - o **Focus:** Restructuring, operational improvements, or capital infusions to resolve financial difficulties.
    - o **Investment Structure:** Often involves complex negotiations and strategic interventions to stabilize and grow the business.

2 **Strategies and Approaches in Private Equity**

- Value Creation:
    - o **Operational Improvements:** Implementing efficiencies, streamlining processes, and enhancing management practices.
    - o **Financial Engineering:** Optimizing capital structure,

refinancing debt, and managing cash flows to maximize returns.

- o **Strategic Initiatives:** Expanding market reach, diversifying product offerings, and pursuing strategic acquisitions.

- **Exit Strategies:**
  - o **Initial Public Offering (IPO):** Listing portfolio companies on public stock exchanges to realize gains.
  - o **Secondary Sale:** Seling the company to another private equity firm or strategic buyer.
  - o **Recapitalization:** Distributing dividends or refinancing to return capital to investors while retaining ownership.

2. **Advantages of Private Equity Financing**

- **Flexible Capital:** Tailored financing solutions that suit the specific needs and growth stages of businesses.
- **Operational Expertise:** Access to industry expertise, networks, and strategic guidance from PE firms.
- **Long-Term Focus:** Ability to pursue growth initiatives and operational improvements without the short-term pressures of public markets.
- **Alignment of Interests:** Shared incentives between investors and management to enhance shareholder value.

3. **Challenges and Considerations**

- **Risk and Return:** Higher risk investments with potential for significant returns, but also higher potential for losses.
- **Liquidity Constraints:** Longer investment horizons compared to public markets, with limited exit options until a successful exit strategy is executed.
- **Regulatory Scrutiny:** Compliance with regulatory requirements and scrutiny due to the private nature of transactions.
- **Operational Risks:** Execution challenges in implementing growth strategies and achieving projected returns.

1.3.5. Leveraged Buyouts

Leveraged Buyouts (LBOs) involve the acquisition of a company using a significant amount of borrowed money, often with the assets of the company being used as collateral for the loans. The acquired company's cash flow and assets are typically used to repay the debt, which can be substantial compared to the acquiring company's equity. LBOs are a strategic tool used by private equity firms, corporations, and occasionally management teams to acquire companies, often with the goal of restructuring or improving operations to increase profitability and ultimately sell the company for a profit.

1. **Mechanics of Leveraged Buyouts**

   i. **Acquisition Structure:** LBOs are structured in such a way that a large portion of the purchase price is financed through debt. The acquiring entity, often a private equity firm or a consortium, raises capital from various sources such as banks, institutional investors, and sometimes the acquiring firm's own funds.

   ii. **Debt Financing:** The debt used in an LBO can take

various forms, including senior debt (secured by company assets and given priority in repayment), subordinated or mezzanine debt (higher risk, higher yield), and sometimes seller financing. The debt-to-equity ratio in an LBO is typically high, amplifying potential returns but also increasing risk.

iii. **Financial Engineering:** Post-acquisition, LBOs often involve financial restructuring to improve cash flow and profitability. This may include reducing costs, optimizing capital structure, refinancing debt at lower rates, and sometimes divesting non-core assets.

iv. **Exit Strategy:** The ultimate goal of an LBO is to exit the investment at a higher valuation than the purchase price. Exit strategies include selling the company to another investor or taking it public through an Initial Public Offering (IPO).

2. **Motivations for Leveraged Buyouts**

i. **Return on Investment:** LBOs offer the potential for high returns on equity invested due to the use of leverage. This can significantly amplify investor returns if the acquired company performs well post-acquisition.

ii. **Strategic Transformation:** Acquirers may see opportunities to restructure the acquired company, streamline operations, or unlock value that was not being realized under previous ownership.

iii. **Market Timing:** Economic cycles and market conditions often influence the timing of LBO activity. During periods of low interest rates and economic optimism, LBOs tend to increase as financing costs decrease.

iv. **Ownership and Control:** LBOs allow investors to gain a controlling interest in a company, which can enable more aggressive decision-making and operational changes compared to public companies.

3. **Risks and Challenges of Leveraged Buyouts**

i. **Financial Risk:** High levels of debt increase financial risk, especially if the acquired company's performance deteriorates post-acquisition or if interest rates rise.

ii. **Operational Risk:** Turnaround efforts may not succeed as expected, leading to operational challenges and potential underperformance.

iii. **Liquidity Risk:** The burden of debt repayment can strain cash flow, particularly if the business encounters unexpected challenges or downturns.

iv. **Market and Economic Factors:** LBO success is influenced by broader economic conditions, market trends, and industry-specific challenges.

1.3.6. Initial Public Offerings (IPOs)

An IPO is the process through which a private company becomes publicly traded by offering shares of its stock to the general public for the first time. This transition typically occurs when a company seeks to raise capital for growth, acquisition, debt repayment, or other strategic purposes.

The IPO marks the company's entry into the stock market, where its shares can be bought and sold by investors. Historically, IPOs have played a crucial role in the growth of capital markets worldwide. The first recorded public offering dates back to the Dutch East India Company in 1602, which offered shares to the public to finance its expeditions and trade ventures. Since then, IPOs have evolved significantly in terms of regulation, structure, and global reach.

1.3.6.1. Regulatory Framework

The regulatory framework for IPOs varies by country but generally involves stringent requirements to protect investors and ensure transparency. In the United States, for instance, the Securities and Exchange Commission (SEC) plays a pivotal role in overseeing the IPO process through the Securities Act of 1933 and subsequent regulations. Companies must file a registration statement with the SEC, which includes detailed financial information, business operations, and risks associated with investing in the company.

Other countries have similar regulatory bodies and requirements tailored to their respective legal and financial systems. These regulations aim to safeguard investor interests, prevent fraud, and maintain the integrity of the capital markets.

1.3.6.2. IPO Process

The IPO process is complex and involves several key stages:

1. **Preparation and Due Diligence**: The company selects underwriters (investment banks) to manage the IPO process. Due diligence is conducted to ensure all financial and legal aspects are in order.
2. **Registration and Filing:** The company files a registration statement with the regulatory authority (e.g., SEC in the U.S.). This statement includes financial disclosures, business operations, management details, and potential risks.
3. **Roadshow:** The company and underwriters conduct a roadshow to market the IPO to institutional investors. This involves presentations and meetings to gauge investor interest and set the IPO price.
4. **Pricing:** Based on investor feedback and market conditions, the underwriters determine the IPO price. This price reflects the valuation of the company and the number of shares offered.
5. **Trading:** The IPO shares are allocated to investors, and trading begins on the designated stock exchange. The company's shares are now publicly traded, and the IPO proceeds are received by the company.

1.3.6.3. Benefits of IPOs

IPOs offer several benefits to companies and investors:

- Access to Capital: Companies can raise substantial funds to finance growth, research, and development, or pay off debts.
- Enhanced Visibility and Prestige: Being publicly traded can enhance a company's profile, credibility, and brand recognition.
- Liquidity for Founders and Investors: Existing shareholders, including founders and early investors, can

monetize their investments by selling shares on the open market.

1.3.6.4. Challenges and Risks

Despite the benefits, IPOs present significant challenges and risks:

- **Cost and Complexity:** The IPO process is expensive and time-consuming due to regulatory requirements, legal fees, and underwriting expenses.
- **Market Volatility:** Market conditions can impact the success of an IPO, affecting pricing and investor demand.
- **Loss of Control:** Going public means increased scrutiny from shareholders, analysts, and regulatory authorities, potentially limiting management's autonomy.

1.3.7. Mezzanine Financing

Mezzanine financing is a hybrid system of financing, which incorporates the features of equity and debt, both. It gives the lender a right to convert their debt into equity shares, in case of a default.

Mezzanine debt is subordinated debt, and close to being the last to be paid off. It is senior only to equity shares. Hence, it is high-risk debt and carries a very high rate of interest, as compared to any other debt.

1.3.7.1. How Does Mezzanine Financing Work?

This form of financing is typically used in acquisitions, as it bridges the gap between debt and equity. Borrowers generally take on mezzanine debt after they have exhausted other sources of financing. Mezzanine financing is used more by well-established companies to fund projects and growth, rather than companies in the start-up phase.

There are various ways in which mezzanine debt can be structured, the most common being a legal right to convert to equity, in case the debt is not repaid on time or repaid in full. The percentage of interest can be structured differently, with some portion being fixed and some portion variable. In mezzanine financing, interest can also be paid by increasing the principal amount, instead of frequent cash payouts.

1.3.7.2. Mezzanine Financing Rate of Return

The basic form of mezzanine financing is unsecured debt and preferred stocks. As mezzanine financing is unsecured, it carries higher risks, and investors require a higher rate of return than secured lenders. Typically, it pays an investor 12–20%, which is higher than the rate of return on ordinary debt.

Mezzanine investors can earn returns from the following available sources:

1. **Cash Interest:** Based on the portion of the outstanding mezzanine funding balance, investors receive cash periodically. The interest rate may either be set or may fluctuate over the loan period.
2. **Payment in Kind (PIK) Interest:** It is also a periodic method of payment. However, the interest amount is not paid in cash. Instead, it is added to the principal sum of the security, and the total amount is paid at the end of the loan period. For example, a $50 million bond with a 10% PIK interest rate will amount to $55 million at the end of the period, and there will be no cash interest payment.

3. **Ownership:** Similar to a convertible bond, mezzanine financing often includes an equity interest in the form of a conversion feature or warrant. Usually, the PIK interest or the cash interest follows the ownership portion of the securities.
4. **Participation Payout:** In place of equity, investors may take a return on equity in the form of a percentage of the company's performance as measured by net sales or EBITDA, or profit.
5. **Arrangement Fee:** Mezzanine investors are also required to be paid an arrangement fee upon closing the transaction.

1.3.7.3. Advantages and Disadvantages of Mezzanine Financing

- Advantages:
  1. Lenders are assured of receiving regular interest payments, and these interest rates are much higher than regular debt.
  2. Mezzanine financing is typically unsecured debt, and there is more flexibility involved for the borrower while taking on the debt, as no assets need to be given on lien.
  3. Mezzanine investors target a lower cost of capital, as compared to private equity investors.
  4. Mezzanine debt is tax-deductible for the borrower.
  5. Deferment of interest payments may be possible with mezzanine debt, but usually not with any other form of debt.
  6. It helps borrowers get additional sources of income when they have exhausted all other options.
- Disadvantages:
  1. It is a very expensive form of financing for a company.
  2. Mezzanine lenders are paid off only after senior debtors; hence, they could also risk losing their investment as there is generally no lien on the assets.
  3. Owners need to sacrifice equity and control in the event of something going wrong.
  4. Mezzanine lenders are ones who wish to have a long-term strategic relationship with the company, rather than only get a quick return on investment.

1.3.8. Asset-Backed Financing (ABF)

Asset-backed financing (ABF) involves leveraging assets owned by a company as collateral to secure a loan or credit. The underlying principle is straightforward: by pledging tangible or intangible assets, businesses can obtain financing they need for various purposes, from expanding operations to managing cash flow. This form of financing has gained prominence due to its flexibility and ability to mitigate risk for lenders.

1.3.8.1. Types of Assets Used in Asset-Backed Financing

Assets that can be utilized in asset-backed financing span a wide range, depending on the nature of the business and its operations:

1. **Accounts Receivable:** Often referred to as invoice financing or factoring, where businesses sell their outstanding invoices to a lender at a discount in exchange for immediate cash.
2. **Inventory:** Inventory can be used as collateral, especially in industries where maintaining stock levels is crucial. Lenders may advance funds based on the value of the inventory.
3. **Equipment:** Machinery and equipment owned by a business can be pledged as collateral to secure financing. This is common in industries requiring substantial capital investment in equipment.
4. **Real Estate:** Property owned by a business can be leveraged to secure loans. Real estate-backed financing is prevalent in commercial real estate and development projects.
5. **Future Revenue Streams:** In industries such as entertainment or pharmaceuticals, where revenue is expected from royalties or future sales, these streams can be securitized and used to obtain financing.

1.3.8.2. Mechanics of Asset-Backed Financing

The process of asset-backed financing typically involves several key steps:

1. **Asset Evaluation:** Lenders assess the value and quality of the assets being offered as collateral. This may involve appraisals, audits, or verification of ownership.
2. **Structuring the Transaction:** Based on the asset's value, a financing structure is proposed. This includes determining the loan amount, interest rates, repayment terms, and any additional fees.
3. Legal Documentation: Contracts and legal agreements are drafted to outline the terms of the financing arrangement, rights and obligations of both parties, and procedures in case of default.
4. **Disbursement of Funds:** Once the agreement is finalized, funds are disbursed to the borrower. These funds can be used for various purposes outlined in the agreement.
5. **Monitoring and Management:** Lenders typically monitor the performance of the collateralized assets to ensure compliance with the agreement terms. This may involve periodic audits or reporting requirements.

1.3.8.3. Benefits of Asset-Backed Financing

Asset-backed financing offers several advantages to both borrowers and lenders:

1. **Access to Capital:** Businesses can access capital that might otherwise be tied up in assets, enabling growth opportunities or addressing short-term liquidity needs.
2. **Lower Cost of Financing:** By pledging collateral, businesses may secure lower interest rates compared to unsecured loans, as the risk to the lender is reduced.
3. **Flexible Financing Options:** Asset-backed financing can be structured to meet specific needs, such as seasonal fluctuations in cash flow or financing large-scale projects.
4. **Risk Mitigation for Lenders:** Lenders have recourse to the collateral in case of default, reducing the overall risk compared to unsecured lending.

5. **Improved Cash Flow Management:** Financing based on assets allows businesses to optimize their cash flow by converting assets into working capital.

1.3.8.4. Risks Associated with Asset-Backed Financing

Despite its benefits, asset-backed financing carries certain risks:

1. **Asset Value Fluctuation:** The value of collateralized assets may fluctuate over time, impacting the amount of financing available or the terms of the agreement.
2. **Default Risk:** If the borrower fails to repay the loan or comply with the agreement terms, the lender may seize and liquidate the collateral. However, liquidation values may be lower than expected.
3. **Operational Risks:** Depending on the type of asset, there may be operational risks such as damage, obsolescence, or regulatory changes affecting its value.
4. **Legal and Regulatory Risks:** Asset-backed financing transactions involve complex legal and regulatory considerations, which if not managed properly, can lead to disputes or compliance issues.
5. **Market Risks:** External market factors such as economic downturns or industry-specific challenges can impact the value of collateralized assets and the ability to secure financing.

1.3.8.5. Role of Asset-Backed Financing in Financial Markets

Asset-backed financing plays a significant role in modern financial markets by enhancing liquidity, promoting economic growth, and supporting diverse industries:

1. **Capital Formation:** By unlocking capital tied up in assets, asset-backed financing facilitates investment in new projects, innovation, and expansion.
2. **Risk Management:** It allows businesses to manage risk more effectively by diversifying funding sources and securing financing against specific assets.
3. **Industry-Specific Applications:** Different industries leverage asset-backed financing tailored to their needs, such as technology companies financing equipment or real estate developers using property as collateral.
4. **Investment Opportunities:** Asset-backed securities (ABS), where pools of assets are securitized and sold to investors, provide opportunities for diversification and yield in investment portfolios.
5. **Global Impact:** Asset-backed financing is not limited by geographical boundaries, enabling businesses worldwide to access capital markets and foster international trade and investment.

1.3.8.6. Challenges and Future Trends

Looking ahead, asset-backed financing faces several challenges and opportunities:

1. **Technological Advancements:** Digital platforms and blockchain technology could streamline asset evaluation, transaction processing, and risk management in asset-backed financing.
2. **Regulatory Environment:** Evolving

regulations governing financial markets and collateralized lending require careful monitoring and adaptation by stakeholders.

3. **Sustainability and ESG Factors:** There is increasing focus on integrating environmental, social, and governance (ESG) considerations into asset-backed financing practices.
4. **Market Innovation:** Continued innovation in structuring asset-backed transactions, such as using non-traditional assets or hybrid financing models, could expand the market.
5. **Resilience to Economic Shocks:** Asset-backed financing's resilience during economic downturns could be tested, highlighting the need for robust risk management frameworks.

CASE STUDY

RESTRUCTURING AN INVESTMENT AND FINANCIAL SERVICES FIRM

Founded in 2000, our client is a leading finance and investment company in Kuwait, listed on multiple stock exchanges. In addition it had also floated funds and manages substantial Assets under Management portfolio.

The Challenge

Our Client was initially incorporated as a finance company and had operated successfully with this business model. The Client received an Investment license which allowed them to establish their Assets under Management division as well as float multiple funds. Shareholder confidence and market appetite allowed the company to increase its equity through multiple increases in the last 10 years.

However the Client gradually invested into private equity during FY 2007 to FY 2008, which was majorly funded using short to medium term debt. The global financial meltdown led to major asset value declines. This in addition to the lack of liquidity led to the Company facing the prospects of a major default on debt due to both Local as well as International banks and possible liquidation.

The Client was in the process of reassessing and reviving its operational departments and identifying assets to be exited for which it required services of AB to develop a Re-Organization and an extensive Capital Restructuring plan under multiple scenarios. The main intention included:

- Allowing the Client to continue as a going concern
- Preserve Shareholder reputation by avoiding default
- Capital, Assets & Operations restructuring to ensure sustainability of the Client.

Our Approach

AB worked along with the Client's investments, operations & finance department to analyze performance, identify inefficiencies and sub-optimal utilization of resources as well as means to improve revenue generation. Investment exits were discussed and ways to increase economic value of strategic stakes were also considered to improve exit values.

During this exercise, certain areas were identified where the costs could be reduced. AB also arrived at a sustainable debt level post assets & operations restructuring.

AB projected a major revamp of the current capital structure based on multiple scenarios that considered major debt to equity swaps, additional capital increase by current shareholders and assess overall returns to both the debt holders as well as the equity holders.

Conclusion

We assisted the client in their numerous meetings & discussions with different banks and presenting the Reorganization Plan which would enable the Client to meet the Restructured Debt obligations that were proposed to the Banks.

CLASS ACTIVITY

Students will analyze financial statements to assess company performance, create a capital budgeting proposal for a hypothetical project, and discuss the impact of financial decisions on shareholder value and market competitiveness.

SUMMARY

- Corporate finance plays a vital role in maximizing the financial soundness of an organization and its stockholders. The departments that work under this branch of finance mainly manage the financial activities of a company. They make important decisions about investments, capital allocation and organizational budgeting.
- Capital financing is the central pillar that entails deciding how to finance investments at an optimal level. Financing happens through a company's debt, equity, or both. Long-term financing for significant investments or expenditures may come from issuing debt securities through investment banks or selling company stocks.
- The capital budgeting process reveals the viability of investment proposals and enables businesses to invest in profitable projects. Its primary goal is to enhance growth and maximize profitability. Part of capital budgeting entails analyzing the present and future values of various investment alternatives to interpret risk-return ratios in relation to organizational goals. Only the most profitable projects are given priority in corporate financing.
- Working capital, also known as net working capital (NWC), is the difference between a company's current assets—such as cash, accounts receivable/customers' unpaid bills, and inventories of raw materials and finished goods—and its current liabilities, such as accounts payable and debts. It's a commonly used measurement to gauge the short-term health of an organization.
- Capital structure refers to the mix of different sources of funds, including equity and debt, used by a company to finance its operations and investments. It represents the way that a company finance its assets and is essential in determining its financial health and risk profile.
- Equity finance is a method of raising fresh capital by selling shares of the company to public, institutional investors, or financial institutions. The people who buy shares are referred to as shareholders of the company because they have received ownership interest in the company.
- Debt financing occurs when a company raises money by selling debt instruments to investors. Debt financing is the opposite of equity financing, which entails issuing stock to raise money. Debt financing occurs when a firm sells fixed income products, such as bonds, bills, or notes.
- Private equity is ownership or interest in entities that aren't publicly listed or traded. A source of investment capital, private equity comes from firms that buy stakes in private companies or take control of public companies with plans to take them private and delist them from stock exchanges.

REVIEW QUESTIONS

1. Define corporate finance and explain its primary objectives.
2. What are the key components or elements of corporate finance? Provide examples of each.
3. Explain the concept of capital budgeting. How does it contribute to corporate financial decision-making?
4. Describe the concept of cost of capital. How is it calculated and why is it important for corporate finance decisions?
5. Explain the differences between mergers and acquisitions (M&A) and initial public offerings (IPOs) as methods of corporate finance.

REFERENCES

1. Black, F., & Scholes, M. (1974). The effects of dividend yield and dividend policy on common stock prices and returns. *Journal of Financial Economics, 1*(1), 1–22.
2. Cameron, R., & Bovykin, V. I. (1991). *International Banking: 1870–1914*. New York, NY: Oxford University Press. ISBN 978-0-19-506271-7.
3. Cassis, Y. (2006). *Capitals of Capital: A History of International Financial Centers, 1780–2005*. Cambridge, UK: Cambridge University Press. ISBN 978-0-511-33522-8.
4. Correia, C., Flynn, D. K., Uliana, E., & Wormald, M. (2007). *Financial Management*. Juta and Company Ltd. ISBN 978-0-7021-7157-4.
5. Damodaran, A. (1989). The weekend effect in information releases: A study of earnings and dividend announcements. *Review of Financial Studies, 2*(4), 607–623.
6. Ederington, L., & Lee, J. H. (1996). The impact of macroeconomic news on financial markets. *Journal of Applied Corporate Finance, 9*(1), 41–49.
7. Gherghina, Ş. C. (2021). Corporate finance. *Journal of Risk and Financial Management, 14*(2), 44. https://doi.org/10.3390/jrfm14020044.
8. Jensen, M. C., & Smith, C. W. (2000). The theory of corporate finance: A historical overview. In M. C. Jensen & C. W. Smith Jr. (Eds.), *The Modern Theory of Corporate Finance* (pp. 2–20). McGraw-Hill. SSRN 244161.
9. Kieso, D. E., Weygandt, J. J., & Warfield, T. D. (2007). *Intermediate Accounting* (12th ed.). New York: John Wiley & Sons. ISBN 978-0-471-74955-4.
10. McMenamin, J. (2002). *Financial Management: An Introduction*. Routledge. ISBN 978-1-134-67624-8.
11. Roberts, R. (2008). *The City: A Guide to London's Global Financial Center*. Economist. ISBN 978-1861978585.

CHAPTER 2

Time Value of Money

LEARNING OBJECTIVES

After studying this chapter, you will be able to:

- Explain the concept of time value of money
- Discuss the three rules of time travel
- Describe valuing a stream of cash flows
- calculating the net present value
- Explain perpetuities and annuities
- Describe using an annuity spreadsheet or calculator
- Define non-annual cash flows
- Elaboration the solving for the cash payments
- Define the internal rate of return

KEY TERMS FROM THIS CHAPTER

Annuity
Compound interest
Discounting
Future value
Growing perpetuity
Net present value
Present value
Timeline
Annuity spreadsheet
Compounding
Financial decisions
Growing annuity
Internal rate of return
Perpetuity
Stream of cash flows

INTRODUCTION

The time value of money (TVM) is a fundamental concept in corporate finance that underscores the principle that the value of money is not static over time. Instead, it appreciates or depreciates depending on various factors, including interest rates, inflation, and investment risk. In essence, TVM posits that a dollar received today is worth more than a dollar received in the future due to its potential earning capacity.

The two core concepts in TVM are present value (PV) and future value (FV). Present value is the current worth of a future sum of money or stream of cash flows given a specific rate of return. Conversely, future value is the value of a current asset at a future date, considering a specific rate of interest or growth over time. Calculating these values requires the application of discounting (for PV) or compounding (for FV) techniques, which factor in the time period and the rate of return.

Discounting is the process of determining the present value of a payment or a stream of payments that will be received in the future. It is essentially the reverse of compounding, which is used to determine the future value of a current sum of money or cash flow. The discount rate reflects the opportunity cost of capital, inflation, and the risk associated with future cash flows.

TVM is pivotal in various aspects of corporate finance, including capital budgeting, investment analysis, and financial planning. For instance, when evaluating potential investment projects, firms use TVM to calculate the net present value (NPV) and internal rate of return (IRR) to assess profitability and make informed decisions. It also aids in determining loan schedules, valuing bonds and stocks, and planning for retirement.

The time value of money helps corporations make informed financial decisions by understanding the real value of their investments and the cost of capital. It ensures that businesses can accurately assess the profitability of long-term projects, determine the best financing options, and optimize their capital allocation to maximize shareholder value.

The time value of money is a crucial principle in corporate finance, enabling businesses to make sound investment decisions, plan for future financial needs, and maintain the overall health of their financial operations by understanding and leveraging the time-related value of money.

2.1. CONCEPT OF TIME VALUE OF MONEY

The idea behind time value of money (TVM) is that an amount of money has more value now than it will have later because of its potential for earnings in the interim. One of the fundamental ideas of finance is the time value of money. A sum of money that is paid now is worth more than the same amount that must be paid later. The present discounted value is another name for the time value of money.

Getting money now is more appealing to investors than getting the same amount later. Any amount of money increases over time if it is invested. Therefore, investing the money they receive today is more valuable than waiting until tomorrow to receive it. For instance, interest is paid on funds deposited into savings accounts. Interest is accrued over time and added to the principal, earning interest. That is the way compound interest works.

The money loses value over time if it is not invested. You will forfeit the extra money your $1,000 mattress would have made if it had been invested over the course of three years. When you retrieve it, its purchasing power will be even less due to inflation.

Let's take another scenario where you can choose to receive $10,000 now or $10,000 in two years. $10,000 today has greater value and utility than it will in two years, even though its face value is equal. This is because there are opportunity costs linked to the delay. Stated differently, an untimely payment represents a squandered chance.

There is a negative correlation between inflation and the time value of money. Recall that an increase in the cost of goods and services is known as inflation. Because of this, you can't buy as much as you could in the past when prices rise because a dollar loses value.

2.2. THE TIMELINE

We start by going over some basic terminology and tools before looking at the valuation of cash flows over multiple periods. A stream of cash flows is a sequence of cash flows that spans multiple time periods. A timeline, which depicts the expected cash flows in a linear fashion, can be used to visualize a stream of cash flows. When organizing and subsequently resolving a financial issue, timelines are a crucial first step. They are used frequently in this text.

Consider that you owe money to a friend in order to demonstrate how to create a timeline. He has committed to paying back the loan in two installments of $10,000 at the conclusion of the following two years. We display this data as follows on a timeline:

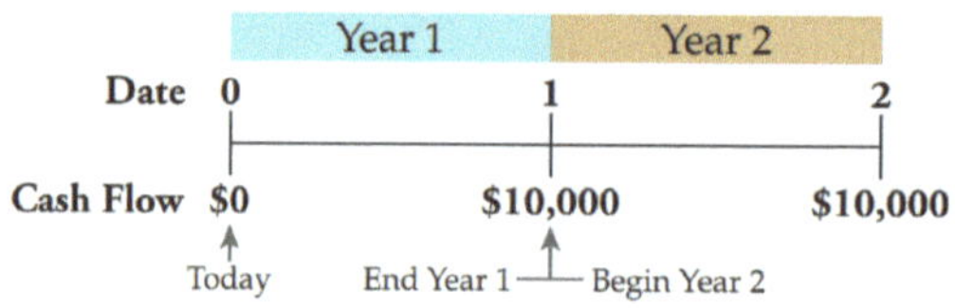

The present is represented by date 0. One year later, on Date 1, the first year comes to an end. At the end of the first year, you will receive the $10,000 cash flow below date 1. Date 2 denotes the end of the second year and is two years from now. At the end of the second year, you will receive the $10,000 cash flow below date 2.

Interpret each point on the timeline as a specific date in order to track cash flows. The time interval between these dates—in this case, the first year of the loan—is then represented by the space between dates 0 and 1. Date 0 marks the start of the first year, and Date 1 marks its conclusion. In a similar vein, date 1 marks the start of the second year and date 2 its conclusion. Date 1 represents the start of year 2 as well as the end of year 1 when time is represented in this manner, which makes sense since those dates are essentially the same point in time.

Both of the cash flows in this example are inflows. Nonetheless, a financial choice will frequently involve both inflows and outflows. We give each type of cash flow a distinct sign in order to distinguish it from the other: inflows are positive cash flows, while outflows are negative cash flows.

To give an example, let's say you agreed to lend your brother $10,000 today because you're still feeling giving. Your brother has consented to pay back the loan in two $6,000 installments at the conclusion of the following two years. The chronology is given below:

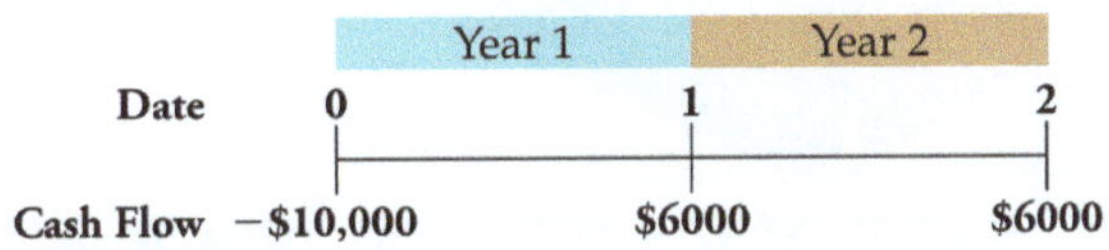

Observe that since it is an outflow, the first cash flow at date 0 (today) is shown as -$10,000. Because they are inflows, the ensuing $6,000 in cash flows are positive.

To illustrate the cash flows that happen at the end of each year thus far, we have done so using timelines. In actuality, cash flows that occur at the conclusion of any time period can be represented by timelines. If you pay rent on a monthly basis, for instance, you could use a timeline similar to the one in our first example to show two rental payments; just swap out the "year" label for "month."

A large number of the timelines in this chapter are fairly basic. As a result, you might think that creating them is not worth the effort or time. But as you get to more challenging issues, you'll discover that timelines help you see aspects of an investment or transaction that are simple to miss. You'll make bad financial decisions if you don't see these cash flows.

2.3. THE THREE RULES OF TIME TRAVEL

Cash flows that occur at various points in time must frequently be compared or combined in order to make financial decisions. This section presents three fundamental principles that are essential to financial decision-making and enable us to combine or compare values.

2.3.1. Rule 1: Comparing and Combining Values

First of all, values can only be combined or compared at the same moment in time. You can only compare or combine cash flows that are in the same units. A dollar now is not the same as a dollar in a year. Money that you have now is more valuable than money that you will have later because you can earn interest on it. Cash flows that occur at different points in time must first be converted into the same units or moved to the same point in time in order to be compared or combined. The cash flows on the timeline can be rearranged according to the next two rules.

2.3.2. Rule 2: Moving Cash Flows Forward in Time

Suppose we have $1000 today, and we wish to determine the equivalent amount in one year's time. If the current market interest rate is 10%, we can use that rate as an exchange rate to move the cash flow forward in time. That is;

($1000 today) * (1.10 $ in one year/$ today) = $1100 in one year

In general, if the market interest rate for the year is r, then we multiply by the interest rate factor, (1 + r), to move the cash flow from the beginning to the end of the year. This process of moving a value or cash flow forward in time is known as compounding. Our second rule stipulates that to move a cash flow forward in time, you must compound it.

We can apply this rule repeatedly. Suppose we want to know how much the $1000 is worth in two years' time. If the interest rate for year 2 is also 10%, then we convert as we just did:

($1100 in one year) * (1.10 $ in two years/$ in one year) = $1210 in two years

Let's represent this calculation on a timeline as follows:

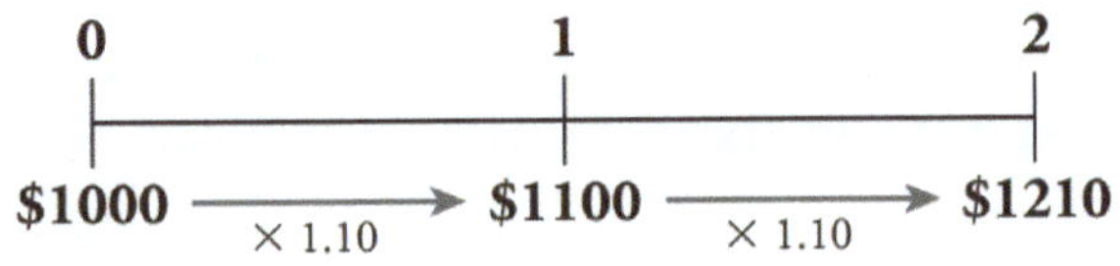

Given a 10% interest rate, all of the cash flows—$1000 at date 0, $1100 at date 1, and $1210 at date 2—are equivalent. They have the same value but are expressed in different units (different points in time). An arrow that points to the right indicates that the value is being moved forward in time—that is, compounded. A cash flow's future value is the amount that is added when it is transferred forward in time. In the example above, $1210 represents the value of $1000 in two years from now. Keep in mind that the value increases as we move the cash flow forward in time. The time value of money is represented by the difference in value between money today and money tomorrow. This illustrates the idea that having money early allows you to invest it and earn more money later on. Also take note of the fact that the equivalent value increases by $110 in the second year but by $100 in the first. We earn interest on both our initial $1000 investment and the $100 in interest we received in the first year during the second year. Compound interest is the term for this result of earning "interest on interest."

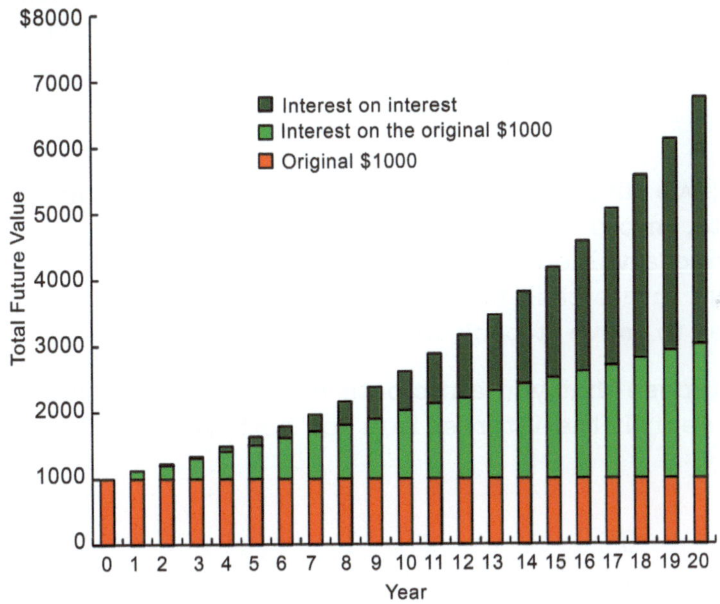

Figure 2.1. *The composition of interest over time. This graph shows the account balance and the composition of interest over time when an investor starts with an initial deposit of $1,000, shown in red, in an account earning 10% interest over a 20-year period. Note that the turquoise area representing interest on interest grows, and by year 15 has become larger than the interest on the original deposit, shown in green. In year 20, the interest on interest the investor earned is $3727.50, while the total interest earned on the original $1000 is $2000.*

Source. https://vk.com/doc399904795_480298778?hash=sLEzOoz8DP50Y9wyqDdcmJvt0O71bxw1T7jHQuy2Q8T.

How does the future value change if we move the cash flow three years? Continuing with the same approach, we compound the cash flow a third time. Assuming the competitive market interest rate is fixed at 10%, we get:

$$\$1000 * (1.10) * (1.10) * (1.10) = \$1000 * (1.10)^3 = \$1331$$

In general, to take a cash flow C forward n periods into the future, we must compound it by the n intervening interest rate factors. If the interest rate r is constant, then;

Future Value of a Cash Flow

$$FV_n = C \times \underbrace{(1+r) \times (1+r) \times \cdots \times (1+r)}_{n \text{ times}} = C \times (1+r)^n \quad (1)$$

The significance of earning "interest on interest" in the gradual increase of the account balance is illustrated in Figure 2.1. Growth resulting from compounding is referred to as geometric or exponential growth.

2.3.3. Rule 3: Moving Cash Flows Back in Time

The process of moving cash flows backward in time is outlined in the third rule. Let's say you want to calculate the current value of the $1000 you will receive in a year. To calculate this value, convert units and assume that the market interest rate is 10%.

($1000 in one year) ÷ (1.10 $ in one year/$ today) = $909.09 today

In other words, we divide the cash flow by the interest rate factor, (1 + r), where r is the interest rate, in order to move the cash flow backward in time. Discounting is the process of moving a value or cash flow backward in time to determine the current value equivalent of a future cash flow. According to our third rule, we have to discount a cash flow in order to move it back in time.

To illustrate, suppose that you anticipate receiving the $1000 two years from today rather than in one year. If the interest rate for both years is 10%, we can prepare the following timeline:

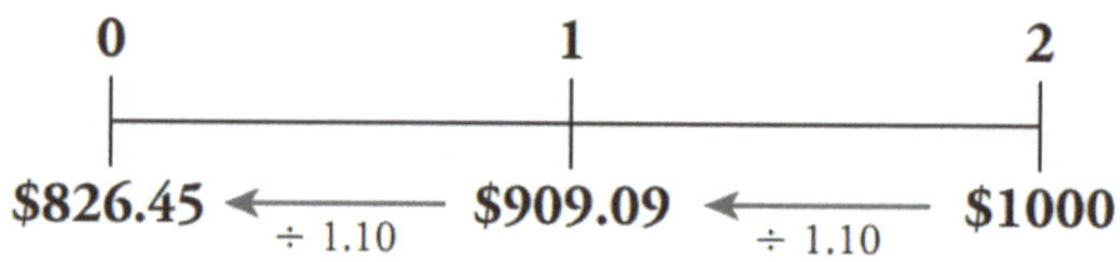

All of the cash flows—$826.45 at date 0; $909.09 at date 1; and $1000 at date 2—are equivalent when the interest rate is 10%. They are different points in time that represent the same value in different units. The value is being discounted or moved backward in time as indicated by the left-pointing arrow. As we move the cash flow further back, you'll notice that the value drops. A future cash flow's present value at an earlier time in the timeline is equal to its value at that earlier point. In other words, the present value of $1000 in two years at date 0 is $826.45. The "do-it-yourself" cost to generate a future cash flow is known as the present value. According to the second law of time travel, we would therefore have a future value of $1000 if we invested $826.45 today for two years at a rate of 10% interest.

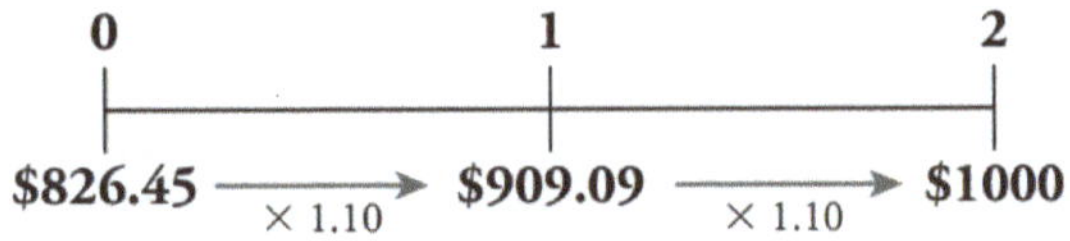

Suppose the $1000 were three years away and you wanted to compute the present value. Again, if the interest rate is 10%, we have

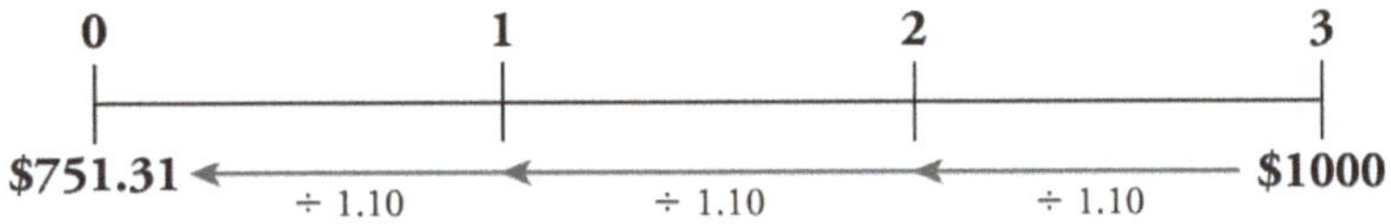

That is, the present value today of a cash flow of $1000 in three years is given by

$$\$1000 \div (1.10) \div (1.10) \div (1.10) = \$1000 \div (1.10)^3 = \$751.31$$

In general, to move a cash flow C backward n periods, we must discount it by the n intervening interest rate factors. If the interest rate r is constant, then;

Present Value of a Cash Flow

$$PV = C \div (1 + r)^n = \frac{C}{(1 + r)^n} \qquad (2)$$

2.3.4. Applying the Rules of Time Travel

Time travel rules enable us to combine and compare cash flows that happen at various times. Assume that we want to set aside $1000 today and another $1000 at the end of the following two years. How much will we have in three years if we earn a fixed 10% interest rate on our savings?

Again, we start with a timeline:

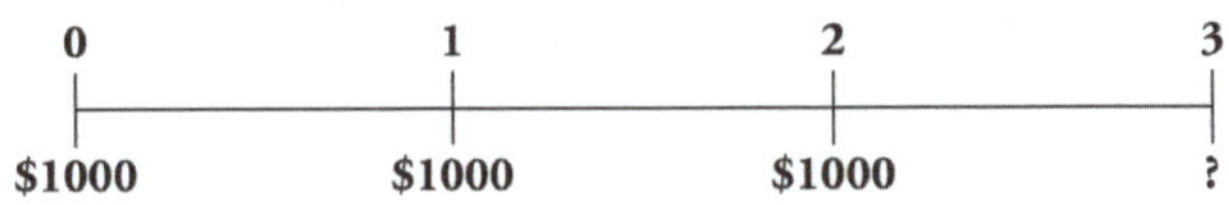

The timeline shows the three deposits we plan to make. We need to compute their value at the end of three years. We can combine and compare cash flows that happen at various times thanks to the laws of time travel. Let's say our goal is to save $1,000 today and $1,000 at the end of the following two years. What will our savings be worth in three years if we earn a fixed 10% interest rate?

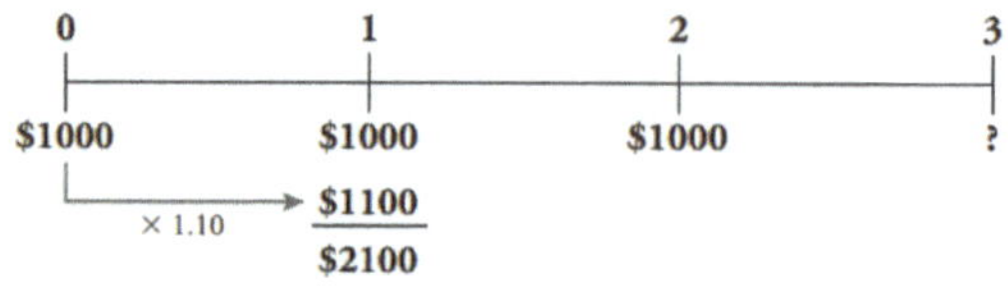

Using the first two rules of time travel, we find that our total savings on date 1 will be $2100. Continuing in this fashion, we can solve the problem as follows:

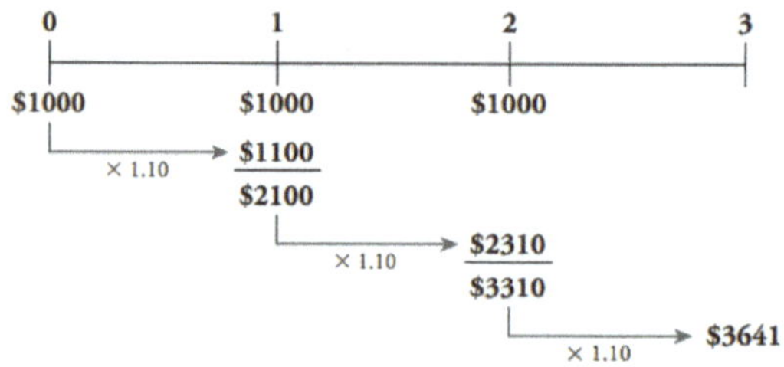

The total amount we will have in the bank at the end of three years is $3641. This amount is the future value of our $1000 savings deposits.

Another approach to the problem is to compute the future value in year 3 of each cash flow separately. Once all three amounts are in year 3 dollars, we can then combine them. The future value is the same for both calculations. We obtain the same outcome as long as we abide by the rules. It makes no difference what order we apply the rules in. Whichever calculation works best for the given situation is the one we'll go with. The three-time travel rules and the formulas that go along with them are compiled in Table 2.1.

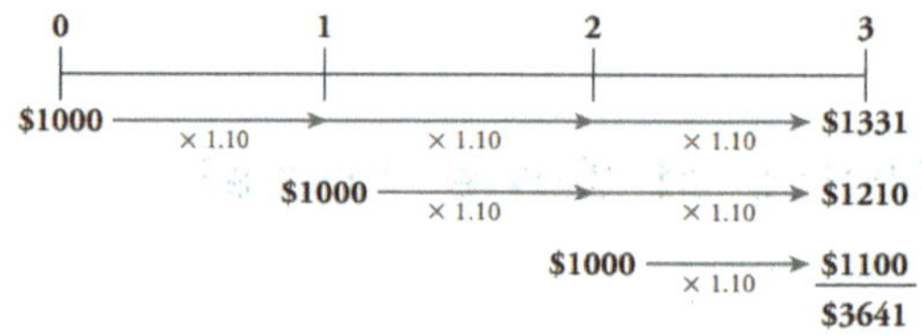

Table 2.1. The Three Rules of Time Travel

Rule 1	Only values at the same point in time can be compared or combined.	
Rule 2	To move a cash flow forward in time, you must compound it.	Future Value of a Cash Flow $FV_n = C \times (1+r)^n$
Rule 3	To move a cash flow backward in time, you must discount it.	Present Value of a Cash Flow $PV = C \div (1+r)^n = \frac{C}{(1+r)^n}$

Source. https://vk.com/doc399904795_480298778?hash=sLEzOoz8DP50Y9wyqDdcmJvt0O71bxw1T7jHQuy2Q8T.

2.4. VALUING A STREAM OF CASH FLOWS

The majority of investment opportunities feature several cash flows that happen at various times. To value these cash flows, we used the time travel rules. We now derive a general formula for the valuation of a stream of cash flows, formalizing this approach.

Consider a stream of cash flows: C_0 at date 0, C_1 at date 1, and so on, up to C_N at date N. We represent this cash flow stream on a timeline as follows:

Using the time travel techniques, we compute the present value of this cash flow stream in two steps. First, we compute the present value of each individual cash flow. Then, once the cash flows are in common units of dollars today, we can combine them.

For a given interest rate r, we represent this process on the timeline as follows:

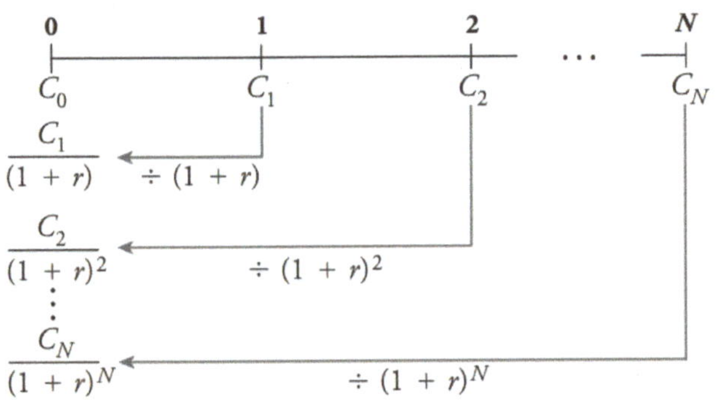

This timeline provides the general formula for the present value of a cash flow stream:

$$PV = C_0 + \frac{C_1}{(1+r)} + \frac{C_2}{(1+r)^2} + \cdots + \frac{C_N}{(1+r)^N} \quad (3)$$

We can also write this formula as a summation:

$$PV = \sum_{n=0}^{N} PV(C_n) = \sum_{n=0}^{N} \frac{C_n}{(1+r)^n} \quad (4)$$

The summation sign, Σ, means "sum the individual elements for each date n from

0 to N." Note that $(1 + r)^0 = 1$, so this shorthand matches precisely Eq. 3. That is, the present value of the cash flow stream is the sum of the present values of each cash flow. We defined the present value as the dollar amount you would need to invest today to produce the single cash flow in the future. The same idea holds in this context. The present value is the amount you need to invest today to generate the cash flow stream C_0, C_1, ..., C_N. That is, receiving those cash flows is equivalent to having their present value in the bank today.

2.5. CALCULATING THE NET PRESENT VALUE

After establishing the time travel laws and figuring out how to calculate present and future values, we can now move on to our main objective, which is weighing the advantages and disadvantages of a project in order to assess a long-term investment choice. According to our first time travel rule, we must value cash flows at a single point in time in order to compare them. Using present values is a convenient option. In particular, we define the net present value (NPV) of an investment decision as follows:

$$NPV = PV(\text{benefits}) - PV(\text{costs}) \quad (5)$$

The cash inflows are the benefits in this scenario, and the cash outflows are the costs. Any decision we make about investments can be shown as a cash flow stream on a timeline, with positive cash flows representing inflows and negative cash flows representing outflows. Thus, the NPV of an investment opportunity is also the present value of the stream of cash flows of the opportunity:

$$NPV = PV(\text{benefits}) - PV(\text{costs}) = PV(\text{benefits} - \text{costs})$$

The NPV of an investment opportunity like the Chevy Volt that lasts more than one period has been computed, and we have demonstrated how to answer the question we posed at the beginning of the chapter: How should financial managers evaluate the cash flows from undertaking a multi-year project like the Chevy Volt? In actuality, the computations can get laborious when there are more than four or five cash flows—which they almost certainly will. Thankfully, there are a few unique situations where treating each cash flow separately is not necessary.

2.6. PERPETUITIES AND ANNUITIES

We are able to determine the current or future value of any cash flow stream using the formulas we have created thus far. This section examines perpetuities and annuities, two unique forms of cash flow streams, and teaches us quick methods for valuing them. The cash flows have a regular pattern, which makes these shortcuts possible.

2.6.1. Perpetuities

A perpetuity is an endless stream of equal cash flows that happen on a regular basis. The British government bond known as a consol, also known as a perpetual bond, is one instance. Consol bonds guarantee the owner a consistent annual cash flow for all time.

Here is the timeline for a perpetuity:

Note from the timeline that the first cash flow does not occur immediately; it arrives at the end of the first period. This timing is sometimes referred to as payment in arrears and is a standard convention that we adopt throughout this text.

Using the formula for the present value, the present value of a perpetuity with payment C and interest rate r is given by

$$PV = \frac{C}{(1+r)} + \frac{C}{(1+r)^2} + \frac{C}{(1+r)^3} + \cdots = \sum_{n=1}^{\infty} \frac{C}{(1+r)^n}$$

Notice that $C_n = C$ in the present value formula because the cash flow for a perpetuity is constant. Also, because the first cash flow is in one period, $C_0 = 0$.

It may seem impossible to find a finite sum for an infinite number of positive terms, even with a shortcut, but it would take an eternity to find the value of a perpetuity one cash flow at a time.

The explanation is that the future cash flows are discounted for a growing number of periods, which causes their contribution to the total to eventually disappear.

We compute the value of a perpetuity by constructing our own perpetuity in order to derive the shortcut. The perpetuity's present value can then be determined because, according to the Law of One Price, its value must equal the expense we would incur if we were to create it ourselves.

As an example, let's say you have $100 that you could invest in a bank account that pays you 5% interest annually for eternity. You will have $105 in the bank after a year—your initial $100 plus $5 in interest. Let's say you take the $5 interest out and put the $100 back in for a second year. After a year, you will have $105 once more, from which you can take out $5 and reinvest $100 for an additional year. You can withdraw $5 annually indefinitely by following this procedure year after year:

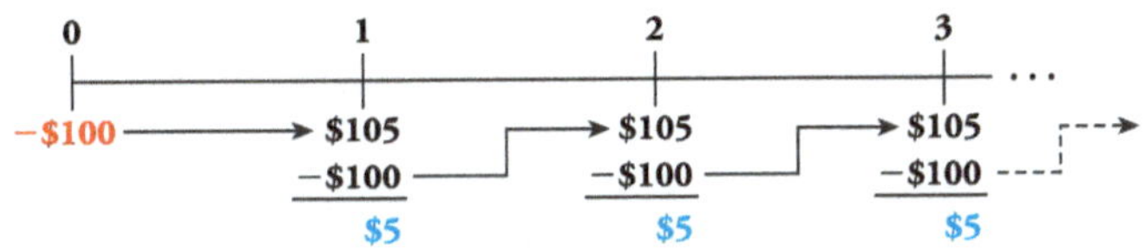

Put $100 in the bank today and you can practically create a perpetuity that pays $5 annually. According to the Law of One Price, a good must be priced the same in every market. The present value of the $5 annually in perpetuity is this $100 "do-it-yourself" cost because the bank will "sell" us (let us create) the perpetuity for $100.

Now let's generalize this argument. Suppose we invest an amount P in the bank. Every year we can withdraw the interest we have earned, C = r * P, leaving the principal, P, in the bank. The present value of receiving C in perpetuity is therefore the upfront cost P = C/r. Therefore,

$$PV(C \text{ in perpetuity}) = \frac{C}{r} \quad (6)$$

In other words, by depositing the amount C/r today, we can withdraw interest of (C/r) * r = C each period in perpetuity. Thus, the present value of the perpetuity is C/r.

Take note of our argument's logic. The present value of a cash flow stream was calculated by calculating the "do-it-yourself" cost of producing the same cash flows at the bank. This is a much faster and more straightforward method than summing those infinite terms, and it is incredibly powerful and helpful.

2.6.2. Annuities

A stream of N equal cash flows paid at regular intervals is called an annuity. An annuity ends after a certain number of payments, which is how it differs from a perpetuity. Annuities include most mortgages, auto loans, and some bonds. The cash flows of an annuity are shown as follows on a timeline.

Note that just as with the perpetuity, we adopt the convention that the first payment takes place at date 1, one period from today. The present value of an N-period annuity with payment C and interest rate r is

$$PV = \frac{C}{(1+r)} + \frac{C}{(1+r)^2} + \frac{C}{(1+r)^3} + \cdots + \frac{C}{(1+r)^N} = \sum_{n=1}^{N} \frac{C}{(1+r)^n}$$

2.6.2.1. Present Value of an Annuity

We apply the same strategy we used for the perpetuity to find a more straightforward formula: figure out how to generate an annuity. As an example, let's say you deposit $100 into a bank account that offers 5% interest. You will have $105 in the bank after a year—your initial $100 plus $5 in interest. Let's say you withdraw the $5 interest and reinvest the $100 for a second year using the same method as for a perpetuity. After a year, you will have $105 once more, and you can continue the process each year by withdrawing $5 and reinvesting $100. You left the principal in place for all eternity.

Alternatively, you might decide after 20 years to close the account and withdraw the principal. In that case, your cash flows will look like this:

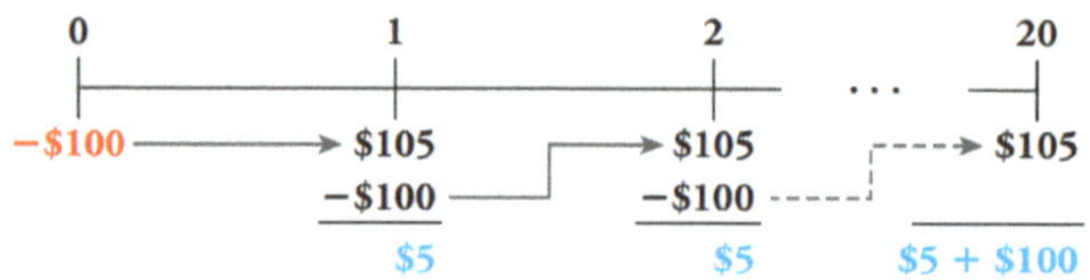

With your initial $100 investment, you have created a 20-year annuity of $5 per year, plus you will receive an extra $100 at the end of 20 years. By the Law of One Price, because it took an initial investment of $100 to create the cash flows on the timeline, the present value of these cash flows is $100, or

$100 = PV(20-year annuity of $5 per year) + PV($100 in 20 years)

Rearranging terms gives;

$$PV(\text{20-year annuity of \$5 per year}) = \$100 - PV(\text{\$100 in 20 years})$$
$$= 100 - \frac{100}{(1.05)^{20}} = \$62.31$$

So the present value of $5 for 20 years is $62.31. Intuitively, the value of the annuity is the initial investment in the bank account minus the present value of the principal that will be left in the account after 20 years.

We can use the same idea to derive the general formula. First, we invest P in the bank, and withdraw only the interest C = r * P each period. After N periods, we close the account. Thus, for an initial investment of P, we will receive an N-period annuity of C per period, plus we will get back our original P at the end. P is the total present value of the two sets of cash flows, or

P = PV(annuity of C for N periods) + PV(P in period N)

By rearranging terms, we compute the present value of the annuity:

$$PV(\text{annuity of } C \text{ for } N \text{ periods}) = P - PV(P \text{ in period } N)$$
$$= P - \frac{P}{(1+r)^N} = P\left(1 - \frac{1}{(1+r)^N}\right) \quad (7)$$

Recall that the periodic payment C is the interest earned every period; that is, C = r * P or, equivalently, solving for P provides the upfront cost in terms of C,

P = C/r

Making this substitution for P, in Eq. 7, provides the formula for the present value of an annuity of C for N periods.

$$PV(\text{annuity of } C \text{ for } N \text{ periods with interest rate } r) = C \times \frac{1}{r}\left(1 - \frac{1}{(1+r)^N}\right) \quad (8)$$

2.6.2.2. Future Value of an Annuity

Finding a straightforward formula for an annuity's future value is simple now that we have a basic formula for its present value. We advance the present value N periods forward on the timeline, or compound the present value for N periods at interest rate r:, if we wish to know the value N years from now.

$$FV(\text{annuity}) = PV \times (1+r)^N$$
$$= \frac{C}{r}\left(1 - \frac{1}{(1+r)^N}\right) \times (1+r)^N$$
$$= C \times \frac{1}{r}\left((1+r)^N - 1\right) \quad (9)$$

This formula is useful if we want to know how a savings account will grow over time. Let's apply this result to evaluate a retirement savings plan.

2.6.3. Growing Cash Flows

Thus far, we have solely examined cash flow streams with consistent cash flow throughout each period. We can also get a straightforward formula for the present value of the future stream if, on the other hand, it is anticipated that the cash flows will increase at a steady rate during each period.

2.6.3.1. Growing Perpetuity

A stream of cash flows that happens regularly and grows at a steady rate indefinitely is known as a growing perpetuity. For instance, the following timeline applies to a growing perpetuity with a $100 initial payment and a 3% growth rate:

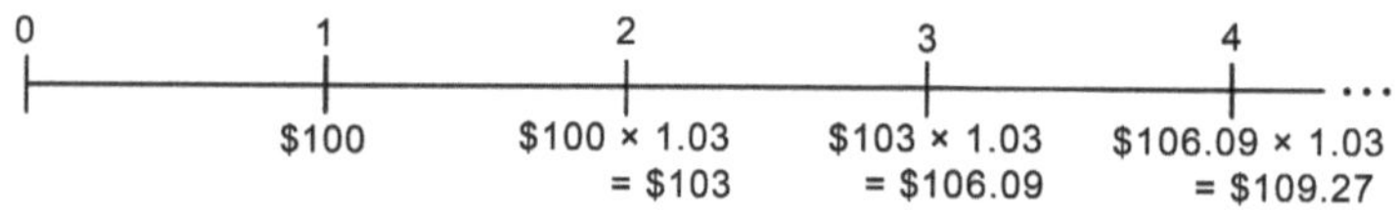

In general, a growing perpetuity with a first payment C and a growth rate g will have the following series of cash flows:

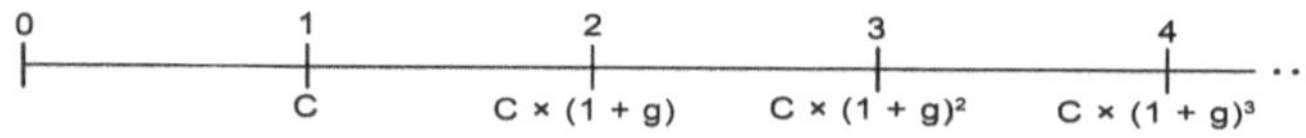

Similar to perpetuals with equal cash flows, we follow the custom of the first payment being made on date 1. Keep in mind another crucial convention: growth is not included in the first payment. In other words, even though the first payment is only one period away, it is C. In a similar vein, there are only n – 1 periods of growth in the cash flow in period n. The general formula for the present value of a cash flow stream can be modified by substituting the cash flows from the previous timeline, as follows.

$$PV = \frac{C}{(1+r)} + \frac{C(1+g)}{(1+r)^2} + \frac{C(1+g)^2}{(1+r)^3} + \cdots = \sum_{n=1}^{\infty} \frac{C(1+g)^{n-1}}{(1+r)^n}$$

Suppose $g \geq r$. Then the cash flows grow even faster than they are discounted; each term in the sum gets larger, rather than smaller. In this case, the sum is infinite! What does an infinite present value mean? Remember that the present value is the "do-it-yourself " cost of creating the cash flows. An infinite present value means that no matter how much money you start with, it is impossible to sustain a growth rate of g forever and reproduce those cash flows on your own. Growing perpetuities of this sort cannot exist in practice because no one would be willing to offer one at any finite price. A promise to pay an amount that forever grew faster than the interest rate is also unlikely to be kept (or believed by any savvy buyer).

In order for each subsequent term in the sum to be smaller than the preceding term and for the total sum to be finite, the only sustainable growing perpetuities are those in which the perpetual growth rate is smaller than the interest rate. Consequently, for a growing perpetuity, we assume that $g < r$.

We use the same reasoning as for a regular perpetuity to determine the formula for the present value of a growing perpetuity: Determine how much you would have to deposit today to establish the perpetuity on your own. In the instance of a regular perpetuity, we reinvested the principal and withdrew the annual interest to create a constant payment for all time. The principal that we reinvest every year needs to rise in order to raise the amount we can withdraw annually. As a result, we take out less money than we earn in interest each period, adding to our principal with the interest that remains.

Let's look at a particular instance. Assuming you invest \$100 in a bank account that yields a 5% interest rate, you can establish a perpetuity growing at a rate of 2%. You will have \$105 in the bank after a year—your initial \$100 plus \$5 in interest. You will have \$102 to reinvest—2% more than you started with—even if you take out just \$3. The following year, this sum will increase to \$102 * 1.05 = \$107.10, from which you can withdraw \$3 * 1.02 = \$3.06, leaving you with a principle of \$107.10 – \$3.06 = \$104.04. Keep in mind that \$102 * 1.02 equals \$104.04. In other words, the principal you reinvest and the amount you withdraw both increase by 2% annually. These cash flows appear as follows on a timeline:

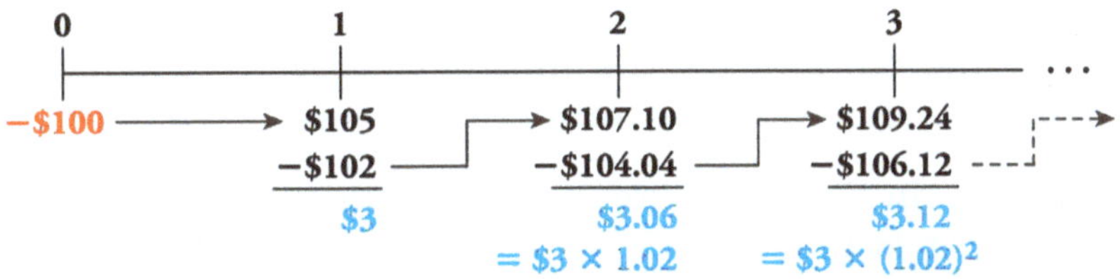

You have established a growing perpetuity with a \$3 starting point and a yearly growth rate of 2% by employing this strategy. The present value of this increasing perpetuity needs to match the \$100 cost.

This is a generalizable argument. We put P in the bank and withdrew the interest every year in the event of an equal-payment perpetuity. We could continue in this pattern indefinitely since we consistently left the principal P in the bank. The principal in the bank must increase by the same factor g if we wish to raise the amount we withdraw from it annually. In other words, we should reinvest $P(1 + g) = P + gP$ in the second year rather than P. We can only remove $C = rP - gP = P(r - g)$ in order to raise our principal by gP. This equation yields the present value of a growing perpetuity with initial cash flow C when P, the initial amount deposited in the bank account, is solved for:

$$PV(\text{growing perpetuity}) = \frac{C}{r-g} \tag{10}$$

Start with the formula for a perpetuity in order to gain an intuitive understanding of the formula for a growing perpetuity. In the previous instance, depositing sufficient funds into the bank was necessary to guarantee that the interest yielded aligned with the cash flows of the regular perpetuity. You must deposit more money in the bank in the event of a growing perpetuity because the growth in cash flows must be financed. How much more? If the bank pays interest at a rate of 5%, the difference (5% – 2% = 3%) is all that needs to be removed in order to ensure that the principal grows by 2% annually. Hence, the present value of the perpetuity is now divided by the difference between the growth rate and the interest rate, rather than being the first cash flow divided by the interest rate.

2.6.3.2. Growing Annuity

A stream of N growing cash flows paid at regular intervals is called a growing annuity. It's a perpetual growth that eventually draws to an end. The timeline that follows displays a growing annuity with an initial cash flow of C that grows at a rate of g each period until period N.

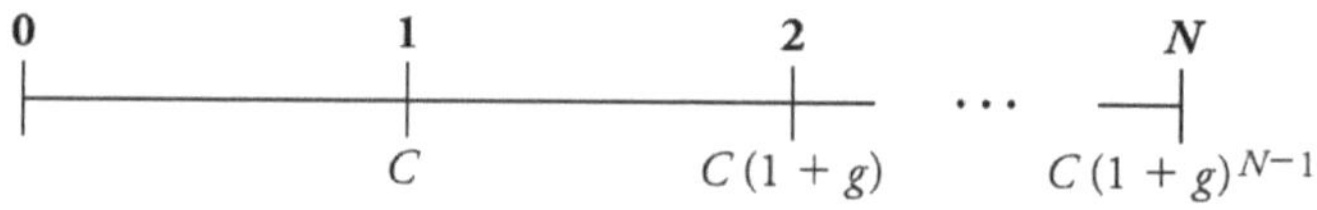

The preceding conventions remain valid: (1) the first cash flow is received at the conclusion of the first period; and (2) the first cash flow is not increasing. Thus, only N − 1 growth periods are shown in the most recent cash flow.

The present value of an N-period growing annuity with initial cash flow C, growth rate g, and interest rate r is given by

$$PV = C \times \frac{1}{r-g}\left(1 - \left(\frac{1+g}{1+r}\right)^N\right) \tag{11}$$

Because the annuity has only a finite number of terms, Eq. 11 also works when g > r. The process of deriving this simple expression for the present value of a growing annuity is the same as for a regular annuity.

The formula for the growing annuity encompasses all of the other formulas in this section. To see how to derive the other formulas from this one, first consider a growing perpetuity. It is a growing annuity with $N = \infty$. If g < r, then

$$\frac{1+g}{1+r} < 1,$$

and so,

$$\left(\frac{1+g}{1+r}\right)^N \to 0 \quad \text{as} \quad N \to \infty.$$

The formula for a growing annuity when $N = \infty$ therefore becomes

$$PV = \frac{C}{r-g}\left(1 - \left(\frac{1+g}{1+r}\right)^N\right) = \frac{C}{r-g}(1-0) = \frac{C}{r-g},$$

which is the formula for a growing perpetuity. The formulas for a regular annuity and perpetuity also follow from the formula if we let the growth rate g = 0. So, if you remember the growing annuity formula, you've got them all!

2.7. USING AN ANNUITY SPREADSHEET OR CALCULATOR

Numerous functions in spreadsheet programs like Excel and popular financial calculators carry out the calculations that finance professionals use them for most frequently. The functions are NPER, RATE, PV, PMT, and FV in Excel. The timeline of an annuity serves as the foundation for all functions.

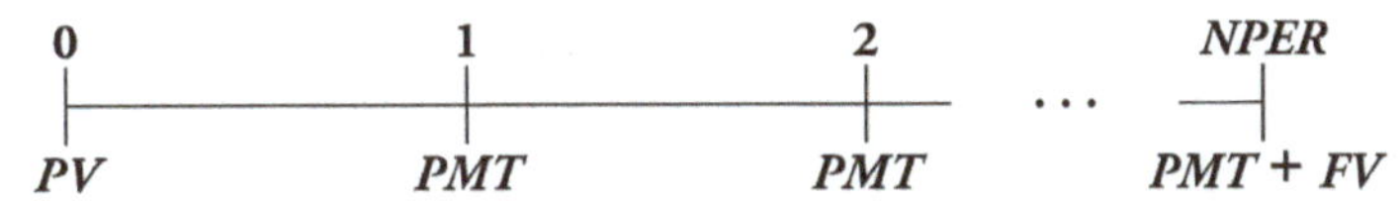

The interest rate used to discount these cash flows is denoted by RATE. Thus, there are a total of five variables: NPER, RATE, PV, PMT, and FV. Each function takes four of these variables as inputs and returns the value of the fifth one that ensures that the NPV of the cash flows is zero. That is, the functions all solve the problem

$$NPV = PV + PMT \times \frac{1}{RATE}\left(1 - \frac{1}{(1+RATE)^{NPER}}\right) + \frac{FV}{(1+RATE)^{NPER}} = 0 \tag{12}$$

In words, the present value of the annuity payments PMT, plus the present value of the final payment FV, plus the initial amount PV, has a net present value of zero. Let's tackle a few examples.

This spreadsheet is what WE call the annuity spreadsheet. To compute a variable, simply enter the four input variables on the top line and leave it blank. The fifth variable is calculated by the spreadsheet, and the result is shown on the bottom line. The Excel function that is used to obtain the answers is also shown in the spreadsheet. Now let's work through a more complex example that demonstrates the annuity spreadsheet's convenience. The same computations can also be performed with a portable financial calculator. The annuity spreadsheet and the calculators function pretty much in the same way. The calculator determines the fifth variable when you enter any four of the 5 variables.

2.8. NON-ANNUAL CASH FLOWS

Until now, we have only considered cash flow streams that occur at annual intervals. Do the same tools apply if the cash flows occur at another interval, say monthly? The answer is yes: Everything we have learned about annual cash flow streams applies to monthly cash flow streams so long as:

1. The interest rate is specified as a monthly rate.
2. The number of periods is expressed in months.

For example, suppose you have a credit card that charges 2% interest per month. If you have a \$1000 balance on the card today, and make no payments for six months, your future balance in one year's time will be:

$$FV = C \times (1+r)^n = \$1000 \times (1.02)^6 = \$1126.16$$

We apply the future value formula exactly as before, but with r equal to the monthly interest rate and n equal to the number of months.

2.9. SOLVING FOR THE CASH PAYMENTS

Thus far, we have computed the cash flow stream's present value or future value. On occasion, though, we are aware of the future or present value but not the cash flows. The best example is a loan; you are aware of the interest rate and the amount you wish to borrow (the present value), but you are unsure of the annual repayment amount. Let's say you want to start a business that needs a $100,000 down payment. The manager of your bank has consented to lend you this money. According to the loan terms, you will pay an interest rate of 8% and make equal annual payments for the next 10 years. The first payment is due one year from today.

From the bank's perspective, the timeline looks like this:

The bank will give you $100,000 today in exchange for 10 equal payments over the next decade. You need to determine the size of the payment C that the bank will require. For the bank to be willing to lend you $100,000, the loan cash flows must have a present value of $100,000 when evaluated at the bank's interest rate of 8%. That is;

100,000 = PV(10-year annuity of C per year, evaluated at the loan rate)

Using the formula for the present value of an annuity;

$$100{,}000 = C \times \frac{1}{0.08}\left(1 - \frac{1}{1.08^{10}}\right) = C \times 6.71$$

Solving this equation for C gives;

$$C = \frac{100{,}000}{6.71} = \$14{,}903$$

You will be required to make 10 annual payments of $14,903 in exchange for $100,000 today.

We can also solve this problem with the annuity spreadsheet:

	NPER	RATE	PV	PMT	FV	Excel Formula
Given	10	8.00%	100,000		0	
Solve for PMT				**– 14,903**		=PMT(0.08,10,100000,0)

Generally speaking, the amount borrowed (the loan principal) should be considered the present value of the payments when calculated using the loan rate. If the loan payments are an annuity, we can use the annuity formula inverted to find the loan payment. Formally speaking, we start this process with the following timeline (as seen from the bank's point of view) for a loan with principal P that needs N periodic payments of C and interest rate r.

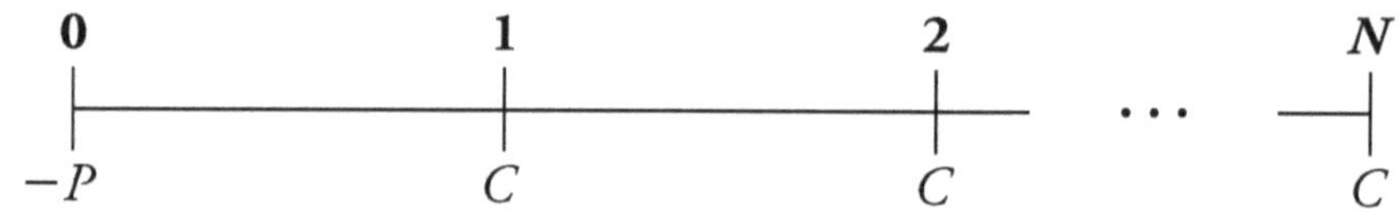

Setting the present value of the payments equal to the principal,

$$P = PV(\text{annuity of } C \text{ for } N \text{ periods}) = C \times \frac{1}{r}\left(1 - \frac{1}{(1+r)^N}\right)$$

Solving this equation for C gives the general formula for the loan payment in terms of the outstanding principal (amount borrowed), P; interest rate, r; and number of payments, N:

$$C = \frac{P}{\frac{1}{r}\left(1 - \frac{1}{(1+r)^N}\right)} \quad (13)$$

Note that the cash flow for a perpetuity is simply C = rP. Rewriting (13) as $C = rP/(1 - 1/(1 + r)^N)$, we can see that the payment for an annuity always exceeds the payment of the equivalent value perpetuity, which makes sense because the annuity will eventually end.

When we know the future value instead of the present value, we can apply the same method to calculate the cash flows. For instance, let's say you recently gave birth to a child. You make the wise decision to begin saving for her college expenses this year. You hope to have saved $60,000 by the time your daughter turns 18.

The timeline for this example is:

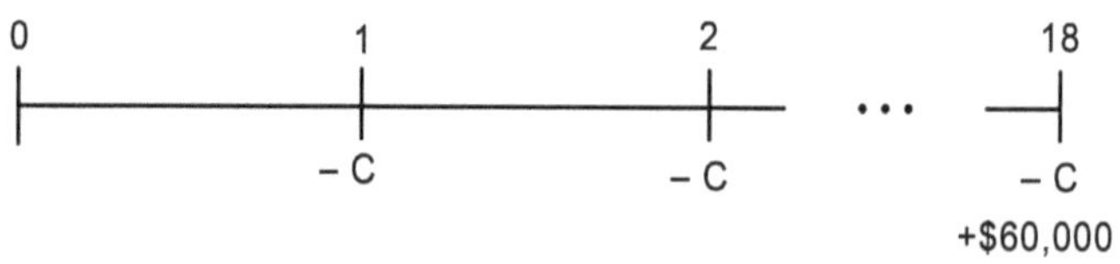

That is, you plan to save some amount C per year, and then withdraw $60,000 from the bank in 18 years. Therefore, we need to find the annuity payment that has a future value of $60,000 in 18 years. Using the formula for the future value of an annuity from Eqn. 9.

$$60{,}000 = FV(\text{annuity}) = C \times \frac{1}{0.07}(1.07^{18} - 1) = C \times 34$$

Therefore, $C = \frac{60{,}000}{34} = \$1765$. So you need to save $1765 per year. If you do, then at a 7% interest rate, your savings will grow to $60,000 by the time your child is 18 years old.

Now let's solve this problem with the annuity spreadsheet:

	NPER	RATE	PV	PMT	FV	Excel Formula
Given	18	7.00%	0		60,000	
Solve for PMT				**−1765**		=PMT(0.07,18,0,60000)

Once again, we find that we need to save $1765 for 18 years to accumulate $60,000.

2.10. THE INTERNAL RATE OF RETURN

In certain cases, you are aware of an investment opportunity's cash flows and present value, but you are unsure of the interest rate that would be required to equalize them. The interest rate that causes the net present value of the cash flows to equal zero is known as the internal rate of return, or IRR.

For example, suppose that you have an investment opportunity that requires a $1000 investment today and will have a $2000 payoff in six years. On a timeline;

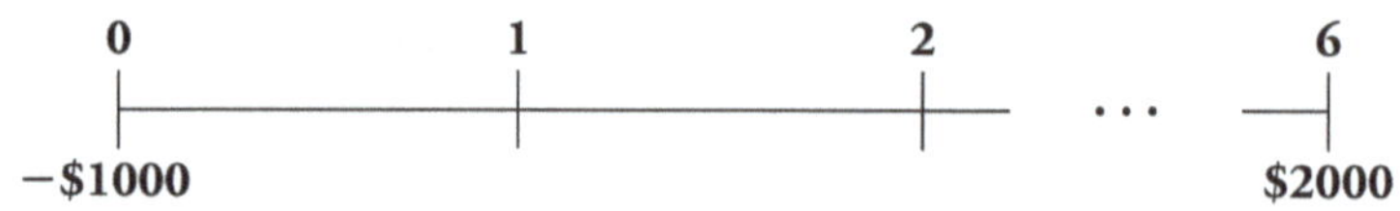

One way to analyze this investment is to ask the question: What interest rate, r, would you need so that the NPV of this investment is zero?

$$NPV = -1000 + \frac{2000}{(1+r)^6} = 0$$

Rearranging gives

$$1000 \times (1+r)^6 = 2000$$

That is, r is the interest rate you would need to earn on your $1000 to have a future value of $2000 in six years. We can solve for r as follows:

$$1 + r = \left(\frac{2000}{1000}\right)^{1/6} = 1.1225$$

or r = 12.25%. This rate is the IRR of this investment opportunity. Making this investment is like earning 12.25% per year on your money for six years.

When there are just two cash flows, as in the preceding example, it is easy to compute the IRR. Consider the general case in which you invest an amount P today, and receive FV in N years. Then the IRR satisfies the equation $P * (1 + IRR)^N = FV$, which implies;

$$IRR \text{ with two cash flows} = (FV/P)^{1/N} - 1 \tag{14}$$

Note in the formula that we take the total return of the investment over N years, FV/P, and convert it to an equivalent one-year return by raising it to the power 1/N.

More generally, if we invest P and receive a perpetuity with initial cash flow C and growth rate g, we can use the growing perpetuity formula to determine;

$$IRR \text{ of growing perpetuity} = (C/P) + g \tag{15}$$

Let's now look at a more complex example. Let's say your company needs to buy a new forklift. The dealer presents you with two options: (1) the forklift's price if you pay cash, or (2) the yearly payments if you borrow money from the dealer. You should compare the interest rate on the loan with what your bank is willing to give you in order to assess the loan that the dealer is offering you. How do you calculate the interest rate that the dealer charges given the loan payment that the dealer quotes?

We must calculate the dealer loan's internal rate of return in this instance. Assume the dealer offers financing with no down payment and four $15,000 annual payments, even though the forklift has a cash price of $40,000. The loan has the subsequent timeframe:

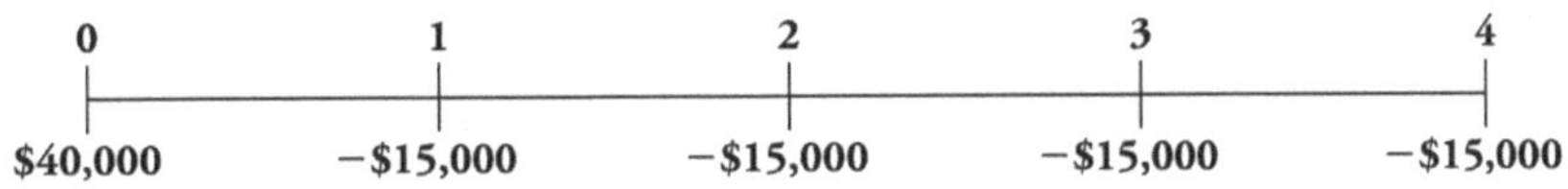

The timeline makes it evident that the loan is an annuity with a four-year term, a $15,000 annual payment, and a $40,000 present value. The present value of the payments must match the purchase price in order to set the net present value (NPV) of the cash flows to zero.

$$40{,}000 = 15{,}000 \times \frac{1}{r}\left(1 - \frac{1}{(1+r)^4}\right)$$

The interest rate applied to the loan is the value of r that provides the solution to this equation, or the IRR. The only way to solve this equation is to guess values of r until you find the correct one. Sadly, there is no easy way to solve for the interest rate r. in this instance.

Start by guessing r = 10%. In this case, the value of the annuity is:

$$15{,}000 \times \frac{1}{0.10}\left(1 - \frac{1}{(1.10)^4}\right) = 47{,}548$$

The present value of the payments is too large. To lower it, we need to use a higher interest rate. We guess 20% this time:

$$15{,}000 \times \frac{1}{0.20}\left(1 - \frac{1}{(1.20)^4}\right) = 38{,}831$$

Now the present value of the payments is too low, so we must pick a rate between 10% and 20%. We continue to guess until we find the right rate. Let us try 18.45%:

$$15{,}000 \times \frac{1}{0.1845}\left(1 - \frac{1}{(1.1845)^4}\right) = 40{,}000$$

The interest rate charged by the dealer is 18.45%.

Using a spreadsheet or calculator to automate the guessing process is a simpler solution than estimating the IRR and manually computing values. The annuity spreadsheet in Excel can be used to calculate the internal rate of return (IRR) when the cash flows are annuities, as in this example. Note that Eqn. can be solved using the annuity spreadsheet. 12. It guarantees that investing in an annuity has no net present value (NPV). It will find the interest rate—the IRR—that causes the NPV to equal zero when the interest rate is the unknown variable. Specifically in this instance.

	NPER	RATE	PV	PMT	FV	Excel Formula
Given	4		40,000	−15,000	0	
Solve for Rate		18.45%				=RATE(4,−15000,40000,0)

The annuity spreadsheet correctly computes an IRR of 18.45%.

CASE STUDY

THE IMPACT OF TIME VALUE OF MONEY ON INVESTMENT DECISIONS

Background

Jane Doe, a recent graduate in finance, has just started her first job at a small investment firm. As part of her onboarding process, Jane is given the task of evaluating two potential investment opportunities for a client. The first option is a conservative bond with a guaranteed return, while the second option is a riskier startup investment with higher potential returns but more uncertainty. Jane must use the principles of the time value of money (TVM) to make a recommendation.

Investment Options

1. **Bond Investment:**
    i. **Principal Investment:** $10,000

    ii. **Annual Interest Rate:** 5%

    iii. **Duration:** 5 years

    iv **Return Type:** Fixed

2. **Startup Investment:**
    i. **Principal Investment:** $10,000

    ii. **Expected Annual Return:** 12%

    iii. **Duration:** 5 years

    iv. **Return Type:** Variable and high-risk

Problem Statement

Jane needs to determine the future value of both investments and assess which investment option would be more beneficial for the client, considering the risk tolerance and financial goals. She will apply the TVM concept to calculate the future values and analyze the risk-adjusted returns.

Calculations

Step 1: Calculate the Future Value of the Bond Investment

The future value (FV) of a bond investment can be calculated using the formula:

$FV=PV\times(1+r)^n$

where:

- PV is the present value (initial investment).
- r is the annual interest rate.
- n is the number of years.

For the bond investment:

- PV=$10,000
- r=0.05 (5%)
- n=5

$FV_{bond}=10{,}000\times(1+0.05)^5$

$FV_{bond}=10{,}000\times1.27628$

$FV_{bond}=\$12{,}762.80$

Step 2: Calculate the Expected Future Value of the Startup Investment

For the startup investment, the future value is more complex to calculate due to its variability. However, assuming the expected return of 12% is consistent, we can use the same formula:

For the startup investment:

- PV=$10,000
- r=0.12 (12%)
- n=5n = 5n=5

$FV_{startup}=10{,}000\times(1+0.12)^5$

$FV_{startup}=10{,}000\times1.76234$

$FV_{startup}=\$17{,}623.40$

Step 3: Analyze Risk-Adjusted Returns

While the startup investment shows a higher future value, it also carries more risk.

The bond investment, being fixed, is less risky and provides a guaranteed return. Jane must weigh the potential higher returns of the startup against the risk of loss, as the expected return is not guaranteed.

Recommendation

Considering the client's risk tolerance and investment goals, Jane makes the following recommendation:

- If the client has a low risk tolerance and prefers a guaranteed return, the bond investment is more suitable. It ensures the principal and provides a modest but reliable return of $12,762.80 after five years.
- If the client is willing to take on more risk for a potentially higher return, the startup investment might be more attractive. Despite the inherent risks, it has a projected future value of $17,623.40.

Conclusion

This case study highlights the importance of the time value of money in making informed investment decisions. By understanding TVM, Jane can provide valuable insights into the potential growth of investments over time and advise her client on the best course of action based on their financial objectives and risk appetite.

This analysis also underscores the critical role of balancing potential returns with associated risks, ensuring that the client's financial goals and risk tolerance are aligned with their investment choices.

CLASS ACTIVITY

You are head of the Schwartz Family Endowment for the Arts. You have decided to fund an arts school in the San Francisco Bay area in perpetuity. Every five years, you will give the school $1 million. The first payment will occur five years from today. If the interest rate is 8% per year, what is the present value of your gift?

SUMMARY

- The time value of money (TVM) is a fundamental concept in corporate finance that underscores the principle that the value of money is not static over time.
- Discounting is the process of determining the present value of a payment or a stream of payments that will be received in the future.
- The time value of money (TVM) is the concept that a sum of money is worth more now than the same sum will be at a future date due to its earnings potential in the interim.
- A perpetuity is a stream of equal cash flows that occur at regular intervals and last forever.
- An annuity is a stream of N equal cash flows paid at regular intervals. The difference between an annuity and a perpetuity is that an annuity ends after some fixed number of payments.
- A growing perpetuity is a stream of cash flows that occur at regular intervals and grow at a constant rate forever.
- A growing annuity is a stream of N growing cash flows, paid at regular intervals. It is a growing perpetuity that eventually comes to an end.
- Spreadsheet programs such as Excel, as well as common financial calculators, have a set of functions that perform the calculations that finance professionals do most often.

REVIEW QUESTIONS

1. What is the present value of $1,000 paid at the end of each of the next 100 years if the interest rate is 7% per year?
2. You are thinking of building a new machine that will save you $1,000 in the first year. The machine will then begin to wear out so that the savings decline at a rate of 2% per year forever. What is the present value of the savings if the interest rate is 5% per year?
3. A rich aunt has promised you $5,000 one year from today. In addition, each year after that, she has promised you a payment (on the anniversary of the last payment) that is 5% larger than the last payment. She will continue to show this generosity for 20 years, giving a total of 20 payments. If the interest rate is 5%, what is her promise worth today?
4. Suppose you currently have $5000 in your savings account, and your bank pays interest at a rate of 0.5% per month. If you make no further deposits or withdrawals, how much will you have in the account in five years?
5. Your firm spends $5,000 every month on printing and mailing costs, sending statements to customers. If the interest rate is 0.5% per month, what is the present value of eliminating this cost by sending the statements electronically?

REFERENCES

1. Bodie, Z. (1976). Common stocks as a hedge against inflation. *Journal of Finance, 31*(2), 459–470.
2. Brealey, R. A., Myers, S. C., & Allen, F. (2020). *Principles of Corporate Finance*. McGraw-Hill Education.
3. Brigham, E. F. (1965). The impact of inflation on the time value of money. *Journal of Financial and Quantitative Analysis, 1*(4), 5–19.
4. Brigham, E. F., & Ehrhardt, M. C. (2013). *Financial Management: Theory & Practice*. Cengage Learning.
5. Damodaran, A. (2014). *Corporate Finance: Theory and Practice*. John Wiley & Sons.
6. Fabozzi, F. J., & Peterson, P. P. (2003). *Financial Management and Analysis*. John Wiley & Sons.
7. Fisher, I. (1930). The theory of interest. *Journal of Political Economy, 38*(5), 488–515.
8. Freeman, R. N., & Tse, S. Y. (1992). A nonlinear model of security price responses to unexpected earnings. *Journal of Accounting Research, 30*(2), 185–209.
9. Gitman, L. J., & Zutter, C. J. (2015). *Principles of Managerial Finance*. Pearson.
10. Gordon, M. J., & Shapiro, E. (1956). Capital equipment analysis: The required rate of profit. *Management Science, 3*(1), 102–110.
11. Higgins, R. C. (2018). *Analysis for Financial Management*. McGraw-Hill Education.
12. Khan, M. Y., & Jain, P. K. (2007). *Financial Management: Text, Problems and Cases*. Tata McGraw-Hill Education.
13. Levy, H., & Sarnat, M. (1972). Investment and portfolio analysis. *Journal of Finance, 27*(5), 1169–1173.
14. Moore, J. C., & Flory, S. M. (1993). Time value of money: Conceptual development and pedagogical implications. *Journal of Accounting Education, 11*(1), 99–113.
15. Petty, J. W., Keown, A. J., & Scott, D. F. (2016). *Foundations of Finance: The Logic and Practice of Financial Management*. Pearson Education.
16. Phelan, C. M. (1997). The effects of financial education on the financial knowledge of undergraduate business students. *Financial Services Review, 6*(4), 325–338.
17. Ross, S. A., Westerfield, R. W., & Jaffe, J. (2015). *Corporate Finance*. McGraw-Hill Education.
18. Siegel, J. J. (1992). Risk, interest rates, and the time value of money. *Financial Analysts Journal, 48*(3), 67–71.
19. Van Horne, J. C., & Wachowicz, J. M. (2008). *Fundamentals of Financial Management*. Pearson Education.
20. Weber, E. U., & Chapman, G. B. (2005). Risk tolerance and the time value of money. *Journal of Risk and Uncertainty, 31*(2), 203–228.

CHAPTER 3

Interest Rates

LEARNING OBJECTIVES

After studying this chapter, you will be able to:

- Understand the interest rates
- Understand the different ways interest rates are quoted
- Use quoted rates to calculate loan payments and balances
- Know how inflation, expectations, and risk combine to determine interest rates
- See the link between interest rates in the market and a firm's opportunity cost of capital

KEY TERMS FROM THIS CHAPTER

Annual percentage rate
Bond
Cost of capital
Effective annual rate
Face value
Nominal interest rates
Rate of return
Risk-free interest rate
Annual percentage yield
Compound interest
Cost of debt
Equal credit opportunity act
Federal funds rate
Opportunity cost
Real interest rate
Simple interest

INTRODUCTION

The amount of interest owed on a loan, deposit, or borrowing amount expressed as a percentage of the principal sum is known as the interest rate. The principal amount, interest rate, frequency of compounding, and duration of loan, deposit, or borrowing all affect the total interest on the amount borrowed or lent.

The interest rate compounded annually is the rate for a full year. Other interest rates are typically annualized and apply over varying time periods, like a day or a month.

An index of the preference for a dollar of present [income] over a dollar of future income has been defined as the interest rate (Fisher Irving, 1907). The borrower is prepared to pay an expense, known as the interest rate, in exchange for the ability to access money more quickly.

This chapter examines the variables that impact interest rates and goes over how to figure out the right discount rate for a given set of cash flows. We start by discussing interest rates and how they are quoted. We also demonstrate how to compute the effective interest paid over the course of a year using various quoting conventions. Next, we examine two primary factors that affect interest rates: inflation and economic expansion. Due to the fluctuating nature of interest rates, investors will demand varying interest rates for varying investment horizons. This will depend on their expectations and the level of risk associated with longer time horizons.

3.1. UNDERSTANDING INTEREST RATES

The amount a lender charges a borrower, expressed as a percentage of the principal amount loaned, is known as the interest rate. Usually, a loan's interest rate is stated annually and represented as an annual percentage rate (APR).

A certificate of deposit (CD) or savings account may also have an interest rate. In this instance, the account holder receives a portion of the money deposited from a bank or credit union. The interest earned on these deposit accounts is referred to as the annual percentage yield, or APY.

In essence, interest is a fee assessed to the borrower for the utilization of an asset. Borrowed assets may consist of money, merchandise, automobiles, and real estate. As a result, interest rates can be compared to the cost of money, with higher rates resulting in higher borrowing costs for the same amount of money.

The majority of lending and borrowing transactions involve interest rates. People take out loans to buy houses, finance initiatives, start or grow businesses, or cover college expenses. Companies borrow money to finance capital projects and grow by investing in long-term and fixed assets like real estate, machinery, and buildings. Repayment of borrowed funds can be made in monthly installments or as a lump amount by a prearranged deadline.

In the case of loans, the principal—the total amount of the loan—is subject to the interest rate. The cost of debt for the borrower and the rate of return for the lender are represented by the interest rate. Due to the fact that lenders demand payment for the money they cannot use during the loan term, the amount owed is typically greater than the amount borrowed. Rather than giving out a loan during that time, the lender could have invested the money, which would have yielded income from the asset. The interest charged is the difference between the total amount repaid and the original loan.

The borrower will typically pay a lower interest rate if the lender deems them to be low risk borrowers. A higher interest rate will be applied to a borrower deemed to pose a greater risk, thereby increasing the cost of the loan.

A prospective borrower's credit score is usually used by lenders to determine risk, so having a high score is crucial to being eligible for the best loans.

3.1.1. Simple Interest Rate

Borrowers must pay lenders simple interest as a fee in exchange for a loan. Compound interest is not included; the principal is the only factor used in the calculation. Simple interest is applicable to a variety of loans. It also refers to the kind of interest that banks give their savings account holders.

If you borrow $300,000 from a bank and the loan agreement states that the interest rate is 4% simple interest, you will be required to repay the bank the $300,000 principle plus (4% x $300,000) = $300,000 + $12,000 = $312,000 that was borrowed.

The example above was calculated based on the annual simple interest formula, which is:

Simple interest = principal x interest rate x time

If the loan was only for a year, the person who took it out will have to pay $12,000 in interest at the end of the year. The interest payment, assuming the loan was a 30-year mortgage, would be:

Simple interest = $300,000 x 4% x 30 = $360,000

A yearly interest payment of $12,000 is calculated using a basic interest rate of 4%. The borrower would have paid $360,000 in interest after 30 years, or $12,000 x 30 years. This illustrates how banks profit from loans, mortgages, and other forms of lending.

3.1.2. Compound Interest Rate

Compound interest refers to interest that is applied to both the original principal of a loan or investment as well as the interest that has accrued over time. Stated differently, compound interest is the accumulation of interest on interest.

The borrower pays even more in interest when using the compound interest method, which is preferred by some lenders. In addition to the principal, compound interest—also known as interest on interest—is applied to the interest that has accrued over earlier periods. The borrower is assumed to owe the bank the principal amount plus interest for the first year at the end of the loan. Additionally, the bank assumes that the borrower will owe the principal amount plus interest from the first year plus interest on interest at the end of the second year.

Compounding results in a higher interest payment than the simple interest method. Monthly interest is assessed on the principal amount, which includes interest that has accumulated over the previous months. The calculation of interest for both approaches will be comparable for shorter time periods. However, the difference between the two methods of interest calculations gets larger as the lending period gets longer.

Using the example above, at the end of 30 years, the total owed in interest is almost $700,000 on a $300,000 loan with a 4% interest rate.

The following formula can be used to calculate compound interest:

$$\text{Compound interest} = p \times [(1 + \text{interest rate})^n - 1]$$

Where:

p = principal

n = number of compounding periods

Let's look at another example. Ben takes out a three-year loan of $10,000 at an interest rate of 5%, which compounds annually. In the end, as worked out in the calculation below, he pays $1,576.25 in interest on the loan:

$$\$10,000\ [(1 + 0.05)^3 - 1] = \$10,000\ [1.157625 - 1] = \$1,576.25$$

3.1.3. Compound Interest and Savings Accounts

Compound interest is a benefit when using a savings account to save money. The account holder receives compensation for allowing the bank to use their deposited funds in the form of compound interest earned on these accounts.

For instance, the bank may take $300,000 out of your $500,000 deposit into a high-yield savings account and use it as a loan for a mortgage. The bank credits your account with an annual interest rate of 5% as compensation. Thus, the bank earns 3% in interest while deducting 8% from the borrower and giving the account holder 5%. Saver money is essentially lent to the bank, which then disburses funds to borrowers in exchange for interest.

Even during extremely low interest rates, the compounding effect of interest rates can help you accumulate wealth over time. Investopedia Academy's Personal Finance for Grads course teaches students how to build a nest egg and preserve wealth.

3.1.4. Borrower's Cost of Debt

Interest rates are a cost of debt for the borrower even though they represent interest income to the lender. Businesses compare the cost of borrowing to the cost of equity, which includes dividend payments, in order to ascertain which funding source will be the least expensive. Since most businesses raise capital through the issuance of equity or the taking on of debt, it is necessary to assess the cost of capital in order to establish an ideal capital structure.

3.1.4.1. APR vs. APY

Annual percentage rates, or APRs, are commonly used to quote interest rates on consumer loans. Lenders require this rate of return in exchange for allowing borrowers to access their funds. An APR, for instance, is used to express the interest rate on credit cards. The APR for the borrower or mortgage in the aforementioned example is 4%. Compound interest for the year is not taken into account by the APR.

The interest rate on a savings account or certificate of deposit (CD) at a bank or credit union is known as the annual percentage yield, or APY. Compounding is taken into consideration in this interest rate.

3.1.4.2. How Are Interest Rates Determined?

Bank interest rates are influenced by various factors, including the overall health of the economy. The interest rate, which each bank uses to determine the APR range they offer, is set by the central bank of that nation (e.g., the Federal Reserve in the United States). The cost of debt increases when interest rates are set high by the central bank. A high cost of debt deters people from taking out loans and reduces demand from consumers. Inflation tends to drive up interest rates.

Banks may raise reserve requirements, create a tighter money supply, or increase credit demand in order to fight inflation. People save more money when interest rates are high because they get more money from their savings rate. Due to investors' preference for taking advantage of the higher savings rate over investing in the stock market, which offers lower returns, the stock market suffers. Additionally, businesses can only obtain a limited amount of capital funding through debt, which causes the economy to contract.

Because borrowers can obtain loans at low interest rates, economies are frequently stimulated during low interest rate periods. Low interest rates on savings make it more likely for individuals and businesses to spend money on riskier investments like stocks. Spending like this stimulates the economy and injects capital into the markets, which leads to economic growth.

Lower interest rates are preferred by governments, but they eventually cause market disequilibrium, which increases inflation when demand exceeds supply. Interest rates rise in response to inflation, which could be connected to Walras' law.

The average interest rate in February 2024 for a 30-year fixed-rate mortgage. This represents an increase from 6.50% one year ago and 3.89% two years prior.

3.1.4.3. Interest Rates and Discrimination

In the United States, systemic racism persists despite legislation, such as the Equal Credit Opportunity Act (ECOA), that forbids discriminatory lending practices.

There is proof that White applicants are granted mortgage approvals more frequently. Black, Hispanic-White, and Asian applicants were denied conventional mortgage loans 16.4%, 11.1%, and 9.2% of the time in 2022, according to data reported under the Home Mortgage Disclosure Act, the most comprehensive publicly available information on mortgage market activity. Conversely, White applicants had significantly lower rejection rates (5.8%).

Additionally, data points to the possibility that race affects interest rates. Using mortgage data from 2018 and 2019, Realtor.com found that mortgages with interest rates 13 basis points higher are offered to homebuyers in predominantly Black communities than to those in White communities.

Other sources that have verified evidence of discrimination in interest rates with mortgages include Harvard University and the think tank Urban Institute, which stated in 2022 that the average Black homeowner pays approximately $250 more in interest annually and is charged an interest rate 33 basis points higher than the average White homeowner.

There are those who disagree with these results. No race receives preferential treatment, according to a study by Federal Reserve Board economists. However, the study's authors conjectured that the reason for other reported disparities may be that Black and Hispanic borrowers typically choose slightly higher interest rates in exchange for lower upfront costs.

The Federal Reserve Board attributes the improvement in discrimination, at least in part, to increased automated underwriting and more stringent adherence to the ECOA and Fair Housing Act.

3.1.5. History of Interest Rates

Interest rates have been set in different ways over the last 200 years by central banks or national governments. For instance, the base rate of the Bank of England fluctuated between 0.5% and 15% from 1989 to 2009, the Federal Reserve federal funds rate in the United States fluctuated between approximately 0.25% and 19% from 1954 to 2008, and rates in Germany ranged from nearly 90% in the 1920s to approximately 2% in the 2000s.

In an effort to stop the hyperinflation that was spiraling out of control, the Central Bank of Zimbabwe raised borrowing rates to 800% in 2007. There have never been such high long-term rates since the creation of modern capital markets as there were in the late 1970s and early 1980s when it came to prime credits. These rates were higher than US peaks since 1800, British peaks since 1700, and Dutch peaks since 1600. There have been accounts that savings deposits could achieve an annual return of at least

25% and up to 50% before the advent of modern capital markets (Homer, Sidney et al., 1996).

3.1.6. Why Are Interest Rates on 30-Year Loans Higher Than 15-Year Loans?

Interest rates are determined by opportunity cost and default risk. Longer-term debts and loans carry a higher inherent risk because the borrower has a longer window of opportunity to default. Longer time periods also result in a higher opportunity cost since the principal is locked up and cannot be utilized for any other reason during that time.

3.1.7. How Does the Fed Use Interest Rates in the Economy?

Interest rates are a tool used by the Federal Reserve and other central banks worldwide to implement monetary policy. The central bank can affect many other interest rates, including those on personal loans, business loans, and mortgages, by raising the cost of borrowing among commercial banks. This raises the cost of borrowing money generally, which reduces demand for money and cools an overheated economy. Conversely, lowering interest rates facilitates borrowing, which encourages investment and spending.

3.1.8. Why Do Bond Prices React Inversely to Interest Rate Changes?

A bond is a type of debt instrument that, during the course of its life, usually pays interest at a fixed rate. Assume that the current interest rate is 5%. A bond will pay bondholders $50 annually if it is priced at par, or $1,000, and has a 5% interest rate (coupon). The interest rate on newly issued bonds will double, to 10%, i.e., $100 for every $1,000 face value. For someone to want to purchase an existing bond that only pays $50, it must be sold at a steep discount. In the same way, new bonds will only pay $10 for every $1,000 in face value if interest rates fall to 1%. Because of this, a $50 bond will be highly sought after and its price will rise significantly.

3.2. INTEREST RATE QUOTES AND ADJUSTMENTS

You can literally find dozens of interest rates discussed and advertised in newspapers if you take the time to look through them. These rates include those for auto loans, savings accounts, and interest paid on government debt. It is obvious that interest rates are essential to any financial system's operation. It's crucial to consider interest rates as a cost—the cost of using money—in order to comprehend interest rates. When you take out a loan to purchase a car, you are borrowing money from the bank and will eventually repay it. The cost you incur to be able to turn your future loan payments into a car today is the interest rate on your loan. In a similar vein, by funding a savings account, you grant the bank access to your funds until you take them out at a later time. The cost the bank incurs to use your money (e.g., to make car loans) is the interest it pays you on your deposit.

Interest rates are determined by market factors, such as the supply and demand for funds, just like any other price. In the event that borrowing is scarce and savings are abundant, low interest rates will result. In addition, risk and anticipated inflation have an impact on interest rates.

Understanding how interest rates are quoted is necessary for us to be able to study and use them. In actuality, interest rates are quoted differently and interest is paid in various ways. In mid-2006, for instance, New Century Bank offered daily interest-paying savings accounts at 5.12%, while Internet bank ING Direct offered savings accounts with an interest rate of 5.25% paid at the end of a year. The length of the investment horizon can also affect interest rates. When it came to risk-free investments, investors could earn over 5% on 15-year investments, but only about 1% on one-year investments in January 2004. Risk has an impact on interest rates as well. The US government, for instance, can borrow money at a lot cheaper interest rate than General Motors.

It is frequently necessary to modify the interest rate to a time period that corresponds with our cash flows because interest rates can be quoted for a variety of time periods, including monthly, semiannual, or annual. In this section, we examine these interest rate mechanics.

3.2.1. The Effective Annual Rate

When interest is compounded over a specified period of time, the rate of interest actually earned on an investment or paid on a loan is known as the Effective Annual Rate (EAR). It is used to compare various financial products that compute annual interest with various compounding periods—weekly, monthly, yearly, etc.—and is typically higher than the nominal rate. When more compounding periods are added, the effective annual interest rate rises over time (Figure 3.1).

Effective Annual Rate

$$\left[1 + \frac{\text{Nominal interest rate}}{\text{\# of compounding periods}}\right]^{\wedge(\text{number of compounding periods})} - 1$$

Figure 3.1. *Effective annual rate.*

Source: https://corporatefinanceinstitute.com/resources/commercial-lending/effective-annual-rate/.

Typically, the effective annual rate exceeds the nominal rate since the latter expresses a yearly percentage rate without taking compounding into account. The effective annual rate is higher than the nominal rate when the number of compounding periods is increased. Put another way, an annual compounding investment will have an effective annual rate that is equal to its nominal rate. The effective annual rate would be higher, though, if the same investment were compounded on a quarterly basis.

The formula for the EAR is:

Effective Annual Rate = (1 + (nominal interest rate/number of compounding periods)) ^ (number of compounding periods) – 1

For instance, Union Bank provides Mr. Obama, a bank customer, with a certificate of deposit at a nominal interest rate of 12%. The client committed to a one-year interest compounding period and an initial $1,000 investment. Even though the interest is only offered at 12%, compounding results in an effective interest rate of 12.683%, meaning that the money increased by $126.83 over the course of a year.

Effective annual rate (EAR) and annual percentage yield (APY), which show the total interest that will be earned at the end of a year, are common terms used to describe interest rates. Thus far, we have quoted the interest rate in this context using this method, and in our time value of money calculations, we have used the EAR as the discount rate r. For example, with an EAR of 5%, a $100 investment grows to;

$$\$100 \times (1 + r) = \$100 \times (1.05) = \$105$$

in one year. After two years it will grow to:

$$\$100 \times (1 + r)^2 = \$100 \times (1.05)^2 = \$110.25$$

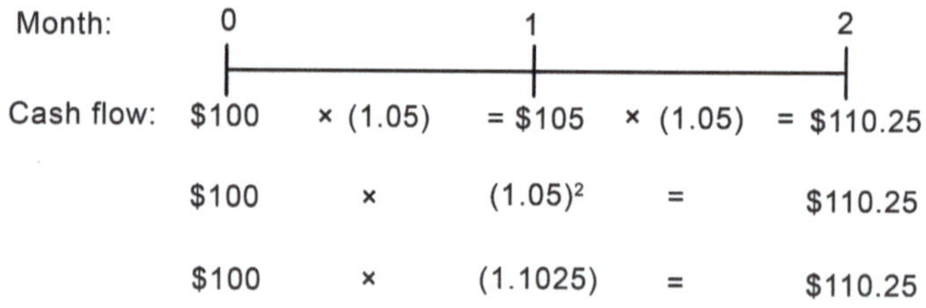

3.2.2. Adjusting the Discount Rate to Different Time Periods

The preceding example shows that earning an effective annual rate of 5% for two years is equivalent to earning 10.25% in total interest over the entire period:

$$\$100 \times (1.05)^2 = \$100 \times 1.1025 = \$110.25$$

Generally speaking, we can compute an equivalent interest rate for a longer time period by increasing the interest rate factor to the appropriate power.

For time periods shorter than a year, we can determine the equivalent interest rate using the same procedure. We increase the interest rate factor to the proper fractional power in this instance. For example, earning 5% interest in one year is equivalent to receiving

$$(1 + r)^{0.5} = (1.05)^{0.5} = \$1.0247$$

for each $1 invested every six months (0.5 years). That is, a 5% effective annual rate is equivalent to an interest rate of approximately 2.47% earned every six months. We can verify this result by computing the interest we would earn in one year by investing for two six-month periods at this rate:

$$(1 + r)^2 = (1.0247)^2 = \$1.05$$

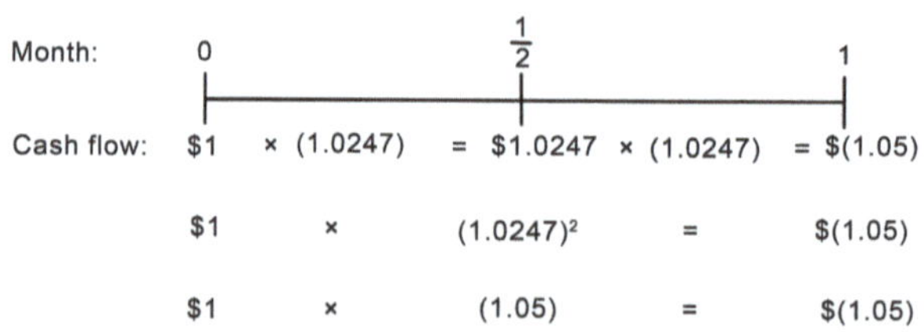

In general, we can convert a discount rate of r for one period to an equivalent discount rate for n periods using the following formula:

$$\text{Equivalent } n\text{-period Discount Rate} = (1 + r)^n - 1 \qquad (1)$$

When using this formula, n can be either larger than 1 (to calculate a rate over a longer period of time) or smaller than 1 (to compute a rate over a shorter period of time). You should modify the discount rate to correspond with the cash flows' time period when calculating present or future values. Applying the perpetuity or annuity formulas to non-annual cash flows requires this modification, as seen in the example below.

3.2.2.1. Example 3.1. Valuing Monthly Cash Flows

- **Problem:** Suppose your bank account pays interest monthly with an effective annual rate of 6%. What amount of interest will you earn each month?

  If you have no money in the bank today, how much will you need to save at the end of each month to accumulate $100,000 in 10 years?
- Solution:

  - **Plan:** We can use Eqn. 1 to convert the EAR to a monthly rate, answering the first question. The second question is a future value of an annuity question. It is asking how big a monthly annuity we would have to deposit in order to end up with $100,000 in 10 years. However, in order to do this problem, we need to write the timeline in terms of monthly periods because our cash flows (deposits) will be monthly:

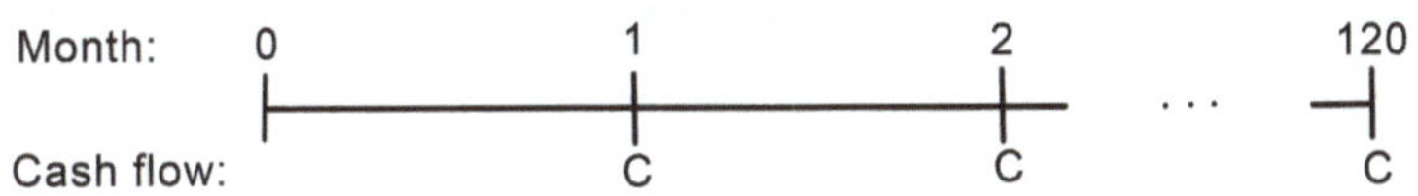

    That is, we can view the savings plan as a monthly annuity with 10 × 12 = 120 monthly payments. We have the future value of the annuity ($100,000), the length of time (120 months), and we will have the monthly interest rate from the first part of the question. We can then use the future value of an annuity formula to solve for the monthly deposit.
  - **Execute:** From Eqn.1, a 6% EAR is equivalent to earning $(1.06)^{1/12} - 1 = 0.4868\%$ per month. The exponent in this equation is 1/12 because the period is 1/12th of a year (a month).

    To determine the amount to save each month to reach the goal of $100,000 in 120 months, we must determine the amount C of the monthly payment that will have a future value of $100,000 in 120 months, given an interest rate of 0.4868% per month. Now that we have all of the inputs in terms of months (monthly payment, monthly interest rate, and total number of months), we use the future value of annuity formula to solve this problem:

$$FV(\text{annuity}) = C \times \frac{1}{r}[(1 + r)^n - 1]$$

    We solve for the payment C using the equivalent monthly interest rate r =

0.4868%, and n = 120 months:

$$C = \frac{FV(\text{annuity})}{\frac{1}{r}[(1+r)^n - 1]} = \frac{\$100{,}000}{\frac{1}{0.004868}[(1.004868)^{120} - 1]} = \$615.47 \text{ per month}$$

We can also compute this result using a financial calculator or spreadsheet:

	N	I/Y	PV	PMT	FV
Given:	120	0.4868	0		100,000
Solve for:				**−615.47**	
Excel Formula: = PMT(RATE,NPER,PV,FV)=PMT(0.004868,120,0,100000)					

- **Evaluate:** Thus, if we save $615.47 per month and we earn interest monthly at an effective annual rate of 6%, we will have $100,000 in 10 years. Notice that the timing in the annuity formula must be consistent for all of the inputs. In this case, we had a monthly deposit, so we needed to convert our interest rate to a monthly interest rate and then use total number of months (120) instead of years.

3.2.2.2. Using the EAR in the Annuity Formula

Many students erroneously attempt to use the EAR in the annuity formula at this point. The annuity formula's interest rate and the cash flow frequency must coincide. For this reason, in Example 3.1, we computed the monthly loan payments using the annuity formula after first converting the EAR into a monthly rate. In this instance, a common error would be to calculate the annual cash flows using the annuity formula's EAR and then divide those cash flows by 12 to determine the monthly payments.

The incorrect answer will be obtained by this method. Examine the timing of the first deposit in Example 3.1 to understand why. The annuity formula, which uses a monthly rate and monthly payments, projects that the first payment will be made in a month. After that, it makes the assumption that you will deposit 11 more times each month before the first year ends. As soon as you make a deposit, it will all begin to accrue interest. On the other hand, the formula for calculating an annual cash flow using an EAR assumes that you will make your first deposit in a year, meaning you will miss out on a full year of interest before you begin to earn anything. As you can see, the EAR approach ignores the fact that you are increasing your interest-earning principal more frequently than once a year because you are making deposits earlier and more frequently than once a year.

3.2.3. Annual Percentage Rates

The interest rate applied to a loan, mortgage loan, credit card, etc., for an entire year (annualized) as opposed to just a monthly fee or rate is known as the annual percentage rate of charge (APR), which can also refer to a nominal APR or an effective APR (EAPR). It is a finance charge that is stated as an annual percentage (O'Sullivan,

Steven M. Sheffrin, & Arthur O'Sullivan, 2010). In certain nations or legal systems, those terms have official, legal definitions; however, in the US:

- The nominal *APR* is the simple-interest rate (for a year).
- The effective *APR* is the fee+compound interest rate (calculated across a year).

In certain regions, the effective interest rate that a borrower will pay on a loan is represented by its simplified counterpart, the annual percentage rate (APR). As a kind of consumer protection, lenders (like banks) are compelled in numerous nations and jurisdictions to reveal the cost of borrowing in a uniform manner. The purpose of the (effective) APR is to facilitate lender and loan option comparison (Chen James, 2021).

The annual percentage rate (APR), which represents the amount of simple interest earned in a year—that is, the amount of interest earned without the effect of compounding—is the most widely used unit of measurement for interest rates. The APR quote is often less than the actual amount of interest you will earn because it does not account for the compounding effect. You must first convert the annual percentage rate (APR) to an effective annual rate in order to determine the actual amount you will earn in a year.

For instance, let's say Granite Bank offers savings accounts with monthly compounding interest rates of 6% APR. Granite Bank actually implies that you will make money each month when it quotes a rate in this manner. In other words, rather than quoting an annual interest rate, an APR with monthly compounding actually quotes a monthly interest rate. In this instance, the bank quotes an annual percentage rate (APR) by multiplying the actual rate by 12 months, even though the rate is actually 0.5% per month. Because the interest compounds each month, you will actually have;

$$\$1 \times (1.005)^{12} = \$1.061678$$

at the end of one year, for an effective annual rate of 6.1678%. Because of compound interest, which allows you to earn interest on interest paid in previous months, the 6.1678% that you earn on your deposit is higher than the 6% APR that is quoted. In conclusion, an actual monthly rate of 0.5% can be expressed in one of the following ways:

- 6% APR, compounded monthly
- EAR of 6.1678%, which is the actual rate earned per year

It's crucial to keep in mind that the APR by itself cannot be used as a discount rate since it does not accurately represent the total amount you will earn over the course of a year. Instead, the APR is a way of quoting the actual interest earned each compounding period:

$$\text{Interest Rate per Compounding Period} = \frac{APR}{m}$$
$$(m = \text{number of compounding periods per year}) \quad (2)$$

Eqn. (1) can be used to calculate the equivalent interest rate for any other time interval after we have calculated the interest earned per compounding period using Eqn. (2). Therefore, the following conversion formula yields the effective annual rate that corresponds to an APR:

Converting an APR to an EAR

$$1 + EAR = \left(1 + \frac{APR}{m}\right)^m$$
$$(m = \text{number of compounding periods per year}) \quad (3)$$

The effective annual rates with various compounding intervals that translate to a

6% annual percentage rate are displayed in Table 3.1. Because interest on interest can be earned sooner, the EAR rises as compounding frequency increases. Compounding occurs even more frequently than daily for investments. The compounding interval could theoretically occur every hour or every second. Practically speaking, compounding more often than once a day has very little effect on the effective annual rate and is rarely done.

When working with APRs, before assessing the present or future value of a set of cash flows, we must first convert the APR to an EAR using Eq. (3), or to a discount rate per compounding interval using Eq. (2).

Table 3.1. Effective Annual Rates for a 6% APR with Different Compounding Periods

Compounding Interval	Effective Annual Rate
Annual	$\left(1+\frac{0.06}{1}\right)^{1}-1=6\%$
Semiannual	$\left(1+\frac{0.06}{2}\right)^{2}-1=6.09\%$
Monthly	$\left(1+\frac{0.06}{12}\right)^{12}-1=6.1678\%$
Daily	$\left(1+\frac{0.06}{365}\right)^{365}-1=6.1831\%$

3.2.3.1. Example 3.2. Converting the APR to a Discount Rate

- **Problem:** Your firm is purchasing a new telephone system that will last for four years. You can purchase the system for an upfront cost of $150,000, or you can lease the system from the manufacturer for $4,000 paid at the end of each month. The lease price is offered for a 48-month lease with no early termination—you cannot end the lease early. Your firm can borrow at an interest rate of 6% APR with monthly compounding. Should you purchase the system outright or pay $4,000 per month?
- Solution

o **Plan:** The cost of leasing the system is a 48-month annuity of $4,000 per month:

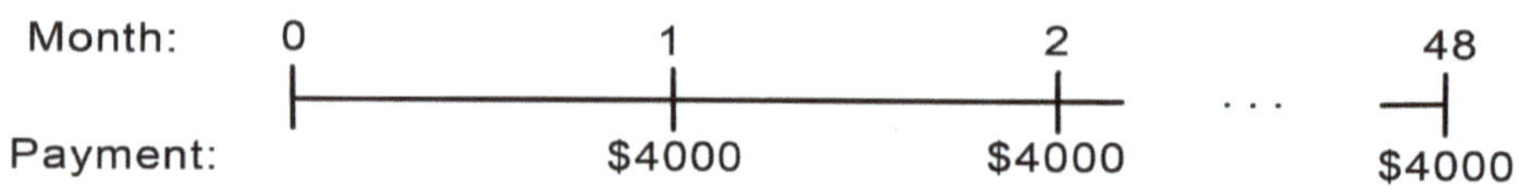

We can compute the present value of the lease cash flows using the annuity formula, but first we need to compute the discount rate that corresponds to a period length of one month. To do so, we convert the borrowing cost of 6% APR with monthly compounding to a monthly discount rate using Eqn. 2. Once we have a monthly rate, we can use the present value of annuity formula

$C \times \frac{1}{r}\left(1 - \frac{1}{(1+r)^N}\right)$ to compute the present value of the monthly payments and compare it to the cost of buying the system.

- **Execute**

  As Eqn. 2 shows, the 6% APR with monthly compounding really means 6%/12 = 0.5% every month. The 12 comes from the fact that there are 12 monthly compounding periods per year. Now that we have the true rate corresponding to the stated APR, we can use that discount rate in the annuity formula to compute the present value of the monthly payments:

$$PV = 4000 \times \frac{1}{0.005}\left(1 - \frac{1}{1.005^{48}}\right) = \$170{,}321.27$$

  Using a financial calculator or spreadsheet:

	N	I/Y	PV	PMT	FV
Given:	48	0.5		−4000	0
Solve for:			170,321.27		
Excel Formula: =PV(RATE,NPER,PMT,FV)=PV(0.005,48,−4000,0)					

- **Evaluate:** Thus, paying $4000 per month for 48 months is equivalent to paying a present value of $170,321.27 today. This cost is $170,321.27 − $150,000 = $20,321.27 higher than the cost of purchasing the system, so it is better to pay $150,000 for the system rather than lease it. One way to interpret this result is as follows: At a 6% APR with monthly compounding, by promising to repay $4000 per month your firm can borrow $170,321 today. With this loan it could purchase the phone system and have an additional $20,321 to use for other purposes.

3.3. APPLICATION: DISCOUNT RATES AND LOANS

After describing how to calculate the discount rate from an interest rate quote, let's use the idea to resolve two typical financial issues: figuring out how much a loan payment is and how much is left on the loan.

3.3.1. Computing Loan Payments

APR with monthly compounding is used to quote many loans with monthly payments, including mortgages and auto loans. These loans are amortizing loans, which means that in addition to the principal amount, you also pay interest on the loan each month. The loan is completely repaid with the final payment, which is the same as each monthly installment. A new car loan might have terms like "6.75% annual percentage rate for 60 months." If the APR's compounding interval isn't specified clearly, it's equivalent to the time between payments, which in this case is one month. According to this quote, the loan will be paid back in 60 equal monthly installments, calculated at an annual percentage rate of 6.75% with monthly compound interest. Sometimes it helps to consider the loan from the perspective of the bank: you will receive $30,000 in cash from the bank today to be used toward the purchase of the car. In exchange, beginning one month from now, you will make 60 equal payments to the bank every month for 60 months. The present value of what you will give the bank, discounted at the interest rate on the loan, must match the amount of cash the bank is giving you now for the bank to be willing to accept this exchange. Consider the timeline for a $30,000 car loan with these terms:

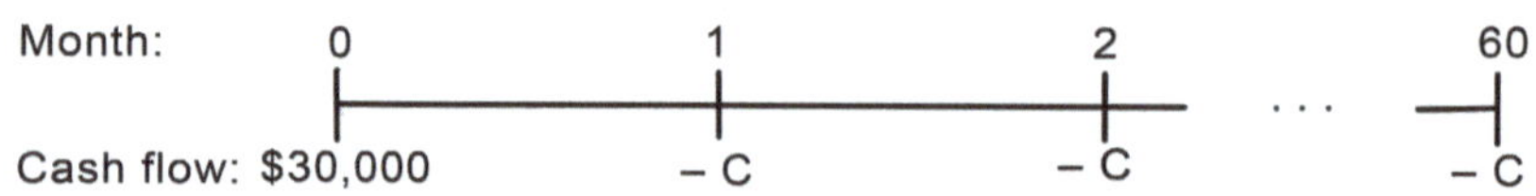

The payment, C, is calculated so that the loan interest rate and the present value of the cash flows equal the $30,000 initial principle. In this instance, the monthly compounded annual percentage rate of 6.75% results in a one-month discount rate of 6.75%/12 = 0.5625%. We can move forward because we have a monthly loan payment and a monthly discount rate in this case, which is crucial given the frequency of the cash flows. Because the loan payments are an annuity:

$$C = \frac{P}{\frac{1}{r}\left(1 - \frac{1}{(1+r)^N}\right)} = \frac{30{,}000}{\frac{1}{0.005625}\left(1 - \frac{1}{(1+0.005625)^{60}}\right)} = \$590.50$$

Alternatively, we can solve for the payment C using a financial calculator or spreadsheet:

	N	I/Y	PV	PMT	FV
Given:	60	0.5625	30,000		0
Solve for:				−590.50	
Excel Formula: =PMT(RATE,NPER,PV,FV)=PMT(0.005625,60,30000,0)					

Monthly principal repayment and interest are deducted from your loan payment, lowering the remaining balance. The interest charged on the loan balance decreases monthly as a result of the loan balance (the total amount you still owe) decreasing. The portion of your payment that is required to cover interest each month is therefore continuously decreasing, and the portion that is left over to further reduce the principal is continuously increasing, even though your payment remains the same for the full 60-month term of the loan. Figure 3.2's panel (a) provides an illustration of this effect by showing the percentage of each monthly loan payment that goes toward interest (red) and the remaining percentage (turquoise) that goes toward principal reduction. You can see that, out of your initial $590.50 payment, $168.75 is required to cover interest that has accumulated during the first month ($30,000 × 0.005625 = $168.75). But by the time the loan is over, almost all of your payment will have gone toward principal due to the amount gradually declining.

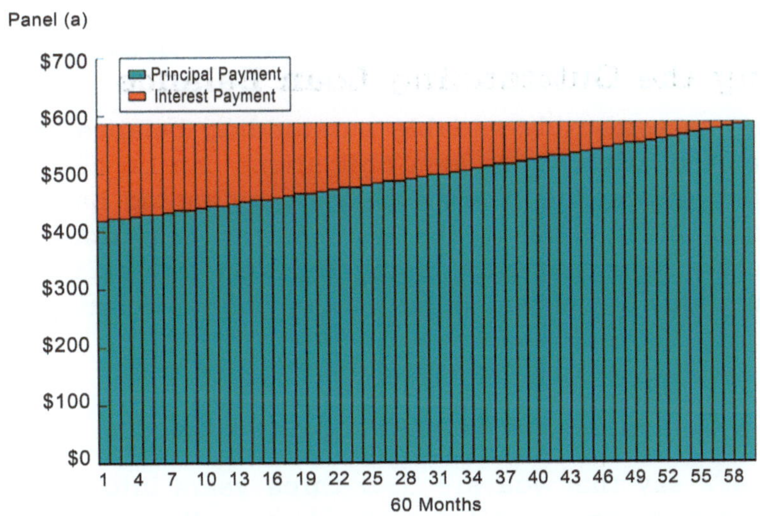

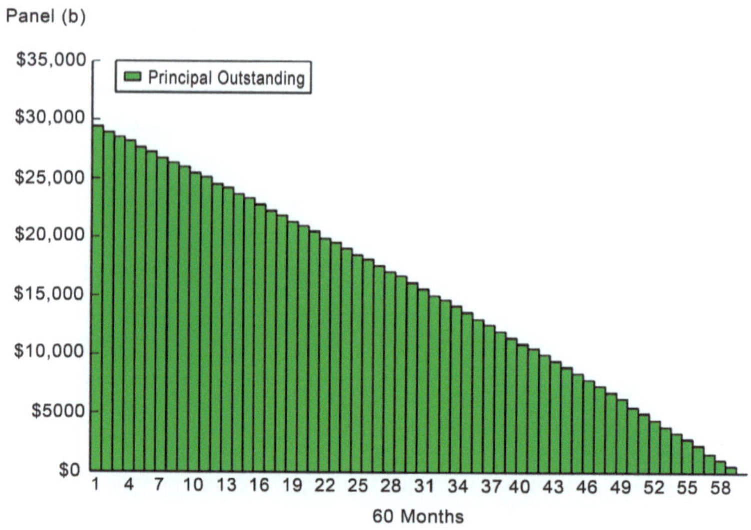

Figure 3.2. *Amortizing loan. Panel (a) shows how the interest (red) and principal portions (turquoise) of the monthly payment on the $30,000 car loan change over the life of the loan. Panel (b) illustrates the effect on the outstanding balance (principal) of the loan. Note that as the balance decreases, the amount of the payment needed to cover interest on that balance decreases, allowing more of the payment to be used to reduce the principal.*

Figure 3.2's Panel (b) illustrates how your loan balance is affected by your payments. When you make your initial $590.50 payment, $168.75 goes toward paying off the loan's interest, leaving $421.75 to lower the principle to $30,000 − $421.75 = $29,578.25. The remaining portion of your $590.50 payment goes toward further reducing the principal because you only owe interest on the $29,578.25 loan balance—or $166.38—the following month. As a result of this ongoing effect, every month you are able to contribute a larger portion of your payment toward principal reduction, which causes the principal to decrease quickly as the loan nears its conclusion.

3.3.2. Computing the Outstanding Loan Balance

An amortizing loan has a monthly variable outstanding balance, as shown in Figure 3.2. The present value of your future loan obligations can be used to determine how much you owe at any given time. Therefore, the outstanding balance, also known as the outstanding principal, is equal to the loan interest rate times the present value of the remaining future loan payments. Using the loan rate as the discount rate, we compute the present value of the remaining loan payments to arrive at the outstanding loan balance.

3.3.2.1. Example 3.3. Computing the Outstanding Loan Balance

- **Problem:** Let's say that you are now three years into your $30,000 car loan from the previous section and you decide to sell the car. When you sell the car, you will need to pay whatever the remaining balance is on your car loan.

After 36 months of payments, how much do you still owe on your car loan?

- **Solution**
    - **Plan:** We have already determined that the monthly payments on the loan are \$590.50. The remaining balance on the loan is the present value of the remaining 2 years, or 24 months, of payments. Thus, we can just use the annuity formula with the monthly rate of 0.5625%, a monthly payment of \$590.50, and 24 months remaining.
    - **Execute**

$$\text{Balance with 24 months remaining} = \$590.50 \times \frac{1}{0.005625}\left(1 - \frac{1}{1.005625^{24}}\right) = \$13{,}222.32$$

Thus, after three years, you owe \$13,222.32 on the loan.

Using a financial calculator or spreadsheet:

	N	I/Y	PV	PMT	FV
Given:	24	0.5625		−590.50	0
Solve for:			13,222.32		

Excel Formula: =PV(RATE,NPER,PMT,FV)=PV(0.005625,24,−590.50,0)

You could also compute this as the FV of the original loan amount after deducting payments:

	N	I/Y	PV	PMT	FV
Given:	36	0.5625	30,000	−590.50	
Solve for:					13,222.56

Excel Formula: =FV(RATE,NPER,PMT,PV)=FV(0.005625,36,−590.50,30000)

The 24 cent difference is due to rounding on the payment amount.

- **Evaluate:** At any point in time, including when you first take out the loan, you can calculate the balance of the loan as the present value of your remaining payments. Recall that when the bank gave you the \$30,000 in the first place, it was willing to take 60 monthly payments of \$590.50 in return only because the present value of those payments was equivalent to the cash it was giving you. Any time that you want to end the loan, the bank will charge you a lump sum equal to the present value of what it would receive if you continued making your payments as planned. As the second approach shows, the amount you owe can also be thought of as the future value of the original amount borrowed after deducting payments made along the way.

3.4. THE DETERMINANTS OF INTEREST RATES

After learning how interest rates are quoted and applied to loans, we can ask more general questions about how interest rates are set. At their core, market forces based on the relative supply and demand of funds determine interest rates. The willingness of people, banks, and businesses to lend, save, and borrow in turn determines this supply and demand. Interest rate fluctuations have an impact on consumer choices, including how much you can borrow for a mortgage or auto loan. Interest rate changes also affect the firm's capital budgeting decisions broadly because they alter the present value of future cash flows. This section examines some of the variables that could affect interest rates, including projected future growth, inflation, and current economic activity.

3.4.1. Inflation and Real Versus Nominal Rates

The purchasing power of a given amount of money decreases as prices rise, and this is measured by inflation. The adage, "A dollar just doesn't buy what it used to," has been heard a lot. Prices have been steadily rising; for instance, the cost of your morning coffee is probably higher now than it was five years ago. Our assessment of the interest rates that banks and other financial institutions are quoting is impacted by inflation. These interest rates, along with the ones we used to discount cash flows, are nominal interest rates, which show you how much money will grow if you invest it for a specific amount of time. Naturally, the nominal interest rate does not accurately reflect the real increase in purchasing power that comes from investing if inflation is also driving up prices in the economy.

As an illustration, suppose the price of a cup of coffee is $1 this year. One could purchase 100 coffees with $100. Alternatively, if you invest that $100 in a bank account that yields 5.06% annually, you will end up with $105.06 at the end of the year. However, the actual amount of improvement in your situation will rely on the rate of price growth over the same year. At the end of the year, the cost of that cup of coffee would have increased by 3%, or $1.03, if inflation was 3% annually. You would therefore only be 2% better off if you took your $105.06 and used it to purchase $105.06/$1.03 = 102 coffees.

That 2% is your real interest rate: the rate of growth of your purchasing power, after adjusting for inflation. Just as in the example, we can calculate the rate of growth of purchasing power as follows:

$$\text{Growth in Purchasing Power} = 1 + \text{Real Rate} = \frac{1 + \text{Nominal Rate}}{1 + \text{Inflation Rate}} = \frac{\text{Growth of Money}}{\text{Growth of Prices}} \quad (3.4)$$

We can rearrange Eq. 3.4 to find the following formula for the real interest rate, together with a convenient approximation for the real interest rate when inflation rates are low:

The Real Interest Rate

$$\text{Real Rate} = \frac{\text{Nominal Rate} - \text{Inflation Rate}}{1 + \text{Inflation Rate}} \approx \text{Nominal Rate} - \text{Inflation Rate} \quad (3.5)$$

That is, the real interest rate is approximately equal to the nominal interest rate less the rate of inflation.

The history of nominal interest rates and inflation rates in the US since 1955 is displayed in Figure 3.3. Be aware that the nominal interest rate typically follows changes in inflation. It makes sense that people's willingness to save will be influenced by the anticipated growth in their purchasing power, which is determined by the real interest rate. Therefore, a higher nominal interest rate is required to encourage people to save when the rate of inflation is high. This was made clear in the late 1970s and early 1980s when US inflation hit double digits and nominal rates rose accordingly.

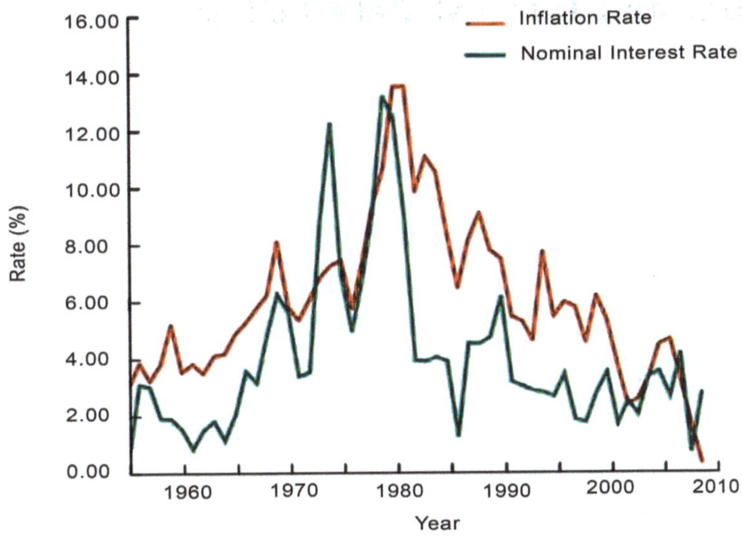

Figure 3.3. *U.S. interest rates and inflation rates, 1955–2009. The graph shows U.S. nominal interest rates (in blue) and inflation rates (in red) from 1955–2009. Note that interest rates tend to be high when inflation is high. Interest rates are average three-month Treasury bill rates and inflation rates are based on annual increases in the U.S. Bureau of Labor Statistics' consumer price index.*

3.4.1.1. Example 3.4. Calculating the Real Interest Rate

- **Problem:** In the year 2000, short-term U.S. government bond rates were about 5.8% and the rate of inflation was about 3.4%. In 2003, bond rates were about

1% and the rate of inflation was about 1.9%. What was the real interest rate in 2000 and 2003?

Solution

- **Plan:** The bond rates tell us the nominal rates. Given the nominal rates and inflation rates for each year, we can use Eq. 3.5 to calculate the real interest rate.
- **Execute:** Eqn. 3.5 says:

$$\text{Real Rate} = \frac{\text{Nominal Rate} - \text{Inflation Rate}}{1 + \text{Inflation Rate}}$$

Thus, the real interest rate in 2000 was (5.8% – 3.4%)/(1.034) = 2.32% (which is approximately equal to the difference between the nominal rate and inflation: 5.8% – 3.4% = 2.4%). In 2003, the real interest rate was (1% – 1.9%)/(1.019) = -0.88%.

- **Evaluate:** Note that the real interest rate was negative in 2003, indicating that interest rates, given by the bond rates, were insufficient to keep up with inflation. As a result, investors in U.S. government bonds were able to buy less at the end of the year than they could have purchased at the start of the year.

3.4.2. Investment and Interest Rate Policy

Interest rates have an impact on businesses' incentives to raise capital and make investments as well as people's tendency to save. Think about a $10 million upfront investment that will yield $3 million in cash flow over the course of four years. If the interest rate is 5%, this investment's benefits have a PV of:

$$PV = \frac{3}{1.05} + \frac{3}{1.05^2} + \frac{3}{1.05^3} + \frac{3}{1.05^4} = \$10.638 \text{ million}$$

If the interest rate is 9%, the PV falls to;

$$PV = \frac{3}{1.09} + \frac{3}{1.09^2} + \frac{3}{1.09^3} + \frac{3}{1.09^4} = \$9.719 \text{ million}$$

and the investment is no longer profitable given its $10 million cost. Naturally, the explanation is that the positive cash flows are being discounted at a higher rate, which lowers their present value. Nonetheless, the $10 million cost happens now, so the discount rate has no bearing on its present value.

An increase in interest rates will generally make an investment less appealing when its costs outweigh its benefits. Higher interest rates will therefore typically result in fewer quality investments being available to businesses, all other things being equal. When attempting to steer the economy, the Federal Reserve in the United States and central banks in other nations make use of this relationship between interest rates and investment incentives. When the economy is slowing down, they frequently try to boost investment by lowering interest rates; conversely, when the economy is "overheating" and inflation is rising, they try to decrease investment by raising interest rates.

3.4.3. The Yield Curve and Discount Rates

The term or horizon of the loan or investment determines the interest rate that banks charge on loans and offer on investments. Let's say, for illustration purposes, that you are willing to invest your money in a certificate of deposit (CD) that matures in two years and cannot be refunded earlier without incurring penalties. Compared to putting your money in a statement savings account, where you can take money out whenever you want, the bank will give you a higher interest rate on this CD. The term structure of interest rates refers to the connection between the interest rate and the investment term. This relationship can be shown on a graph known as the yield curve. The term structure and matching yield curve of US interest rates that were accessible to investors in November of 2006, 2007, and 2008 are displayed in Figure 3.4. Remember that the interest rate in each scenario is contingent upon the time horizon, and that in 2008, there was a notable disparity between short- and long-term interest rates. Interest rates for US Treasury securities, which are thought to be free of any default risk (the US government won't default on its loans), are plotted. As a result, each of these rates is a risk-free interest rate, or the interest rate at which funds can be borrowed or lent for a predetermined amount of time without incurring any risks.

Term	Date		
(years)	Nov-06	Nov-07	Nov-08
0.5	5.23%	3.32%	0.47%
1	4.99%	3.16%	0.91%
2	4.80%	3.16%	0.98%
3	4.72%	3.12%	1.26%
4	4.63%	3.34%	1.69%
5	4.64%	3.48%	2.01%
6	4.65%	3.63%	2.49%
7	4.66%	3.79%	2.90%
8	4.69%	3.96%	3.21%
9	4.70%	4.00%	3.38%
10	4.73%	4.18%	3.41%
15	4.89%	4.44%	3.86%
20	4.87%	4.45%	3.87%

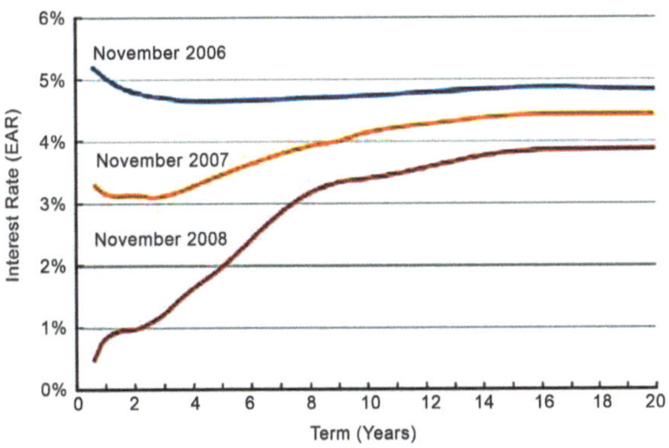

Figure 3.4. *Term structure of risk-free U.S. interest rates, November 2006, 2007, and 2008. The figure shows the interest rate available from investing in risk-free U.S. Treasury securities with different investment terms. In each case, the interest rates differ depending on the horizon. For example, in 2008,* the interest rate on a 10-year loan (3.41%) was more than three times the rate on a 1-year loan (0.91%).

The term structure can be used to calculate the risk-free cash flow's present and future values over various investment horizons. For example, $100 invested for one year at the one-year interest rate in November 2008 would grow to a future value of:

$$\$100 \times 1.0091 = \$100.91$$

at the end of one year, and $100 invested for 10 years at the 10-year interest rate in November 2008 would grow to:

$$\$100 \times (1.0341)^{10} = \$139.84$$

The same reasoning can be used to determine the present value of cash flows with various maturities. The two-year interest rate should be used to discount risk-free cash flows received in two years, and the 10-year interest rate should be used to discount cash flows received in 10 years. In general, a risk-free cash flow of C_n received in n years has the present value

$$PV = \frac{C_n}{(1 + r_n)^n} \tag{3.6}$$

where r_n is the risk-free interest rate for an n-year term. In other words, when computing a present value we must match the term of the cash flow and term of the discount rate.

Combining Eqn. 3.6 for cash flows in different years leads to the general formula for the present value of a cash flow stream:

Present Value of a Cash Flow Stream Using a Term Structure of Discount Rates

$$PV = \frac{C_1}{1 + r_1} + \frac{C_2}{(1 + r_2)^2} + \cdots + \frac{C_N}{(1 + r_N)^N} \tag{3.7}$$

Based on the rate from the yield curve with the same term, we use a different discount rate for each cash flow in this instance. The yield curve is said to be flat when interest rates are nearly identical across maturities because it resembles a flat line. The difference between using different rates for each cash flow is relatively small when the yield curve is relatively flat, as it was in November 2006, and is frequently disregarded by discounting using a single "average" interest rate. However, Eq 3.7 should be used when short-term and long-term interest rates vary greatly, as they did in November 2008.

Note: All of our financial calculators and annuity and perpetuity formulas, which are quick ways to calculate present values, rely on discounting each cash flow at the same rate. When cash flows need to be discounted at various rates, they cannot be applied.

3.4.3.1. Example 3.5. Using the Term Structure to Compute Present Values

- **Problem:** Compute the present value of a risk-free 5-year annuity of $1000 per year, given the yield curve for November 2008 in Figure 3.3.
- **Solution**
  - o **Plan:** The timeline of the cash flows of the annuity is:

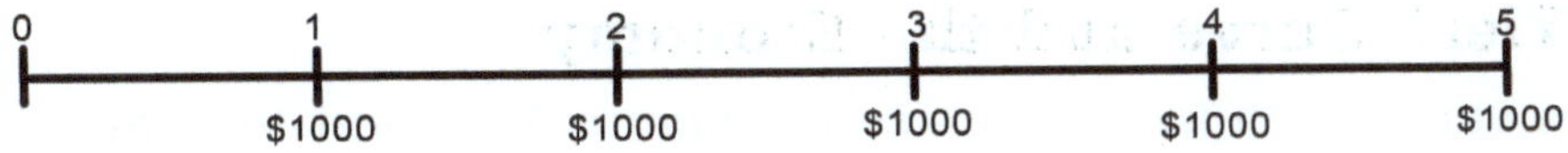

We can use the table next to the yield curve to identify the interest rate corresponding to each length of time: 1, 2, 3, 4, and 5 years. With the cash flows and those interest rates, we can compute the PV.

- Execute: From Figure 3.3, we see that the interest rates are: 0.91%, 0.98%, 1.26%, 1.69%, and 2.01%, for terms of 1, 2, 3, 4, and 5 years, respectively.

  To compute the present value, we discount each cash flow by the corresponding interest rate:

$$PV = \frac{1000}{1.0091} + \frac{1000}{1.0098^2} + \frac{1000}{1.0126^3} + \frac{1000}{1.0169^4} + \frac{1000}{1.0201^5} = \$4775$$

- **Evaluate:** The yield curve tells us the market interest rate per year for each different maturity. In order to correctly calculate the PV of cash flows from five different maturities, we need to use the five different interest rates corresponding to those maturities. Note that we cannot use the annuity formula here because the discount rates differ for each cash flow.

3.4.3.2. Using the Annuity Formula When Discount Rates Vary

Even though interest rates fluctuate with the length of the investment horizon, a common error made when calculating the present value of an annuity is to apply the annuity formula with a single interest rate. For instance, the five-year interest rate from November 2008 is insufficient to calculate the present value of the five-year annuity in Example 3.5.

$$PV \neq \$1000 \times \frac{1}{0.0201}\left(1 - \frac{1}{1.0201^5}\right) = \$4712$$

We must first compute the annuity's present value using Eq. 3.7 and then solve for its rate of return in order to determine the single interest rate that we could use to value the annuity. We utilize a spreadsheet or financial calculator to determine the annuity's 1.55% rate of return in Example 3.5. As in this example, the annuity's rate of return is always between the highest and lowest discount rates used to determine its present value.

	N	I/Y	PV	PMT	FV
Given:	5		−4775	1000	0
Solve for:		1.55			
	Excel Formula: =RATE(NPER,PMT,PV,FV)=RATE(5,1000,−4775,0)				

3.4.4. The Yield Curve and the Economy

The yield curve varies with time, as shown in Figure 3.5. Short-term and long-term rates can differ significantly at times, or they can be similar in other situations. What is the reason behind the yield curve's shifting shape?

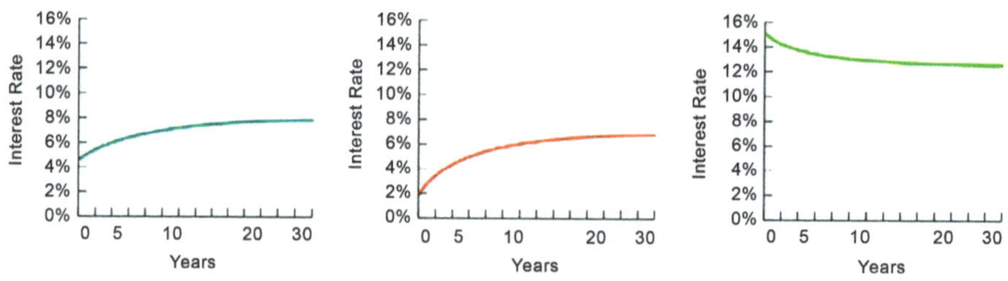

Figure 3.5. *Yield curve shapes. The figure shows three different yield curve shapes. The blue line represents a "normal" yield curve. Most of the time the yield curve has this shape—moderately upward sloping. The red line depicts a steep yield curve—note the larger than normal difference between short-term rates (2%) and long-term rates (7%), making the yield curve look steeper than normal. This example of a steep yield curve is from October 1991. Finally, the green line depicts an inverted yield curve, so called because it slopes downward instead of upward. This happens when short-term rates are higher than long-term rates as they were in January 1981. We discuss why the shape of the yield curve changes over time in the rest of this section.*

3.4.4.1. Interest Rate Determination

The federal funds rate, or the rate at which banks can borrow cash reserves overnight, is influenced by the Federal Reserve, which in turn sets very short-term interest rates. Every other interest rate on the yield curve is determined by the market and is changed until each loan term's supply and demand of credit are equal. The yield curve's shape is largely determined by investors' willingness to lend money or borrow it for longer periods of time, as we will see in a moment, based on their expectations about future changes in interest rates.

Assume that the interest rates on short- and long-term loans are the same. Long-term investments would not be desired by investors if rising interest rates were predicted in the future. They would be better off making short-term investments and then reinvesting when interest rates rise. In order to draw in investors, long-term interest rates will typically be higher than short-term rates if rising interest rates are anticipated.

Similarly, borrowers would not want to borrow at long-term rates that are equal to short-term rates if it is anticipated that interest rates will decline in the future. They would benefit more from taking out a short-term loan and renewing it when interest rates drop. In order to draw in borrowers, long-term rates will typically be lower than short-term rates if a decline in interest rates is anticipated.

3.4.4.2. Yield Curve Shape

These arguments suggest that interest rate expectations will have a significant impact on the yield curve's shape. In general, a steeply rising yield curve, where long-term rates are significantly higher than short-term rates, suggests that future interest rate increases are anticipated. An anticipated drop in future interest rates is typically indicated by a decreasing (inverted) yield curve, where long-term rates are lower than short-term rates. An inverted yield curve is frequently seen as a poor indicator of future economic growth because interest rates typically decline in reaction to a slowdown in the economy. In fact, as Figure 3.6 shows, the yield curve was inverted prior to each of the previous seven recessions in the US (notice the red shaded areas preceding the gray bars signifying a recession). On the other hand, when the economy emerges from a recession and interest rates are anticipated to rise, the yield curve typically becomes steeper, which is why it is colored blue.

The yield curve typically has a moderate upward slope. If investors consistently held the belief that interest rates would increase in the future, then this would be the situation. However, since that is improbable, other factors must be at play for long-term interest rates to typically be higher than short-term rates. The main justification given is that long-term loans carry greater risk than short-term loans. The present value of the loan payments you receive if you take out a 30-year loan today and lock in the interest rate is highly susceptible to even slight fluctuations in market interest rates. This sensitivity results from the compounding of interest rate changes over a 30-year period. Examine this effect by thinking about the example that follows.

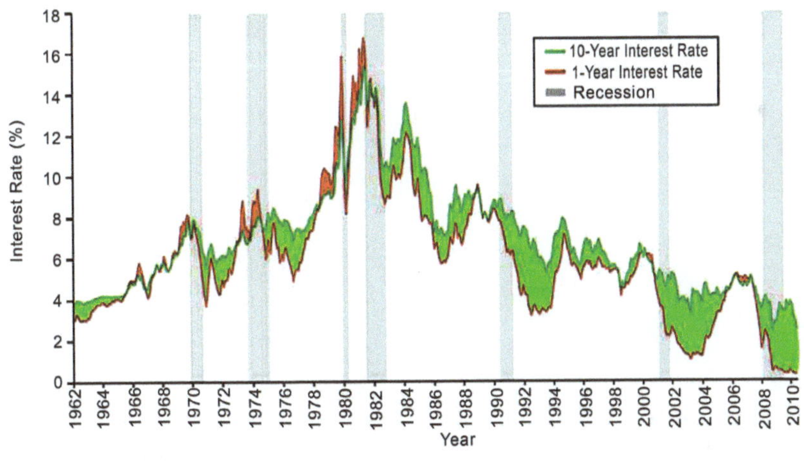

Figure 3.6. *Short-term versus long-term U.S. Interest Rates and Recessions. 1-year and 10-year U.S. Treasury rates are plotted, with the spread between them shaded in green if the shape of the yield curve is increasing (the one-year rate is below the 10-year rate) and in red if the yield curve is inverted (the one-year rate exceeds the 10-year rate). Gray bars show the dates of U.S. recessions as determined by the National Bureau of Economic Research. Note that inverted yield curves tend to precede recessions as determined by the National Bureau of Economic Research. In recessions, interest rates tend to fall, with short-term rates dropping further. As a result, the yield curve tends to be steep coming out of a recession.*

3.4.4.3. Example 3.6. Long-Term Versus Short-Term Loans

- **Problem:** You work for a bank that has just made two loans. In one, you loaned \$909.09 today in return for \$1000 in one year. In the other, you loaned \$909.09 today in return for \$15,863.08 in 30 years. The difference between the loan amount and repayment amount is based on an interest rate of 10% per year. Imagine that immediately after you make the loans, news about economic growth is announced that increases inflation expectations, so that the market interest rate for loans like these jumps to 11%. Loans make up a major part of a bank's assets, so you are naturally concerned about the value of these loans. What is the effect of the interest rate change on the value to the bank of the promised repayment of these loans?

Solution:

- Plan: Each of these loans has only one repayment cash flow at the end of the loan. They differ only by the time to repayment:

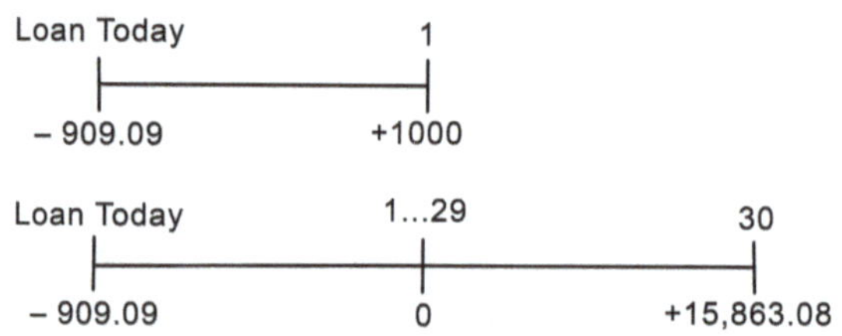

The effect on the value of the future repayment to the bank today is just the PV of the loan repayment, calculated at the new market interest rate.

- **Execute:** For the one-year loan:

$$PV = \frac{\$1000}{(1.11)^1} = \$900.90$$

For the 30-year loan:

$$PV = \frac{\$15{,}863.08}{(1.11)^{30}} = \$692.94$$

- **Evaluate**: The value of the one-year loan decreased by \$909.09 – \$900.90 = \$8.19, or 0.9%, but the value of the 30-year loan decreased by \$909.09 – \$692.94 = \$216.15, or almost 24%! The small change in market interest rates, compounded over a longer period, resulted in a much larger change in the present value of the loan repayment. You can see why investors and banks view longer-term loans as being riskier than short-term loans.

It not only indicates the discount rates for risk-free cash flows with varying time horizons, but it may also be a leading indicator of future economic expansion. These characteristics make the yield curve a very valuable tool for business managers.

3.5. THE OPPORTUNITY COST OF CAPITAL

When a company decides to invest money in an internal project instead of a marketable security, it forfeits a portion of its potential return on investment, which is known as the opportunity cost of capital. Therefore, if one were to base their decision solely on the expectation that the internal project's projected return would be lower than the expected rate of return on a marketable security, they would not invest in it. What separates the two projects' returns is their opportunity cost of capital. For instance, senior management of a company may invest $10,000,000 over time in a new manufacturing facility with the expectation of earning 8%, or it may choose to put the money into stocks with a projected 12% long-term return. Investing $10,000,000 in stocks is a better use of the money, barring any other factors. Given that the two investment opportunities have different returns, investing in the manufacturing facility has an opportunity cost of capital of 2%.

It helps to picture yourself as a financial manager vying with financial managers at other companies for investors' money (capital) in order to comprehend the meaning of opportunity cost of capital. You must be able to give creditors and investors an expected return that is at least as good as what they could get elsewhere in the market for the same risk and length of investment if you want them to lend money to your company or invest in it. Investors in your company are forfeiting their chance to invest their money elsewhere, which makes the origin of the phrase "opportunity cost of capital" clearer. They are facing an opportunity cost, which you must overcome by providing them with a return that meets or exceeds their opportunity cost of capital. The reasoning holds true even if you already have the money to invest internally at your company. You have two options: either reinvest the money in a new project or give it back to your shareholders to use for other investments. Reinvesting money should only be done if it will yield a higher return than the shareholders' other options.

The return an investor forfeits when making a new investment is known as the opportunity cost of capital. It will usually match the interest rate on US Treasury securities with a comparable term for a project that is risk-free. However, the cost of capital is a much broader idea that also applies to investments that carry some risk.

Example 3.7. The Opportunity Cost of Capital

- **Problem:** Suppose a friend offers to borrow $100 from you today and in return pay you $110 one year from today. Looking in the market for other options for investing the $100, you find your best alternative option that you view as equally risky as lending it to your friend. That option has an expected return of 8%. What should you do?

- **Solution:**
  - **Plan:** Your decision depends on what the opportunity cost is of lending your money to your friend. If you lend her the $100, then you cannot invest it in the alternative with an 8% expected return. Thus, by making the loan, you are giving up the opportunity to invest for an 8% expected return. You can make your decision by using your 8% opportunity cost of capital to value the $110 in one year.
  - **Execute:** The value of the $110 in one year is its present value, discounted at 8%:

$$PV = \frac{\$110}{(1.08)^1} = \$101.85$$

    The $100 loan is worth $101.85 to you today, so you make the loan.
  - **Evaluate:** The Valuation Principle tells us that we can determine the value of an investment by using market prices to value the benefits net of the costs. As this example shows, market prices determine what our best alternative opportunities are, so that we can decide whether an investment is worth the cost.

3.5.1. Cost of Capital

The required return for the company is its cost of capital. Lenders and owners of the company want payment for delaying their own consumption and taking on investment risk; they do not give out financing for free. In order to satisfy its debt and equity investors, the company must achieve a benchmark return, which is established in part by the cost of capital.

The most popular technique for figuring out capital costs is to weigh each capital investment source differently and then modify the needed return.

A company's cost of capital would be the same as its cost of debt if it were fully funded by bonds or other loans. On the other hand, the cost of capital and the cost of equity would be the same if the company were fully funded by the issuance of common or preferred stock. WACC assists in combining the cost of debt and cost of equity into a single, useful figure, since the majority of businesses combine debt and equity financing.

3.5.1.1. Meaning of Cost of Capital

The cost incurred by the business when employing money from shareholders and creditors is known as the cost of capital. The cost of a company's long-term funding sources—debt, preferred equity, and common equity—is known as its cost of capital.

"Cost of capital is the minimum required rate of earnings or cutoff rate of capital expenditure," according to Ezra Solomon.

As per Mittal and Agarwal, "the cost of capital refers to the lowest expected rate of return that a company should achieve from a proposed project in order to maintain its market price and earn no less than its share price per equity shareholder."

"The minimum rate of return that a firm must earn on its investment for the market value of the firm to remain unchanged" is what Khan and Jain define as cost of capital.

According to Hampton, John, the term refers to the rate of return that a company needs from investments in order to raise its market value.

3.5.1.2. Characteristics of Cost of Capital

The following are the basic characteristics of cost of capital:

i. Cost of capital is a rate of return, it is not a cost as such.
ii. This return, however, is calculated on the basis of actual cost of different components of capital.
iii. A firm's cost of capital represents minimum rate of return that will result in at least maintaining (If not increasing) the value of its equity shares.
iv. It is related to long term capital funds.

3.5.1.3. Components of Cost of Capital

Cost of capital consists of three components:

a. **Return at Zero Risk Level:** This refers to the expected rate of return when a project involves no risk whether business or financial.
b. **Premium for Business Risk:** Business risk is possibility where in the firm will not be able to operate successfully in the market. Greater the business risk, the higher will be the cost of capital.
c. **Premium for Financial Risk:** It refers to the risk on account of pattern of capital structure. In other words, a firm having a higher debt content in its capital structure is more risky as compared to a firm which has a comparatively low debt content.

3.5.1.4. Importance of Cost of Capital

When making financial decisions, the cost of capital is a crucial concept. Cost of capital refers to how much an investor must forego in order to invest with the hope of receiving a reasonable return on his capital in the future in exchange for deferring his immediate needs. However, from the perspective of the company using the capital, the cost of capital is the amount paid to the investor for the use of the capital that he supplied. The compensation for using capital is thus the cost of capital. When making financial decisions, progressive management always likes to take the cost of capital into account because it's important in the following areas:

1. **Designing the Capital Structure:** When creating a firm's ideal and balanced capital structure, the cost of capital is a crucial consideration. The management must keep the goal of minimizing capital costs and optimizing the firm's value in mind when designing it. By evaluating the distinct expenses of multiple capital sources, a financial manager can determine which source of funding is most cost-effective and create a well-rounded capital structure.
2. **Capital Budgeting Decisions:** When making decisions about capital budgeting, the cost of capital sources is a very helpful tool. Any proposal for investment will either be accepted or rejected based on the cost of capital. A proposal cannot be approved until its rate of return exceeds the capital cost. Through a variety of discounted cash flow techniques, cost of capital assesses the viability of each investment proposal by discounting the cash flows and evaluating the financial performance.

3. **Comparative Study of Sources of Financing:** There are several ways to finance a project. By comparing the costs of various funding sources, one can determine which of these should be used at a given time. One would choose the source with the lowest capital cost. Even though the cost of capital plays a significant role in these choices, maintaining control and minimizing risks also matter.
4. **Evaluations of Financial Performance:** The cost of capital can be used to assess how financially successful capital projects are. These kinds of assessments can be carried out by contrasting the project's actual profitability with the capital costs incurred in raising the funds for it. A project's performance can be deemed satisfactory if its actual profitability exceeds its actual cost of capital.
5. **Knowledge of Firms Expected Income and Inherent Risks:** Investors can learn about a company's expected income and associated risks by looking at its cost of capital. When a company's cost of capital is high, it indicates that its risk profile is broader, its earnings rate is lower, and its capital structure is unbalanced. As a result, investors anticipate a higher rate of return.
6. **Financing and Dividend Decisions:** When making other crucial financial decisions, it is convenient to use the concept of capital as a tool. Based on this, choices can be made about working capital sources, dividend policy, and profit capitalization.

In summary, the cost of capital is significant because it is used to assess new projects for businesses and makes calculations simple enough to ensure that investors receive the minimal return on their investment in the company.

3.5.1.5. Significance of Cost of Capital

1. **Maximization of the Value of the Firm**: A company seeks to minimize its average cost of capital in order to maximize its value. A company's capital structure should have a sensible balance between debt and equity to prevent the company from taking on excessive financial risk.
2. **Capital Budgeting Decisions**: When a company is making capital budgeting decisions, a correct estimate of the cost of capital is crucial. The discount rate used to determine whether an investment project is desirable is typically the cost of capital. If a project's rate of return exceeds its cost of capital, it will be approved under the internal rate of return method. The cost of capital is used as the discounting rate to get the net present value of the project's anticipated future cash flows. Consequently, the cost of capital serves as a benchmark for deciding how best to allocate the company's investible funds. Because of this, the terms cutoff rate, target rate, hurdle rate, minimum required rate of return, etc., are also used to refer to cost of capital.
3. **Decisions Regarding Leasing**: Estimation of cost of capital is necessary in taking leasing decisions of business concern.
4. **Management of Working Capital**: The cost of capital can be used in working capital management

to assess alternative receivables policies and determine how much it costs to carry an investment in receivables. Additionally, inventory management makes use of it.

5. **Dividend Decisions**: Cost of capital is significant factor in taking dividend decisions. The dividend policy of a firm should be formulated according to the nature of the firm—whether it is a growth firm, normal firm or declining firm. However, the nature of the firm is determined by comparing the internal rate of return (r) and the cost of capital (k) i.e., $r > k$, $r = k$, or $r < k$ which indicate growth firm, normal firm and decline firm, respectively.
6. **Determination of Capital Structure**: The capital structure of a company is influenced by cost of capital. Due consideration is given to the firm's overall, or weighted average, cost of capital when designing the ideal capital structure, which is the ratio of debt to equity. The company's goal should be to select this debt/equity ratio in order to minimize its overall cost of capital.
7. **Evaluation of Financial Performance**: The financial performance of upper management can be assessed using the cost of capital concept. This can be achieved by contrasting the firm's investment project's actual profitability with its total cost of capital.

3.5.1.6. Classification of Cost of Capital

The lowest rate of return a company needs to achieve on its investment to appease investors and preserve its market value is known as the cost of capital. It is the required rate of return for investors. The discount rate that is applied to ascertain the present value of projected future cash flows is also referred to as the cost of capital. The major classification of cost of capital are:

1. **Historical Cost and Future Cost**: The term "historical cost" refers to the expenses already paid for project financing. It is determined using historical data. Future cost is the estimated cost of funds that need to be raised in order to finance a project. When compared to standard costs, historical costs offer an assessment of past performance and aid in cost prediction for the future. Future costs are more important in financial decisions than past costs.
2. **Specific Costs and Composite Cost**: The term "specific costs" describes the expenses associated with a particular source of funding, such as retained earnings, equity shares, preference shares, and debentures. The total cost of different sources of funding is referred to as the composite cost of capital. To put it another way, the cost of capital is weighted average. "Overall costs of capital" is another name for it. A capital expenditure proposal should be evaluated using the composite cost of capital as a criterion for acceptance or rejection. Decision-makers should take into account the composite cost rather than the specific cost when a business uses capital from multiple sources. However, the unique costs of those sources of capital alone must be taken into account when the business uses capital from a single source.
3. **Average Cost and Marginal Cost**:

The term "average cost of capital" refers to the weighted average cost of capital, which is determined by factoring in the costs of each capital source according to their proportion of the total capital funds. The phrase "cost of obtaining another dollar of new capital" can be used to characterize marginal cost of capital. Marginal cost is the specific or explicit cost incurred when a company raises additional capital from a single source (as opposed to multiple sources). When making decisions about financing and capital budgeting, marginal cost is given more weight. Marginal cost typically rises in direct proportion to the amount of debt.

4. **Explicit Cost and Implicit Cost**: The value of an investment or the present value of cash outflows is equal to the discount rate, which is known as the "explicit cost." The internal rate of return that a business pays to obtain funding is, therefore, the explicit cost of capital. A company that takes out an interest-free loan will have no explicit costs because there is no cash outflow in the form of interest. Conversely, the implicit cost denotes the potential rate of return on investment when money is allocated to alternative investments. The implicit cost is, in other words, the opportunity cost of the funds. Implicit cost is the rate of return that, if the project the company is currently considering is approved, would be forfeited and represents the best investment opportunity for the company and its shareholders. Therefore, implicit costs only appear when money is invested; otherwise, they do not. The implicit cost of retained earnings, for instance, is the rate of return that the shareholder would have received as a dividend from the company instead of investing these funds. For this reason, costs are implicit when they are used and explicit when they are raised.

3.5.2. Discount Rate

A discount rate is the rate of return used in corporate finance to reduce future cash flows to their present value. This rate is frequently a company's required rate of return, weighted average cost of capital (WACC), or the hurdle rate, or expected rate of return, that investors anticipate earning in relation to investment risk. The discount window rate set by the central bank and rates obtained from probability-based risk adjustments are examples of other discount rates (Figure 3.7). A new project must be profitable for a company to move forward; in other words, it must be expected to generate more revenue than costs. It is feasible to calculate the present value of the project's future cash flows by applying a discount rate.

Only after the company has estimated the project's free cash flow can an appropriate discount rate be chosen. The free cash flow figure that the company has arrived at can then be discounted to get the net present value (NPV).

Determining the discount rate is not always simple. While WACC is a popular substitute for the discount rate among businesses, there are alternative approaches as well. It could be advisable to include a risk premium in cases where the new project is significantly riskier or less risky than the business's regular operations in case the project's cash flow is less than anticipated or the cost of capital is underestimated.

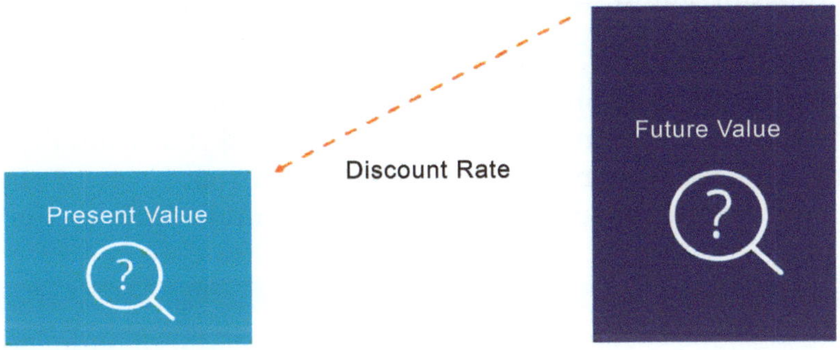

Figure 3.7. *Discount rate.*

Source: https://corporatefinanceinstitute.com/resources/valuation/discount-rate/.

The risk of investing is taken into account by raising the cost of capital by a risk premium and using the result as the discount rate. Because of this, the discount rate is typically greater than the capital cost.

3.5.2.1. Why Is a Discount Rate Used?

A discount rate is used to calculate the Net Present Value (NPV) of a business as part of a Discounted Cash Flow (DCF) analysis. It is also utilized to:

- Account for the time value of money
- Account for the riskiness of an investment
- Represent opportunity cost for a firm
- Act as a hurdle rate for investment decisions
- Make different investments more comparable

3.5.2.2. Types of Discount Rates

In corporate finance, there are only a few types of discount rates that are used to discount future cash flows back to the present. They include:

- Weighted Average Cost of Capital (WACC) – for calculating the enterprise value of a firm
- Cost of Equity – for calculating the equity value of a firm
- Cost of Debt – for calculating the value of a bond or fixed-income security
- A pre-defined hurdle rate – for investing in internal corporate projects
- Risk-Free Rate – to account for the time value of money

3.5.2.3. Discount Rate Example (Simple)

A screenshot of a hypothetical investment that pays out seven times a year, each time $100, can be seen below. An analyst uses a 5% hurdle rate to determine the investment's net present value, arriving at $578.64. This is in contrast to a $700 non-discounted total cash flow.

In essence, the investor is expressing that they hold no preference between receiving a single payment of $578.64 immediately or receiving $100 annually for a period of 7 years. The investor's decision considers the perceived risk level of the investment and the opportunity cost, which represents potential earnings from a similar investment.

		1	2	3	4	5	6	7
Case Flows		$100	$100	$100	$100	$100	$100	$100
Discount Rate	5.0%							
NPV	$578.64	= NPV (E6,F4,G4,H4,I4,J4,K4,L4)						
		NPV(rate, value1, [value2], [value3], [value4], [value5], [value6], [value7], [value8],[value9],...)						
Sum of Cash Flow	$700							

3.5.2.4. Issues with Discount Rates

There are numerous assumptions that are merely "best guesses" about what will happen in the future, even though the computation of discount rates and their application in financial modeling may seem scientific.

Furthermore, while interest rates and risk profiles are actually continually changing dramatically, only one discount rate is utilized at a time to value all future cash flows. The calculation relies on a company's beta, a measure of the historical volatility of returns on investment, when using the WACC as a discount rate. One should not assume that historical return volatility is a reliable indicator of future risk.

3.5.3. Cost of Capital vs. Discount Rate

There is a lot of overlap between the terms cost of capital and discount rate, making them easily confused. When determining whether a new project or investment will be profitable, both are essential due to their significant differences.

The return needed by debtors and equity holders to justify an investment or project is referred to as the cost of capital. The kind of funding that was utilized to pay for the project or investment is specifically to blame for this. The necessary return, in the event that it is financed with equity, is known as the equity cost. Debt interest is referred to as the cost of debt if it is financed through debt.

In a discounted cash flow (DCF) analysis, the present value of future cash flows is calculated using the discount rate. Considering the project's perceived risk, this helps ascertain whether the project's future cash flows will be worth more than the capital expenditure required to fund it now. The return required to cover the cost of capital needed for the investment is known as the discount rate, whereas the cost of capital is the rate necessary to justify the expense and risk of a new venture.

When budgeting for a new project, many businesses compute their weighted average cost of capital (WACC) and use it as their discount rate.

- **What Is Cost of Capital?:** The required return for a company is its cost of capital. It aids in setting a benchmark return that the business needs to hit in order to appease its debt and equity investors.
- **What Is Discount Rate?:** The interest rate used to determine the present value of future cash flows from a project or investment is called the discount rate. It allows for the estimation of the present value of the project's future cash flows.
- **How Can Cost of Capital Be Calculated?:** To calculate cost of capital, three factors must be considered: cost of debt, cost of equity, and weighted average cost of capital (WACC). The formula is cost of debt + cost of equity = cost of capital.
- **How Can Discount Rate Be Calculated?:** Two primary formulas are used to determine discount rate: the weighted average cost of capital (WACC) and the adjusted present value (APV).

The WACC discount formula is WACC = E/V × Ce × D/V × Cd × (1-T), where:

- E = Value of equity
- D = Value of debt
- Ce = Cost of equity
- Cd = Cost of debt
- V = D + E
- T = Tax rate

The APV discount formula is APV = NPV + PV of the impact of financing, where:

- NPV = Net present value
- PV = Present value

CASE STUDY

BANKING: DELAYED NEW ACCOUNT OPENING RESULTS IN CONFUSION ABOUT INTEREST RATE TO BE APPLIED

This complaint relates to the delay in opening a new fixed deposit account causing confusion with the interest rate applied.

Mr B opened a fixed-term deposit account with the bank in May 2020 for a term of one year. The interest rate initially advised upon application was 0.96%. Mr B completed the account application and requested a transfer of funds from his other bank to this newly opened fixed-term deposit account. The bank contacted Mr B the same day of the transfer to confirm the interest rate had dropped since his initial application to 0.87%. Although dissatisfied, Mr B continued with the transfer as it was already organized. A few days later, Mr B was notified by the bank that the account had not actually been opened in time to receive the transferred funds; that there was also a one-day delay caused by the transferring bank and the interest rate had again dropped to 0.82%.

Mr B complained to the bank and the bank advised that the interest rate applied to the newly opened account was the rate at the time the transfer had been received from the transferring bank, suggesting the delay was caused by the transferring bank and not by the delay in opening the new account. Mr B contacted the bank to confirm that the transferring bank had delayed the transfer by one day, but as the account had not actually been opened until the following week, Mr B believed this is what caused the delay resulting in a lower interest rate. The bank confirmed that the interest rate applied to the account was the same as the interest rate from the day the transferring bank had made the transfer. Therefore, the delay in opening the bank account had not impacted the interest rate that was applied. However, the bank did offer Mr B the interest that would have accumulated during the two-day delay in opening the account but did not offer to change the applied interest rate.

CIFO investigated and found the bank's interest rates to be correct and that the delay from the transferring bank had resulted in the lower interest rate being applied. CIFO felt the bank's offer to compensate Mr B for the interest lost due to the delay in opening the account was appropriate and upheld the complaint but noted the compensation already offered for the economic loss was sufficient. CIFO also recommended that the Bank compensate Mr B an additional £30 for the distress and inconvenience he had endured whilst trying to clarify the issue. The bank initially refused to do so, but after further communication with CIFO, credited Mr B's account for the additional £30 of compensation recommended for the unnecessary distress and inconvenience caused.

CLASS ACTIVITY

You have been accepted into college. The college guarantees that your tuition will not increase for the four years you attend college. The first $10,000 tuition payment is due in six months. After that, the same payment is due every six months until you have made a total of eight payments. The college offers a bank account that allows you to withdraw money every six months and has a fixed APR of 4% (semiannual) guaranteed to remain the same over the next four years. How much money must you deposit today if you intend to make no further deposits and would like to make all the tuition payments from this account, leaving the account empty when the last payment is made?

SUMMARY

- An interest rate is the amount of interest due per period, as a proportion of the amount lent, deposited, or borrowed (called the principal sum). The total interest on an amount lent or borrowed depends on the principal sum, the interest rate, the compounding frequency, and the length of time over which it is lent, deposited, or borrowed.
- Simple interest is an interest charge that borrowers pay lenders for a loan. It is calculated using the principal only and does not include compounding interest. Simple interest relates not just to certain loans. It's also the type of interest that banks pay customers on their savings accounts.
- Compound interest is interest that applies not only to the initial principal of an investment or a loan, but also to the accumulated interest from previous periods. In other words, compound interest involves earning, or owing, interest on your interest.
- The Effective Annual Rate (EAR) is the rate of interest actually earned on an investment or paid on a loan as a result of compounding the interest over a given period of time. It is usually higher than the nominal rate and is used to compare different financial products that calculate annual interest with different compounding periods – weekly, monthly, yearly, etc. Increasing the number of compounding periods makes the effective annual interest rate increase as time goes by.
- The term annual percentage rate of charge (APR), corresponding sometimes to a nominal APR and sometimes to an effective APR (EAPR), is the interest rate for a whole year (annualized), rather than just a monthly fee/rate, as applied on a loan, mortgage loan, credit card, etc. It is a finance charge expressed as an annual rate.
- Many loans, such as mortgages and car loans, have monthly payments and are

quoted in terms of an APR with monthly compounding. These types of loans are amortizing loans, which means that each month you pay interest on the loan plus some part of the loan balance. Each monthly payment is the same, and the loan is fully repaid with the final payment.

- Interest rates affect not only individuals' propensity to save, but also firms' incentive to raise capital and invest. Consider an opportunity that requires an upfront investment of $10 million and generates a cash flow of $3 million per year for four years.
- The Federal Reserve determines very short-term interest rates through its influence on the federal funds rate, which is the rate at which banks can borrow cash reserves on an overnight basis. All other interest rates on the yield curve are set in the market and are adjusted until the supply of lending matches the demand for borrowing at each loan term.
- The opportunity cost of capital is the incremental return on investment that a business foregoes when it elects to use funds for an internal project, rather than investing cash in a marketable security. Thus, if the projected return on the internal project is less than the expected rate of return on a marketable security, one would not invest in the internal project, assuming that this is the only basis for the decision. The opportunity cost of capital is the difference between the returns on the two projects.
- The cost of capital is the company's required return. The company's lenders and owners don't extend financing for free; they want to be paid for delaying their own consumption and assuming investment risk. The cost of capital helps establish a benchmark return that the company must achieve to satisfy its debt and equity investors.
- A discount rate is the rate of return used to discount future cash flows back to their present value. This rate is often a company's Weighted Average Cost of Capital (WACC), required rate of return, or the hurdle rate that investors expect to earn relative to the risk of the investment. Other types of discount rates include the central bank's discount window rate and rates derived from probability-based risk adjustments.

REVIEW QUESTIONS

1. What is an interest rate?
2. What is the effective annual rate?
3. What is the difference between an EAR and an APR quote?
4. Why can't the APR be used as a discount rate?
5. How is the principal repaid in an amortizing loan?
6. Why does the part of your loan payment covering interest change over time?
7. What is the difference between a nominal and real interest rate?
8. How are interest rates and the level of investment made by businesses related?

9. What is the opportunity cost of capital?
10. Can you ignore the cost of capital if you already have the funds inside the firm?

REFERENCES

1. Chen, J. (2021). Annual percentage rate (APR). *Investopedia*. Retrieved from: https://www.investopedia.com (accessed on 16 July 2024).
2. Fisher, I. (1907). *The Rate of Interest: Its Nature, Determination and Relation to Economic Phenomena* (p. 8). New York: The MacMillan Company. ISBN 1578987458.
3. Homer, S., Sylla, R. E., & Sylla, R. (1996). *A History of Interest Rates*. Rutgers University Press. ISBN 978-0-8135-2288-3. Retrieved from: https://rutgersuniversitypress.org (accessed on 16 July 2024).
4. O'Sullivan, A., & Sheffrin, S. M. (2010). *Economics: Principles in Action* (p. 514). Upper Saddle River, NJ: Prentice Hall. ISBN 978-0-13-063085-8.
5. Wigglesworth, R. (2012). Schatz yields turn negative for first time. *Financial Times*. Retrieved from: https://www.ft.com (accessed on 16 July 2024).

CHAPTER 4

Discounted Cash Flow (DCF) Analysis

LEARNING OBJECTIVES

After studying this chapter, you will be able to:

- Understand the overview of discounted cash flow (DCF) analysis
- Discuss on alternative approaches to DCF
- Explain the practical use of DCF analysis for valuation
- Define the discounted dividend model
- Focus on effects of errors

KEY TERMS FROM THIS CHAPTER

Capital asset pricing model (CAPM)
Cash flows
Cost of equity
Discount rate
Dividend discount model (DDM)
Enterprise value (EV)
Foreign exchange risk
GDP growth
Net present value (NPV)
Price earnings (P/E)
Capital expenditure
Cost of Capital
Country Risk
Discounted Cash Flow (DCF)
Earnings per share (EPS)
Financial planning and analysis
Free cash flow (FCF)
Mergers and acquisitions
Present values (PVs)
Sales revenue forecast

INTRODUCTION

Discounted Cash Flow (DCF) analysis is a financial valuation method used to determine the present value of an investment or company based on its expected future cash flows. This method involves forecasting the free cash flows (FCFs) that the investment is expected to generate and then discounting these cash flows to their present value using an appropriate discount rate, typically the weighted average cost of capital (WACC). The rationale behind DCF analysis is that a dollar today is worth more than a dollar in the future due to its potential earning capacity. Therefore, future cash flows are discounted back to the present value to account for the time value of money. The steps in a DCF analysis include projecting the future cash flows of the investment, estimating the terminal value, and selecting a discount rate. The free cash flows are projected over a specific period, often five to 10 years, based on reasonable assumptions about revenue growth, operating margins, taxes, and capital expenditures. The terminal value represents the value of the investment at the end of the projection period and can be calculated using either the perpetuity growth model or the exit multiple method. The WACC, which reflects the average rate of return required by all of the company's investors, is used as the discount rate. It incorporates the cost of equity and the cost of debt, weighted by their respective proportions in the company's capital structure. The present value of the projected free cash flows and the terminal value are then summed to arrive at the total enterprise value (EV) of the investment. DCF analysis is widely used in finance due to its theoretical soundness and flexibility, allowing for adjustments to various assumptions. However, it also has limitations, such as its sensitivity to input assumptions, including growth rates, discount rates, and terminal value calculations. Small changes in these inputs can significantly affect the valuation, making the process both an art and a science. Despite these challenges, DCF analysis remains a cornerstone of investment valuation and corporate finance, providing a structured approach to estimate the intrinsic value of an asset based on its expected future performance. This method is particularly useful for evaluating investments with predictable and stable cash flows, such as established companies and long-term projects.

4.1. OVERVIEW OF DISCOUNTED CASH FLOW (DCF) ANALYSIS

The net present value (NPV) of anticipated cash flows that are accessible to all capital providers, net of the money required to be invested in order to achieve the anticipated growth, is represented by the discounted cash flow (DCF) analysis. The foundation of DCF valuation is the idea that an asset's or business's intrinsic value is determined by its capacity to produce cash flows for capital providers. To that extent, the DCF is a more theoretical approach based on multiple assumptions and depends more on the business's basic expectations than on variables from the public market or historical precedents. With a DCF analysis, the total value of a company is determined (i.e., company value), which takes into account debt and equity.

4.1.1. History of Discounted Cash Flow (DCF)

Discounted cash flow (DCF) analysis became a popular technique for stock valuation after the 1929 stock market crash. The discounted cash flow (DCF) method was first formally expressed in modern economic terms by Irving Fisher in his 1930 book "The Theory of Interest" and by John Burr William in his 1938 text "The Theory of Investment Value."

Later, in the late 1950s and early 1960s, Gordon (1962) added a dividend growth component to the William model. The dividend DIV is still a popular tool for estimating stock value.

The body of research pertaining to valuing equity and firms has grown significantly in recent years. The current pioneers in modeling the free cash flow to the firm—which is widely used to determine the firm's value—were Copeland, Koller and Murrin (1990, 1994, 2000), Rappaport (1988, 1998), Stewart (1991), and Hackel and Livnat (1992).

A recent equity valuation model based on discounting a stream of free cash flows to equity at a required rate of return to shareholders was introduced by Copeland, Koller and Murrin (1994) and Damodaran (1998). Furthermore, Damodaran (2001) offers a number of methods for estimating a company's value in the absence of comparable firms, operate earnings, and a substantial quantity of cash flow data. Fama's (1970) efficient market research cast doubt on intrinsic valuation models' applicability.

4.1.2. Components of a DCF

- **Free Cash Flow (FCF)**: Cash generated by the assets of the business (tangible and intangible) available for distribution to all providers of capital. FCF is often referred to as unlevered free cash flow, as it represents cash flow available to all providers of capital and is not affected by the capital structure of the business.

- **Terminal Value (TV)**: Value at the end of the FCF projection period (horizon period).
- **Discount Rate**: The rate used to discount projected FCFs and terminal value to their present values.

4.1.3. DCF Methodology

In order to determine the net present value (NPV) of the total expected cash flows of the business or asset, the DCF method of valuation entails projecting FCF over the horizon period, determining the terminal value at the end of that period, and discounting the projected FCFs and terminal value using the discount rate.

Advantages	Disadvantages
• Theoretically, the DCF is arguably the most sound method of valuation. • The DCF method is forward-looking and depends more on future expectations rather than historical results. • The DCF method is more inward-looking, relying on the fundamental expectations of the business or asset, and is influenced to a lesser extent by volatile external factors. • The DCF analysis is focused on cash flow generation and is less affected by accounting practices and assumptions. • The DCF method allows expected (and different) operating strategies to be factored into the valuation. • The DCF analysis also allows different components of a business or synergies to be valued separately.	• The accuracy of the valuation determined using the DCF method is highly dependent on the quality of the assumptions regarding FCF, TV, and discount rates. As a result, DCF valuations are usually expressed as a range of values rather than a single value by using a range of values for key inputs. It is also common to run the DCF analysis for different scenarios, such as a base case, an optimistic case, and a pessimistic case, to gauge the sensitivity of the valuation to various operating assumptions. While the inputs come from a variety of sources, they must be viewed objectively in the aggregate before finalizing the DCF valuation. • The TV often represents a large percentage of the total DCF valuation. Valuation, in such cases, is largely dependent on TV assumptions rather than operating assumptions for the business or the asset.

4.1.4. Application of DCF

In discount cash flow analysis, all future cash flows are estimated and discounted by using cost of capital to give their present values (PVs). The sum of all future cash flows, both incoming and outgoing, is the net present value (NPV) investors can assess whether a stock is undervalued or overvalued compared to its current market price. This helps in making informed buy or sell decisions, thereby enhancing portfolio returns.

In corporate finance, DCF analysis is used for evaluating major projects and capital expenditures. Companies rely on DCF to decide whether to pursue new ventures, expand operations, or invest in new technology. By projecting future cash flows from a project and discounting them at the firm's cost of capital, managers can determine the net present value (NPV) of the project. A positive NPV indicates that the project is expected to generate value above its cost, making it a viable investment. This application ensures that corporate resources are allocated efficiently to maximize shareholder value.

DCF analysis is also crucial in mergers and acquisitions (M&A). During the due diligence process, acquirers use DCF to assess the value of target companies. By analyzing the target's expected future cash flows and discounting them, acquirers can determine a fair acquisition price. This helps in negotiating deals and structuring transactions that are beneficial for both parties. Additionally, DCF provides a basis for understanding the potential synergies and cost savings from the merger, which are factored into the overall valuation.

In capital budgeting, DCF assists in evaluating long-term investment decisions. Public sector entities and corporations use DCF to appraise infrastructure projects, real estate developments, and other capital-intensive investments. By forecasting the cash inflows and outflows associated with a project and discounting them, decision-makers can assess the viability and profitability of the investment. This ensures that funds are committed to projects that are expected to yield positive returns over time.

Furthermore, DCF is used in financial planning and analysis (FP&A) for budgeting and forecasting. By projecting future cash flows based on historical performance and market conditions, companies can develop strategic plans and set financial targets. This application helps in resource allocation, performance evaluation, and long-term planning.

Overall, the application of DCF analysis is fundamental in various financial contexts, providing a robust framework for valuing investments, assessing project feasibility, and making strategic decisions. Its ability to incorporate time value of money and future cash flow projections makes it an indispensable tool in finance.

4.1.5. Use Discounting Methods With Care

The widely accepted economic theory that an asset's value is determined by the total present value of the future cash flows that the asset holder will receive forms the foundation of discounting techniques. A factor based on the discount rate is used to convert the cash flows into terms of present value. Discounting techniques provide "intrinsic" or "true" value in the context of economics, but it's important to recognize the practical challenges. An owner may receive cash flows as a result of capital distributions, tax breaks, takeovers, rights or entitlements, regular or special dividends, etc. Certain cash flows are unique to particular owners and are not available to all. Furthermore, it's possible that these cash flows won't happen at all. In a similar vein, the present value of the future "investor" cash flows is determined by an uncertain discount rate. This is attested to by the discount rate treatises that hang on the utility regulators' walls. It is a common misconception that even small adjustments to the discount rate can have a big impact on value. For instance, if a company with perpetually growing cash flows had a correct discount rate of 10% but an incorrect rate of 9% was used, the enterprise value would be a whopping 50% too high! In addition, if debt represented, say, 50% of the correct enterprise value, the equity value would be 100% too high!

Lastly, the discount rate's level, the timing and size of the cash flows, and all of them are dynamic. Each could, for instance, be subject to abrupt changes brought about by the annual budget or to gradual changes brought about by changes in the macroeconomy. Using the DCF approach is frequently impossible or impractical due to the challenges associated with estimating cash flows and determining the discount rate. Conventional methods typically circumvent these issues by presuming implicitly that a company's growth profile and discount rate are comparable to those of its comparators. Naturally, there are situations in which this presumption is incorrect, as shown in companion documents in the UBS Valuation Series.

4.1.6. Purpose of DCF

This study aims to investigate the methods and analyze the theories of business valuation models. determining the essential inputs that are used in the valuation models and then figuring out how to forecast these inputs more accurately. A review of the literature and an accompanying questionnaire survey will be used to achieve this. Analyzing the application of the discounted cash flow method in firm valuation is the aim of the literature review. Investigating the method's shortcomings and the causes of the trouble spots is the goal. Additionally, the study will be carried out to identify justifications and counterarguments for these issues' solutions. The next questionnaire survey's goals are to demonstrate the validity of the null hypothesis and highlight significant ramifications of the model's empirical flaws and restrictions regarding discounted cash flow (DCF). According to the null hypothesis H_0, various methods of business valuation will yield identical outcomes. The alternative hypothesis H1 makes the assumption that different business valuation methods won't yield the same outcomes.

4.2. ALTERNATIVE APPROACHES TO DCF

When utilizing DCF valuation techniques to determine absolute value, caution should be exercised due to their limitations. However, the technique opens the possibility of other approaches to valuation:

- **Implied Market Discount Rate:** Cash flows, discount rate, and value are the three variables that a DCF relates to one another; any two of these three can be used to determine the third. Therefore, the implied discount rate can be computed using the current market value and the anticipated cash flows. Of the three variables, the assessment of the discount rate presents the biggest challenge, which makes this an appealing process (because analysts would likely have a reasonable degree of confidence in their cash flow forecasts and current market value can be determined precisely). Based on this, an analysis would aim to rank companies based on implied discount rate; any anomalies in the ranking would then be found, either subjectively or objectively, by comparing implied discount rate to theoretical rate.
- **Scenario Analysis:** Conducting scenario analyzes is arguably the most effective use of a DCF analysis. Generally, a forecast would include three cash flow scenarios that correspond to important strategic options. For food retailers, for instance, one could think about an aggressive price war, sensible product pricing, or player collusion of some kind. A DCF would be used to value each scenario, with the same discount rate applied to each. After that, the value differences can be evaluated. The advantage of this technique is that:
    - Compared to traditional valuation techniques that consider just a single point in time forecast, the effects of cash flow differences between scenarios that occur over several years can be valued.
    - Any systematic errors in the cash flow forecast and/or discount rate will be neutralized when the percentage differences between the DCF valuation for each scenario is calculated.

Note that while the discount rate handles the systematic risks (interest rates, exchange rates, etc.), company-specific (non-systematic) factors should be modeled in the cash flow scenarios.

4.2.1. Defining Cash Flow

Cash flow declared after capital expenditure but prior to interest and dividends (i.e., the free cash flow to the firm or FCFF) is always required for a discounted cash flow. Cash flows are sometimes taken after capital expenditures for maintenance; this is incorrect and ought to never be done. Cash flow, which should take into account the effects of matured debt, loan note conversion, share option exercise, and other events, must always be reported following the completion of capital expenditures. A pre-tax cost of capital should be applied when analyzing cash flows that are taken before taxes, as some analysts do. An after-tax cost of capital should be used if cash flows are reported after taxes, but before interest and dividends. The tax charge that will be applied to the after-tax cash flow should include both the actual cash tax paid and the tax shelter that the company has access to as a result of interest payments. The capitalized value of the item and the capitalized value of net interest (i.e, net debt) should be deducted from the DCF value in order to calculate the equity value if cash flows are reported before any item other than net interest and dividends. For instance, if an analyst thought a business would eventually have to pay a windfall profit tax but wasn't sure when the cash outflow would occur, the tax could be disregarded as long as the tax's present value was deducted from the DCF value.

Naturally, it is challenging to determine present value precisely when timing is unknown, but an estimate is typically adequate. This is a crucial point: the model may increase or decrease the value of the "phantom" retained cash if the cash outflow is not modeled. It is evident from the above example that in addition to deducting the present value of the tax from the DCF value, the present value of the value added to or deducted from the "phantom" retained cash should also be deducted. Although a windfall profit tax has been taken into consideration, the cash flow forecast purposefully leaves out numerous other one-time or recurring expenses of a similar nature. The DCF value must be changed where this occurs.

4.2.2. Incorporate Financial and Non-Financial Performance Data

Diverse accounting methodologies may result in disparate depictions of a firm's worth. The usual protocols entail obtaining the financial information, applying various modifications to it, carrying out the necessary calculations, and ultimately creating a comprehensive depiction of the company's worth. Relative valuation and the asset-based method don't really address future forecasting. The goal of relative valuation is to assign a value to assets based on the market prices of comparable assets. If projections for the future are created, like with the discounted cash flow (DCF) approach, they are mostly predicated on historical data. forecasts of discounted cash flow (DCF) for both the short and long term. Based on information about things like machine replacements and product introduction, the cash flows may be adjusted.

Nevertheless, the methodology lacks a thorough framework for examining and integrating the company's overall operational and strategic performance metrics. Based on historical financial data, financial forecasts make the assumption that the future will be the same as the past, which may not be accurate given the dynamic nature of today's business environment. Not all of the operational and strategic viewpoints related to managing a business and appraising its operations are taken into account by the financial valuation techniques used today. The valuation process needs to take a more holistic approach to total value. "Accountants must now establish the value of a specific business capability—which includes things like quantifying the value of contracting out supply chain logistics or human resource management—in order to determine the true cost of a company's various business activities" (Goldman 2002).

Macroeconomic factors are a good place to start when creating scenarios involving cash flows because they have an impact on the performance of emerging market companies and industries. Next, match those macroeconomic scenarios with particular company and industry scenarios. Here, developed and emerging markets differ only slightly in that macroeconomic performance will be less erratic in developed markets. Since value is frequently more erratic in emerging markets, it is advised to create multiple scenarios.

Inflation rates, GDP growth, foreign exchange rates, and frequently interest rates are the main macroeconomic variables that need to be predicted. The connections between these things need to take economic realities into account. For example, inflation and GDP growth are significant factors influencing foreign exchange rates. Because of purchasing power parity, make sure that foreign exchange rates, when creating a high inflation scenario, ultimately reflect inflation. According to the purchasing power parity theory, exchange rates should gradually change to bring about a roughly equal price for goods in any two countries.

4.2.3. Calculating Discount Rate

The returns that each capital provider (such as debt, convertible debt, preference shares, ordinary shares, etc.) demands are represented by the cost of capital. It should come as no surprise that the weighted average cost of capital (WACC) is the cost of capital, which is a weighted average of all these various financing costs. The percentage of total capital that each instrument represents, expressed in terms of market value, serves as the basis for weighting. For example, if the company was financed by just debt and equity then:

$$\text{WACC} = \frac{G}{(1+G)}.\text{COD}.(1 - T) + \frac{1}{(1+G)}.\text{COE}$$

The cost of debt (COD) and the cost of equity (COE), which are calculated after corporation tax and before investor tax, respectively, in this equation need to be modified to account for the equity risk that the company's financial structure introduces. T is the marginal corporate tax rate, and G is the company's gearing (net debt/equity) based on the market values of debt and equity. Recall that the same method can be applied if net debt is negative (i.e., net cash), as long as the cash flow is reported prior to net interest received and the net cash is added to the DCF value to determine the equity value. Analysts will occasionally compute WACC using the accounting value of debt and equity. This is incorrect; market values should always be used.

4.2.3.1. Cost of Debt

The cost of debt is a straight-forward calculation:

$$COD = R_f + \text{debt risk premium}.$$

The risk-free rate (R_f) is given in Table 4.1. The debt risk premium is relatively small, at between 40bp and 120bp. For large, high-quality businesses with high interest cover a debt risk premium at the lower end of this range is appropriate and vice versa. To simplify the calculation, we use one of three risk premia:

Table 4.1. Estimating the Debt Risk Premium

Debt risk premium	Comment
0.4%	High-quality corporate, high interest cover, typically AA+ rated
0.8%	Average-quality corporate, average interest cover, typically A rated
1.2%	Low-quality corporate, low interest cover, typically BBB rated

Source: .

4.2.3.2. Cost of Equity

The entire return that equity investors demand on their investment is known as the cost of equity. As the risk to those returns rises, investors will demand higher returns on their investments, and vice versa. The relationship between risk and reward is a key idea in the computation of equity cost. The capital asset pricing model (CAPM) is a popular model used to express this relationship.

Cost of equity and of capital, breaks down the return into two principal components:

- The returns on 'risk free' investments (government debt). This is generally known as the risk free rate (R_f).
- The additional return required to compensate for the uncertainty associated with investing in the company.

This latter component is further broken down into two parts:

- The return that the market as a whole will deliver over and above the risk free rate. This is known as the market risk premium (R_p).
- The risk of the company relative to that of the market. This is known as the company's beta (β). This risk represents both the sensitivity of the underlying business (systematic business risk) to macro influences and the risk to equity investors from the capital structure of the company (financial risk). The way these components are combined is straightforward and is shown in the equation below:

$$COE = R_F + \beta \,.\, R_P$$

1. **Market Risk Premium:** We view the risk premium as a premium that looks ahead, predicated on the market's anticipated long-term returns. Capital and

equity costs deducted from the risk-free rate. This usually ranges from 2 to 4%, depending on the market.

2. **Beta (β):** The final component of the COE calculation is the risk measure (beta or β). We estimate, within certain guidelines, a forward looking β. To introduce some consistency into the calculation of β across various sectors and countries, we base the risk measurement on two factors:

   i. **Systematic Business Risk:** Business risk, in general, refers to the risk that the company as a whole bears, excluding any risks arising from financing decisions. There are two types of risks associated with this: company-specific risks and risks that impact all companies. The possibility of a rival altering their pricing strategy or the possibility of industrial action are examples of the former, whereas shifts in interest rates or inflation are examples of the latter. When estimating β, only risks that are applicable to all companies are taken into consideration. Systematic risks are what these dangers are called. These hazards ought to be assessed in comparison to a "average" business. It is best to use financial modeling and scenario analysis to address company-specific risks rather than adjusting the discount rate.

   ii. **Financial Risk:** The equity risk that arises from the company's capital structure, or gearing, is this. The formula in Cost of Equity and of Capital shows how gearing affects β. When estimating the degree of gearing, the market average should be taken into consideration. Business and financial risk categories are taken into consideration when creating Table 4.2. There is a slight narrower range than the historical βs for the maximum and minimum βs from Table 4.2, which are 1.6 and 0.4, respectively. Given that βs typically exhibit mean reversion, or gradually shift towards 1.0, this is appropriate.

Table 4.2. Company Risk Premium: β (β= 1 + A + B)

Systematic business risk		Financial risk	
Risk category of company rel. to market avg.	Risk adjustment (A)*	Company gearing %**	Risk adjustment (B)***
Lower quintile	-0.4	-20	-0.2
Next quintile	-0.2	0	-0.1
Next quintile	+0.0	20	+0.0
Next quintile	+0.2	40	+0.1
Upper quintile	+0.4	60	+0.2

Source: http://pricing.online.fr/docs/DiscountedCashFlow.pdf.

In using Table 4.2, if there is a significant change in gearing over the forecast period then the analyst should adjust the COE for these changes.

4.2.3.3. Cost of other Types of Capital

Although debt and equity financing have been discussed, other forms of funding, such as convertibles and preference shares, can also be utilized. It is best to estimate the costs of these financing options based on the fact that they will have some traits in common with debt and equity. Assigning each type of instrument to debt or equity is a straightforward substitute in cases where the other instruments make up less than 10% of the capital base.

4.2.3.4. Foreign Exchange Risk (FOREX)

There are three types of FOREX risk exposure.

- **Transaction Exposure:** Transaction exposure is defined as the uncertain domestic currency value of an open position denominated in a foreign currency with respect to a known transaction.
- **Economic Exposure:** Economic exposure is the impact of exchange rate changes on the uncertain foreign currency stream of corporate cash flows.
- **Accounting or Translation Exposure:** Accounting or translation exposure is caused by the uncertain domestic value of a net accounting position denominated in a foreign currency at a certain future date.

4.2.3.5. Sales Revenue Forecast

The two areas that is important when conducting a valuation,

1. How to limit the subjectivity of the assumptions and estimations behind the valuation
2. How to make an accurate forecast of the future sales revenue

Forecasts are one of the most crucial tools managers create to help them in the decision-making process, according to Bernstein (1996), who was mentioned in the section on key concepts. Almost all significant operational decisions rely to some degree on forecasts (Hanke, 2001). This raises the issue of how to project future sales revenue accurately. The foundation of a business's free cash flow is its revenue forecast. There is enough demand for the product to sustain five years of strong growth if the company keeps itself busy meeting the demand, has strong marketing channels, and upgraded, efficient factories. After that, the market will become saturated as new competitors enter the market. Arguably, the most significant and challenging assumption an analyst can make about a company's future cash flows is a revenue forecast. Forecasting revenue growth requires taking a number of things into account. These include the company's market share performance and whether it is growing or shrinking. It's also important to think about whether any new products are driving sales or if price adjustments are about to happen. Nevertheless, it is wise to take into account multiple scenarios since the future is never guaranteed.

Four Ps marketing in sales i.e., Product, pricing, place, and promotion make up the company's marketing mix. In the end, these dictate the sales figures. Sales regional managers can forecast possible deals in their pipeline with the help of the sales revenue-forecasting engine, which also gives management a precise picture of the sales organization. This strong engine gives the sales manager the precise data required to project for upcoming years while enabling in-depth examination of prior months, quarters, and years. When businesses divide their sales into smaller, more manageable chunks, forecasting becomes generally simpler. While not every business sells in units, the majority do. Add the product lines for each month after estimating the sales for each product line month by month. Next, multiply the total quantity by the unit sales price to convert them into a value.

By dissecting things into their constituent parts, forecasting becomes simpler.

4.2.3.6. Cost of Goods Sold (Cogs)/General and Administrative Expenses

For manufacturing products the best way to calculate the cost of the product, is to prepare the cost of the product according to the recipe of the product based on current raw material prices in order to arrive at cost per kilogram. The total number of units sold multiplied by the weight of each product yields the total weight of sales, which is then multiplied by the cost per kilogram to determine the cost of goods sold. For future years, find out the percentage of inflation rate and increase by that percentage year on year basis. The analyst will also be able to calculate the cost of general and administrative expenses per kilogram, multiply that figure by the weight of the sales quantity to determine the total expenses, and then add the annual inflation rate to determine the expenses for subsequent years. The analyst must examine the historical percentage of the company's cost of goods sold (cogs), expressed as a percentage of revenues, if the cost per kilogram cannot be determined. When forecasting, analysts must err on the side of caution and assume that, as the company is forced to lower its prices over time in order to remain competitive, operating costs will increase as a percentage of revenues.

4.2.3.7. Taxation

The official corporate tax rate is often not paid by many businesses on their operating profits. For example, businesses that invest a lot of capital are eligible for tax benefits. As a result, it makes sense to divide profits before income tax by the average annual income tax paid over the previous few years in order to determine the tax rate.

4.2.3.8. Capital expenditure (CAPEX)

Businesses must continue to invest in capital goods like real estate, machinery, and plants in order to support growth. Future years' capital expenditures can be projected using the company's investment plan.

4.2.3.9. Change in Working Capital

Working capital is the amount of money needed by a company to run its daily operations or, more precisely, the short-term loans needed to keep up current assets like inventory. A business will require more cash for working capital and investments the faster it grows. Current assets less current liabilities is the formula for calculating working capital. The difference in working capital levels from one year to the next is known as the net change in working capital. An increase in working capital is recognized as a cost against free cash flow when there is a greater cash commitment than in the prior year. In order to keep up with the growth in sales revenues, a larger investment in inventory and receivables will be required because working capital usually rises with revenue growth. Working capital is taken into account when calculating cash flows because investments in it are viewed as squandering money that do not yield a reasonable rate of return. As a result, inventory costs money that is squandered because it remains on the shelves and generates no revenue. It is not appropriate to include short-term debt in current liabilities when calculating working capital. Current liabilities should include supplier credit, accounts payable, and accrued expenses like taxes and salaries, among other things.

4.2.4. Calculating the Terminal Value

After estimating the free cash flow

generated during the forecast period, we must calculate the reasonable estimate of the cash flows that the company will generate beyond that period when the company has settled into middle age and maturity. The challenge lies in predicting cash flows in the long run. We employ a "terminal value" strategy, which entails making certain assumptions about long-term cash flow growth, to help with the task's difficulty.

4.2.4.1. Gordon Growth Model

There are several ways to estimate a terminal value of cash flows, but one well-known method is to value the company as a perpetuity using the Gordon growth model. The model uses this formula:

Terminal value = Final projected year cash flow/(Discount rate – Long term cash flow growth rate)

This formula rests on the big assumption that the cash flow of the last projected year will stabilize and continue at the same rate forever.

$$TV = (FCF_n)/(k-g)$$

Where; TV is the terminal value; FCF_n is the free cash flow generated by the firm in year n; n is the last year of the projections; and g is the constant rate of increase in perpetual free cash flows; k -discount rate.

4.2.5. Country Risk and Cost of Capital

Country risk and the cost of capital are closely intertwined in international finance, as country risk significantly impacts the required rate of return on investments in a particular country. Country risk encompasses the economic, political, and social risks associated with investing in a foreign country, including factors such as political instability, economic volatility, currency fluctuations, and regulatory changes. These risks can affect the predictability of cash flows and the overall stability of the investment environment. To compensate for these risks, investors demand a higher return on their investments, which is reflected in the cost of capital. The cost of capital is the required return necessary to make a capital budgeting project, such as building a new factory, worthwhile. In the context of international investments, the cost of capital includes the risk-free rate, typically based on long-term government bonds, and a risk premium that accounts for the specific risks associated with the country in question. This risk premium is often estimated using sovereign credit ratings, political risk assessments, and economic indicators. A higher country risk leads to a higher risk premium, thereby increasing the cost of capital. This elevated cost of capital affects the valuation and feasibility of potential investments, as projects must yield returns that exceed this higher threshold to be considered viable. Therefore, understanding and accurately assessing country risk is crucial for multinational corporations and investors when evaluating international investment opportunities. By incorporating country risk into the cost of capital calculations, investors can better gauge the potential rewards and challenges of investing in different regions, ultimately aiding in more informed and strategic decision-making.

4.2.6. Calculating Total Enterprise Value (EV)

To arrive at a total enterprise value (EV), we simply have to take the present value of the cash flows and terminal value, divide them by the discount rate and finally add up the results.

$$EV = FCF_1 / (1+WACC)^1 + FCF_2 / (1+WACC)^2 + \ldots\ldots + FCF_n / (1+WACC)^n + TV / (1+WACC)^n$$

Where; EV is enterprise value; FCF is free cash flow of the enterprise; WACC is weighted average cost of capital; n is the number of years; TV is the terminal value.

4.2.7. Calculating the Value of Equity (V_e)

Enterprise value includes the company's debt. Investors are interested in the value of the enterprise's shares alone. The value of the enterprise's equity is equal to enterprise value less net debt of that enterprise.

$$EV = V_e + V_d$$

$$V_e = EV - V_d$$

Where: V_e is the value of equity
V_d is the value of debt
EV is the enterprise value.

4.2.8. How Do the Analysts Value a Business That Is Losing Money?

Currently, businesses that are losing money present a number of challenges for analysts trying to value them. There are number of reasons why a business might have negative earnings, and the response will vary depending upon the reason:

The best course of action for a cyclical firm experiencing a decline in earnings due to a recession is to normalize earnings by calculating the average earnings over the course of a full business cycle. A good example would be Ford or Chrysler in 1991, when the recession caused both businesses to have negative earnings.

Normalized net income = Average ROE * Current book value of equity

Normalized after tax operating income = Average ROC * Current book value of assets

Once earnings are normalized, the growth rate used should be consistent with the normalized earnings, and should reflect the real growth potential of the firm rather than the cyclical effects.

If the earnings of a firm are depressed due to a one-time charge, the best response is to estimate the earnings without the one-time charge and value the firm based upon these earnings. For example, it would apply to firms that had significant restructuring charges.

If the earnings of a firm are depressed due to poor management, i.e., the firm is a poor performer in a sector with healthy earnings; the average return on equity or capital for the industry can be used to estimate normalized earnings for the firm. The implicit assumption is that the firm will recover back to industry averages, once management has been removed.

Normalized net income = Industry average ROE * Current book value of equity

Normalized after tax operating income = Industry average ROC * Current book value of assets

Use the industry average operating or profit margins along with revenues to arrive at normalized earnings if the negative earnings over time have led to a significant decline in the book value. Note that this normalization will not happen instantly, but rather gradually over the course of a discounted cash flow valuation. Therefore, it is reasonable to assume that a company with negative operating income today will converge on normalized earnings in five years. (This would be the strategy to use for a company like Digital Equipment, which reported low earnings in 1996 while other companies in the same industry reported record profits.) If a company's earnings are low or negative due to the early stages of its industry, the discounted cash flow valuation will be influenced by the expectation of operating margins and return on equity (ROE) as the industry matures. The best course of action in cases where high leverage is causing a decline in equity earnings is to value the company as a whole rather than just the equity and account for the gradual reduction of leverage.

4.2.9. Pros and Cons of Discounted Cash Flow DCF

After going over the discounted cash flow analysis's mechanics, it's time to look at the method's advantages and disadvantages. The best justification is that it yields a value that is most similar to an intrinsic stock value. Relative valuation measures are alternatives to discounted cash flow (DCF) that compare stocks within a sector using multiples. The price to earnings (P/E), enterprise value to earnings before interest, tax, depreciation and amortization (EV/EBITDA), and price to sales ratios are examples of relative valuation metrics that are easy to compute, but they are not very helpful if a market or sector as a whole is overvalued or undervalued. A well-crafted discounted cash flow (DCF) can be employed as a management tool to seize opportunities and lessen risks to the business in order to optimize shareholder value. Discounted cash flow (DCF), in contrast to conventional valuation instruments like the P/E ratio, is dependent on free cash flows. Free cash flow is a reliable metric that eschews most of the subjectivity found in reported earnings. Discounted cash flow (DCF) analysis has many advantages, but it also has some drawbacks. The value created for the company won't be accurate if the inputs—free cash flow forecasts, discount rates, and perpetuity growth rates—are inaccurate because of uncertainties. The nature of discounted cash flow (DCF) analysis is dynamic, requiring ongoing attention to detail and adjustment. The model prioritizes long-term value; it is not appropriate for short-term investing. A well-designed discounted cash flow (DCF) could save you from purchasing a bubble, but it might also cause you to miss out on potentially profitable short-term increases in share prices.

4.3. PRACTICAL USE OF DCF ANALYSIS FOR VALUATION

The practical use of Discounted Cash Flow (DCF) analysis for valuation involves a structured process to determine the intrinsic value of a business, project, or investment. This method is favored for its ability to provide a detailed and theoretically sound valuation based on future cash flow projections.

4.3.1. How Should DCF Valuations Be Undertaken?

The process of performing a DCF valuation involves figuring out the total present value of all future free cash flows. The discount rate is used to determine the present value. The term "free cash flows" refers to the cash flows that are reported following capital expenditures and taxes, but prior to the payment of dividends and net interest. Stated differently, the cash flow that is exclusively available to debt and equity holders. This method of calculation yields the enterprise value; hence, in order to determine the equity value, net debt must be subtracted. To determine equity value, the total value of any claims made against the business should also be deducted from the DCF value if, for whatever reason, the discounted free cash flows are used to pay off other obligations. In these situations, extreme caution should be exercised to guarantee that the appropriate discount rate is applied. Generally speaking, DCF valuations provide an absolute value, so unlike other approaches, there is no comparators problem. However, the possibility of inaccurate analyst forecasts exists when utilizing DCFs to compute absolute values. Generally speaking, these mistakes are more likely to be systematic than random. Since systematic errors won't affect these differences, DCFs are the most appropriate tool for evaluating the percentage differences between the values of different strategies in these situations. Lastly, the implied discount rate for one stock can be compared to the implied discount rate for other stocks if the DCF technique is applied to calculate it.

4.3.2. Where Should DCF Be Used?

Any business can do a DCF analysis, but there are some real-world challenges. Applying a DCF valuation technique is challenging if cash flows are highly cyclical, volatile, or prone to disruptions because it necessitates forecasting cash flows over extended periods of time. Having said that, there are issues with other approaches as well, and a DCF approach is generally far superior to other approaches and is in no way inferior to them. The technique is superior because it requires the analyst to forecast the cash flow profile explicitly, which forces them to address the business and strategic issues the company faces. The sectors that benefit most from a DCF analysis are those with easily defined systematic risks and steady, predictable cash flows.

4.3.3. What Influences DCF Valuations?

The projected cash flow profile and the cost of capital required to bring that profile into present value terms have an impact on a DCF valuation. It goes without saying that the caliber of the analyst's model and the caliber of the input assumptions affect the projected cash flow profile. The latter is a cerebral quality, whereas the former is mechanical. The cost of capital is the second factor that affects value, and it also necessitates some mechanical and mental computation. Since cash flows are not always predictable in practice, some assumptions are made about their characteristics after the explicit forecast period. These presumptions are used to determine a terminal value, and it is obvious that they will also have an impact on the result. Poor cash flow forecasts, incorrect terminal value computations, and improperly estimated discount rates are the main causes of DCF valuation failures.

4.4. DISCOUNTED DIVIDEND MODEL

The present value of the anticipated flow of all future cash payments to an investor, including dividend payments and the proceeds from the share's final sale, is what economists refer to as a share's intrinsic value. The most accurate model for firm valuation, according to theory, is the dividend discount model (DDM). The market price is established by the anticipated dividends that the newly acquired security will yield during their ownership tenure. This means that dividends can eventually replace the market price in terms of stock value, since a dividend stream can always replace it.

$$V_0 = D_1/(1+k) + D_2/(1+k)^2 + \ldots + D_t/(1+k)^t + P_t/(1+k)^t \text{ with}$$

$$P_t = D_{t+1}/(1+k)^{t+1} + D_{t+2}/(1+k)^{t+2} + \ldots + D_n/(1+k)^n$$

$$\text{becomes } V_0 = \sum_{t=1}^{n} D_t/(1+k)^t \qquad (1)$$

V_0 = Value of the stock in t=0

D_t = Dividend received in period t

P_t = Market price in period t

k = Discount rate

n = Number of years over which the asset will generate dividends for investors.

The most widely known discounted dividend model (DDM) is the Gordon growth model (Gordon, 1962). It expresses the value of a stock based on a constant growth rate of dividends so that $D_t = D_{t-1}(1 + g)$ where g is the expected constant growth rate in dividends. For any time t, D_t equals the t=0 dividends, compounded at g for t periods:

$D_t = D_0(1+g)^t$. If D_t is substituted into eqn. 1, we obtain

$$V_0 = \sum_{t=1}^{n} D_t(1+g)^t/(1+k)^t$$

As this represents a geometric series, the equation can be simplified into the Gordon growth model.

$$V_0 = D_0(1+g)/k\text{-}g \text{ or even simplified to } V_0 = D_1/k\text{-}g$$

These formulas demonstrate how the current dividend, growth rate, and discount rate all affect a stock's value. The discounted dividend model (DDM) has significant shortcomings when it comes to its actual use, despite being the most accurate theoretical valuation model for common stocks. The primary issue is that the observed dividends have no direct bearing on the company's ability to create value and, consequently, on future dividend payments. Miller and Modigliani (1961) claim that current dividend observations are unreliable unless the payout policy is connected to the creation of value within the organization. According to Penman (1992), price is determined by future dividends; however, price is not inferred from observed dividends. Because payout ratios are hard to predict, there is a problem with dividend forecasting as a result of the missing connection between value creation and distribution. First, it is important to realize that the discounted cash flow valuation method is an entity or enterprise approach in which the value of the cash flows from all sources of capital is determined, and the value of equity is obtained by deducting the debt. One method that is very similar to discounted cash flow (DCF) is the dividend discount model. In essence, it provides the same result as the enterprise approach by taking the free cash flows and discounting them to the shareholders at the cost of equity.

4.4.1. Relative Valuation

The goal of discounted cash flow (DCF) valuation is to determine an asset's value based on its cash flow, growth, and risk attributes. The goal of relative valuation is to determine an asset's value by looking at how comparable assets are currently valued by the market. As such, relative valuation consists of two parts. The first is that prices must be standardized in order to value assets relative to one another. This is typically accomplished by converting prices into multiples of sales, book values, or earnings. To ascertain the relative adequacy of the standardized multiples, it is necessary to locate comparable firms and compare them. The challenge with valuing equity in businesses is that different businesses in the same industry may have different risk profiles, potential for growth, and cash flow profiles. When comparing a multiple across multiple firms, the issue of how to account for these variations becomes crucial. Although relative valuation is simple to apply and intuitive, it can also be abused with ease.

Main methods using different multiples are commonly used in the relative approach to valuation.

- Relative earnings valuation method: P/E ratio or earnings multiple, PEG ratio

  P/E = Price/Earnings per share

  PEG = P/E/g, where g is the expected growth rate of earnings.
- Relative revenue valuation method: P/S ratio

  P/S = Price/ Sales per share.
- Relative cash flow valuation method.

  P/EBIT, P/EBITDA, P/CFO ratios Where EBIT is earnings before interest and tax

  EBITDA earnings before interest, tax, depreciation and amortization

  CFO cash flow from operation.

When analysts have strong confidence in the accuracy of past and future earnings per share (EPS) and when EPS growth is anticipated, earnings multiples are frequently employed. When earnings are declining or negative, or when earnings are not comparable or indicative of the future, the revenue-based valuation method is applied. Cash flow ratios are employed by cyclical companies with high earnings volatility or by industries with low or negative earnings per share (EPS) as a result of significant non-operating expenses.

4.4.2. Reasons for Popularity

It requires less time and resources than valuation using discounted cash flow (DCF). Compared to relative valuation, discounted cash flow (DCF) valuation requires a lot more information. Relative valuation presents a less time-consuming option for analysts who are limited in their access to information and have limited time. Relative valuations, in which the value used for a multiple is frequently derived from what the market is paying for similar firms, are far more difficult to defend than discounted cash flow (DCF) valuations, which have lengthy lists of explicit forecasts and explanations of how the discount rate works. Since relative valuation aims to measure relative value rather than intrinsic value, it is much more likely to reflect the current state of the market. For investors who assess relative value, this is significant.

4.4.3. Potential Pitfalls

Relative valuations have advantages, but they also have disadvantages. Although a relative valuation can be constructed by combining a multiple with a set of similar companies, it can also lead to erroneous value estimates that neglect important factors like risk, growth, and cash flow potential. Since multiples are a good indicator of the state of the market, it follows that estimating an asset's value using relative valuation may lead to values that are either too high or too low depending on whether the market is overvaluing or undervaluing comparable businesses. Relative valuations are susceptible to manipulation because the assumptions behind them are opaque.

4.4.4. Reconciling Relative and Discounted Cash Flow Valuations

Different estimates of value will typically be produced for the same business using the two valuation techniques—discounted cash flow valuation and relative valuation. Moreover, you can arrive at different estimates of value even within relative valuation, depending on the multiple you use and the businesses you used as the basis for the relative valuation. Different perspectives on market efficiency or inefficiency account for the value discrepancies between discounted cash flow valuation and relative valuation. The concepts of relative valuation and discounted cash flow (DCF) diverge greatly philosophically. We try to determine an asset's intrinsic value through discounted cash flow (DCF) valuation, taking into account the asset's potential to produce cash flows in the future. By examining what the market is willing to pay for comparable assets, we can determine the value of an asset through relative valuation. In relative valuation, we use comparable asset prices to determine an asset's value. In order to compare prices, we first convert prices into standardization multiples and then compare these multiples between businesses that meet our criteria for comparability. Profits, book value, revenue, and industry-specific factors can all be used to standardize prices.

4.5. EFFECTS OF ERRORS

Although the intrinsic value of the projected cash flows at a specific discount rate can be found through a DCF analysis, calculating these two amounts is difficult. Furthermore, because cash flows cannot be predicted forever, a terminal value—which frequently draws on conventional valuation methods—is determined at the conclusion of the explicit forecast period. Any one or all of these three items:

i. Cash flow forecast.
ii. Terminal value.
iii. Discount rate.

4.5.1. Cash Flow Forecast and Terminal Value

One possible issue with DCF analyzes is shown in Tables 4.3 and 4.4, where there is a general lack of value related to the explicit forecast period. Less than 20% of the company's value will come from the cash flows in the explicit forecast period for typical discount rates (after-tax, weighted-average cost of capital of 8% to 12%), free cash flow growth rates (5% to 7%), and five-year explicit forecasts. The explicit cash flows only account for about 30% of value, even over an explicit forecast period of 10 years. The percentages for high-growth businesses could be as low as 5% or 10% for 8% and 12% discount rates, respectively. It is evident that a DCF only scratches the surface of valuation in most practical cases; the terminal value contains the majority of the value. Indeed, figuring out terminal value would likely be a much better use of time and resources than attempting to project cash flow for the next 5 or 10 years, with the exception of low-growth businesses.

Table 4.3. Percentage of Value Accumulated in Explicit Forecast Period

Duration of explicit forecast (years)	Growth rate / discount rate*			
	0.0	0.3	0.6	0.9
1	7	5	3	1
2	14	10	6	1
3	21	15	9	2
4	26	19	11	3
5	32	23	14	4
6	37	27	17	4
7	42	31	19	5
8	46	35	21	6
9	50	38	24	6
10	54	41	26	7

Source: http://pricing.online.fr/docs/DiscountedCashFlow.pdf.

Table 4.4. Percentage of Value Accumulated in Explicit Forecast Period

Duration of explicit forecast	Growth rate / discount rate 0	0.3	0.6	0.9
1	11	8	4	1
2	20	14	8	2
3	29	21	12	3
4	36	27	16	4
5	43	32	20	5
6	49	37	23	6
7	55	42	26	7
8	60	46	30	8
9	64	50	33	9
10	68	54	35	10

Source: http://pricing.online.fr/docs/DiscountedCashFlow.pdf.

4.5.1.1. Effect of Forecast Errors

A cursory glance through our research archive indicates that analysts project cash flows one year from now with an accuracy of ±30%, within 80% confidence limits. Assuming analysts can accurately predict the 5th year's cash flows to within ±30%, we have been generous in Figure 4.1 and also the terminal value.

For a typical growth rate and discount rate, the resulting valuation errors could very easily range from 50% to 180%. Even though these mistakes are significant, they still represent errors in the company's total value. The analyst must deduct the non-equity components in order to value the equity. Generally speaking, these can be evaluated rather quickly and accurately. As a result, errors in the company's overall value will be magnified when evaluating the equity on its own. For instance, the equity value error would be 0% to 230% off if the 50% to 180% value errors mentioned above happened in a company with 50% debt (by market value)! To put this into perspective, it would be as if an analyst proposed a fair value P/E of 0.0 or 37.0x for the German market (actual P/E of about 16x). The analyst would, quite rightly, be laughed out of court.

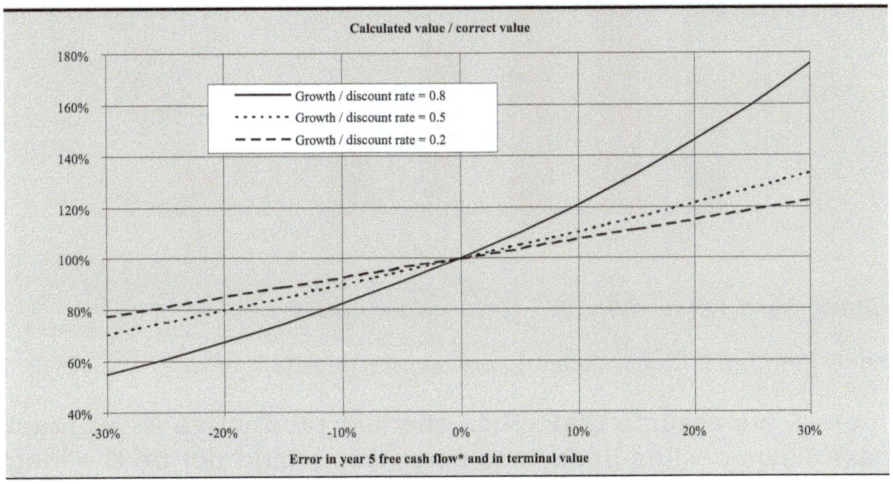

Figure 4.1. *Same errors in the fit year forecast and terminal value.*

Source: http://pricing.online.fr/docs/DiscountedCashFlow.pdf.

4.5.2. Calculating Terminal Value

The value of the cash flows that are expected to occur after the specific forecast period is represented by the terminal enterprise value. The terminal value is typically the best way to capture the majority of a business's true value.

There are several ways in which terminal value can be calculated:

- Constant cash flow growth.
- Zero value added.
- Constant (operating) profit growth.
- Market multiples and financial ratios.

Although "zero value added" is our preferred method of determining terminal value, constant cash flow growth and constant operating profit growth are closely behind. Financial ratios and market multiples are overly ambiguous.

4.5.2.1. Zero Value Added

Terminal value based on "zero value added" makes the assumption that management will receive an economic return on future investments equal to the cost of capital at the conclusion of the explicit forecast period. Stated differently, the present value of the future cash flow from new assets will be DM80m if DM80m of the gross cash flow is invested in them. This means that we can simply discount the gross cash flows from current assets since new investments don't add value.

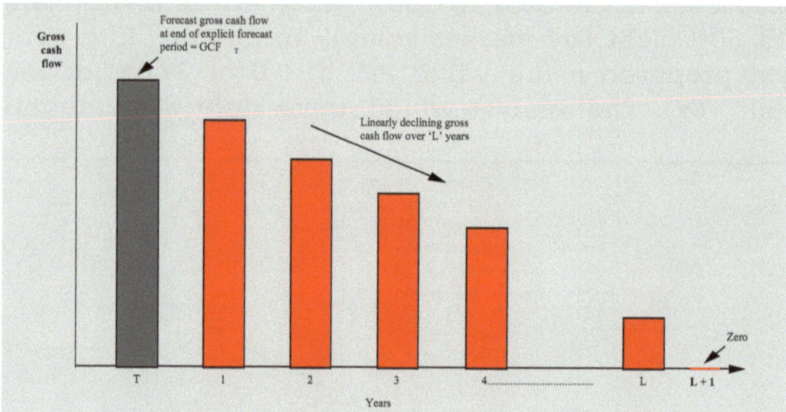

Figure 4.2. *Declining cash flows underlies 'zero value added.'*

Source: http://pricing.online.fr/docs/DiscountedCashFlow.pdf.

For convenience, we assume that when the last productive asset reaches the end of its life, these cash flows decline linearly to zero (this would not be the longest remaining life of the productive assets but would be the average remaining life across all the assets). It's highly likely that some value will endure after all productive assets have reached the end of their useful lives. For instance, the land and building values. The linearly decreasing gross cash flows should be increased by this amount (appropriately discounted). For the sake of simplicity, we will assume that the residual value is zero in the following computations.

From Figure 4.2 we can see that the value (TV) of the declining gross cash flow from GCFFT at the end of the explicit forecast period to zero at L + 1 is given by:

$$TV = \sum_{n=1}^{n=L} \frac{GCFF_T(1 - n/(L+1))}{(1+W)^n} \qquad (2)$$

Where n is the year (first year after the end of the explicit forecast period n = 1, second year n = 2, etc), W is the weighted average cost of capital and L is the life remaining at the end of the explicit forecast period of the longest life asset.

This equation can be re-written as:

$$TV = \frac{GCFF_T}{L+1} \sum_{n=1}^{n=L} \frac{L+1-n}{(1+W)^n}$$

or

$$TV = \frac{GCFF_T}{L+1}\left((L+1)\sum_{n=1}^{n=L}\frac{1}{(1+W)} - \sum_{n=1}^{n=L}\frac{n}{(1+W)^n}\right)$$

This equation can be reduced to:

$$TV = \frac{GCFF_T}{W^2(1+W)^L(1+L)} \left((1+W)^L.(WL-1)+1\right) \qquad (3)$$

In present value terms, the terminal value is given by:

$$\frac{TV}{(1+W)^T} = \frac{GCFF_T.((1+W^L).(WL-1)+1}{W^2(1+L).(1+W)^{(L+T)}} \qquad (4)$$

Where T is the duration of the explicit forecast period in years and GCF is this gross cash flow at the end of the explicit forecast period, W is the weighted average cost of capital and L is the remaining life of the asset base. The terminal value is not brought into present value terms and is divided by GCFF, i.e.:

$$\frac{TV}{GCFF_T} = \frac{((1+W^L).(WL-1)+1)}{W^2(1+L).(1+W)^L} \qquad (5)$$

4.5.2.2. Constant Cash Flow Growth

By considering the growth g in free cash flow to the firm (FCFF) beyond the end of the explicit forecast period T to be constant, we can calculate the terminal value. This is shown below:

$$\frac{TV}{(1 + WACC)^T} = \frac{FCFF\,(1 + g)}{(WACC - g)\,(1 + WACC)^n}$$

In this equation WACC represents the weighted average cost of capital and the FCFF is the last forecast for the explicit forecast period (Kincheloe, 1990)

An essential factor in determining the terminal value is the free cash flow's long-term growth. The expansion of the business can only be fueled by an increase in net new investment (capital expenditure over and above maintenance capital expenditure) if we assume that the company is in a steady state following the explicit forecast period (i.e., return on equity and return on capital are both constant). Therefore, in a steady state, the rate of net new investment will determine the growth rate, and this rate will be equal to or slightly higher than the growth rate of the company's market (i.e., growth rate in new car sales, phone calls, plane orders, etc.). It is helpful to make sure that the level of free cash flow to which the growth is applied is consistent with the rate of investment, even though we can determine growth in free cash flow to the firm by taking into account the "macro" environment in which the company operates. This can be achieved by making sure that the growth rate assumed is consistent with the ratio of free cash flow to gross cash flow, or cash flow after capital expenditure to cash flow before capital expenditure. This ratio is calculated below.

We can relate the gross cash flow (GCFF) to the gross book value (GBV) of assets through the cash flow return on gross book value (gross cash return (GCR)), i.e.:

$$GCR = \frac{GCFF_1}{GBV_0} \qquad (6)$$

Although it might not be a familiar term, the gross cash flow return is the same as the project's initial EBITDA over capital employed (CE). Nevertheless, when accumulated depreciation erodes the capital used, a project's EBITDA/CE will increase. Therefore, the benefit of a gross cash flow return is that it offers a return amount that is constant and unaffected by the rate of investment.

In addition to Eqn. (2) we can say that the gross book value one year to the next is related through the capital expenditure (CX) i.e.:

$$GBV_1 = GBV_0 + CX_1 \qquad (7)$$

From Eqn. (3) we can write the growth in gross book value (which will be the same as the growth in gross cash flow if gross cash flow return is constant) in terms of capital expenditure.

$$\frac{GBV_1 - GBV_0}{GBV_0} = g = \frac{CX_1}{GBV_0} \qquad (8)$$

Eqn. (6) can be substituted into Eqn. (8) to give growth in terms of return and gross cash flow:

$$g = \frac{CX_1 . GCR}{GCFF_1} \qquad (9)$$

Finally, we know that the free cash flow to the firm (FCFF) is related to the gross cash flow as follows:

$$FCFF_1 = GCFF_1 - CX_1 \qquad (10)$$

therefore, substituting (10) in (9) gives:

$$g = \left(\frac{GCFF_1 - FCFF_1}{GCFF_1}\right)GCR$$

or in more general terms:

$$g = \left(1 - \frac{FCFF}{GCFF}\right)$$

It may be more convenient to express the ratio of free cash flow to gross cash flow in terms of growth and gross cash return:

$$FCFF / GCFF = 1 - g / GCR \qquad (11)$$

or to express the level of capital expenditure in terms of gross cash flow, growth and cash return:

$$CX = \frac{g . GCFF}{GCR} \qquad (12)$$

Eqns. (11) or (12) should be used in conjunction with the constant cash flow growth equation to ensure the free cash flow is consistent with the forecast gross cash flow and assumed growth.

4.5.2.3. Constant Operating Profit Growth

Cash flows can be expressed in terms of the operating profit and net new investment (in fixed assets and operating working capital), this is illustrated in Table 4.5 which gives a simplified cash flow statement.

Table 4.5. Simplified Cash Flow Statement

	Cash flow item		
+	After tax operating profit (NOPAT)*		
+	Depreciation	}	
-	Capital expenditure	}	Net increase in assets** (=ΔA)
-	Increase in operating working capital	}	
=	After-tax free cash flow to the firm		
-	Tax shield on interest payments		
-	Cash interest		
-	Cash dividend		
=	Change in net debt		

Source: http://pricing.online.fr/docs/DiscountedCashFlow.pdf.

Thus, we can write:

$$FCFF_n = NOPAT_n - \Delta A_n \quad (13)$$

However, $NOPAT_n$ can be expressed as a return on accounting capital employed, i.e.:

$$NOPAT_n = ROCE_n . BV_{n-1} \quad (14)$$

Where $ROCE_n$ represents the return on capital employed and BV_{n-1} represents the opening capital employed.

If we assume that ROCE remains constant overtime, which would be the case in steady-state conditions, then:

$$NOPAT_n - NOPAT_{n-1} = ROCE . (BV_{n-1} - BV_{n-2}) \quad (15)$$

or

$$NOPAT_n = NOPAT_{n-1} + ROCE . \Delta A_{n-1} \quad (16)$$

In addition, with constant ROCE the growth in NOPAT (gop) will be constant. This growth can be expressed as:

$$gop = (NOPAT_n - NOPAT_{n-1}) / (NOPAT_{n-1}) \quad (17)$$

By substituting Eqn. (17) in Eqn. (16) the net increase in assets can be expressed in terms of operating profit, growth and return;

$$\Delta A_{n-1} = gop . (NOPAT_{n-1}) / ROCE \quad (18)$$

Eqn. (18) can now be substituted into equation (14) to obtain the free cash flow in terms of operating profit, growth and return;

$$FCFF_n = NOPAT_n - g_{op} \, . \, NOPAT_n \, / \, ROCE$$

or;

$$FCFF_1 = NOPAT_1 \, (1 - g_{op} \, / \, ROCE) \qquad (19)$$

If Eqn. (19) is substituted in the constant cash flow growth model, Eqn. (14), and bearing in mind that in steady state conditions gCF = gop = g, we can write the value of the entire business under conditions of constant growth as;

$$\text{Fair enterprise value} = \frac{NOPAT \, . \, (ROCE - g)}{ROCE \, . \, (WACC - g)} \qquad (20)$$

Where the net operating profit after tax (NOPAT) is for the first forecast year.

4.5.3. Market Multiples and Financial Ratios

A terminal enterprise value may occasionally be determined using market multiples. EV/EBITDA is the most often used multiple, though EV/sales is also occasionally employed. Although this method is easy to use and quick, it is not without its drawbacks. For instance, the level of the multiple that is selected is frequently highly arbitrary. Moreover, considering the significance of the terminal value to overall value, it would be more appropriate to value the entire business using the market multiple. As a result, we do not advise performing a DCF analysis using market multiples to determine terminal values.

4.5.3.1. Market Multiples for Terminal Value of Equity

Instead of valuing the company, market multiples are occasionally used to determine the terminal value of equity. In order to determine the value of equity over the explicit forecast period, if these multiples are utilized, the enterprise value over the period must be subtracted from the present value of the non-equity over the same period. To get the total equity value, this can then be added to the equity's terminal value.

This is shown in Table 4.6 Below:

Table 4.6. Assessing Terminal Value of Equity

	Component of value
+	Present value of free cash flow over the explicit forecast period
-	Present value of non-equity cash flow over the explicit forecast period
=	Present value of the equity over explicit forecast period
+	Terminal value of equity based on market multiples
=	Total value of equity

Source: http://pricing.online.fr/docs/DiscountedCashFlow.pdf.

In general, one of the following four multiples will be used:

- P/E (price to earnings per share).
- Yield.
- P/cash flow.
- P/NAV (price to net asset value).

Although analysts find the market multiple approach to terminal value more understandable than EV multiples, it is still a poor approach and, if possible, alternative approaches should be employed. We reason as follows: it is challenging to evaluate a terminal multiple. The current multiple, which represents the cash flow through and beyond the explicit forecast period, will not be related to it. Instead, the terminal multiple only accounts for the cash flows that occur after the stated forecast period. In this regard, selecting a terminal multiple will be just as, if not more, subjective than valuing the share using a current multiple and completely eschewing the discounted cash flow method. This is further supported if the reader remembers that the terminal value represents at least 80% of a share's total value; if this is determined by a fictitious market multiple, there can be little trust in the value as a whole.

An alternative to using market multiples is the use of embedded value measures. At UBS two measures have been used:

1. Liquidation value.
2. Replacement cost.

1. **Liquidation Value:** When the explicit forecast period ends, the liquidation value is determined by deducting the liabilities from the estimated proceeds of the business's asset sale. In any case, it is very difficult to determine this value and is typically quite arbitrary. The industries with tradable assets—financial, like insurance policies—commodities, like tin mines with defined reserves, or, to a lesser degree, land and property—are the ones that benefit most from its application. For companies with substantial physical asset bases—such as oil refineries, power plants, shipping fleets, etc.—where the liquidation value might be as little as the scrap value, this strategy is not especially appropriate. Finally, this strategy ought to be applied only in cases where it is anticipated that the assets will be sold.

2. **Replacement Cost:** Economists often refer to this method as the optimum net deprival value. Replacement cost can be understood in two ways: first, as the cost of replacing the existing assets with like ones. Secondly, as the cost of replacing the existing assets with ones that will provide the end customer with the same product or service. One instance of this latter technique would be swapping out a fixed telecom network for a mobile one or an optimal power distribution network for a suboptimal one (built, for instance, to supply energy to industrial clients that no longer exist). The "new" cost in both cases needs to be depreciated to account for the assets' remaining economic life rather than their accounting life. The replacement cost approach is especially well-suited for businesses with substantial physical asset bases, like telecom, electricity, and chemical companies.

4.5.4. Calculating the Value of Equity

Non-equity claims on the company A DCF valuation provides the total business value. The value of non-equity claims on the business must be deducted from the business's value in order to determine the equity's value. There are two main non-equity claims on the business:

i. Debt and any other non-equity funding such as preference shares
ii Unfunded liabilities such as German pensions.

- **Debt:** There are two common ways of valuing the net debt of a business:

i. Book value of net debt.
ii. Market value of net debt.

While most analysts in the US use market value, most analysts in the UK and continental Europe use book value. It is not very justified to use the book value of debt, any more so than it is to use the book value of equity! An easy way to test this is to take two companies that are exactly the same except that one is funded by debt that has a lower coupon than the other. It is obvious that the pre-interest cash flows will be the same, and as a result, the businesses' values will be the same. That being said, a company with lower interest costs will have more cash on hand for its shareholders, increasing the equity's value. As a result, each has a different market value for debt even though their book values are equal.

Market value of debt = book value of debt × coupon/current interest rate

It is crucial to understand that the "current interest rate" in the formula above refers to the rate that would apply to debt whose term structure is exactly the same as the remaining term structure of the book debt. In Europe, because debt was typically issued at a floating rate, the discrepancy between book value and market value has frequently been disregarded. The coupon to current interest rate ratio is one when dealing with floating rate debt. Since fixed-rate debt is more prevalent in the US, market value and book value may not always coincide. However, fixed rate debt is becoming more and more common among European businesses.

- **Other Non-Equity Funding:** If the cash flows that have been discounted have been stated before any funding (excluding debt) such as;
- Preference shares
- Off-balance sheet debt (or more generally, non-equity)
- Warrants, etc.

The DCF value should then be reduced by the capitalized value of these expenses, which is the cumulative present value of future costs. There is a gray area that goes beyond these instances and could involve derivative contracts, leasing, etc. In order to modify the enterprise value, the analyst must have a thorough understanding of the costs of funding that have been included and excluded from the free cash flow.

- **Unfunded Liabilities:** To determine the value of equity, any liability that would be financed by the cash flows utilized in the DCF valuation must be subtracted. German corporations have a pension liability, for example. Pensions are paid out of a pension provision funded by a P and L charge by German corporations on a cash basis. However, a liability for more future pensioners is created because the cash charge (the charge impacting cash flows) only covers the demands of the current pensioners. Naturally, projections for future cash flow may include cash pension charges, and the terminal value computation may take into account their growth.

However, it is preferable to state cash flows prior to pension costs and deduct the total present value of the pension liability from the computed enterprise value rather than forecasting annual cash pension over the explicit forecast periods. Unfortunately, it is evident that, generally speaking, the balance sheet pension provision is insufficient to meet the future pension liabilities where German companies have issued financial statements under US GAAP. As a result, the analyst will still need to estimate the total pension liability.

CASE STUDY

APPLYING DCF ANALYSIS TO EVALUATE AN INVESTMENT OPPORTUNITY

Discounted Cash Flow (DCF) analysis is a fundamental financial tool used by businesses and investors to assess the value of an investment or project. In this article, we will delve into the intricacies of DCF analysis and explore how it can be harnessed for comprehensive decision-making, negotiation strategies, and financial forecasting.

XYZ Company, a tech startup, is considering an investment opportunity to expand its product line by developing a new software application. To assess the feasibility and potential return on investment, the company decides to employ Discounted Cash Flow (DCF) analysis. This case study will demonstrate how various DCF concepts are applied to evaluate this investment opportunity.

Scenario: XYZ Company is contemplating the development of a new software application that is expected to generate revenue over the next five years. The company has gathered the following information:

1. **Historical Financial Data:** XYZ Company has collected its past financial statements to analyze revenue trends and expense patterns over the last five years.
2. **Key Drivers:** Market research indicates that the new software's success will depend on factors such as market size, pricing strategy, and customer acquisition costs.
3. **Capital Expenditures:** The development of the software will require significant capital expenditures, including research and development costs, marketing expenses, and equipment purchases.
4. **Long-Term Growth Rate:** The company expects the software's growth rate to be in line with the industry average, which has historically been around 8%.
5. **Weighted Average Cost of Capital (WACC):** The WACC for XYZ Company is determined to be 10%, representing the minimum rate of return required by its investors and lenders.
6. **Terminal Value:** The company assumes that it will continue to generate cash flows indefinitely, and the terminal value is estimated based on a perpetuity model.

Application of DCF Concepts

1. **Historical Financial Data:** XYZ Company begins the DCF analysis by reviewing its historical financial data, including revenue, expenses, and net income. By examining these trends, the company gains insights into its historical performance

and identifies any seasonality or growth patterns that may impact future cash flows.

2. **Key Drivers:** To assess the potential success of the new software application, XYZ Company carefully considers key drivers such as market size, pricing strategy, and customer acquisition costs. Market research and competitive analysis provide valuable data for making informed assumptions about these drivers.
3. **Capital Expenditures:** The company estimates the capital expenditures required for software development, including research and development costs, marketing expenses, and equipment purchases. Accurate CAPEX estimation ensures that the cash flow projections are realistic.
4. **Long-Term Growth Rate:** Based on industry benchmarks and historical performance, XYZ Company sets a long-term growth rate of 8% for the new software. This rate aligns with the industry average and provides a reasonable projection of future performance.
5. **Weighted Average Cost of Capital (WACC):** The WACC, determined to be 10%, serves as the discount rate for calculating the present value of future cash flows. It represents the minimum return that investors and lenders expect from the investment.
6. **Terminal Value:** To estimate the terminal value, XYZ Company assumes that it will continue generating cash flows indefinitely. The terminal value is calculated using the perpetuity model, taking into account the expected cash flows beyond the explicit forecast period.

By applying DCF analysis to evaluate the investment opportunity, XYZ Company gains a comprehensive view of the potential return on its new software application. This analysis considers historical financial data, key drivers, capital expenditures, long-term growth rates, WACC, and terminal value to arrive at a present value estimate of the investment. This informed decision-making process allows XYZ Company to assess the feasibility of the project, negotiate financing terms, and make strategic choices regarding the expansion of its product line.

CLASS ACTIVITY

AN ANALYSIS OF DISCOUNTED CASH FLOW (DCF) APPROACH TO BUSINESS

Please tick your answer:

1. What is the priority of your firm's valuation technique?

1st 2nd 3rd

1. Asset based valuation
2. Discounted Cash Flow
3. Relative valuation

2. Do you carry out SWOT analysis of your firm and incorporate the results when you carry out future forecast of sales?

Ye......No......

SUMMARY

- Discounted cash flow (DCF) analysis tries to work out the value of a company today based on projections of how much money it will generate in the future. The basic idea is that the value of any company is the sum of cash flows that it produces in the future, discounted to the present at an appropriate rate.
- Discounted cash flow (DCF) analysis treats a company as a business rather than just a stock price, and it requires you to think through all the factors that will affect the company's performance. What DCF analysis really gives you is an appreciation for what drives stock values.
- International Valuation Standards (IVS) identifies three principal approaches to valuations: the market approach, the income approach and the cost approach.
- Investment value (or worth) can be affected by particular participants and perspectives, but market value and investment value (initially termed calculation of worth) are different bases of valuation and are not to be confused. Investment value can be different to market value regardless of individual investor perspectives due to market mispricing of assets or segments/sectors.
- Discounted cash flow analysis can provide investors and companies with information on whether planned investments are worthwhile. It's an analysis that provides reasonable estimates of future cash flows.

- If the cash flows are determined to continue indefinitely, a terminal value is usually added to the discrete period to represent this continued steady state of cash flows.
- Revenues and expenses of subsidiary companies are consolidated into a parent company's financials according to the accounting regulations if certain conditions are met. This is true even if the parent company does not own 100% of the subsidiary. Minority interests must be valued and considered when valuing the entire business.
- Time value of money (risk-free rate) – according to the theory of time preference, investors would rather have cash immediately than having to wait and must therefore be compensated by paying for the delay.

REVIEW QUESTIONS

1. Who is credited with the development of the Discounted Cash Flow (DCF) method?
2. Why is the terminal value important in a DCF analysis?
3. Describe the role of DCF in corporate finance decision-making.
4. Why is it important to use discounting methods carefully in DCF analysis?
5. What type of problems have you faced with when using the valuation models and how do these problems affect your firm's final decisions?
6. What are the limitations of the valuation model your firm use?
7. How do the analysts value a business that is losing money?
8. Describe the pros and cons of discounted cash flow (DCF).

REFERENCES

1. Chan, L. K. C., Karceski, J., & Lakonishok, J. (2001). The level and persistence of growth rates. Cambridge, MA.
2. Copeland, T. E., Koller, T., & Murrin, J. (2000). *Valuation: Measuring and Managing the Value of Companies*. New York: John Wiley & Sons.
3. Damodaran, A. (2005). Valuation approaches and metrics: A survey of the theory and evidence. *Foundations and Trends in Finance, 1*(8), 693–784. https://doi.org/10.1561/0500000013.
4. Damodaran, A. (2013). Equity risk premiums (ERP): Determinants, estimation and implications—The 2013 edition. *SSRN Electronic Journal*. https://doi.org/10.2139/ssrn.2238064.
5. Fama, E. F., & French, K. R. (2003). The capital asset pricing model: Theory and evidence. *SSRN Working Paper Series, 18*(3), 25–46. https://doi.org/10.2139/ssrn.440920.

6. Kincheloe, S. C. (1990). The weighted average cost of capital—The correct discount rate. *Appraisal Journal, 58*(1), 88–95.
7. Lim, A., & Lim, A. (2019). Choosing the discount rate in an economic analysis. *Emergency Medicine Australasia, 31*(5), 898–899.
8. Pratt, S., Reilly, R. F., & Schweihs, R. P. (2000). *Valuing a Business*. McGraw-Hill Professional.
9. Reilly, R. F., & Schweihs, R. P. (2016). *Guide to Intangible Asset Valuation*. McGraw-Hill Education.
10. Rosenbaum, J., & Pearl, J. (2009). *Investment Banking: Valuation, Leveraged Buyouts, and Mergers & Acquisitions*. Hoboken, NJ: John Wiley & Sons.
11. Sawhney, C. (2012). Discounted cash flow–The prominent income approach to valuation. *Corporate Valuations*. Retrieved from: http://www.corporatevaluations.in (accessed on 16 July 2024).
12. Sroufe, R. (2018). *Integrated Management: How Sustainability Creates Value for Any Business*. Emerald Publishing.

CHAPTER

5 Return on Investment (ROI)

LEARNING OBJECTIVES

After studying this chapter, you will be able to:

- Understand the basics of return on investment (ROI)
- Describe ROI extensions
- Define the term ROI virtualizations
- Discuss about ROI and the need for smart IT investment decisions
- Describe return on investment metrics: insights for smarter decision making

KEY TERMS FROM THIS CHAPTER

Accounting records	Asset utilization
Financial accounting metrics	Financial accounts
Investment returns	Monetary value
Monetary value	Public sectors
Relative error	ROI analysis
ROI assessment process	ROI assessments
ROI calculations	Social return on investment (SROI)

INTRODUCTION

One of the most widely used performance measurement and evaluation metrics in business analysis is return on investment (ROI). When used properly, ROI analysis is a potent tool for assessing current information systems and helping decision-makers with software purchases and other endeavors. Long ago, ROI was first used in finance and meant to refer to a notion that came from a thorough and measurable examination of costs and returns. ROI is currently widely acknowledged and accepted in both the public and private sectors of business and financial management. However, due to the widespread adoption of the ROI method, it is now frequently perceived as a loose, ambiguous collection of different methodologies that is subject to bias and inaccuracy.

The return on investment (ROI) metric is used in business to determine whether or not to make an investment by calculating the rates of return on capital invested in an economic entity over a given period of time. Additionally, it serves as an indicator for contrasting various investments held in a portfolio. Although the spread of ROI over an investment's lifetime should also be considered, the investment with the highest ROI is typically given priority. The idea has recently been extended to scientific funding organizations (like the National Science Foundation) and their investments in open-source hardware research, with the goal of obtaining direct digital replication returns.

A snapshot of profitability is provided by ROI and related metrics, which are adjusted for the size of the investment assets linked to the business. ROI is frequently contrasted with required or expected rates of return on investment. Unlike net present value, for example, ROI is not time-adjusted; instead, most textbooks model it using an initial investment of "Year 0" and two to three years of income.

Although there is a clear potential link between marketing decisions and ROI (profits), these decisions also frequently affect how assets are used and how much capital is needed (think of receivables and inventories as examples). Marketers need to be aware of their company's position as well as the anticipated returns. When reporting a marketing program's ROI percentage to executives, it is necessary to separate its effects from extraneous factors. In a survey of nearly 200 senior marketing managers, 77% responded that they found the "return on investment" metric very useful.

Return on investment can mean more than just monetary gain. Social return on investment (SROI), for instance, is a principles-based technique that quantifies the value of resources invested in relation to extra-financial value (i.e., environmental and social value not currently reflected in conventional financial accounts). Any organization can use it to assess the effects on stakeholders, find strategies for raising performance, and improve the return on investments.

5.1. BASICS OF RETURN ON INVESTMENT (ROI)

ROI is a performance metric that can be used to compare the effectiveness of several different investments or to assess how efficient an investment is. ROI is calculated by dividing the investment's benefit (return) by its cost. The result is given as a percentage or ratio.

It is important to understand that figuring out a business's profit and figuring out the return on an investment are two different things. A company's cash flow is the only factor that determines profit.

The amount of money left over after expenses are subtracted is known as net profit. Net income is divided by the total cost of financing to determine the return on investment.

A performance metric called ROI is used to compare the effectiveness of multiple projects or evaluate the profitability or efficiency of an investment. ROI makes an effort to determine how much of a return an investment has in relation to its cost (Chmielewski & Phillips, 2002). To calculate ROI, one must divide the investment's benefit (or return) by its cost. The result is expressed as a ratio or a percentage. ROI is a widely used statistic due to its simplicity and adaptability.

In essence, ROI can be interpreted as a rough gauge of an investment's profitability. This could be the yield from a real estate transaction, a manufacturing expansion, or an investment in stocks. With its wide range of uses, the computation is not too complicated and is easy to understand. An investment is unquestionably advantageous if the return on it is net positive. Still, these signals can help investors filter out or choose the best options if there are other opportunities with higher returns. Additionally, investors should steer clear of negative ROIs, which denote a net loss.

The ROI formula comes in a variety of forms. The two most usually used are seen below:

ROI = Net Income/Investment Cost

or

ROI = Return on Investment/Investment Base

5.1.1. Benefits of ROI

Listed below are some of the benefits of ROI:

1. **Improved Profitability Measurement:** By linking net income to divisional investments, divisional profitability can be estimated more precisely. Divisional

managers are incentivized to maximize asset utilization since they know that their performance will be evaluated based on how they utilized resources to create profit.

Additionally, it ensures that assets are only purchased in compliance with the organization's policies and only when they are certain to generate profits. As a result, the required amount of investment is the main emphasis of ROI.

As a result, they can choose an investment that will maximize their current investments and enhance divisional and organizational profit performance.

2. **Comparative Analysis:** ROI makes it possible to contrast the asset utilization and profitability of various business units. If the companies whose results are being compared are similar in size and operate in the same industry, it can be used for inter-firm comparisons. When selecting investment options, ROI is a useful metric because it is simple to compare to the associated cost of capital.
3. **No Need for a Separate Accounting System:** ROI is based on the financial accounting of your business. There is no requirement for a new or distinct accounting measurement in order to produce ROI data. The figures required to compute ROI are all included in your financial statements.
4. **Matching with Accounting Metrics:** Financial accounting metrics, which are frequently employed in traditional accounting, form the basis of ROI. To obtain data for ROI calculations, it is not required to develop a new accounting metric. Financial statements produced by a traditional accounting system contain all the data required to compute ROI. To calculate ROI, some changes to the current accounting data might be necessary, but this is not a problem.
5. **ROI as an Indicator of Other Performance Factors:** ROI, which takes into account various aspects of a business unit's performance, is thought to be the most important indicator of an investment division's performance.

   An investment center that has a higher return on investment (ROI) is likely doing well in other areas as well, like cost control, efficient asset utilization, selling price strategy, marketing and promotional strategy, and so forth.

5.1.2. Calculation

Various methods can be used to calculate return on investment based on the application and goal. This is the most complete formula:

Return on investment (%) = (current value of investment if not exited yet or sold price of investment if exited + income from investment – initial investment and other expenses)/initial investment and other expenses x 100%.

Example with a share of stock: You bought 1 share of stock for US$100 and paid a buying commission of US$5. Then over a year you received US$4 of dividends and sold the share 1 year after you bought it for US$200 paying a US$5 selling commission.

Your ROI is the following:

$$ROI = (200 + 4 - 100 - 5 - 5)/(100 + 5 + 5) \times 100\% = 85.45\%$$

As the duration of this investment is 1 year, this ROI is annual.

For a single-period review, divide the return (net profit) by the resources that were committed (investment):

return on investment = Net income/ Investment

Where:

Net income = gross profit – expenses.

investment = stock + market outstanding + claims.

or

return on investment = (gain from investment – cost of investment)/cost of investment

or

return on investment = (revenue – cost of goods sold)/cost of goods sold

or

return on investment = (net program benefits/program costs) x 100

5.1.2.1. Property

When a second mortgage is obtained or real estate is refinanced, there may be issues with the ROI calculation. When the revised figures are incorporated into the ROI calculation, interest rates on a second, or refinanced, loan could go up and fees might be assessed, both of which could lower the ROI. If the owner of a residential rental or commercial property pays these expenses, there may also be an increase in maintenance costs, property taxes, and utility rates.

When purchasing real estate with an adjustable rate mortgage (ARM), which has a variable, escalating interest rate that is charged annually for the term of the loan, intricate calculations might also be necessary.

5.1.2.2. Marketing Investment

Marketing has an impact on investment levels in addition to net profits. Three major investment categories that are impacted by marketing decisions are new plants and equipment, inventories, and accounts receivable. RoA, RoNA, RoC, and RoIC, in particular, are similar measures with variations on how 'investment' is defined. Due to marketing budget allocation, return on investment (ROI) is a popular metric among marketing heads. Return on Investment aids in determining which marketing mix initiatives should be maintained and which should be discontinued.

5.1.3. How to Use Return on Investment?

Recognizing how your investment will affect your company. It is evident that a change needs to be made if you find yourself spending money on an expense. Many different forms of ROI may assist you in making key business choices, including, but not limited to:

1. **Buying a New Tool**: It could be beneficial to add new products, machinery, and tools to your company, but you have to make wise choices when doing so. You can assess the value of your new purchase and decide what kind of equipment to invest in down the road by calculating the return on investment (ROI) on an equipment purchase.
2. **Hiring New Workers**: Is your new employee improving or decreasing

the profitability of your company? Tracking your workers' return on investment will help you better identify the kind of individuals to hire (or fire).

3. **Adding a New Department**: If it increases profitability, expanding your company's operations by hiring a new department or employee may prove to be a prudent decision. This is not the place to hazard a guess; calculate return on investment to gauge departmental profitability and identify areas for expansion.
4. **Sales Strategies**: Did a certain tactic contribute to a sale? Tracking which kind of sales methods produce results will offer you an idea of how to increase your company's profitability.

5.1.4. The Factors Determining the Return on Investment (ROI)

The factors determining the return on investment (ROI) are given as follows:

- **Investment Type**: The nature of the investment, whether it's in stocks, real estate, marketing campaigns, or research and development, greatly influences the potential ROI.
- **Timeframe**: The duration over which the investment generates returns affects the overall ROI. Short-term investments might yield quicker returns, while long-term investments may require more patience.
- **Costs:** The initial cost of the investment, along with any ongoing expenses, impacts the ROI. Higher costs can reduce the overall profitability.
- **Market Conditions**: External factors such as economic conditions, industry trends, and market demand can significantly influence the success of an investment.
- **Risk**: Risk and ROI often go hand in hand. Investments with higher risk may offer the potential for greater returns, but they also come with an increased chance of loss.
- **Management & Strategy**: How well an investment is managed and the strategies employed to maximize returns play a pivotal role in determining ROI.

5.1.5. Maximize Return on Investment (ROI)

Effective execution, well-informed decision-making, and strategic planning are necessary to maximize return on investment (ROI). Here are some strategies to enhance your investment returns:

- **Thorough Research**: Conduct extensive research before investing. Understand the market trends, potential risks, and growth prospects to make informed decisions.
- **Diversification**: Spread your investments across different assets or industries to minimize risk. Diversification can help protect your portfolio from significant losses.
- **Set Clear Objectives**: Define clear investment objectives and goals. Are you seeking short-term gains or long-term stability? Having a clear vision guides your investment choices.
- **Risk Management**: Assess and manage risk effectively. While higher-risk investments can yield substantial returns, it's essential to balance risk with potential rewards.

- **Continuous Monitoring**: Regularly monitor the performance of your investments. Be prepared to make adjustments based on changing market conditions and new opportunities.
- **Invest In Learning**: Stay informed about the investment landscape. Continuous learning about financial markets and trends can help you make informed decisions.
- **Cost Reduction**: Minimize unnecessary costs associated with your investments. High fees and expenses can eat into your returns over time.
- **Optimize Marketing Efforts**: In the context of business, optimizing marketing campaigns is essential. Use data-driven insights to allocate resources effectively and target the right audience.
- **Customer Satisfaction**: For businesses, delivering exceptional customer experiences can lead to repeat business and positive word-of-mouth, ultimately contributing to increased revenue.
- **Innovation & Research**: Invest in R&D to produce cutting-edge goods and services that will give you a competitive advantage and open up new revenue streams.
- **Employee Training**: Investing in the training and development of employees can benefit businesses by increasing customer satisfaction, productivity, and quality—all of which are beneficial to the bottom line.

5.2. ROI EXTENSIONS

The goal of creating ROI Extensions was to address some of the shortcomings of the Traditional ROI and expand the scope of its application. Conventional ROI computation is done retroactively, for projects that have already been finished. The ROI Extensions are primarily unique in that they are based on projected project outcomes (though historical data may be included). The final calculation, which divides net returns by costs, is the same. Included are the same kinds of expenses and returns. But costs and benefits for upcoming projects cannot be found in accounting records. Through estimation procedures, their amounts are projected. Furthermore, the inclusion of the time value of money and the impact of risks is frequently the foundation of ROI Extensions (Kingma & Schisa, 2010).

5.2.1. Estimating Costs

Costs and returns numbers were gathered or retrieved from accounting value:

$$PV = FV/(1 + Rate)^n$$

- Rate – discount rate; the same as an interest rate;
- n – number of periods.

Organizations generally employ discount rates ranging from 8% to 16%, depending on the conditions of their present setting, according to Forrester Consulting. Future values and time-adjusted present values may diverge significantly. For instance, time-adjusted values for the second through fifth years of a five-year project with a 10-% discount rate and annual future values of $1,000 will be $909, $826, $751, $683, and $621. The ROI amounts determined using time-adjusted costs and returns will therefore be different from those of "simple" ROIs.

5.2.2. Another Time-Related Issue is Calculation of the Multi-Period ROI

Because there is no accepted method or consensus for calculating ROI, this can be challenging. Take a three-year project, for instance (see Figure 5.1). The three-year project has total costs of 60 and returns of 90 (million or thousand). The ROI calculations are presented in the table in four different ways, each represented by a row. The table's three middle columns display the distribution of costs and returns by year. The ROI computation results for each of the four scenarios are shown in the right column. Below is an explanation of each scenario. The time value of money is not taken into account in order to streamline computations.

Scenario 1. Calculating ROI based on the total 3-year numbers results in ROI1 = 50%.

Scenario 2. Same overall numbers (90–60), but they are provided annually and distributed evenly over the years (30–20), and calculations are done for each year and then summed up. Result: ROI2 = 150%. Some vendors and consultants would recommend this approach to calculations.

Scenario 3. Same overall numbers (90–60) provided annually but distributed differently, and calculations are done for an individual year and then summed up. Result: ROI3 = 450%.

To optimize the ROI amount, the following actions are prompted by this calculation method. Maximum costs should be moved to the year (probably the first year) where the ROI will be negative because, in any case, the ROI will never fall below -100%. Aim for the year with the highest returns on the most benefits; the ROI will be multiplied.

Scenario 4. Same as Scenario 3 as far as year by year returns and costs. However, calculation is done based on the cumulative numbers, that is, cumulative return for a year equals to the sum of this year and previous years.

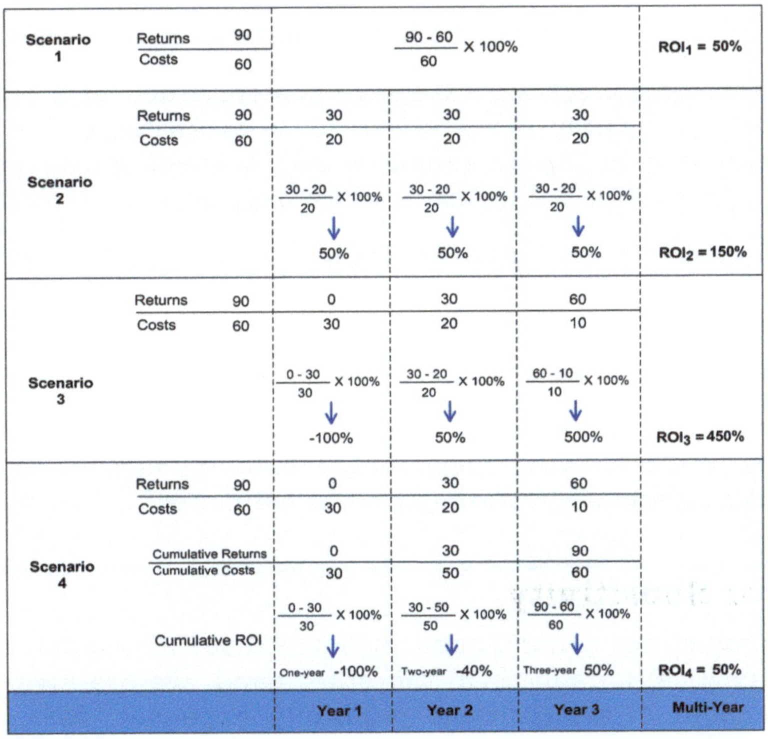

Figure 5.1. *Multi-period ROI calculations.*

Source: https://www.researchgate.net/figure/Multi-period-ROI-Calculations_fig1_216356259.

This example shows how different methods can yield completely different results (with order of magnitude variances) when calculating ROI for a project with the same total numbers. Therefore, in the absence of extensive details that clearly explain how it was calculated, the ROI number may be unclear. The actual amount of money gained in each of the scenarios is the same – 30 (not including cost of borrowing, taxes, etc.).

By presenting these instances, we are not endorsing any particular strategy (what's right and wrong). In order for you to know what to ask when you are presented with multi-period ROI calculations, we want to make you aware of what is used.

Speaking about the time frame, the most fundamental question is how many years should be included in the calculations: 1 or 2 or 3 or the life cycle? There is no consensus on this issue. That's why this parameter must be explicitly provided with the ROI number (otherwise, ROI number is absolutely unclear).

5.2.3. Risks in the ROI Context

Uncertainties must be considered from the moment we begin to describe future projects. A risk is an occurrence or circumstance that, if it materializes, could have a favorable or unfavorable impact on the initiative's expenses or financial returns. Events that lower expenses and/or boost financial returns are considered positive risks. Events that raise expenses and/or lower financial returns are considered negative risks. A project may encounter numerous issues, some of which could have an impact on expenses or profits.

For instance, a project involving extensive customization of a novel software type carried out by outside consultants might lead to an extension of the hours required of the consultants, resulting in higher expenses and a lower return on investment. For instance, there is a chance of a 2-month activity overrun with probability 0.5.

Risk-Adjusted Cost = Initial Estimate + 0.5 x (2-month labor cost)

Based on the PERT approach calculations are performed according to the formula:

(best case + worst case + 4 x most likely case estimates)/6

Analyzing the general project risks should be the first step in identifying ROI risks. Next, pay attention to the "related" risks and include any additional specific ROI risks. The procedure lacks objectivity. Determining the estimates' accuracy is challenging.

5.2.4. ROI Error Sensitivity

As previously mentioned, the general public believes that ROI is a precise instrument that is based on mathematical formulas. On the other hand, we are aware that calculating ROI requires a number of assumptions regarding expenses, returns, schedule, and surroundings. ROI follows naturally from the accuracy of the cost, return, and time estimates entered into the formula.

The project management methodology states that the estimations' accuracy is contingent upon the stage of the initiative's life cycle. Rough order of magnitude (ROM) accuracy is typically estimated for the initiation phase, with a range of +/-50%. Subsequently, it might narrow to within +/-10%. Additionally, there is a level of accuracy associated with estimates of each type of costs and returns.

Let's consider the effects of estimating errors on ROI accuracy on a simple example. The scenario: costs – $500,000; returns – $600,000. So, ROI = 20%

If we estimated Costs as X1 and real costs are X2, and we made an error (e.g., due to uncertainty of future vendor prices), which can be characterized by the absolute error Delta=X1 – X2 or relative error Delta/X1, this error will then affect the ROI magnitude – so called propagation of uncertainty.

Assuming we made a relative error of +/-10% in our cost and/or return estimates/ calculations, the costs' absolute error will range from 0 to 50,000. When the project moves forward into its later stages of the life cycle, that kind of error might be encountered.

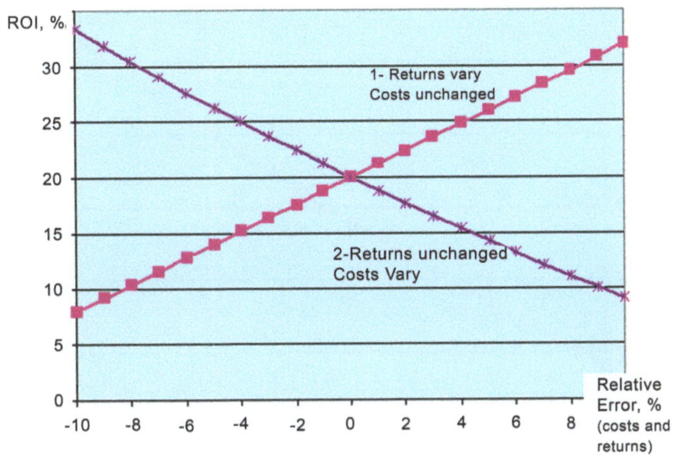

Figure 5.2. *ROI sensitivity to error.*

Source: https://www.researchgate.net/figure/ROI-Sensitivity-to-Error_fig2_216356259.

A two-line diagram is depicted in Figure 5.2: Line 1 represents ROI in the scenario where costs were predicted with zero error and the relative error for the returns changed from -10 to +10%; Line 2 represents ROI in the scenario where returns were predicted with zero error and the relative error for the costs changed from -10. In these instances, ROI is fluctuating between 8 and 33% (compared to the initial estimate of 20%).

When costs errors are positive (+10%) and returns errors are negative (-10%), the effect of the errors is maximized. As seen in Figure 5.3, this is explained. The ROI range is expanding from 2% to about 50%, making it harder to classify as "highly accurate." Keep in mind that, from an initial "true" ROI of 20%, ROI becomes "negative" at some "worst case" point.

Observations from this exercise:

- ROI is not immune from errors. Unavoidable uncertainties/errors of estimating costs and returns propagate through the ROI formula and affect the result.
- "Precise" ROI is more an exception than the rule. Results of the ROI calculations with decimal places are most likely questionable.

- For prudent analysis, an ROI number should be accompanied with characteristics of the accuracies of costs and returns estimates and evaluation of the accuracy of the final ROI number.

This exercise's value lies in its ability to illustrate the methodology and ROI accuracy level for a standard CRM project. While the study focused on a particular case and did not assert any universal significance, it did demonstrate that even minor inaccuracies of roughly 10% in cost and return estimations can result in notable discrepancies in return on investment. A measure of accuracy should be included with a ROI number in order to give it significance.

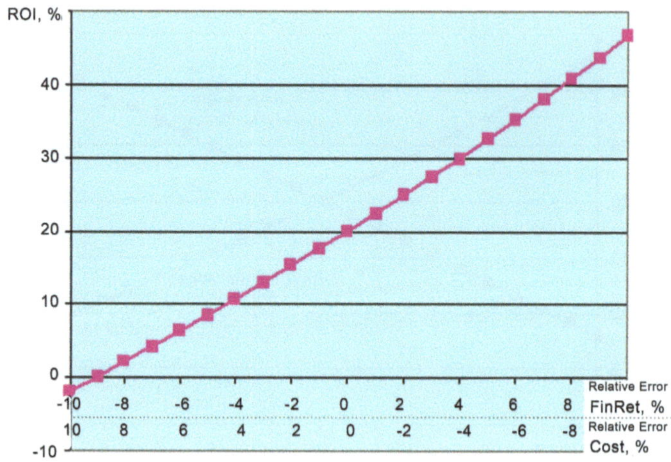

Figure 5.3. *ROI sensitivity to error (worst case scenario).*

Source: https://www.researchgate.net/figure/ROI-Sensitivity-to-Error-worst-case-scenario_fig3_216356259.

5.3. ROI VIRTUALIZATIONS

The main differentiator of ROI Virtualizations is the inclusion of intangible returns/ benefits in ROI calculations.

5.3.1. Intangible Benefits – Examples

Benefits that are hard to quantify and put a monetary value on are known as intangibles. Hao, Jager, Cheng, and Hulten, for instance, propose that intangible assets can be divided into three categories: economic competencies, computerized information, and innovative property.

Some examples of intangibles include the following:

- **Better Information:** Information systems are intended to provide relevant information for decision-making, contributing to better decisions, and therefore enhancing the return on investment.
  - More timely information.
  - Accurate and faster access to data for timely decisions.
  - Uniform reporting according to corporate standards.
- Improved effectiveness of decision-making processes facilitating:
  - Strategic planning and operations.
  - Resource control and asset utilization
  - Organizational planning.
  - Organizational flexibility and transparency.

The aforementioned examples demonstrate a broad range of intangibles; each has a distinct "level of intangibility." Certain ones are simpler to quantify in relation to other variables that are thought to be quantifiable, like productivity or time. For others, locating a suitable "proxy" is challenging.

Even the border between intangibles and tangibles is fuzzy. The same type such as "labor cost savings" may represent two significantly different entities:

- **Tangible:** For example, in a Traditional ROI "labor cost savings" due to a reduction of three FTE positions – resulting in real hard/tangible amount of $210,000 dollars.

Intangible. "Labor cost savings" of 6 min per day for 200 people. Numerically it is the same savings of 111.75 hours per week with $210,000 "saved" annually. However, realization of this amount is more than questionable.

Analyzing intangibles requires considering particular case circumstances. In certain situations, something that is intangible (like an information system or environment) may become tangible.

5.3.2. Reasons to Include Intangibles

It is widely acknowledged that the value of information systems extends well beyond their apparent advantages. Numerous projects and solutions generate value that is greater than what can be calculated in monetary terms.

In general, the definition of intangibles is far broader than how ROI evaluations use it. Whether intangible assets belong in corporate financial statements has been a topic of much discussion for the past 15 to 20 years. It is prompted by studies conducted at various economic levels that demonstrate intangible assets account for a sizeable and continuously increasing portion of market value (Pearce, 2016).

Another subjective argument for including intangibles is that, frequently, the return on investment (ROI) of information systems that rely on monetary gains (or "tangible" benefits) is either zero or too low to support investment decisions. Lastly, the situations where ROI is assigned a role as the primary performance metric exhibit the greatest use of intangibles. In these situations, intangibles can mean anything from easily quantifiable financial gains or returns to anything of perceived value, such as improved information.

Table 5.1. Inclusion of Intangibles

PROS	CONS
On the macro level, US investment in intangibles ($1.6 trillion in 2007) has been exceeding tangible investment since 1996, reflecting a shift from a manufacturing to knowledge-based economy. Same trend exists in other developed countries. In 2000s, US financial sector earned over 40% of the domestic corporate profits.	Macro level assessments lack structured definition of intangibles. Summing up R&D investments (which may result in an absolutely tangible product) and value of new products in the financial industry (especially in the wake of 2008), doubtfully may lead to a convincing conclusion.
On the company level, the value of accumulated intangible assets is comparable or even greater than the book value of other assets (e.g., for Microsoft in 2006, intangible assets amounted to $66 billion in addition to the $70 billion assets on the balance sheet)	Company level intangibles (e.g., value of the corporate image) are prone to frequent (if not daily) variations. For example, BP (British Petroleum) corporate image a day before and after the Gulf spill in 2010 will have a significantly different value. That makes the use of intangibles justifiable only during a time-limited process of company acquisition.

"Responsible ROI analysis demands that all factors be quantified in money terms. Whether recognized or not, the decision maker is placing a quantified monetary value on the intangible benefits... Thus for example, putting a dollar value on relieving pain and suffering may seem impossible and even inappropriate; but every day, health care providers make thousands of such determinations when allocating limited resources among competing demands." Politicians are putting a dollar value to the lives of people setting certain value to terror security systems. Aircraft designers are putting a dollar value on lives of passengers by embedding certain level of reliability.	Quantification of certain values (e.g., value of the project team members' collaboration provided by a new information system) and translating them into financial terms are prone to subjective judgment and inaccuracies. Resulting numbers have a false impression of rigor.

Source: Alexei Botchkarev and Peter Andru A Return on Investment as a Metric for Evaluating Information Systems: Taxonomy and Application, DOI: 10.28945/1535.

Though proponents of intangibles have made some progress in the current academic discourse, there is still much work to be done. A considerable amount of time must pass before intangibles are officially included in financial statements due to sound conservatism in accounting practice (apart from corporate acquisition transactions). Even with this scientific uncertainty and financial practitioners' reluctance to accept intangibles, it has become standard procedure to include intangibles in ROI analyzes.

5.3.3. Sample ROI Claims Analysis

A typical place to start when conducting ROI evaluations for intangibles is by estimating "a conservatively" how much time a new information system will save each employee each day—for instance, five minutes. These cost savings could come from shorter sales cycles, improved teamwork among project participants, and higher worker productivity. Once this estimate is established, the ROI assessment procedure is simplified to a simple calculation: five minutes multiplied by the hundreds of people's salary savings over a three-year period yields numbers that are convincingly high for "intangible benefits." When estimates are presented at the first step (savings of five minutes), they often make sense or at the very least state something like, "Our assumptions are so conservative that even the most determined skeptic couldn't challenge them." Adding ratios of "partial capturing the benefits" (e.g., only 70% of the intangible benefits will be captured/realized) or "incremental uptake" (e.g., for a three-year implementation project, during the first year the system will be used by only 20% of the employees, and additional 30% and 50% will be given access in the second and third years respectively; system benefits will be realized based on the portion of the employees actually using the system) are common ways authors/consultants build on this positive impression.

Some experts, while agreeing that not all time potentially saved will be used productively, state that lower-level employees are more likely to turn extra time into more work and offer the following rule-of-thumb percentage of time converted into increased output:

- Assembly-line workers: 95–100%.
- Call-center support: 90–95%.
- Administrative and support help: 70–80%.
- Engineering (technical): 75%.
- Engineering (non-technical): 65–75%.
- General staff within a group (marketing, PR, accounting): 60%.
- Companywide general staff: 50%.
- Middle management (large corporations): 40–55%.

The aforementioned "concessions" to those who oppose the inclusion of the intangibles are made in order to deflect attention from the fundamental concerns regarding the initial estimate (those five minutes) and to make the results appear more realistic. How was this number arrived at? Why is the amount five and not 3 or 10 minutes? What was the objective rationale behind this assessment? These questions are usually left unanswered and allow opponents of including intangibles argue that ROI assessments of intangibles can easily vary by +/– 100% or more and that such variance indicates a wide window for subjectivity and misjudgment in the results of ROI calculations.

5.3.4. Intangible Costs

It is assumed by participants in general discussions about intangibles that there are both intangible costs and benefits (costs that are difficult/impossible to predict and/or quantify). Intangible costs, however, are rarely taken into account when calculating ROI.

Some examples of intangible costs are:

- Cost of upsetting customers from system change.
- Cost of failure due to inappropriate system or faulty implementation.
- Incompatibility with other systems leading to unexpected costs of software amendments, tailoring, and maintenance.
- Cost of errors due to lack of experience in using new system (IT dept, users).
- Cost of losing staff morale.
- Cost of losing a competitive edge.
- Cost of declining company image.
- Loss of investment in prior systems.

5.4. ROI AND THE NEED FOR SMART IT INVESTMENT DECISIONS

Decision-makers in government must respond to the growing demands for new technology and improved performance while also making the most of limited resources. Consequently, there is an increasing need to make prudent IT investments. As resources become more scarce, rising demand prompts critical inquiries and careful examination of new investment proposals. Furthermore, the appalling track record of government IT investments in terms of failure begs reasonable questions concerning the effectiveness of these expenditures and the reasons behind their frequent inability to meet expectations or function at all. Consequently, in order to support new IT investments, IT planning procedures frequently incorporate—or even mandate—a thorough business case. These include methods for determining the expenses and anticipated returns from that investment, such as ROI analysis.

Methods of return on investment analysis are becoming increasingly popular as there is a growing interest in evaluating the returns on IT investments. On specific techniques or best practices for evaluating ROI, there is, nevertheless, little consensus. A wide range of potential strategies are presented in expert white papers and trade journals. Government executives and decision makers thus struggle to select or create a return on investment analysis that is workable and suitable for their purposes. It provides an overview of ROI's goals and concepts, as well as an introduction to fundamental techniques and sample cases, to assist administrators and decision makers in making these decisions. For individuals who would like to delve deeper into any particular topic, it also provides links to other resources. ROI analysis is a useful tool for IT project planners and designers to convince decision makers to support their work. An IT investment proposal can benefit from, and in some cases even require, a return on investment analysis to help decision makers assess the proposal. Either way, the circumstances surrounding the design and execution of an ROI analysis will influence it (Daneva & Wieringa, 2008).

Many factors usually influence the decision of what kind of return on investment analysis to perform, or if one should be performed at all. ROI analysis might or might not make sense in the overall framework of making investment decisions. Situations where decisions must be made quickly or with strict adherence to policy guidelines may not allow for a thorough analysis. Scale is also important. It would be difficult to justify a lengthy ROI analysis for a low-risk, small-scale project that needs to be decided quickly.

Large, complex projects, on the other hand, are usually high-risk ventures for which the extra time and expense of a thorough ROI analysis would be entirely justified. Although justified, ROI analysis is not utilized at all in some environments when assessing potential investments; instead, best practice reviews or benchmarking are preferred. The practices of today differ greatly. For instance, the state of Iowa provides a uniform framework, complete with business case and ROI analysis requirements, to all agencies submitting proposals for IT projects. Federal agencies are subject to similar requirements from the US Office of Management and Budget. In other states, local governments and agencies are free to create their own internal business cases and ROI specifications.

5.4.1. An Approach to Understanding and Using ROI Analysis

Understanding the nature of the methods and how they fit into the business environment is essential for making decisions regarding the application of ROI analysis. In general, ROI analysis encompasses a wide range of techniques, abilities, resources, pursuits, and concepts. They could all be helpful in determining an investment's relative worth over time. But these approaches are not a single formula or preset computation that will provide a straightforward yes-or-no response to the query of how to invest. ROI is not a miracle cure. Actually creating and implementing any type of ROI analysis necessitates selecting numerous concepts and techniques and performing an analysis suitable for the given decision-making scenario. Various decisions will lead to varying outcomes.

As such, it is far easier said than done to conduct a meaningful analysis of returns on investment in information technology. Decisions regarding the execution of a ROI analysis ought to be grounded in fundamental knowledge regarding:

- the strategic objective(s) of the analysis;
- the place of the proposed IT investment in the overall enterprise3;
- exactly how the analysis should be done (i.e., what data and methods of analysis are best suited to those objectives); and
- how the ROI analysis fits in the overall decision context for IT investments.

5.4.2. Understanding Strategic Objectives in ROI Design

The final method and application of a ROI analysis will depend on how well you comprehend its strategic goals. There are two connected aspects to the topic of strategic objectives. One addresses the goals and circumstances surrounding the suggested investment. The second covers the goals and background of the actual ROI work. The answers to these important questions, which are outlined below, are necessary for a sufficient understanding of the first portion of the strategic objective.

- **What Are the Programmatic and Business Goals of the Proposed Investment?:** The business process using the new technology and the programmatic goals are directly related to the value of an investment. For instance, rather than just producing faster or more complex accounting reports, the strategic goal of investing in a new financial management system would be to improve the quality of financial decision making and control of resource flows. Instead of concentrating solely on the technology, consideration of the strategic objectives keeps the focus more broadly on the types of benefits sought and how to measure them. Maintaining focus on the strategic and business objectives will also help you comprehend the entire range of benefits that you can anticipate from the investment.

- **What Are the Needs or Interests of the Primary Customers and Other Key Stakeholders with Respect to Products or Services Involved and Impacts on Business Processes?:** Stakeholders are essential to the success of new initiatives. The success of an investment is greatly endangered when their role is ignored or undervalued, and this can result in significant unforeseen expenses or lost opportunities. Without consulting the employees who answered customer calls, a sizable organization recently created a comprehensive new customer help desk application. The day before the new system went online, those employees were made aware of it. Lower returns and higher costs were the outcome, along with subpar performance and a severe blow to employee morale.
- **How Extensive Is the Analysis to be? What Range of Costs and Returns Are Expected? What Resources and Frameworks Are Available or Required for the ROI Analysis Itself?:** A ROI analysis may require a sizable financial outlay on its own. It is a waste of resources to expand its scope, level of detail, or complexity beyond what is necessary for making decisions that are well-informed. It will also be a waste of resources to attempt a ROI analysis that is outside the scope or capabilities of the organization. Thus, selecting a suitable scope for the analysis is an essential step in the procedure. The types of data used, whether hard or soft estimates will suffice, the types of projections, quantitative or qualitative data that are required, and which financial or non-financial outcomes (customer/user satisfaction, social or political outcomes, improved equity) are all significant are some of the decisions that determine the specifics of the ROI analysis itself. The types of employees, equipment, and other resources required are then determined by the responses to these questions.
- **What Are the Risk Factors and How Might They Affect the Project's Costs and Results?:** The ROI analysis should always take risk into account. The project's inherent characteristics (complexity, size, novelty), its organizational context (difficulty, resource limitations, high-level support, time constraints), and the broader environment (political unrest, crises, and policy changes) all provide risk factors.

5.4.3. Defining and Measuring the Costs and Returns from IT Investments

There would be a single, straightforward method for calculating the expenses, benefits, and returns if a ROI analysis were a single, straightforward item. In actuality, though, a ROI analysis may be asked a wide range of questions, necessitating the use of various measurement techniques to address them. The remaining pieces of the puzzle involve figuring out how to recognize these measures and use them in analysis.

Gaining an understanding of the variations in the questions posed by a ROI analysis is necessary to solve that puzzle. Questions of the financial, effectiveness, efficiency, and impact types are the four distinct but related categories.

- **Can We Afford This? and Will it Pay for Itself?:** In order to respond to these inquiries, data regarding costs and returns in terms of the monetary value of the resources used (inputs), as determined and documented by conventional financial factors, is needed. In its most basic form, a ROI analysis based on this kind of question would compute the return by comparing the dollar cost of all new system expenses to the expected savings and revenue increases (if any). To illustrate a payback period or calculate the present value of future returns, the costs, savings, and revenues may be projected over a number of years.
- **How Much 'Bang for the Buck' Will We Get Out of This Project?:** Information regarding the project's expenses in relation to its contribution to reaching program objectives and yielding the intended outcomes is necessary to respond to effectiveness inquiries. The metrics will be more intricate, requiring computations of unit cost or activity cost. The evaluation of returns will encompass performance metrics in relation to program or project objectives, in addition to cost reductions or revenue growth.
- **Is This the Most We Can Get for This Much Investment?:** Information about whether the project will yield the highest possible value in relation to its costs is necessary to answer questions about efficiency. Analysis issues relating to efficiency are very problematic. Either a thorough analysis of numerous options or a valid simulation of performance are needed to prove that a specific outcome is the best of all possible outcomes. For certain types of systems with enough resources and data, this is possible, but it can significantly raise the cost and complexity of the analysis.
- **Will the Benefits to Society (Our State or Our City) Justify the Overall Investment in This Project?:** Information about a project's larger social and economic costs and benefits is necessary to respond to impact questions. These queries present two challenging issues. The amount of data needed to measure an investment's overall social and economic costs is far more than what most financial systems can offer. It can be even more difficult to quantify or even identify the entire spectrum of social and economic benefits from a government IT project. Calculating a cost/benefit ratio is a desirable but rarely practical idea. Although not impossible, this type of analysis is rarely found in IT investment planning due to its breadth and complexity.

There are several differences between the four types of measurement questions and approaches. One significant distinction is the selection of pertinent metrics. While some methods only consider financial metrics (costs or returns expressed in dollars), others also take into account metrics related to the production output, such as client or customer satisfaction and the caliber of the goods or services. Metrics can be used to measure social and political outcomes as well as organizational elements like morale. Impacts on social equity, political support, social or human capital, and quality of life are a few examples. Table 5.2 provides a summary of these variations.

Table 5.2. Approaches to Cost and Return Measurement

Measurement Question	Measuring Costs	Measuring Returns/ Benefits
Can we afford this and will it pay for itself?	Financial metrics; defined by policy and accepted accounting principles; reporting and control-oriented; standards based or consistent; not linked to business process; ignores important cost factors; short time frame; data routinely collected/reported	Savings as measured in accounting categories; narrow in focus and impact; increased revenues, reduced total costs, acceptable payback period
How much 'bang for the buck' will we get out of this project?	Financial and outcome/ quality metrics; operations and management oriented; defined by program and business process; may or may not be standardized; often requires new data collection; may include organizational and managerial factors	Possible efficiency increases; increased output; enhanced service/product quality; enhanced access and equity; increased customer/client satisfaction; increased organizational capability; spillovers to other programs or processes
Is this the most we can get for this much investment?	Financial and organizational metrics; management and policy oriented; non-standardized; requires new data collection and simulation or analytical model; can reveal hidden costs	Efficiency increases; spillovers; enhanced capabilities; avoidance of wasteful or suboptimal strategies
Will the benefits to society (our state, our city, etc.) justify the overall investment in this project?	Financial, organizational, social, individual metrics; individual and management oriented; nonstandard; requires new data collection and expanded methods; reveals hidden costs; potentially long time-frame	Enhanced capabilities and opportunities; avoiding unintended consequences; enhanced equity; improved quality of life; enhanced equity; enhanced political support

Source: Anthony M. Cresswell, Return on Investment in Information Technology: A Guide for Managers, https://www.ctg.albany.edu/media/pubs/pdfs/roi.pdf.

5.4.4. Understanding ROI Decisions in their Political and Policy Context

Political and policy factors play a role in the public sector when making investment decisions, whether they are related to technology or not. Regardless of the quality or technical sophistication of an ROI analysis, it is unlikely to be the only factor considered when making an investment decision. Therefore, considering potential political and organizational factors is helpful when determining how to prepare and present a ROI analysis. This kind of external factor analysis could influence the approach, focus, or methods of presentation used to incorporate ROI analysis into decision-making processes. These factors, which are covered in more detail below, may also aid in gaining support for the analysis's conclusions and providing direction for describing or defending the analysis's methodology. 6 These factors can all be categorized as distinct kinds of risks.

5.4.4.1. Political Risk Factors

- **Public Exposure of Failure or Error**: Public business is the domain of government. The majority of novel concepts are applied in broad daylight. Any mishandled investment puts at risk not just money but also an agency's and its leadership's credibility with lawmakers, executive officials, and the general public. Therefore, government tends to rely on the "tried and true" in order to reduce risks. Failure risk can be reduced by being cautious not to overstate the advantages of new initiatives and by making sure that sufficient strategic planning is in place to lower the likelihood of failure. Excessive caution may also put you at risk for another type of failure: passing up chances to work on worthwhile projects.
- **Divided Authority:** Rarely do public executives have a direct line of command over the activities of their agencies. Existing laws, financial and budgetary restraints, civil service structures, political limitations, and a host of rules enforced by legislatures and courts all serve to limit their decision-making. These limitations make it difficult to manage the intricacies of multimillion-dollar IT projects in a technological environment that is changing quickly.
- **Multiple Stakeholders:** Usually, stakeholders have conflicting objectives. IT projects involve stakeholders such as customers, constituents, vendors, service providers, elected officials, professional staff, and others. It helps to prevent unanticipated problems to understand how various choices may affect and be affected by each stakeholder group.
- **Annual Budgets:** The amount and availability of resources in the future are uncertain due to government budget cycles. This makes it harder for government organizations to successfully implement or maintain new IT innovations, particularly ones that require a lot of time to develop.
- **Highly Regulated Procurement:** The experimentation and learning that are frequently necessary for successful IT investments are not well suited for the regulations found in the traditional competitive

bidding process. Regulations pertaining to procurement frequently cause issues and delays even though they support justice and integrity. These become particularly problematic when organizations draft requests for proposals (RFPs) based solely on the scant knowledge they have amassed via insufficient experience and investigation.

5.4.4.2. Organizational Risk Factors

- **Complex Program Networks:** Numerous intricate connections exist between government programs and non-governmental organizations, as well as between programs within the same or different agencies. There are instances when the links are clear-cut and formal. They are frequently inadvertent or informal. Program changes may have unanticipated effects on a number of other people, increasing expenses and complicating the investment project.
- **Misalignment of Goals:** An IT project's objective may be viewed in more limited, potentially contradictory terms by some organizational components. For instance, the technical elegance of a database or office automation project may captivate an IT unit. However, the system's end users might require features that the new technology cannot support. In the absence of goal alignment, a project is doomed to fail.
- **Lack of Leadership Support and Organizational Acceptance:** Support from upper management is crucial for any technology initiative. In a similar vein, gaining acceptance and support across the entire organization—especially from those who will be utilizing the technology or its products—is crucial but frequently more challenging. Comprehending and improving assistance mitigates or restricts hazards.

5.4.4.3. Business Process Risks

- **Reality of the Process**: Innovations in IT are integrated into business operations. Significant risks are introduced when project design and implementation fail to recognize and take this reality into account. Systems that don't meet business needs, are too costly for the meager productivity gains they offer, or aren't adaptable enough to change with the times are frequently designed.

5.4.4.4. Technology Risk Factors

- **Rapid Change:** Risk of obsolescence arises from the moment a project selects its technology. The rate at which technology is developing makes it challenging for planners to stay abreast of new advancements and fully comprehend how each new technical tool functions or might be replaced. Technology decisions that are informed by long-term plans and closely aligned with corporate objectives can reduce a lot of the risks associated with quickly evolving technologies.
- **Technology Interactions:** The idea that "you can't do just one thing" is fundamental to system analysis. "Old technologies and work processes interact with new technologies." Both the older and newer technologies may benefit from

the interactions, or they may cause problems for both. Thorough examination of these interactions will reveal potentially dangerous circumstances and offer advice on how to prevent issues and mistakes.

- **Scale and Complexity:** The size and complexity of IT projects directly correlate with increased risk. Some of these risks can be reduced by carefully planning an incremental development process with backup plans, which will help prevent unanticipated issues when moving from small to large, complex systems.

5.5. RETURN ON INVESTMENT METRICS: INSIGHTS FOR SMARTER DECISION MAKING

Metrics known as return on investment (ROI) are crucial instruments used by organizations to assess the success and profitability of their investments. These metrics facilitate more informed decision-making and strategic planning by offering insightful information about the financial performance of a project, initiative, or investment. Businesses can assess the return on their investments, pinpoint areas for development, and make well-informed decisions about their next investments by examining ROI metrics.

Organizations frequently use a number of important ROI metrics to assess the success of their investments. The return on investment ratio (ROI ratio) is one such metric that determines the proportion of an investment's net profit to its initial cost. The ROI ratio, for example, would be 2 ($20,000/$10,000) if a business invests $10,000 in a marketing campaign and makes a net profit of $20,000. This means the business has made twice as much money as it initially invested. The Payback Period, which gauges how long it takes an investment to produce enough cash flow to cover its initial cost, is another often used ROI metric. For instance, the payback period would be five months ($50,000/$10,000) if a business invested $50,000 in a new production line and anticipated to generate $10,000 in monthly cash flows. Businesses can use this metric to determine how quickly their investments can yield returns and adjust their strategy accordingly.

5.5.1. Understanding the Importance of ROI Metrics in Decision Making

1. **ROI Metrics: A Key to Smart Decision Making:** Using and comprehending ROI metrics is essential for making well-informed business decisions. ROI metrics offer significant insights into the profitability and efficacy of diverse business endeavors, facilitating prudent resource allocation and optimizing decision-making procedures for organizations. Decision-makers can assess the possible advantages and hazards of various projects, investments, or tactics by

examining ROI metrics. This section will examine the importance of ROI metrics and their role in facilitating more informed decision-making.

2. **Examples of ROI Metrics:** ROI metrics can take various forms depending on the specific context and objectives of a business decision. Some common examples include:
   - **Marketing ROI:** This metrics evaluates the return on investment from marketing campaigns or projects. Organizations can assess the success of their marketing strategies and adjust resource allocation by monitoring revenue generated and comparing it to the investment made in marketing efforts.
   - **Investment ROI:** Calculating the return on investment (ROI) is crucial for companies thinking about investing in new initiatives or projects. Decision-makers can make better decisions by using this metric to assess the risks and possible returns of various investment opportunities.
   - **Employee ROI:** Programs for the training and development of employees are investments that can provide substantial returns for businesses. Businesses can evaluate the return on investment (ROI) of their training initiatives and make data-driven decisions about future investments in employee development by tracking the effects of these programs on worker productivity and performance.
3. **Tips for Effective Use of ROI Metrics:** To leverage ROI metrics effectively in decision-making, consider the following tips:
   - **Clearly Define Goals and Objectives:** Prior to calculating ROI, it is essential to set specific, quantifiable objectives. By doing this, it is ensured that the metrics are meaningful and in line with the intended results.
   - **Use Consistent Measurement Techniques:** When it comes to measuring ROI, consistency is crucial. Organizations can make better decisions by accurately comparing the return on investment (ROI) of various projects or initiatives through the use of standardized measurement techniques.
   - **Consider Both Financial and Non-Financial Impacts:** When evaluating ROI, non-financial effects should also be taken into account, even though financial returns are crucial. These could include things like staff morale, customer satisfaction, and brand reputation, all of which have an impact on a project's or investment's overall success.

5.5.2. Key ROI Metrics for Evaluating Investments

A thorough understanding of return on investment (ROI) metrics is crucial when evaluating investments because it can lead to more informed decisions. These metrics give you important information about the performance and profitability of your investments, enabling you to evaluate their success and make wise decisions about your next round of investments. In this article, we'll look at three crucial ROI indicators that all investors need to know.

1. **Return on Investment (ROI):** Possibly the most popular metric for assessing investments is return on investment (ROI). By comparing the gain or loss realized to the initial investment cost, it determines how profitable an investment is. The following is the formula to determine return on investment:

ROI = (Net Profit/Investment Cost) x 100

For example, let's say you have invested $10,000 in a project, and it generates a net profit of $2,000. The ROI would be calculated as follows:

ROI = ($2,000/$10,000) x 100 = 20%

An investment with a higher return on investment (ROI) is considered more profitable than one with a lower ROI. You can order which investments have the highest potential returns by comparing their returns on investment (ROI).

2. **Return on Equity (ROE):** The profitability of shareholders' investments is the primary focus of the return on equity (ROE) metric. It assesses the effectiveness with which a business or endeavor uses shareholders' equity to produce profits. The following formula is used to determine ROE:

ROE = (Net Income/Shareholders' Equity) x 100

For example, if a company has a net income of $100,000 and shareholders' equity of $500,000, the ROE would be calculated as follows:

ROE = ($100,000/$500,000) x 100 = 20%

A higher ROE indicates that the company is generating more profit per unit of shareholders' equity, making it a more attractive investment option.

3. **Payback Period:** A metric called the payback period is used to calculate how long it will take an investment to produce sufficient cash flows to cover its initial cost. It is especially helpful when assessing projects with tight budgets or when liquidity is an issue. The payback period can be calculated using the following formula:

Payback Period = initial Investment Cost/ Annual Cash Inflows

For example, if you invest $50,000 in a project that generates $10,000 in annual cash inflows, the payback period would be calculated as follows:

Payback Period = $50,000/$10,000 = 5 years

A shorter payback period suggests a faster return of investment, which can be beneficial in situations where you need to recoup your initial investment quickly.

5.5.3. Calculate and Interpret Return on Investment

One important metric that businesses and individuals use to evaluate the effectiveness and profitability of an investment is return on investment (ROI). You can compute ROI to find out how much money you made or lost on an investment in relation to how much it cost. Making wise decisions and assessing the return on your investments requires an understanding of how to compute and interpret ROI. This section will explore the process of calculating ROI and offer guidance on interpreting the findings.

1. **Calculating ROI:** To calculate ROI, you need to divide the net profit generated by an investment by the initial cost of the investment. The formula for calculating ROI is as follows:

ROI = (Net Profit/Cost of Investment) × 100

For example, suppose you invest $10,000 in a marketing campaign, which generates a net profit of $15,000. Plugging these values into the formula, the calculation would be:

ROI = ($15,000/$10,000) × 100 = 150%

This means that for every dollar invested, you earned a return of $1.50, resulting in a 150% ROI.

2. **Interpreting ROI:** Interpreting ROI involves assessing the profitability and efficiency of an investment. A positive ROI indicates that the investment has generated a profit, while a negative ROI suggests a loss. The higher the ROI percentage, the more profitable the investment. However, it is important to consider the context and compare the ROI to industry benchmarks or alternative investment opportunities to gain a better understanding.

5.5.4. Limitations and Challenges of ROI Metrics

Return on investment (ROI) metrics are essential in the business world for assessing the effectiveness of different plans and projects. It's crucial to recognize that ROI measurements have drawbacks and difficulties. Knowing these restrictions can assist decision-makers in making better decisions and avoiding possible pitfalls. Let's examine some of the main difficulties and factors to take into account when applying ROI metrics.

1. **Difficulty in Measuring Intangible Benefits**: Quantifying intangible benefits presents a significant challenge when using ROI metrics. ROI is frequently used to determine ROI, but it frequently undervalues intangible benefits like brand reputation, customer satisfaction, and employee morale because it is primarily focused on measurable financial gains. For example, funding employee training initiatives can result in increased productivity and long-term growth even though they may not pay off right away. It is crucial to take into account a wider range of metrics that cover both concrete and intangible benefits in order to get around this restriction.
2. **Timeframe and Delayed Impact:** ROI metrics are frequently employed to evaluate an investment's profitability over a given period of time. This strategy might not take long-term advantages and delayed effects into consideration, though. Certain investments, like R&D or marketing campaigns, might not yield noticeable returns right away. Underestimating the possible long-term gains can happen if short-term ROI is the only thing on your mind. To fully understand the impact of investments, decision-makers should think about incorporating additional metrics such as market share or customer lifetime value.
3. **Inaccurate Data and Assumptions**: The quality of the data and the underlying assumptions used in

the computations have a significant impact on ROI metrics' accuracy. Incomplete or inaccurate data can produce deceptive ROI calculations, which may lead to poor decision-making. It is imperative to guarantee data precision and carry out comprehensive examination prior to depending on ROI metrics. This problem can be lessened by routinely checking and updating data sources and verifying assumptions.

4. **External Factors and Attribution**: ROI metrics can be greatly impacted by outside variables that are beyond an organization's control. For instance, shifts in the economy, industry trends, or market conditions may have an impact on the results of investments. It can be deceptive to attribute an investment's success or failure exclusively to internal factors. When interpreting ROI metrics, it's critical to take outside influences into account and refrain from basing decisions only on transient swings.
5. **Industry-Specific challenges**: Measuring return on investment can present certain challenges for different industries. For example, businesses that provide services frequently find it difficult to measure how customer experience affects return on investment. On the other hand, manufacturing industries might find it difficult to correctly allocate expenses and profits to particular projects or products. Accurate decision-making can be improved by comprehending industry-specific challenges and customizing ROI metrics accordingly.
6. **Balancing ROI with Other Metrics**: When making decisions, there are numerous metrics to take into account, ROI being just one of them. If ROI metrics are all that are considered, then other crucial aspects such as customer satisfaction, employee engagement, and environmental impact may be missed. In order to capture various facets of business performance and make more comprehensive decisions, decision-makers should aim for a balanced approach and take a variety of metrics into consideration.

In summary, ROI metrics are useful instruments for assessing the return on investments, but there are drawbacks and difficulties that must be taken into account. Decision-makers can choose more wisely and accurately if they are aware of these constraints and take into account supplementary metrics. It's critical to keep in mind that ROI measurements should be considered as a component of a larger framework that facilitates more informed decision-making.

5.5.5. Tips for Using ROI Metrics Effectively in Decision Making

1. **Define Clear Objectives:** Establishing specific goals is essential before using ROI metrics to guide decision-making. This will enable you to pinpoint the precise results you hope to attain and adjust your metrics appropriately. For instance, you can monitor the number of new visitors or the conversion rate to determine ROI if your goal is to increase website traffic.

2. **Choose Relevant Metrics:** Making the right metrics choices is crucial to making decisions that work. Choose the metrics that are most important to your goals and concentrate on them. For example, you may want to use customer feedback scores or repeat purchase rates to gauge return on investment if your objective is to increase customer satisfaction.
3. **Establish a Baseline:** By creating a baseline, you can precisely assess the influence of your choices. You can ascertain whether your efforts are yielding benefits by comparing outcomes to a baseline. If you launch a new marketing campaign, for example, comparing the ROI before and after the campaign will assist you in determining its efficacy.
4. **Consider the Time Frame:** The ROI metrics can change based on the period of analysis. While long-term metrics can show whether a decision was successful or unsuccessful overall, short-term metrics may offer insights into impacts that are felt right away. Select metrics based on the appropriate time frame for your decision. When launching a new product, for instance, you might first concentrate on short-term ROI metrics to gauge how well it does.
5. **Include All Relevant Costs:** Incorporating all pertinent expenses related to a choice is crucial for obtaining a precise ROI. This covers both direct and indirect costs, such as salary and training expenditures, in addition to direct costs. You can make better decisions if you weigh all the costs associated with a choice. For example, consider expenses like installation, training, and licensing fees when assessing the return on investment of deploying a new software system.
6. **Analyze ROI in Conjunction with Other Metrics:** ROI is a useful metric, but it shouldn't be the only consideration when making decisions. To obtain a complete picture of the situation, compare ROI analysis with other pertinent metrics. For instance, take into account metrics like employee satisfaction, productivity, and retention rates if you are thinking about investing in employee training.
7. **Use Benchmarking:** By contrasting your ROI metrics with those of competitors or industry norms, benchmarking can yield insightful information. You can use this to pinpoint areas in which you might be falling short or exceeding expectations, which empowers you to make more informed choices. For instance, if your return on investment (ROI) for a particular marketing channel is less than the industry standard, this could mean that your approach needs to be adjusted or optimized.
8. **Involve Stakeholders:** Engaging stakeholders in the process of making decisions can result in a more precise and efficient application of ROI metrics. Obtain feedback from pertinent individuals or teams to guarantee that all viewpoints are taken into account. For instance, involve management, end users, and IT personnel when assessing the return on investment (ROI) of a

new technology system in order to obtain information from a variety of sources.

9. **Regularly Review and Update Metrics:** ROI measurements ought to be flexible. Make sure your metrics are still pertinent and in line with your goals by reviewing and updating them on a regular basis. Your metrics should change as your company does. For example, when your business enters new markets, you might need to modify your ROI metrics to take into consideration the particular opportunities and difficulties that those markets present.

You can use ROI metrics to your advantage when making decisions if you pay attention to these pointers. Recall that ROI is only one component of the puzzle; making better decisions requires taking into account a variety of other factors as well.

CASE STUDY

CALCULATING ROI FOR SERVICE DESIGN IMPROVEMENTS: A CASE STUDY APPROACH

ROI, or Return on Investment, is a financial metric that measures the profitability of an investment. It's commonly used in business to evaluate the success of projects and initiatives based on the amount of money invested versus the amount of return generated.

ROI can be calculated by dividing the net profit (revenue minus expenses) by the total investment cost and then multiplying by 100 to get a percentage. This percentage represents how much money was earned in relation to how much was spent.

In service design, ROI is often used to justify investments in improving customer experience or employee satisfaction. By analyzing ROI before implementing changes and after they are made, companies can determine if their efforts were successful and make informed decisions about future investments.

It's important to note that ROI should not be viewed as the only factor when making business decisions. Other factors such as brand reputation, customer loyalty, and long-term sustainability should also be taken into account for comprehensive decision-making.

How to Calculate ROI for Service Design Improvements

Calculating the return on investment (ROI) for service design improvements is an important step in understanding the effectiveness of any changes made. This will give you a clear picture of how much value your organization has derived from these improvements.

To calculate ROI, you need to compare the costs incurred during service design improvement with the benefits that resulted from it. These benefits could be tangible, such as increased revenue or reduced operating costs, or intangible, such as improved customer satisfaction or employee engagement.

The formula to calculate ROI is simple: ROI = (Gain from Investment — Cost of Investment)/Cost of Investment * 100

This formula takes into account both the gain and cost associated with implementing service design improvements and expresses this as a percentage. The higher the percentage, the greater your return on investment.

When calculating ROI for service design improvements, it's crucial to consider all relevant cost factors such as direct costs like salaries and overheads along with indirect costs like training expenses. In addition to financial gains, it's important to measure other factors too such as customer satisfaction levels before and after implementation of new services. By being thorough in measuring returns through multiple metrics including qualitative feedback surveys can also help organizations identify areas that require more attention for better outcomes.

Case Study #1: Improving Customer Satisfaction

Customer satisfaction is a crucial aspect of any service-based business. To improve this, many companies invest in service design improvements. One such company was able to achieve significant results by implementing a few changes.

The company first identified the key pain points for customers and designed solutions accordingly. They trained their employees to be more responsive and empathetic towards customers' needs, which helped them understand the problem better and resolve it quickly.

They also improved their user interface to make it more intuitive, enhancing the overall experience for users. This made it easier for customers to navigate through different sections of their website or app seamlessly.

As a result of these changes, the company saw an increase in positive feedback from customers and an improvement in online ratings. The new design led to higher customer retention rates as well as attracting new clients who were impressed with the improved services.

Investing time and resources into improving customer satisfaction can have tangible benefits on your bottom line. By understanding your clientele's needs and finding innovative ways to solve problems that arise during interactions with your brand, you can gain loyal customers who will recommend you to others.

Case Study #2: Reducing Waiting Times

Reducing waiting times can greatly improve the customer experience. A case study conducted by a medical clinic found that reducing wait times from 30 minutes to 15 minutes resulted in a significant increase in patient satisfaction scores.

To calculate the ROI for this service design improvement, the clinic measured the number of patients seen per day and estimated how much revenue each patient brought in. They then calculated how much additional revenue could be generated if they were able to see more patients due to reduced wait times.

The clinic also took into consideration the cost of implementing this improvement, such as hiring additional staff or restructuring their scheduling system. By comparing these costs to the potential increase in revenue, they were able to determine whether or not it was financially feasible to implement this change.

Case Study #3: Improving Employee Satisfaction

This is an essential aspect of service design improvement as happy employees lead to increased productivity, better customer service and higher retention rates.

In this case study, a company implemented changes in the work environment such as creating more comfortable break areas for employees to relax during their breaks and installing ergonomic chairs at workstations. They also introduced employee recognition programs like "Employee of the Month" awards and birthday celebrations.

The results were remarkable, with a 25% increase in employee satisfaction levels reported through regular surveys conducted by the company's HR department. The happier workforce led to reduced absenteeism rates, improved morale, increased collaboration among teams and ultimately better services provided to customers.

Improving employee satisfaction is not just about making physical improvements but also fostering a positive culture within the workplace that values its staff members' contributions. Employee engagement initiatives can go beyond monetary perks or promotions; it can be something as simple as acknowledging their hard work regularly.

By investing time and resources into improving employee satisfaction levels, companies can create a productive and fulfilling working environment where employees are motivated to provide excellent services daily.

How to Use ROI in Decision Making

After calculating ROI for service design improvements, it's important to use the information in decision-making. Here are some ways that ROI can be used:

Firstly, ROI can help prioritize which service design improvements should be implemented first by identifying those with the highest potential return on investment. This allows organizations to allocate their resources more effectively.

Secondly, ROI can provide a basis for evaluating different options and choosing the most cost-effective solution. By comparing the projected returns of each option against their costs, decision-makers can make informed decisions about which approach is most likely to deliver a positive result.

Thirdly, ROI analysis helps demonstrate the business case for investing in service design improvements. By showing how changes will impact revenue or costs over time, executives and stakeholders will have greater confidence in committing resources towards these initiatives.

Tracking actual results against predicted outcomes enables organizations to learn from experience and improve future decision-making. Adjustments may need to be made based on new data or unforeseen challenges that arise during implementation.

Conclusion

As we have seen from the case studies discussed in this blog post, calculating ROI for service design improvements can be a powerful tool for decision-making. By quantifying the benefits and costs of these improvements, businesses can make informed choices about where to focus their resources.

One key takeaway is that ROI calculations are not one-size-fits-all. The metrics used will depend on the specific improvement being made and its goals. For example, reducing waiting times may require a different set of measurements than improving employee satisfaction.

However, despite these variations, ROI calculations remain relevant across industries and contexts. Whether you're in healthcare or finance, public or private sector, using data to inform your decisions is always valuable.

While there's no magic formula for calculating ROI for service design improvements, taking a case study approach can provide valuable insights into how it works in practice. By investing time and effort into measuring outcomes before making changes to services or products — whether through surveys or other means — businesses stand to benefit both financially and operationally.

CLASS ACTIVITY

Vegan Steaks had the best year ever, with sales of $4,500,000 and operating profit of $950,000. The balance sheet at the beginning of the year showed assets used in production with a cost of $20,000,000 and accumulated depreciation of $5,000,000. The company didn't buy any assets during the year but did have depreciation expense of $1,000,000. Calculate the ROI for the year.

SUMMARY

- Return on Investment (ROI) is one of the most popular performance measurement and evaluation metrics used in business analysis.
- ROI analysis is a powerful tool for evaluating existing information systems and making informed decisions on software acquisitions and other projects.
- In business, the purpose of the return on investment (ROI) metric is to measure, per period, rates of return on money invested in an economic entity in order to decide whether or not to undertake an investment.
- ROI and related metrics provide a snapshot of profitability, adjusted for the size of the investment assets tied up in the enterprise.
- It is crucial to note that determining a company's profit is not the same as calculating the return on an investment. Profit is determined purely by a company's cash flow. This is an example of their instant performance.
- ROI allows you to compare the profitability and asset utilization of different business divisions. It can be used for inter-firm comparisons if the businesses whose results are being compared are comparable in size and in the same industry.
- ROI is determined by your company's financial accounting. To generate ROI data, there is no need for a new or different accounting measurement.
- ROI is regarded as the single most essential metric of an investment division's success, and it covers other components of a business unit's performance.
- Maximizing return on investment (ROI) requires strategic planning, informed decision-making, and effective execution.
- ROI Extensions have been created with the purpose of fixing some deficiencies of the Traditional ROI and widening the area of ROI use.
- Growing interest in assessing returns on IT investments has spawned wide interest in methods of return on investment analysis.
- The value of an investment is directly related to the programmatic goals and business process employing the new technology.
- Investment decisions in the public sector, whether they involve IT or any other expenditure, take place in a context of political and policy influences.

REVIEW QUESTIONS

1. Discuss the benefits of ROI.
2. How to use return on investment? Discus.
3. What are the factors determining return on investment in corporate finance?
4. How can you maximize the return on investment for investors?
5. Discuss the strategic objectives in ROI design.
6. Define and measure the costs and returns from IT investments.

7. Discuss about ROI decisions in their political and policy context.
8. What are the limitations and challenges of ROI metrics.

REFERENCES

1. Anderson, M. L., & Dejoy, J. S. (2011). Corporate social and financial performance: The role of size, industry, risk, R&D and advertising expenses as control variables. *Business and Society Review, 116*(2), 237–256.
2. Anderson, M. L., & Olsen, L. (2011). Corporate social and financial performance: A canonical correlation analysis. *Academy of Accounting and Financial Studies Journal, 15*(2), 17–37.
3. Chew, G., & Walczyk, T. (2012). A Monte Carlo approach for estimating measurement uncertainty using standard spreadsheet software. *Analytical and Bioanalytical Chemistry, 402*(7), 2463–2469.
4. Chmielewski, T. L., & Phillips, J. J. (2002). Measuring return-on-investment in government: Issues and procedures. *Public Personnel Management, 31*(2), 225–237.
5. Cleary, P., Kennedy, T., O'Donnell, D., O'Regan, P., & Bontis, N. (2007). Positioning management accounting on the intellectual capital agenda. *International Journal of Accounting, Auditing and Performance Evaluation, 4*(4/5), 336–359.
6. Daneva, M., & Wieringa, R. (2008). Cost estimation for cross-organizational ERP projects: Research perspectives. *Software Quality Journal, 16*(3), 459–481. https://doi.org/10.1007/s11219-008-9045-8.
7. Dearden, J. (1969). The case against ROI control. *Harvard Business Review, 47*(3), 124–135.
8. Jorgensen, M., & Shepperd, M. (2007). A systematic review of software development cost estimation studies. *IEEE Transactions on Software Engineering, 33*(1), 33–53. https://doi.org/10.1109/TSE.2007.256943.
9. Kingma, B., & Schisa, K. (2010). WISE economics: ROI of quality and consortiums. *Journal of Education for Library and Information Sciences, 51*(1), 43–52.
10. Mogollon, M., & Raisinghani, M. (2003). Measuring ROI in e-business: A practical approach. *Information Systems Management, 20*(2), 63–81.
11. Pearce, J. M. (2016). Return on investment for open-source scientific hardware development. *Science and Public Policy, 43*(2), 192–195. Retrieved from: https://example.com (accessed on 16 July 2024).
12. Schweizer, L., Rogbeer, S., & Michaelis, B. (2015). The dynamic capabilities perspective: From fragments to meta-theory. *Management Research Review, 38*(7), 662–684.
13. Sroufe, R. (2017). Integration and organizational change towards sustainability. *Journal of Cleaner Production, 162*, 315–329.

CHAPTER 6

Fixed Income Securities

LEARNING OBJECTIVES

After studying this chapter, you will be able to:

- Understand basics of fixed-income securities
- Explain bond markets and institutions
- Describe valuing risk-free rate
- Know bond price-interest rate relation
- Focus on bond arbitrage
- Identify interest rate sensitivity of bonds
- Discuss leverage
- Explain forward rates

KEY TERMS FROM THIS CHAPTER

Asset-backed securities (ABS)
Certificate of deposit
Derivatives
Liability
Municipal bond
Preferreds
Treasury bills
Treasury notes
Bond
Corporate bonds
Government bonds
Mortgage-backed bonds (MBS)
Preferred stock
Risk-free rate
Treasury bond

INTRODUCTION

Investment returns on fixed income securities are assured. They represent a risk to the company introducing them to the market. Fixed-income investments yield periodic returns, and regardless of market fluctuations, the interest payable on these securities stays constant. Before the fixed income security is issued, its ultimate value at maturity is determined. At the time of investment, it is disclosed to the investor. This kind of market investment tool is well-liked by those who prefer safe returns on their investments with higher yields over being exposed to risks.

6.1. UNDERSTANDING FIXED-INCOME SECURITIES

Debt instruments known as "fixed-income" securities provide investors with coupon payments equal to a predetermined amount of interest. Typically, semiannual interest payments are made, and upon maturity, the investor receives their principal back. The most popular type of fixed-income securities are bonds. Bonds are investment products that governments and businesses issue to raise money for operations and projects. Bonds issued by corporations and governments have different face values and maturities. The amount that the investor will get when the bond matures is known as its face value. The majority of trade in corporate and government bonds occurs over-the-counter (OTC), not on exchanges. The par value, or $1,000 face value, is typically listed for them.

6.1.1. Credit Rating of Fixed-Income Securities

Various credit ratings are given to bonds according to the issuer's financial stability. Credit-rating agencies use a grading system that includes credit ratings. These organizations evaluate the capacity of corporations and governments to repay loans as well as the creditworthiness of their bonds. Because they outline the risks associated with investing, credit ratings are useful to investors. Investment-grade and non-investment-grade bonds are the two types of bonds. Bonds classified as investment grade have lower interest rates than non-investment grade bonds because they are issued by reliable companies with little chance of default. Because there is a chance that the issuer will default, non-investment grade bonds—also referred to as junk bonds or high-yield bonds—have lower credit ratings. As a reward for taking on the increased risk associated with these debt instruments, investors who purchase junk bonds receive higher interest rates.

6.1.2. Types of Fixed-Income Securities

There are numerous varieties of fixed-income investment options. Let's talk about the various kinds of fixed-income securities that are available for purchase:

1. **Treasury Notes:** The United States issues Treasury notes, or T-notes. Treasury bonds have an intermediate maturity period of 2, 3, 5, 7, or 10 years. T-Notes have fixed coupon rates or interest rates and are issued in $100 increments. Interest payments are made on a semiannual basis. All Treasury marketable securities are backed by the full faith and credit of the United States for principal repayment and interest payments. The government, in order to finance itself, issues these bonds.

2. **Treasury Bond:** The U.S. Additionally, the Treasury issues Treasury bonds, or T-bonds, with a 20- or 30-year maturity. Treasury bonds are offered for auction on the Treasury Direct website, with bids made in $100 increments.
3. **Treasury Bills:** Treasury bills are a type of short-term fixed-income security. The T-bill has an interest-free duration of 4, 8, 13, 17, 26, or 52 weeks. Rather, investors purchase the security at a discount or for less than face value. Investors get paid the face value of the discount note when the bill matures. The difference between the purchase price and the bill's face value is the interest earned or return on investment.
4. **Municipal Bond:** In order to finance capital projects like roads, schools, and hospitals, states, cities, and counties will issue municipal bonds, which are typically sold for $5,000 face value. Federal income tax does not apply to the interest received from these bonds. If an investor lives in the state where the Muni bond is issued, they may be exempt from state and local taxes on the interest they earn. A portion of the principal is due on a periodic basis until the entire principal is paid back on the multiple maturity dates of the municipal bond.
5. **Certificate of Deposit:** A certificate of deposit (CD) is issued by a bank. The bank offers interest to the account holder in exchange for the money they deposit with them for a set amount of time. While most CDs have maturities of five years or less, some can have maturities of even longer durations. Generally speaking, they offer higher rates than traditional savings accounts but lower rates than bonds. A certificate of deposit (CD) is insured up to $250,000 per account holder by the Federal Deposit Insurance Corporation (FDIC).
6. **Corporate Bonds:** Debt instruments called "corporate bonds" are sold by businesses to raise money. Bond investors are not entitled to vote or ownership in the company, unlike owners of company stocks. Bonds are categorized according to how long they take to mature. Bonds are held for four to 10 years for medium-term bonds, more than 10 years for long-term bonds, and less than three years for short-term bonds. Bonds are categorized as investment-grade or non-investment-grade based on the credit rating of the issuer.
7. **Preferred Stock:** Businesses issue preferred stock that pays out a fixed dividend to investors on a predetermined schedule, which can be expressed as a percentage or monetary amount of the share value. Preferred shares are more expensive than most bonds because of inflation and interest rates, and because of their longer duration, they offer higher yields.

6.1.3. Examples of Fixed Income Securities

The most popular kind of fixed income security is a bond, which can be issued by the government or by businesses. Other examples of fixed income securities include derivatives, money market instruments, asset-backed securities, and preferreds.

1. **Bonds:** Bonds constitute a whole field of study in finance or investing on their own. They are generally understood to be loans made by investors to an issuer, with the promise of principal repayment at the designated maturity date and regular coupon payments (usually made every six months) covering interest paid on the loan. These loans have a wide range of purposes. Governments and businesses that are looking for ways to finance operations or projects often issue bonds.
2. **Money Market Instruments:** Securities like commercial paper, banker's acceptances, certificates of deposit (CD), repurchase agreements (or "repos"), and the most traded US government Treasury Bills, or T-bills for short, are examples of money market instruments. The US federal government issues Treasury bills, which are regarded as the safest short-term debt instrument. These securities typically have 28, 91, and 182-day (one month, three months, and six months) maturities, with maturities ranging from one to 12 months. Regular coupon or interest payments are not provided by these instruments. As an alternative, they are offered to investors at a discount to face value, with the interest rate being the difference between the two. For instance, a Treasury bill offering approximately 10% interest would be sold for $90 if its face value, or par value, was $100.
3. **Asset-Backed Securities (ABS):** Fixed income securities known as asset-backed securities (ABS) are backed by financial assets that have undergone a process known as "securitization," including home equity loans, auto loans, and credit card receivables. One such asset group that has been bundled into a single fixed-income security is represented by ABS. Purchasing asset-backed securities is typically a better option for investors than taking on corporate debt.
4. **Preferreds:** These fixed income securities, also referred to as subordinated debt, are ranked lower on the capital stack. The coupon and principal of preferred fixed income securities may not be paid in the event that the issuer's creditworthiness declines. Because of this risk, which is known as loss-absorption, preferreds are occasionally seen as a cross between fixed income and equity securities.
5. **Derivatives:** There have been numerous financial contracts in capital markets with variable payouts based on the performance of other securities. These are referred to as "Derivatives," and in the fixed income industry, derivatives like swaps, options, and structured products are frequently traded for the purposes of speculating, hedging, and gaining access to new markets or assets.

6.1.4. Advantages

Fixed-income securities lower portfolio risk, offer investors consistent interest income, and shield investors from market volatility and swings. Due to the historical volatility of equities relative to bonds, investors may choose to allocate a portion of their portfolios to fixed-income instruments in order to lower their level of risk. Additionally, mutual funds and exchange-traded funds (ETFs) offer fixed-income securities. Fixed-income securities and bonds have fluctuating prices. Fixed-income securities have consistent interest payments, but there is no assurance that their prices will hold steady for the duration of the holding. Gains or losses on an investor's sale of a fixed-income security prior to its maturity are determined by the difference between the purchase and sale prices. Bonds carry the risk of a possible default in addition to price volatility. U.S. government bonds are considered incredibly low-risk as they are backed by the full faith and credit of the United States government. Compared to government bonds, corporate bonds are more susceptible to default and are reliant on the financial stability of the issuing company. Nonetheless, since bondholders will receive their repayment before common and even preferred stockholders, corporate bonds have a good chance of being repaid in the event that a company files for bankruptcy.

6.1.5. Disadvantages

Generally speaking, fixed-income securities offer low returns and sluggish price increases or capital appreciation. This is the cost associated with reduced risk. Their price reductions also tend to be slower. Frequently, the initial principal amount is unreachable, especially in the case of long-term bonds with maturities longer than 10 years. If the bond's current market value is higher than the amount invested, it can be sold to recover the investment early. Regardless of changes in market interest rates, fixed-income securities offer a fixed interest payment. If market interest rates rise above the 2% bond's yield and the investor's money is invested in the bond, the investor will forfeit income from their purchase of the bond. This is also the reason why the market price of bonds declines. The market value of the bond decreases if rates increase above its interest rate. If the rate of inflation exceeds the interest rate of the fixed-income instrument, the return on fixed-rate securities may be negatively impacted. Since bonds are dependent on the issuer's financial stability, they are all subject to credit or default risk. Buying foreign bonds can put you at greater risk of default if the nation is unstable politically or economically.

6.1.6. Risks of Investing in Fixed Income Securities

It's crucial to keep in mind that although some bond kinds carry less risk than others, bonds aren't always safer than stocks. Investors in fixed income securities typically run the following four major risks:

1. **Inflation:** The overall rise in prices over a specific period of time is known as inflation. Rising price levels reduce the purchasing power of the cash flows on Fixed Income Securities, making them riskier for investors because they typically have longer lifespans and most do not have adjustments to account for inflation.
2. **Interest Rate Risk:** the chance that shifts in interest rates could lower an investor's fixed-income security's market value. For instance, if an investor owns a 3% interest 10-year bond, and later on interest rates rise and new 10-year

bonds are issued with a 4% interest rate, the investor's bond with the lower interest rate loses value and its price drops.

3. **Default Risk:** The primary risk pertaining to fixed-income securities is the borrower's susceptibility to nonpayment of debt. These risks are factored into the interest rate or coupon that the security offers; investors will receive a higher interest rate from securities that carry a higher default risk.
4. Additional risks include the possibility of capital controls that would prevent investors from receiving their investment back and the risk of exchange rate volatility if investors purchase securities denominated in foreign currencies.

6.2. BOND MARKETS AND INSTITUTIONS

A bond market is a debt securities market. Both corporate and government-issued debt securities are covered in this market. It makes it possible for capital to move from investors or savers to issuers in need of money for various operations or projects. This sector is also known as the credit market, fixed-income market, or debt market.

6.2.1. Bond Market Meaning

In the bond market, you have two options: you can issue new debt in the primary market or trade debt securities in the secondary market. The most popular kind of trading is with bonds. But notes and bills also work well. The bond market is used by traders, governments, institutional investors, and private citizens. There are three types of bond markets: agency, government, and corporate. Government bonds are the most significant of the three since they can be used to evaluate credit risk and compare other bonds.

6.2.2. Stability of Bond Rates

Businesses are required by contract to return the face value of bonds upon maturity and to pay the specified interest on time. An important issue that typically leads to a company's insolvency is bond default. The available assets of the company will be used to repay bondholders even in the event of a corporation's bankruptcy. Consequently, companies give priority to paying their bonds on time. Because the terms of a bond are known ahead of time, their value will typically move within a relatively narrow range when compared to stocks.

6.2.3. Types of Bond Market

There are many bond markets to investigate when thinking about bond types, such as high-yield or convertible bonds, as well as government, corporate, municipal, and international bond markets. With their unique traits, degrees of risk, and possible profits, each kind offers a range of investment options.

6.2.3.1. Corporate Bonds

Corporate bonds are issued by businesses to raise capital for new manufacturing facilities, product line expansions, or ongoing operations. Corporate bonds are typically longer-term debt instruments with a minimum one-year maturity.

They are typically divided into two types according to the issuer's credit rating and the bond itself. An investment grade bond is one that is of excellent quality and has a low default risk. Different designations, made up of the capital and lowercase letters A and B, are used by bond-rating organizations such as Standard and Poor's and Moody's to indicate a bond's credit quality rating. The risk is higher with junk bonds or high-yield bonds. Junk bonds are bonds issued by financially troubled companies that run a high risk of not meeting their interest payments or paying back the principal to investors. Junk bonds are sometimes referred to as high-yield bonds because they require a higher yield in order to partially offset default risk.

6.2.3.2. Government Bonds

Sovereign or national government bonds are attractive to investors because they pay interest on a regular basis and pay the face value stated on the bond certificate on the designated maturity date. Because of this, conservative investors find government bonds to be the most appealing and least hazardous. In the U.S., government bonds are known as Treasuries and the most active and liquid bond market.

- **Treasury Bill (T-Bill):** a short-term U.S. government debt obligation backed by the Treasury Department with a maturity of one year or less
- **Treasury Note (T-Note):** A commercially viable U.S. securities representing government debt with a fixed interest rate and a 1- to 10-year maturity.
- **Treasury Bonds (T-Bonds):** securities representing government debt that the U.S. Federal agencies with more than 20 years of experience.

Based on anticipated fiscal deterioration over the next three years, a high and rising general government debt burden, and the deterioration of governance relative to AA and AAA peers over the last two decades with repeated debt limit standoffs and premature resolutions, Fitch Ratings downgraded the long-term ratings of the United States to AA+ from AAA in August 2023.

6.2.3.3. Municipal Bonds

States, cities, public utility districts, school districts, publicly owned airports and seaports, and other government-owned organizations issue municipal bonds, also known as Muni bonds, on a local level in an effort to raise money for different projects. Qualified investors who are concerned about taxes find municipal bonds appealing since they are typically tax-free at the federal level and may also be tax-exempt at the state or local level. Government organizations that are not supported by the proceeds of a particular project may issue general obligation bonds (GO bonds). Certain GO bonds are payable from general funds or backed by property taxes. A revenue bond uses taxes on sales, gasoline, hotel occupancy, or other sources to guarantee principal and interest payments. Interest and principal payments are made by a third party when a municipality issues bonds through a conduit.

6.2.3.4. Mortgage-Backed Bonds (MBS)

Pooled mortgages secured by real estate properties make up mortgage-backed security (MBS) issues. Purchasing a mortgage-backed security means that an investor is effectively lending money to homebuyers via their lenders. They usually give interest on a monthly basis. One kind of asset-backed security (ABS) is the MBS. This kind of security was dependent upon failing mortgages to be supported during the subprime mortgage crisis of 2007–2010.

6.2.3.5. Emerging Market Bonds

Compared to domestic or developed bond markets, emerging market economies' governments and businesses offer more risky but potentially profitable bonds. Throughout the 1980s, U.S. Treasury Secretary Nicholas Brady launched a program to use bond issues denominated in U.S. dollars to assist international economies in restructuring their debt dollars. Over the course of the following 20 years, these Brady bonds were issued by numerous Latin American nations, signaling a rise in the issuance of debt by emerging markets. Corporations in Asia, Latin America, Eastern Europe, Africa, and the Middle East issue bonds, as do developing countries. Investing in emerging market bonds entails the standard risks associated with any debt issue, including the issuer's ability to fulfill payment obligations and the issuer's financial or economic performance. The political and economic instability in developing countries can increase these risks. Exchange rate volatility and currency devaluations are additional risks associated with emerging markets.

6.2.4. Bond Investments

Bond prices are expressed as a percentage of par value (100%) and are normally traded in $1,000 increments. Bonds often have minimums that are set by the dealer or the bond itself. Usually, sizes are offered in $10,000 increments. However, anything less than a $100,000 trade is considered an odd lot by broker/dealers. Typically, bonds pay interest at predetermined intervals. Fixed coupon bonds split the stated coupon into segments according to their payment schedule, such as semi-annual pay. Bonds with floating rate coupons have predetermined schedules for computation, with the floating rate determined just prior to the subsequent payment. Bonds with zero coupons don't pay interest. To take into consideration the implied interest, they are issued at a steep discount.

Most bonds are bought as part of a more conservative investment plan because of their consistent income. However, investors can profit or lose money based on market conditions related to the economy, interest rates, and issuers when they actively trade bonds, particularly corporate and municipal bonds. Dividend income is taxed at a favorable rate, whereas bond interest is taxed as ordinary income. Nonetheless, a large number of municipal and government bonds are free from various forms of taxation. Investment companies provide bond funds, closed-end funds, and unit investment trusts as ways for individual investors to get involved in the bond market. The net inflows into bond funds increased by 97% in 2006, from $30.8 billion in 2005 to $60.8 billion. An additional option to trading or investing directly in a bond issue is to use exchange-traded funds (ETFs). Individual investors can overcome significant initial and incremental trading sizes with the help of these securities.

6.2.5. Bond Indices

Just as the Russell Indexes or S&P 500

are used to manage equities portfolios and assess performance, there are numerous bond indices available. The Barclays Capital Aggregate Bond Index, Citigroup BIG, and Merrill Lynch Domestic Master are the three most widely used benchmarks in the United States. The majority of indices are components of larger index families that can be used to gauge bond portfolios globally. Alternatively, they can be further broken down by sector or maturity to manage more specialized portfolios.

6.3. VALUING RISK-FREE RATE

The theoretical rate of return for an investment with no risk is known as the risk-free rate of return. The interest an investor would anticipate from a completely risk-free investment over a given time period is represented by the risk-free rate. You can compute the so-called real risk-free rate by deducting the yield of the Treasury bond that corresponds to the duration of your investment from the current rate of inflation.

6.3.1. Understanding the Risk-Free Rate of Return

The minimal return an investor can anticipate from any investment is the risk-free rate, according to theory. Unless the potential rate of return exceeds the risk-free rate, investors will not take on more risk. The investor's home market needs to be taken into account when determining a stand-in for the risk-free rate of return. A negative interest rate may make matters more difficult. In actuality, there is never a completely risk-free rate since even the safest investments have some degree of risk.

The risk-free rate is determined by using different benchmarks across nations and economic zones. The interest rate on a three-month U.S. Treasury bill (T-bill) is often used as the risk-free rate for U.S.-based investors. The three-month U.S. Treasury bill is a useful proxy because the market considers there to be virtually no chance of the U.S. government defaulting on its obligations. The market's vast size and high level of liquidity add to the sense of security.

A foreign investor whose assets are not denominated in dollars incurs currency risk when investing in U.S. Treasury bills. Currency forwards and options can be used to hedge the risk, but doing so lowers the rate of return. For investors with assets denominated in euros (EUR) or Swiss francs (CHF), the short-term government bills of other highly rated nations, like Germany and Switzerland, provide a risk-free rate proxy. Currency risk is eliminated for investors in German bonds who are based in eurozone nations with lower credit ratings, like Greece and Portugal. In contrast, purchasing a highly-rated government bond will always involve currency risk for an investor holding assets denominated in Russian rubles.

6.3.2. Importance of Risk-Free Rate

Because it is used in financial modeling, investing, and valuations, the risk-free rate is a basic building block of finance. It offers a starting point rate that serves as a standard by which the return on all other investments is evaluated. This is used as the discount rate in valuation models, like discounted cash flow analysis, to calculate the present value of future cash flows. The risk-free rate also aids in the pricing of financial instruments and the determination of suitable rates of return for investment strategies. For example, because it's a crucial component of pricing models, it affects the pricing of bonds, options, and derivatives. Cost-of-capital computations also take the risk-free rate into consideration. It assists businesses in evaluating the necessary return on investment projects and choosing the best capital structure based on what the business could make if it decided not to take on any risk. Lastly, investors place a high value on the risk-free rate. Investors can determine whether the potential return justifies the degree of risk assumed by comparing the expected return of an investment to the risk-free rate. What level of risk would you be willing to accept, for instance, to earn a 7% return if you knew you could earn 5% risk-free? Would your willingness to accept risk change if you knew you could only earn 2% risk-free?

6.3.3. Risk-Free Rate and Financial Asset Pricing

The risk-free rate serves as the benchmark rate of return in valuation models, such as the capital asset pricing model (CAPM), to which the projected returns of riskier assets are contrasted. According to CAPM, an asset's expected return is calculated by multiplying the risk-free rate by a risk premium, which rewards investors for taking on more risk. Therefore, the required rate of return for risky assets is directly impacted by changes in the risk-free rate. Bond yields are determined by the risk-free rate in bond pricing. Bond prices are determined by discounting future coupon payments and principal repayment with the current risk-free rate. This process yields the bond's present value. Bond yields rise in tandem with a fall in bond prices as the risk-free rate rises because it reduces the present value of future cash flows. Conversely, when the risk-free rate falls, the bond's price rises along with the PV of cash flow. As previously mentioned, models like the Black-Scholes model use the risk-free rate to affect how much options and other derivatives are priced. These kinds of option pricing models take the risk-free rate as an input, and the risk-free rate influences the cost of carrying the underlying asset, which impacts the value of options in the same way it does in other models.

6.3.4. Factors That Influence the Risk-Free Rate

The riskless rate is intricate. There are numerous factors that go into determining that rate, and the risk-free rate is not constant. In general, the following are a few of the high-level variables that affect the risk-free rate:

- **Monetary Policy:** The monetary policy decisions made by central banks, specifically the adjustments made to the target interest rates, have an impact on the risk-free rate. For instance, the risk-free rate typically rises when a central bank raises interest rates in an effort to tame inflation or cool an overheating economy. On the other hand, decreasing interest rates can encourage borrowing and boost the economy by lowering the risk-free rate.

- **Economic Conditions:** The risk-free rate is influenced by a number of macroeconomic variables, including consumer sentiment, employment levels, inflation, and economic growth. Higher risk-free rates may result from robust economic growth and low unemployment, which would reflect higher opportunity costs associated with holding risk-free assets. Conversely, recessions or downturns in the economy could lead central banks to cut interest rates, which would lower the risk-free rate.
- **Inflation Expectations:** The real return on risk-free assets can also be influenced by inflation expectations. In order to maintain their purchasing power, investors demand compensation for predicted inflation. Because higher inflation expectations generally translate into higher risk-free rates, variations in inflation expectations can therefore affect the risk-free rate.
- **Supply and Demand for Government Securities:** The yields on government securities and the risk-free rate are frequently closely correlated. Treasury bonds and other similar investments are typically regarded as low-risk investments. Variations in the dynamics of supply and demand for these securities can have an impact on their yields and, in turn, the risk-free rate. Lower risk-free rates can result from rising bond prices and falling yields due to increased demand for government bonds.
- **Market Sentiment and Risk Appetite:** Finally, the risk-free rate is determined in part by investor sentiment and risk appetite. Risk-free assets may be sought after by investors in uncertain or volatile times. As a result, the risk-free rate may decline due to an increase in demand for risk-free assets. Investors may be more willing to take chances when they have a positive outlook on the markets, which implies that there will be less demand for risk-free assets and an increase in the rate.

6.3.5. Proxies for the Risk-Free Rate

In financial analysis and valuation, the risk-free rate is typically represented by a number of different options. Some of those proxies are as follows if you're having trouble obtaining the risk-free rate or need something close in place.

- **Government Treasury Securities:** In many nations, short-term government treasury securities like Treasury bills (T-bills) or longer-term treasury bonds are thought to be the closest thing to risk-free assets. Usually, the yields on these securities are used as a stand-in for the risk-free rate, especially when making short- to medium-term investments. This is due to the widespread belief—at least in some nations—that the government won't declare bankruptcy and stop making debt payments.
- **SOFR:** While LIBOR is no longer available, SOFR has replaced it. Historically, these reference rates have served as a stand-in for the risk-free rate, especially in cases of international trade and contracts with currencies other than the home currency.

- **Central Bank Policy Rates:** Other target rates, like the Federal Reserve's Federal Funds Rate in the U.S., may be set by central banks. Similar rates exist elsewhere in the world as well, such as the primary refinancing rate set by the European Central Bank for the Eurozone.
- **Inflation-Indexed Bonds:** Bonds that track inflation, like the Treasury's inflation-protected securities (TIPS) in the U.S. offer yields that have been indexed for inflation and are occasionally employed as stand-ins for the actual risk-free rate. You can approximate the real risk-free rate by deducting the expected inflation rate from the nominal yield on these bonds.
- **Cash or Cash Equivalents:** Cash or cash equivalents, like money market funds or bank savings accounts, may be used as stand-ins for the risk-free rate for extremely short investment horizons.

6.3.6. Limitations of Risk-Free Rate

Despite its validity and significance in financial analysis, the risk-free rate has a few drawbacks that analysts and investors should be aware of.

- The return an investor can obtain without assuming any risk is represented by the risk-free rate, which is based on the assumption of risk neutrality. But in actuality, even with extremely tiny amounts of risk, all investments carry some level of risk. Consider how unpredictable circumstances can lead to the downfall of even the biggest governments globally.
- Additionally, monetary policy decisions, economic conditions, and investor sentiment all have an impact on the risk-free rate. The risk-free rate may fluctuate over time due to changes in these factors, making it challenging to use it as a reliable benchmark for long-term financial analysis. Furthermore, the real (inflation-adjusted) risk-free rate may be lower than the nominal rate as inflation gradually reduces the purchasing power of money.
- The risk-free rate differs for different currencies and nations. There's a chance that the risk-free rate in Russia and the United States are not the same. This is a reflection of variations in geopolitical risk, monetary policy, and economic conditions. The riskiness of particular markets or geographic areas might not be accurately reflected by using a single risk-free rate for all nations.
- Finally, some risk-free rate proxies, such as the ones mentioned above, might not accurately represent liquidity risk. Liquidity in these markets may dry up during periods of market stress or financial crises. This implies that there may be some volatility in the risk-free rate as well as a potential sharp increase in the price of these goods and a corresponding significant decrease in the rate of return.

The theoretical rate of return that an investor would anticipate on a risk-free investment is known as the risk-free rate of return. A higher rate of return is required for any investment with a risk level higher than zero. In reality, there is never a 100% rate of return because all investments involve some risk, no matter how tiny.

6.4. BOND PRICE-INTEREST RATE RELATION

Bond prices and interest rates frequently move in opposing directions. Bond prices typically decrease when interest rates rise and vice versa.

6.4.1. The Inverse Relationship

The inverse relationship between bond prices and interest rates is one of the key ideas to understand in the bond market. Bond prices decrease when interest rates rise and vice versa. The bond's price is determined by a number of variables, such as the current interest rates, the yield curve, the maturity date, and inflation expectations. But why does this happen? Interest rates rise because borrowing gets more expensive. This makes existing bonds with lower yields less appealing, which drives down the price of those bonds. On the other hand, current bonds with higher yields become more desirable and increase in value when interest rates decline. This dynamic shows how interest rate changes directly affect bond pricing in addition to the yield curve's and other economic indicators' effects.

- **Interest Rates Rise, Bond Prices Fall:** Let's say you have a bond with a 5% coupon rate. Your older bond loses appeal if new bonds with a 6% coupon are issued as a result of rising interest rates. If you issue a bond that pays less interest than newly issued bonds, investors won't pay you the full amount. The price of your bond will therefore decrease because you will need to offer it at a discount in order to sell it.
- **Interest Rates Fall, Bond Prices Rise:** On the other hand, your bond becomes more desirable if interest rates fall to 4% and you own one that pays a 5% coupon. Your bond's price will increase because investors are willing to pay more for it.

6.4.2. Factors Influencing Bond Prices and Interest Rates

Interest rates and bond prices are influenced by a number of factors.

By setting the federal funds rate, among other monetary policies, the central bank has a significant impact on bond yields and interest rates. The Federal Open Market Committee (FOMC) of the Federal Reserve sets this rate, which has a direct effect on short-term interest rates and, consequently, on bond yields and prices. The central bank's position on inflation may be indicated by shifts in the federal funds rate, which could have an impact on investor expectations and market dynamics. An important economic indicator that has a big impact on interest rates and bond prices is the yield curve. Investors' expectations for future inflation, economic growth, and interest rates are reflected in its shape. The yield curve can change from normal to flat or inverted, which can affect how investors perceive the risk and return on bonds and affect market pricing and demand.

- **Economic Policies:** Central banks: the Federal Reserve in the United States, the Reserve Bank of India, etc., as part of their monetary policy, regulate the short-term interest rates. They seek to manage economic growth, stabilize the currency, and rein in inflation—all of which have an impact on bond prices—by changing these rates.
- **Inflation Expectations:** Interest rates are directly impacted by inflation. Central banks may raise interest rates in an effort to curb spending and reduce inflation if an increase in inflation is predicted. Rising interest rates drive down the price of existing bonds with lower rates by making new bonds more profitable with higher yields.
- **Market Demand:** Bond prices and interest rates are also influenced by demand. For instance, low yields on government bonds are frequently the result of strong demand from investors who are prepared to forgo higher returns in exchange for the security and dependability of these bonds.

6.4.3. Real-World Example: The Impact of Global Events

Interest rates and bond prices can be significantly impacted by world events. For example, interest rates fell everywhere in the world during economic uncertainty like the COVID-19 pandemic. It is crucial to examine the current status of the bond market, paying particular attention to recent trends and expert insights that shed light on the dynamics of the current financial environment. Bonds issued prior to the pandemic experienced a sudden surge in value due to their higher interest rates.

6.4.4. Current State of the Bond Market

Current interest rates have a big impact on bond yield trends; they reflect how the economy as a whole is responding to inflation and the Federal Reserve's policy decisions. The bond market is experiencing notable volatility in 2023, which can be attributed to the post-pandemic global economic recovery as well as the disparate monetary policies of central banks worldwide. Bond prices respond inversely to yield expectations on the secondary market, which highlights the real-time effects of interest rate movements. For instance, changes in the Reserve Bank of India's (RBI) repo rate have a direct impact on bond prices and interest rates, and the Indian bond market has responded to these changes with notable reactivity.

6.5. BOND ARBITRAGE

By assuming opposing positions in the market, an investor employing a fixed-income arbitrage strategy can profit from minor price differences while mitigating interest rate risk. As a market-neutral strategy, fixed-income arbitrage aims to make money whether the future trends of the bond market as a whole are positive or negative. The main users of fixed-income arbitrage are investment banks and hedge funds. These funds monitor a variety of fixed-income securities, such as municipal bonds, corporate bonds, government bonds, mortgage-backed securities (MBS), and even more intricate securities like credit default swaps (CDS). Fixed-income arbitrage funds take leveraged long and short positions when there are indications of mispricing in the same or similar issues in order to profit when the market corrects the pricing. The plan calls for taking a short position on the security that looks to be undervalued and a long position on the issue that seems to be overpriced. It is anticipated that even if both of these prices move in opposite directions, the difference between them should narrow and they will eventually approach each other more closely. This strategy presents two primary challenges: first, these securities must be sufficiently liquid; second, the fixed-income securities selected for arbitrage must be sufficiently similar in kind. It will be challenging for traders to profit from a timely narrowing of the price difference in the absence of these two prerequisites.

Risks exist even in basic fixed-income arbitrage transactions. The likelihood that market pricing is inaccurate for a given type of fixed-income security largely depends on the model that is being used to assess the instruments. Models can be incorrect and have been in the past, especially those that deal with bonds issued by businesses and developing economies. A lot of investors still remember Long-Term Capital Management's (LTCM) collapse. LTCM was one of the first funds to engage in fixed-income arbitrage. The strategy's reputation as "picking up nickels in front of a steamroller"—the risks can be crippling and the returns are small—is explained by its association with long-term capital management. As the returns created from closing these pricing gaps are small, fixed-income arbitrage is a strategy for well-capitalized institutional investors. Individual investors are unable to access the levels of leverage required to make meaningful trades.

Fixed-income arbitrage is typically marketed as a capital preservation strategy by funds that use it. Apart from the required capital for engaging in fixed-income arbitrage, there exists an additional obstacle that potential investors must overcome. Opportunities get harder to find, smaller in size, and shorter in duration as more capital is committed to locating and profiting from fixed-income arbitrage. Fixed-income arbitrage fluctuates between times when it is underutilized and extremely profitable and times when it is overused and barely profitable because the market seldom stays at an ideal level for an extended period of time.

6.5.1. Fixed-Income Arbitrage Strategies in the Market

6.5.1.1. Swap Spread Arbitrage

An interest-rate swap is a derivative used in the fixed-income markets that swaps the cash flows from a fixed-rate loan (a fixed-income security) for cash flows from a floating-rate loan (Smith Clifford, Smithson Charles, & Lee Macdonald Wakeman, 1988). The group receiving the fixed-rate (E.g., receiving the fixed-rate on a Treasury Bond), better known as the Yield to Maturity Swap Rate ('YTMsr'), pays the floating Bank Bill Swap Rate ('BBSW'). The net payment to the arbitrageur for each time period is equal to the YTMsr – BBSW, which is then multiplied by the notional principal amount (E.g., A$10,000) as well as the intervals in between payments (E.g., six months) (Scholes Myron, & Pedersen Lasse Heje, 2015). The group paying the fixed-rate, which is the owner of the Treasury bond financed at the repurchased rate, will also receive a fixed-coupon on the yield to maturity (E.g., yield to maturity of the treasury bond), whilst paying interest on the repurchase agreement, known as repo financing. The yield to maturity on the Treasury bond less the swap's fixed rate is known as the swap spread.

Swap Spread = Yield to Maturity of Swap – Yield to Maturity of Treasury Bond

This equation typically yields a positive result. Given that the swap's floating rate is the BBSW, we can infer that it will be higher than the Treasury Bond's yield to maturity because it typically exceeds the repurchase rate. This is because the Treasury Bond's repurchase rate ought to be higher because the BBSW is used as a benchmark for the pricing of AUD derivatives and securities.

6.5.1.2. Yield Curve Arbitrage

Taking long and short positions at various points along the yield curve is known as yield curve arbitrage. This technique entails locating pricing mismatch points on the yield curve, which lead to either rich or cheap points. Investors will bet on the curvature's reversion by re-modeling the bond to identify points at which its actual yield deviates from the yield implied by the model. Once this has been determined, the investor will try to take advantage of the yield curve's rich or cheap spots by selling or buying bonds. These investments will be held by them until the trade converges, at which point it can be sold for a profit. The investor is hedging their investments by taking both long-term and short-term positions on the yield curve. An illustration of this would be placing a wager against a government bond and simultaneously purchasing two bonds to hedge against the wager (Karsimus, 2015).

6.5.1.3. Mortgage Arbitrage

Fixed-income traders use the mortgage arbitrage strategy to trade securities known as mortgage-backed securities (MBSs). MBSs are securities made up of a collection of mortgages guaranteed by an agency and secured by real estate. In this instance, an agency is when the principal has engaged the agent to carry out a task on their behalf; in the instance of MBSs, the agent for the security may be a bank. In the case of MBSs, collateralization would be the sale of the real estate assets to cover the loan losses. Collateralization is the process of using an asset's value to secure a loan, allowing the loan issuer to seize the asset in the event of a default (Cerqueiro Geraldo, Ongena Steven, & Roszbach Kasper, 2016).

By way of securitization, the collection of mortgages that the group possesses, e.g., a bank, bundled into an MBS, and subsequently offered for sale as units or certificates to investors. "Pass-through security" refers to this method of transferring the group of mortgages to the investor (Tanner Glenn & Tanner Glen, 2004). After the original financial institution and the current owner of the security, the cash flows from the mortgages, net of the commissions collected from the mortgage originator, are transferred. In other words, the security's current owner gets paid their portion of the total mortgage payments, which includes principal and interest. In contrast to bonds, which normally only pay interest and return the principal at the end of the tenor, mortgage pass-throughs include both interest and principal with each cashflow (Duarte Jefferson, Longstaff Francis, & Fan Yu, 2007). The fact that each cashflow's payments change over time as the principal is lowered is another significant distinction; as a result, the amount of interest earned on each cashflow will decrease as the principal's capital decreases (Yu Fan, 2006). Because the security is self-liquidating, the investment is finished as soon as the mortgages on the MBSs are settled. Instead of concentrating on capital gains, this strategy aims to provide traders with income (Dunnan Nancy, 1989).

When using the mortgage arbitrage strategy, the trader shorts government bonds or swaps to reduce interest rate risk while investing in long-term MBSs. This is an attempt to capitalize on the yield differential between government bonds and MBS. The overall risk posed by the assets they are secured by is the reason MBSs typically have higher yields. Default risk is what this is. An adverse effect of low interest rates is MBSs. Lower interest rates enable homeowners to make larger prepayments, which shortens the loan's maturity and principal, earning less interest from the asset. Conversely, higher interest rates have a negative impact on mortgage-backed securities (MBS) by affecting homeowners' ability to make mortgage payments, thereby raising the risk of default. Finally, there may be liquidity risks associated with the strategy. An instance of heightened liquidity risk could arise in an environment where a crisis transpired (E.g., the Great Financial Crisis in 2008), when market liquidity starts to decline and lending becomes more challenging for people or organizations.

6.5.1.4. Volatility Arbitrage

The goal of fixed-income volatility arbitrage is to make money by taking advantage of price discrepancies between the implied volatility of options based on the same asset and the projected future price-volatility of fixed income securities. Using this strategy, the arbitrageur must determine whether the implied volatility of a security is overpriced or underpriced, much like in the case of determining the true price of a stock. As an illustration, consider a situation where a stock option is significantly underpriced due to an asset's low implied volatility. The arbitrageur would then decide to open a long call option in addition to a short position in the underlying stock in order to profit from the mispricing.

6.5.1.5. Capital Structure Arbitrage

A popular financial tactic used worldwide is capital structure arbitrage, which aims to make money off of mispricings in the market for security classes that are issued by a single company. The mispricing of these securities is where arbitrageurs try to make their money. Similar to other arbitrage strategies, these mispricings happen when an arbitrageur purchases undervalued securities and sells overpriced securities. The purpose of this strategy is to make money off of the mispricing of a company's other securities and debt. When utilizing this tactic, arbitrageurs frequently gauge the richness and affordability of credit default swap spreads using a structural model. Based on a Company's debt and other securities, the structure model is intended to determine the fair value of such credit default swap spreads (CDS spread). The arbitrageur must determine whether the market misprices the equity value of the CDS market and is not generating fair prices if the model shows that the current market CDS spread differs significantly from the spread that was predicted distinct mispricing scenarios, the arbitrageur will try to make money by spotting these mispricings, selling credit protection, delta-hedging it by selling short delta equities, and waiting for convergence to happen in both cases. The equity position can offset the loss on the CDS position if either the CDS spread widens or the equity price rises, assuming that CDS bid-ask spreads and equity prices move in the same direction [Marra, Miriam, 2017]. In the same way, the equity position's loss can be mitigated by the CDS position. If the spread on the CDS is significantly less than the spread predicted by the structured model, one would purchase delta shares to hedge the position and obtain credit protection.

6.6. INTEREST RATE SENSITIVITY OF BONDS

The analysis of fixed income security price fluctuations to shifts in the market interest rate is known as interest rate sensitivity. The price fluctuations of the security increase with its interest rate sensitivity.

6.6.1. Understanding Interest Rate Sensitivity

One of the main asset classes accessible to investors is fixed income. Through price appreciation and the interest (coupon) rate, investors profit from fixed income. Fixed income coupon payments are determined by market interest rate changes, whereas price fluctuations are the direct result of such changes. The primary market is where fixed income securities are created and first offered for sale. Investors then have the option of selling the fixed income security on the secondary market or holding it until it matures. Interest rate risk is the result of the fixed income price's negative correlation with the market interest rate. Coupon bonds are sold at par value at the time of issuance, with the interest rate determined by the market. The coupon payments on the bond are set for the duration of the loan after it is issued, but the market interest rate is always changing. The prices of outstanding fixed-income securities decrease when the market interest rate rises because newly issued fixed-income securities will pay larger coupon payments. Conversely, since outstanding fixed income securities have larger coupon payments than recently issued fixed income securities, their prices increase in the event that the market interest rate falls.

Thus, while choosing fixed-income securities, it becomes crucial to comprehend interest rate sensitivity. Interest rate sensitivity of a security is influenced by a few factors, including:

- **Maturity Length:** The interest rate sensitivity of the security increases with maturity. This is due to the increased interest rate risk associated with longer-term securities.
- **Coupon Rate:** Because it will bear more interest rate risk, a security with a lower coupon rate will be more sensitive to changes in interest rates.

6.6.2. How Interest Rate Sensitivity Works

Interest rates and fixed-income securities have an inverse relationship. As a result, fixed-income securities' prices typically decline as interest rates rise. Interest rate sensitivity, when used to compute fixed income securities, is referred to as the asset's duration.

This is one method of figuring out how interest rates impact a portfolio of fixed-income securities. A bond or bond fund is more susceptible to changes in interest rates the longer it has been in existence. Investors can gauge a fixed-income security's sensitivity to future changes in interest rates by looking at its duration. Because duration takes into account a variety of bond characteristics, including coupon payments and maturity, it is a useful indicator of interest rate sensitivity. In general, an asset's sensitivity to changes in interest rates increases with its maturity. Bond and fixed-income traders closely monitor changes in interest rates because the ensuing price fluctuations impact the securities' total yield. Investors can protect their fixed-income portfolios from fluctuations in short-term interest rates by comprehending the concept of duration.

6.6.3. Types of Interest Rate Sensitivity

The interest-rate sensitivity of a fixed-income security can be ascertained using four commonly used duration measurements: the Macaulay duration, modified duration, effective duration, and key rate duration. Certain metrics, such as the time to maturity, remaining cash flows, required yield, cash flow payment, par value, and bond price, must be known in order to calculate the Macaulay duration. The yield to maturity (YTM) component is incorporated into the modified duration, which is a modified Macaulay duration calculation. It calculates the amount that the duration would alter for every percentage point that the yield changed. Bonds with embedded options have their duration determined by the effective duration. It calculates the approximate bond price decline in the event that interest rates suddenly increase by 1%. The duration of a fixed-income security or fixed-income portfolio at a given yield curve maturity is determined by the key rate duration.

6.6.4. Example of Interest Rate Sensitivity

The effective duration is one commonly used metric to assess interest rate sensitivity. Take a bond mutual fund, for instance, that has 100 bonds in it that have an average duration of nine years and an average effective duration of 11 years. Based on its effective duration, the bond fund is thus expected to lose 11% of its value if interest rates rise by 1.0% instantaneously. Similarly, a trader may examine a specific corporate bond that has a maturity of six months and a duration of 2.5. The trader can anticipate a 1.25% increase in bond price if interest rates drop by 0.5%.

6.7. LEVERAGE

The idea of using borrowed capital as a funding source is known as financial leverage. When companies invest in themselves for expansions, acquisitions, or other growth strategies, they frequently use leverage. Leverage is another investment strategy that raises the possible return on an investment by using borrowed funds, more precisely, the use of different financial instruments or borrowed capital.

6.7.1. Understanding Financial Leverage

Using debt or borrowed funds to fund an investment or project is known as leverage. It is frequently applied to increase the equity base of an entity. Companies and investors both use the concept of leverage:

- Leverage is a tool used by investors to dramatically raise the possible returns on their investments. They use a variety of tools, such as margin accounts, futures, and options, to leverage their investments.
- Businesses can finance their assets by using leverage. Put another way, rather than issuing stock to raise money, businesses can use debt financing to invest in operations and drive growth.

There are many ways for investors to obtain leverage indirectly if they feel uncomfortable using it directly. They can make investments in businesses that finance or expand operations through leverage in the regular course of business without having to increase their outlay. The purpose and outcome of financial leverage is to increase a project's possible returns. Leverage will also increase the possible downside risk in the event that the investment is a failure. A company, piece of real estate, or investment is said to be highly leveraged if it has more debt than equity.

6.7.2. Risk

Leverage can increase profits as long as the asset's returns exceed the cost of borrowing, but it can also increase losses. During a downturn in the economy, a company that takes on excessive debt may fail or go bankrupt, whereas a less leveraged company may be able to make it. If a stock drops 20%, an investor purchasing it on a 50% margin will lose 40% of their investment. Additionally, the party in question might not be able to reimburse the substantial overall loss that was suffered. Risk could be influenced by how volatile the collateral assets' values are. Brokers may request more money if the value of the securities they are holding drops. When the value of real estate drops below the principal amount of the debt, banks may decide not to renew mortgages. Loans may be called in even if cash flows and profits are enough to cover the continuing costs of borrowing.

There is an implicit assumption in that account, however, which is that the underlying leveraged asset is the same as the unleveraged one. This implies that when the market price declines, leverage increases in proportion to the updated equity value, increasing losses as the prices drop further. This can quickly result in financial disaster because, even in cases where the underlying asset value decline is slight or transient, the debt financing may only be short-term and therefore require immediate repayment. Negotiating the terms of leverage, holding onto unused capacity for further borrowing, and leveraging only liquid assets that can be quickly turned into cash are ways to reduce the risk. But that account makes an implicit assumption that the underlying leveraged asset and the unleveraged asset are the same. In the event that a business takes out a loan to finance modernization, product line expansion, or international expansion, the additional trading profit from increased diversification may exceed the additional risk from leverage. Alternatively, an investor may experience the same volatility and expected return as one who invests the majority of their portfolio in low-risk money market funds and uses the remainder to margin stock index futures, which carries a higher degree of risk. This is known as an unlevered low-risk equity-index fund. Alternatively, the matching and off-setting economic leverage may reduce overall risk levels if a pairs-trading stock strategy holds both long and short positions (Bartram Söhnke, Brown Gregory, & Waller William, 2015).

It is not always the case that a company or investment with leverage is riskier than one without it, even though adding leverage to a particular asset always increases risk. Actually, compared to unlevered bond funds, many highly leveraged hedge funds have lower return volatility. Additionally, equities from heavily indebted, low-risk public utilities are typically less hazardous than those from unlevered, high-risk technology companies.

6.7.3. Financial Leverage Calculation

To determine how much debt a business is leveraging in an effort to maximize profits, a variety of leverage financial ratios are available. These are a few typical leverage ratios.

6.7.3.1. Debt Ratio

By figuring out a company's debt to asset ratio, you can assess its leverage. This ratio shows how much of its assets are generated by debt. A company that has a high debt ratio has likely financed its assets primarily through leverage. A ratio of 1:0 indicates that there is $1 in debt for every $1 in assets held by the company. It has more assets than debt if it is less than 1.0; if it is greater than 1.0, it has more debt than assets.

$$\text{Debt Ratio} = \text{Total Debt} \div \text{Total Assets}$$

Remember that all debt, including both short- and long-term debt vehicles, is used to compute the ratio.

6.7.3.2. Debt-to-Equity (D/E) Ratio

One way to quantify leverage is to look only at the way assets have been financed, as opposed to the company's assets. A comparison between the amount borrowed by the company and the amount raised from shareholders or private investors is made using the debt-to-equity (D/E) ratio.

$$\text{Debt-to-Equity (D/E) Ratio} = \text{Total Debt} \div \text{Total Equity}$$

A company has more debt than equity if its D/E ratio is higher than 1.0. This does not, however, imply that a business is highly leveraged. Every business and sector usually operates differently, which could mean a different ratio. For instance, fledgling technology businesses frequently have to turn to private investors in order to obtain funding. Consequently, a debt-to-equity ratio of.5—that is, one debt for every two equity—might still be regarded as high for this sector of the economy.

6.7.3.3. Debt-to-EBITDA Ratio

By utilizing its Earnings Before Income Tax, Depreciation, and Amortization (EBITDA), you can also evaluate a company's debt in relation to the amount of income it produces over a specific time period. The amount of income available to pay off debt before these operating expenses are subtracted from income is shown by the debt-to-EBITDA ratio. A business that has a high debt-to-EBITDA ratio has a lot of debt relative to its revenue. More leverage indicates a higher debt-to-EBITDA ratio for the company.

Debt-to-EBITDA Ratio = Debt ÷ Earnings Before Interest, Taxes, Depreciation, and Amortization

The fact that EBITDA isn't a true representation of earnings is a problem with using it. This is due to the fact that it excludes necessary expenses. Some businesses use this non-GAAP metric to give the impression of greater profitability.

6.7.3.4. Equity Multiplier

Since total assets and total equity are directly correlated with total debt, debt is implicitly included in the equity multiplier even though it is not taken into account explicitly. The equity multiplier looks at how assets have been financed in an effort to determine a company's ownership weight. A business that has a low equity multiplier is not highly leveraged because a significant amount of its assets have been financed with equity.

Equity Multiplier = Total Assets ÷ Total Equity

The equity multiplier is a tool used in DuPont analysis to quantify financial leverage. The equity multiplier can be computed by dividing the total assets of a company by the total equity. To calculate the return on equity, multiply the total financial leverage by the total turnover of assets and the profit margin.

For instance, the equity multiplier is 2.0 ($500 million ÷ $250 million) if a publicly traded company has $500 million in total assets and $250 million in shareholder equity.

This indicates that equity has been used to finance half of the company's total assets. However, its equity multiplier would be 5.0 if its assets totaled $500 million and its equity was $100 million. Therefore, higher equity multipliers imply that more research is necessary as there may be a greater use of financial leverage.

6.7.3.5. Degree of Financial Leverage (DFL)

Additionally, the degree of financial leverage (DFL) ratio is useful for fundamental analysts. The DFL is computed by dividing the percentage change in a company's earnings before interest and taxes (EBIT) over a given period by the percentage change in its earnings per share (EPS).

Degree of Financial Leverage = % Change in Earnings Per Share ÷ % Change in EBIT

Determining how responsive an organization's earnings per share (EPS) is to variations in operating income is the aim of DFL. A company with a high DFL is probably going to have more volatile earnings; a higher ratio will indicate a higher level of leverage.

6.7.3.6. Consumer Leverage Ratio

The aforementioned formulas are used to assess how much leverage a business uses in its operations. Households, however, can also employ leverage. Households can also use leverage by taking out debt and using their personal income to pay interest charges. The calculation of Consumer Leverage involves dividing the debt of a household by its disposable income. Families with higher computed consumer leverage are highly leveraged because they have higher debt-to-income ratios.

Consumer Leverage = Total Household Debt ÷ Disposable Income

If a consumer's consumer leverage rises too high, they may eventually have trouble getting loans. Lenders, for instance, frequently impose debt-to-income ceilings on households applying for mortgage loans. Financial ratios are most valuable when compared to competitors or over an extended period of time. When comparing the leverage ratios of different companies, keep in mind that different financing arrangements may be appropriate for different industries.

6.7.4. Advantages and Disadvantages of Financial Leverage

- **Advantages:** Some traders and investors use leverage to increase profits. When additional upfront capital is added to your initial investment, trades can become exponentially more profitable. Leverage also gives you access to more costly investment options that a small initial capital contribution would not normally allow. When large amounts of capital are required in short-term, low-risk scenarios, leverage works best. For instance, a growth company may have a short-term capital requirement during acquisitions or buyouts, creating a solid mid-to-long-term growth opportunity. Rather than taking on more debt to fund reckless ventures, astute businesses use leverage to seize opportunities when they present themselves with the goal of rapidly reducing their leveraged position.
- **Disadvantages:** Losses from investments can also be increased with leverage. Leverage can increase downside risk significantly and occasionally lead to losses larger than your initial capital investment. Furthermore, fees, premiums, and margin rates are frequently levied by brokers and contract traders, who also mandate that you keep a margin account open with a certain balance. This implies that you will still be responsible for additional fees even if your trade ends in a loss. The potential drawback of leverage is its complexity. When taking a leveraged position, investors need to be mindful of both the risks associated with it and their current financial situation. This might mean paying closer attention to one's portfolio and contributing more money if the trading account doesn't have enough money in it to meet the broker's minimum requirements.

6.7.5. Example of Financial Leverage

Imagine a business that was founded with investors contributing $5 million. The money that the business can use to run is this equity. The company will have $25 million to invest in business operations and more chances to boost value for shareholders if it uses debt financing and borrows $20 million. Nonetheless, the debt-to-equity ratio would be elevated. An industry's high ratio may or may not be expected given its average ratios and industry. These kinds of positions with significant leverage happen often. For instance, Apple (AAPL) has sold $4.77 billion in Green Bonds since 2016. Apple could use debt financing to increase carbon-free aluminum production and open up recycling opportunities. When bond issuance generates more revenue than debt, this kind of leverage strategy may be effective.

6.8. FORWARD RATES

To put it simply, the forward rate is the estimated yield on a bond that will, in theory, occur in the near future, typically a few months (or even years) from the time of calculation. Almost exclusively, when discussing the purchase of Treasury bills, or T-bills, the forward rate is taken into account.

6.8.1. Exploring the Forward Rate

One of two metrics can be used to determine the forward rate:

1. **Yield Curve:** The correlation between the interest rates on different maturities of government bonds.
2. **Spot Rates:** The yield on a zero-coupon Treasury security that is assumed.

The forward rate is not as frequently determined using spot rates. The yield curve makes the current bond prices and interest rates very evident. It goes above and beyond that, offering plausible predictions for future interest rates based on market assumptions. The yield curve's characteristics make it an almost ideal metric for figuring out the forward rate.

6.8.2. Significance of the Forward Rate

Examine the following example to gain a better understanding of the forward rate's application and importance. A person wishes to purchase a Treasury security with a one-year maturity. Next, two fundamental investment options are presented to them:

- Acquire a T-bill with a six-month maturity period, followed by another T-bill with a similar maturity period.

-or-

- Invest in a single 12-month or 1-year-dated T-bill.

Because interest rates could fluctuate between buying the first and second six-month maturity T-bills, the received yield on the first option might be more erratic. If there was a guarantee that interest rates would remain unchanged, the person would probably choose their option without second thought. In actuality, though, interest rates might change if the investor rolls over their first T-bill investment into a second. The person would obviously profit more from choosing option number one, which involves purchasing one T-bill first, then a second, if rates were higher. On the other hand, six-month T-bill rates may also decrease. In that scenario, opting for the second option, which involved buying a single one-year T-Bill, would have resulted in a higher total yield for the investor. It can be useful to look at the forward rate in order to determine the best course of action in this situation—that is, the course of action most likely to yield the highest yield for the investor. Once more, this is just an estimate of the interest rate that will probably be in effect six months after the investor makes their first purchase of T-bills.

It should be noted that while the forward rate is most frequently applied to T-bills, it can also be computed for securities with longer maturities. However, the estimate of future interest rates is likely to be less accurate the further into the future one looks.

6.8.3. Using the Forward Rate

An investor has three options for calculating the forward rate: simple, yearly compounded, or continuously compounded rates. The interest rate computations will vary slightly from one another. The person must decide which calculation, in their opinion, is the most accurate at that specific moment. Whichever version is used, it is useful to know the forward rate because it allows the investor to select the investment option (purchasing one or two T-bills) that yields the highest likely profit. The computation itself is quite intricate. Thankfully, investors can easily find the current projected forward rate by contacting their brokerage firm or financial advisor, or by visiting any of the numerous websites that provide financial information. Remember that the forward rate is just the market's best guess as to what interest rates will probably be at a given future date. As a result, it's possible that the current estimated forward rate is inaccurate. An investor must ultimately determine whether they think the rate estimate is reliable or whether they think interest rates are likely to be higher or lower than the estimated forward rate when making investment decisions in which the forward rate is a factor to take into account. However, examining the rate at least gives the investor a solid foundation upon which to choose their investment.

CASE STUDY

PROVIDED FIXED INCOME RESEARCH TO IDENTIFY INVESTMENT OPPORTUNITIES FOR A TOP ASSET MANAGEMENT FIRM

Fixed income research services by Outsource2india successfully helped a top asset management firm to identify viable investment opportunities in the volatile international debt markets.

- **The Client:** The client is one of the biggest names in South America, with over 20 years of experience in Asset Management. The client specializes in discretionary mandates, investment funds, as well as advisory services and offers lucrative long-term financial options to their customers. Based out of Sao Paulo, Brazil, the client focuses on finding investment opportunities and monitoring risk tolerance to ensure investments are self-sustainable and profitable.
- **Requirements & Challenges:** The client has extensive experience in investments and credit analysis but needed a qualified and scalable offshore financial research team to support fixed income analysis and report viable investment opportunities in international debt markets. The research involved analyzing corporate financial reports of several organizations that offer bonds and securities. The research reports needed to be updated on real-time basis to avoid changes in the investment scenario, and help the client direct funds for a risk-free investment.
- **Solution:** Outsource2india delivered a pilot program to ensure the quality of our financial research activities met their expectations. As the project required real-time information sharing, we deployed two full-time financial analysts with 15 years of combined research experience. The client deliveries included a list of financial agencies, banks, and other organizations who offer bonds for fixed income investment opportunities. Our dedicated analysts conducted research on those organizations based on the criteria charted by the Service Level Agreements (SLA) to ensure accurate research outcomes.

  Outsource2india conducted Earnings before Interest, Depreciation and Amortization (EBIDA) research, gross debt, net debt, and current capitalization in global currencies to provide the client with simplified financial research reports. O2I also provided updates on company factsheets at the earliest to help the client take quicker decisions. The fixed income analysis reports included Excel sheets and PDFs, which were delivered through secured file and data sharing system.
- **The Outsource2india Advantag**e: Outsource2india is a forerunner in the field of financial research services. We provide tailor-made research reports within

the stipulated time to match client requirements. Our global delivery locations and staff availability across different time zones ensure quick turnaround time. Over the years, our analysts have provided fixed income research services to clients from various industry segments and are familiar with leading market regulations and global economic changes.

CLASS ACTIVITY

WOULD YOU GIVE YOURSELF A LOAN?

Typically, people think they are great candidates for a loan, whether it's a car loan, a personal loan, or mortgage loan. This activity forces students to flip the conversation and discuss what it would take for them to give a loan to someone else or even themselves, especially if their own money or livelihood were on the line. Break your students into small groups of 3–4 members. Assign one group member to act as a bank while the remaining group members act as loan applicants. Once roles have been assigned, tell your students that are acting as bank employees to conduct interviews of loan applicants to determine who they would and would not give a loan to (Students should have the option of using authentic answers or creating a different financial "persona"). Some key components to consider while bankers are interviewing their applicants include:

- **Does the Applicant Have Verifiable Income?** Applicants should be prepared to provide ways to verify income.
- **What Other Proof Would You Need of the Borrower's Ability to Repay?** Ask bankers to decide if income is enough to determine this as well as list what other factors (debts, for example) play a role and why.
- **What Is the Loan for and Who Does the Applicant Owe?** Bankers should ask questions to determine the reason for a loan. This will constitute good and bad reasons for a loan.

SUMMARY

- Fixed-Income securities are debt instruments that pay a fixed amount of interest, in the form of coupon payments, to investors. The interest payments are commonly distributed semiannually, and the principal is returned to the investor at maturity. Bonds are the most common form of fixed-income securities.
- Bonds are assigned different credit ratings based on the financial viability of the issuer. Credit ratings are part of a grading system performed by credit-rating agencies. These agencies measure the creditworthiness of corporate and government bonds and the entity's ability to repay these loans. Credit ratings are helpful to investors because they define the risks involved in investing.
- A bond market is a marketplace for debt securities. This market covers both government-issued and corporate-issued debt securities. It allows capital to be transferred from savers or investors to issuers who want funds for projects or other operations.
- The risk-free rate of return is the theoretical rate of return of an investment with zero risk. The risk-free rate represents the interest an investor would expect from an absolutely risk-free investment over a specified period of time.
- Interest rates and bonds often move in opposite directions. When rates rise, bond prices usually fall, and vice versa.
- Fixed-income arbitrage is primarily used by hedge funds and investment banks. These funds watch a range of fixed-income instruments, including mortgage-backed securities (MBS), government bonds, corporate bonds, municipal bonds, and even more complex instruments like credit default swaps (CDS).
- Interest rate sensitivity is the analysis of fixed income security price fluctuations to changes in the market interest rate. The higher the security's interest rate sensitivity, the greater the price fluctuations.
- When the market interest rate increases, the outstanding fixed-income security prices depreciate because newly issued fixed-income securities will pay higher coupon payments. Vice versa, if the market interest rate decreases, the outstanding fixed income prices appreciate because its coupon payments are higher than newly issued fixed income securities.
- Financial leverage is the concept of using borrowed capital as a funding source. Leverage is often used when businesses invest in themselves for expansions, acquisitions, or other growth methods. Leverage is also an investment strategy that uses borrowed money—specifically, the use of various financial instruments or borrowed capital—to increase the potential return of an investment.
- The forward rate, in simple terms, is the calculated expectation of the yield on a bond that, theoretically, will occur in the immediate future, usually a few months (or even a few years) from the time of calculation.

REVIEW QUESTIONS

1. What are fixed-income securities?
2. Give an example of a fixed-income.
3. What are the risks of investing in fixed-income instruments?
4. What happens to fixed-income securities when the stock market crashes?
5. What is the yield on fixed income securities? How is it different from yield to maturity?
6. What is the impact of inflation on fixed income securities?
7. What are floating rate securities, and how do they differ from fixed-rate securities?
8. What is the institutional use of bond markets?
9. How is bond price related to interest rate?
10. How is financial leverage calculated?

REFERENCES

1. Bartram, S. M., Brown, G. W., & Waller, W. (2015). How important is financial risk? *Journal of Financial and Quantitative Analysis, 50*(4), 801–824. https://doi.org/10.1017/S0022109015000216.
2. Cerqueiro, G., Ongena, S., & Roszbach, K. (2016). Collateralization, bank loan rates, and monitoring. *The Journal of Finance, 71*(3), 1295–1322. https://doi.org/10.1111/jofi.12214.
3. Duarte, J., Longstaff, F. A., & Yu, F. (2007). Risk and return in fixed-income arbitrage: Nickels in front of a steamroller? *The Review of Financial Studies, 20*(3), 769–811. https://doi.org/10.1093/rfs/hhl026.
4. Dunnan, N. (1989). Mortgage-backed securities. *ABA Journal, 75*(4), 108–109. https://www.jstor.org/stable/20760449.
5. Fabozzi, V. K. (2012). *The Handbook of Fixed Income Securities* (7th ed.). New York: Kvrv. ISBN 978-0-07-144099-8.
6. Karsimus. (2015). Yield curve arbitrage in the EUR swap rates market replicating the strategies of quantitative arbitrageurs. Aalto University School of Business. Retrieved from: https://urn.fi/URN:NBN:fi:aalto-201512165791 (accessed on 16 July 2024).
7. Marra, M. (2017). Explaining co-movements between equity and CDS bid-ask spreads. *Review of Quantitative Finance and Accounting, 49*(3), 811–853. https://doi.org/10.1007/s11156-016-0609-6.
8. Scholes, M., & Pedersen, L. H. (2015). Fixed-income arbitrage. In *Efficiently Inefficient* (pp. 241–268). Princeton University Press. https://doi.org/10.2307/j.ctt1287knh.21.
9. Smith, C. W., Smithson, C. W., & Wakeman, L. M. (1988). The market for interest rate swaps. *Financial Management, 17*(4), 34–44. https://doi.org/10.2307/3665765.

10. Tanner, G. (2004). A simpler approach to mortgage-backed securities. *Journal of Financial Education, 30*, 75–86. https://www.jstor.org/stable/41948449 (accessed on 16 July 2024).

11. Yu, F. (2006). How profitable is capital structure arbitrage? *Financial Analysts Journal, 62*(5), 47–62. https://doi.org/10.2469/faj.v62.n5.4282.

CHAPTER

7 Valuing Stocks

LEARNING OBJECTIVES

After studying this chapter, you will be able to:

- Examine the introduction to stocks and shares
- Determine the fundamental analysis of stocks
- Find out the technical analysis of stocks
- Give an overview on stock valuation

KEY TERMS FROM THIS CHAPTER

Business venture
Conservatism
Financial leverage
Information technology
Open market
Portfolio management
Shareholder
Capital asset pricing model (CAPM)
Corporations
General meetings
Insurance policies
Ordinary shares
Rationalism
Stockholders

INTRODUCTION

Stock is a portion of the company's ownership. The claim to the company's assets and profits is represented by its stock. Stated differently, this implies that a larger ownership stake in the company results from holding more stock. A stock certificate, a record attesting to one's ownership interest in the business, represents the stock. A few years ago, the certificates were physically brought to the brokerage firm by the person wishing to buy or sell shares. However, with the advancement of information technology, this stock document is now electronically stored. Trading via a phone call or mouse click has now simplified the transaction process. In the event that there is no ownership claim over the company's assets and profits, the stock certificate is deemed worthless. The limited liability of stock is an additional significant feature. It implies that if the company is unable to pay its debts, the stockholder is exempt from liability. Having stock ensures that the owner will never lose personal assets, even in the event that the company files for bankruptcy (Jackson Thomas, 2001).

A company issues stock because it needs to raise capital. The company has two options for funding this: it can issue stock, or sell a portion of its business, or borrow money from banks or other financial institutions. These means of obtaining capital are referred to as debt financing. Stock issuance is referred to as equity financing. Since the company does not have to repay the money or pay interest, issuing stock is more advantageous. The only thing that the investors receive in exchange for their money is the expectation that the shares will increase in value over time. It should be understood that there is no assurance of principal safety or a consistent return when investing in individual stocks. While some businesses might pay dividends, others might not. The only way for an investor to profit in the absence of dividends is through open market appreciation. Risk does have benefits, even though it may also have drawbacks. A higher return on investment is correlated with increased risk. For this reason, it is reasonable to assume that stocks will perform better than other types of investments, like bonds and savings accounts.

7.1. INTRODUCTION TO STOCKS AND SHARES

A security that denotes ownership of a portion of the issuing company is called an equity, or stock. Shares, also known as units of stock, give the owner the right to a share of the company's assets and earnings in proportion to the number of shares they own. Stocks are the cornerstone of many individual investors' portfolios and are primarily bought and sold on stock exchanges. Regulations enforced by the government are designed to safeguard investors against deceptive activities in the stock market. Companies sell stock to raise money to run their operations. A shareholder may be entitled to a portion of the assets and profits of the company. Depending on how many shares an investor owns in relation to the total number of outstanding shares, they are regarded as owners of the issuing company. In the event that a business issues 1,000 shares of stock, and an individual owns 100 shares, they will own and be entitled to 10% of the business's assets and profits.

Although corporations are a unique kind of organization because they are recognized by the law as legal persons, stockholders do not own corporations. Corporations are able to own property, borrow money, file taxes, and face legal action. A corporation is thought of as a "person" when it comes to its assets. The corporation, not the shareholders, owns a corporate office furnished with desks and chairs. Liability is restricted for both the corporation and the shareholder because corporate property is legally distinct from shareholder property. A judge may order the sale of the company's entire asset portfolio in the event of bankruptcy, but a shareholder's assets are safe. Even though the value of your shares may have decreased, the court cannot order you to sell them. Similarly, in the event of a major shareholder's bankruptcy, the company's assets cannot be sold to satisfy their creditors. The terms "stocks" or "securities" refer to both publicly issued instruments of lending, such as debentures, and ownership, such as shares. A bond or debenture represents the smallest unit of lending, just as a share represents the smallest unit of ownership. Debentures and shares can be of different types.

A shareholder who owns ordinary shares assumes the maximum amount of entrepreneurial risk associated with a business venture as a fractional owner, represented by an ordinary share. There are various aspects to this risk. Generally speaking, an average shareholder gets dividends from operating surplus during the course of a business. This surplus represents the remaining revenue after deducting all operating costs, interest from all loans, different taxes, and dividends owed to non-ordinary shareholders. These days, a number of economic variables, governmental regulations, market dynamics, labor market conditions, management effectiveness, etc., may have an impact on earnings, costs, taxes, interest, etc., in a way that might or might not leave a sufficient surplus for common shareholders at any given time. Once more, even in situations where a company is on the verge of closing, all other parties involved—including the government, preference shareholders, creditors, and employees—remain involved must have their claims satisfied before the ordinary shareholders can split the remaining amount. The ordinary shareholders are the last to receive their claims, and there may or may not be sufficient residual left for them for a variety of reasons. Among all the stakeholders in a business, ordinary shareholders bear the greatest risk in this regard. They might inherit a sizable surplus if they're fortunate and things go well; if not, they might lose out. The risk associated with being an entrepreneur is this potential for earnings fluctuation. Furthermore, since common shareholders take on this risk, it is reasonable for them to anticipate receiving higher earnings in the long run as compensation. Ordinary shareholders have the ability to vote in proportion to the number of shares they own, and they can use this right to influence the company's affairs in a way that best suits their needs given the entrepreneurial risk they assume. Typically, resolutions put before the company are put to a vote during either the Annual or Extraordinary General Meetings.

7.1.1. Shares

A stockholder's ownership of the company is based on their percentage ownership of the company. Each share makes up a stock. A corporation's stock is divided into shares, the total of which is specified at the time the business is formed. The company may go on to issue more shares if the current shareholders approve them. A declared par value, or nominal accounting value, is assigned to each share of stock in some jurisdictions. This value is used to represent the equity on the corporation's balance sheet. However, shares of stock may be issued in other jurisdictions without a corresponding par value. A portion of a company's ownership is represented by shares. Different share types (or classes) with unique ownership restrictions, benefits, or share values may be declared by a business. A stock certificate may be issued to prove ownership of shares. A stock certificate is a legal document that lists the number of shares that a shareholder owns as well as other information about the shares, like the class or, if any, par value. A less common usage of the term "stock" in the UK, Ireland, South Africa, and Australia is to refer to any type of marketable securities.

7.1.2. Types

Shares of common stock or preferred stock are the usual forms of stock. Common stock usually carries voting rights that can be used to influence business decisions as a unit of ownership. Unlike common stock, preferred stock is legally entitled to a certain amount of dividend payments before any dividends can be paid to other shareholders. This is how preferred stock differs from common stock in that it usually does not carry voting rights. Preferred stock with the option to convert its preferred shares into a set number of common shares is known as convertible preferred stock. This conversion can typically occur at any point after a set date. Convertible preferred shares, also known as convertible preference shares in the UK, are the shares of such stock. Specific legal clauses that set the new equity issue apart from the issuer's earlier offerings may be attached. For example, some common stock may be issued with no voting rights at all, or it may have special rights that are only granted to specific parties. New issues may frequently have time restrictions on their ability to be resold if they haven't registered with a securities regulatory body.

Preferred stock can be hybridized by combining the voting rights of common stock with the fixed return characteristics of bonds. In addition, they receive preference over common stock when it comes to dividend payments and when it comes to liquidation. They also have additional dividend accumulation characteristics. Furthermore, a letter designation is typically appended to preferred stock; for instance, Berkshire-Hathaway Class B shares trade under the stock ticker BRK. B, while ORION DHC, Inc.'s Class A shares will trade under the ticker OODHA until the business removes the A, establishing the ticker OODH for its Common shares only designation. This additional letter informs investors that their shares are taken into consideration for exclusive rights, but it does not imply that such rights actually exist. Instead, these rights or privileges could be altered in response to decisions made by the underlying company.

- **Rule 144 Stock:** American shares of stock that are subject to SEC Rule 144: Seling Restricted and Control Securities are referred to as Rule 144 Stock. Restricted and controlled securities are obtained in an unregistered manner in accordance with Rule 144. Investors acquire these securities either from the issuing company (as with restricted securities) or from an affiliate of the issuer (as with control securities) through private sales (or other means, such as via ESOPs or in exchange for seed money). Different regulations apply to investors selling these securities than to those selling conventional common or preferred stock. These people can only liquidate their securities if they fulfill the requirements outlined in SEC Rule 144. Under certain circumstances, restricted securities may be publicly resold in accordance with Rule 144.

7.1.3. Application

A private company's owners might want more money to put toward brand-new initiatives for the business. They might also just want to sell some of their holdings to free up money for personal expenses. They can accomplish these objectives by offering to sell the public company shares via an offering on a stock exchange. The term "IPO" refers to this procedure as an initial public offering. They can sell the company to multiple co-owners in part or in its entirety by issuing shares. A single share can be purchased for actual ownership of the business, a portion of the decision-making authority, and possibly a portion of the profits, which the business may distribute as dividends. Additionally, the owner might inherit debt or even legal action. It is not feasible for thousands of shareholders in a publicly traded corporation to make all of the daily decisions that are necessary to run a business. As a result, during the company's annual board of directors election, shareholders will cast votes using their shares. Typically, one vote is represented by each share. However, corporations have the ability to issue various share classes, each of which could have a unique set of voting rights. The majority shareholder (or shareholders acting in concert) has effective control over the company and can outvote other shareholders if they own the majority of the shares. In this sense, the company's founding owners frequently maintain control over it.

7.1.3.1. Shareholder Rights

A shareholder does not have the right to use a company's building, tools, supplies, or other assets, even though owning 50% of the shares makes them 50% owners of the business. This is so because the business owns all of its assets outright because it is regarded as a legal person. This is crucial in certain situations, like insurance, where the company's name, not the primary shareholder's, is required. The majority of nations owe it to their boards of directors and corporate managers to operate their businesses in the best interests of their investors. However, as Martin Whitman puts it:

> It can safely be stated that there does not exist any publicly traded company where management works exclusively in the best interests of OPMI [Outside Passive Minority Investor] stockholders. Instead, there are both "communities of interest" and "conflicts of interest" between stockholders (principal) and management (agent). This conflict is referred to as the principal–agent problem. It would be naive to think that any management would forego management compensation, and management entrenchment, just because some of these management privileges might be perceived as giving rise to a conflict of interest with OPMIs.

Since the shareholders choose the board of directors, they have some influence over the company's policies even though the board of directors governs the business. Generally, a shareholder's percentage of votes corresponds to the percentage of shares that they own. Therefore, the shareholders have the authority to choose a new board of directors, which in turn can appoint a new management team, provided they concur that the management (agent) is not operating effectively. In actuality, though, fiercely contested board elections are uncommon. Insiders typically hold a sizable portion of the company's stock and can nominate candidates for the board of directors or the board itself. Being a shareholder does not entail taking on debt. If a company goes broke and has to default on loans, the shareholders are not liable in any way. To ensure that shareholders do not receive any money until creditors have been paid (often leaving the shareholders with nothing), all proceeds from the conversion of assets into cash, however, will be used to pay off loans and other debts first.

7.1.3.2. Means of financing

Equity financing is the process of funding a business by selling its stock. As an alternative, debt financing (such as bond issuance) can be used to keep company ownership shares intact. Trade financing, also referred to as unofficial financing, typically supplies the majority of a business's working capital (needs for daily operations).

7.1.4. Stock's Beta

An investor's entire investment portfolio poses a risk, and the impact a given security has on the portfolio as a whole represents the relevant risk associated with that security. A "diversified portfolio" is one in which each investor's holdings are indicative of the market as a whole and have a beta of zero. The beta of a stock indicates how closely the returns of a diversified portfolio follow the security. When a security has a beta of 1.0, it indicates that, on average, the stock price will increase by 10% if the market's total value of securities increases by 10%. A security with a beta of 2.0 will generally see a 20% increase or decrease in price when the market experiences a 10% increase or decrease. When the market drops 20%, a share with a beta of —0.5% will increase by 10%. The weighted average of the individual security betas, where the weights represent the percentages of investments in each security, is the beta of any portfolio of securities. A diversified portfolio's risk is increased when a high beta security (beta greater than 1.0) is added, and the risk of the portfolio is decreased when a low beta security (beta less than zero) is added.

By comparing the historical returns of the security to the return of the market, one can determine the beta coefficient of the stock. A sample of securities is used because it is not practical to take all of the securities. These beta coefficients are used by the Capital Asset Pricing Model (CAPM) to calculate the needed rate of return for the securities. According to the CAPM, a share's required rate is determined by its beta.

The relationship is:

Ke = Riskless rate + Risk premium x Beta

Where; Ke is the expected rate of return.

One can utilize the current rate on government securities as a riskless rate. The risk premium may be represented by the variation in the long-term average rate of return between shares and government securities. The published date provides the beta coefficient, or it can be estimated independently. It is unquestionably preferable to use beta to calculate the cost of equity capital. The main explanation is that, in contrast to other approaches, the method includes risk analysis. Its limited applicability, though, may stem from the laborious nature of determining a stock's beta value.

7.1.4.1. Different Types of Stock Beta

The beta coefficient is a metric used to compare a stock's performance to that of the entire market. Plotting the returns of the market and stocks at discrete intervals over time and fitting (regressing) a line through the resulting data points is how it is calculated. The levered equity beta is the slope of that line. The stock's returns are neither more nor less volatile than market returns when the slope of the line is 1.00. The stock's returns are more erratic than the market's when the slope is higher than 1.000. A crucial element of the Capital Asset Pricing Model (CAPM), which is used to price riskier securities and explains the relationship between risk and expected return, is the beta coefficient. Historical beta, adjusted beta, and fundamental beta are the three main forms of stock beta that are used in financial analysis. The slope of a regression line connecting the returns on a stock and the returns on a market index over a previous period is known as the historical beta. Historical betas can differ dramatically based on how long the holding period is (i.e., weeks, months, or years) as well as the total number of time intervals covered (i.e., the duration of the data used in years). There is no one "theoretically correct" way to do things, and what is "theoretically correct" for any given investor will probably change over time and vary from investor to investor. Investors' time horizons can vary over time; for instance, one may buy stocks with a short time horizon and consider returns over a few days or weeks, while another may buy for the "long haul" and not even check results other than annually.

Generally speaking, adjusted betas are computed as a kind of average between 1.0 and the historical beta, regardless of how it was determined. The reasoning behind adjusted betas is that historical betas that deviate significantly from 1.0 most likely represent transient events that will eventually fade, leading to a tendency for betas to "regress toward the mean of 1.0 over time." The idea of modifying betas is supported by empirical tests, but the precise nature of the adjustment is still up for debate. The notion of fundamental betas considers the possibility that changes in a company's fundamental conditions may occur over time and not be reflected in previous betas. For instance, it is commonly known that a company's beta should increase with the amount of financial leverage it employs. The historical beta, which is what we are really interested in, might not accurately represent the risk for the company going forward, though, if it is determined using, say, five years' worth of monthly data and the company modifies its capital structure near the end of the five years. The future beta may also differ from the historical beta due to other fundamental factors like the assets the company is investing in or the state of its industry (such as the electric utilities as they move from regulated monopolies to competitive companies).

7.1.5. Types of Investors in the Stock Market

When it comes to their investment horizons, styles, mandates, and managed assets, investors vary greatly. Investors are primarily two types of people: individuals who make investments for themselves, or institutions that make investments on behalf of others. Different investor classes have different risk appetites and return requirements, which are important factors in determining the investing styles and strategies used as well as the limitations encountered.

Primarily investors can be categorized into two groups:

1. **Individual Investors:** Although individuals make up the single largest group in terms of numbers in the majority of markets, each investor's portfolio is typically quite small. People vary in what they are willing to risk and what kind of return they need. Some people prefer to take on risk and invest in or speculate in the equity markets, while others may be risk-takers who would rather stick to safe havens like government securities and bank deposits. Individuals' needs also change based on where they are in their life cycle. In India, for instance, a person in the 25–35 age range might plan to buy a house and car; a person in the 35–45 age range might plan for their children's education and marriage; and a person in their fifties would be making plans for their post–retirement lifestyle. The capital required to meet these needs then determines how the investment portfolio is adjusted.
2. **Institutional Investors:** They make up the largest group of participants in the financial markets. Institutions are groups that are representative, i.e., e. they make financial investments on behalf of people, businesses, or other entities. The majority of assets under management are sizable and expertly handled by fund managers. Mutual funds, pension funds, insurance companies, hedge funds, endowment funds, banks, venture capital and private equity firms, and other financial institutions are some examples of these kinds of organizations.

In nutshell we can summarize the discussion on types of investors like this:

The government, businesses, and individuals are the main players in the financial system. Any of these could serve as a fund investor or supplier. People place their savings in a range of investment options that are made available to them, such as savings accounts, debt or equity instruments, insurance policies, etc., depending on their investment goals. However, most people ask for money in order to finance the purchase of real estate, such as homes or cars. Individuals are net suppliers of funds when taking into account both sides, since they invest more money than they withdraw. Government and business, on the other hand, are net recipients of funds since they extract more money from the process than they contribute. Individuals play a crucial role in the overall expansion and development of the financial system as well as indirectly in the growth of the economy.

7.1.6. Portfolio Management

It is a multifaceted process that includes a variety of asset and securities investment activities. Planning, oversight, timing, rationalism, and conservatism are all part of portfolio management when choosing securities to satisfy investors' goals. It involves choosing a list of securities that will give the investor the highest yield while allowing him to take on the level of risk he wants to. Serving a wide range of investors, both individual and institutional, portfolio management is expanding quickly. The assets in a typical investor's portfolio can range from a few 1000 to several crores of rupees.

The topic of portfolio and investment management is relatively new in the nation and is generally misunderstood, despite its increasing significance. The majority of the time, portfolio management has been used as a tool for investment management counseling, advising clients to look for assets with the potential to increase in value and/or generate income. The effective management of securities investments is the focus of portfolio management. The definition of an investment is the temporary current commitment of funds made with the goal of generating future cash flows that will reimburse the investing unit:

- For the time the funds are committed.
- For the expected rate of inflation, and
- For the uncertainty involved in the future flow of funds.

The process of choosing securities from the many opportunities that are available with varying expected returns and carrying varying levels of risk is known as portfolio management. The goal of this process is to provide investors the highest yield possible for a given level of risk or to ensure that risk is minimized for a given level of return. Investors put their money into a portfolio with the hope of earning a healthy return that is commensurate with the risk they are taking. It is necessary to quantify the return obtained from the portfolio and assess its overall performance. It is obvious that building an investment portfolio is a rational investment activity. Every step of the process involved in building and maintaining an investment portfolio is included in portfolio management. Particular topics covered include security analysis, portfolio analysis, selection, revision, and evaluation. Portfolio management employs conceptual theories and analytical techniques for the purpose of rationally allocating funds. The intricate process of portfolio management aims to reduce risk and increase return on investment.

Time horizon and element are involved in portfolio management. Bond and share valuation can benefit from knowing the present value of future returns and cash flows through discounting. When building a portfolio, the investment strategy should have a time horizon of three to five years in order to achieve the intended annual return of 20 to 30%. In addition to portfolio management, one should consider investment incentives and tax benefits.

Since investors receive their returns net of taxes paid, and since inflation is a constant factor, investors who pay taxes will find greater significance in returns net of taxes and inflation. These are supposed to be higher than other returns and are known as net real rates of return. They ought to include a risk-free return along with a fair risk premium on the invested instruments or assets, contingent on the level of risk assumed.

7.1.7. Determine Shares of Stock for a New Business

The first step in starting a new business or company that sells shares to private investors is typically to apply for state authorization. The total number of shares that a company is legally allowed to issue is known as authorized shares. Most companies examine their total book value first before applying for state approval. The validation of the maximum number of authorized shares is aided by this valuation.

- **Company Valuation:** Accounting firms or valuation specialists are frequently hired by private companies to determine their total book value. To do this, the company's total assets and liabilities must be ascertained. Liabilities are the money owed to creditors by the company, and assets are the properties it possesses. This data is utilized to calculate the company's total capital. Because of their greater overall company value, businesses with higher capital are typically permitted to issue more shares. Those with less capital are permitted to issue a lower proportion of shares.
- **Potential Investors:** It is possible for a business to release fewer shares to investors than what is legally permitted. A company that has been authorized to issue 5,000 shares, for instance, might only issue 1,000 of those shares initially. Depending on how many investors have shown interest in the business, this choice might be made. The company may issue more of its authorized shares if additional investors show interest. Capital from early investors can increase the company's equity and the number of shares in circulation.
- **Partnerships:** Companies that intend to implement employee stock ownership plans may take these choices into account when requesting authorization or even before the initial launch. This implies that an owner's application choice for shares may also be influenced by any intended employee compensation plans. As a result, there will be more shares in circulation.
- **Future Prospects:** Depending on the processing time or legal fees involved in applying for shares, some companies seek authorization for the highest number of shares they can afford so they can respond promptly to investor demand and avoid the delays of a subsequent authorization request. Because legal filing fees are costly, some businesses prefer to undergo a one-time authorization process for the highest number of shares and issue those shares as needed.

7.1.8. Calculate Market Price per Share of Common Stock

Some companies request authorization for the maximum number of shares they can afford in order to respond quickly to investor demand and avoid the delays of a follow-up authorization request, depending on the processing time or legal fees involved in applying for shares. Some companies would rather go through a one-time authorization process for the maximum number of shares and issue those shares as needed because legal filing fees can be expensive.

7.1.8.1. Market Value per Share

The most recent price at which shares were sold is always the current market price or market value per share of common stock. In a strict sense, market prices are not determined. Rather, they are the result of the mutual exchange that occurs when sellers and buyers react to market forces. The market price, according to economic theory, tends to move toward an equilibrium point where the quantity of buyers, or demand, equals the quantity of sellers, or supply. The price will tend to rise if there are more purchasers. In contrast, the price tends to decrease if there are fewer buyers or more sellers. The difference between the market price and the book value per share of common stock must be understood. Book value is the accounting value of shareholders' equity as stated on the balance sheet of the company, after the company's liabilities are deducted from its assets. The value of any preferred stock is subtracted from shareholders' equity to determine book value per share of common stock. The remaining amount is then divided by the total number of outstanding common shares. For instance, the book value comes out to $20 per share if a company has $200 million in equity after deducting the value of preferred stock and 10 million shares outstanding. The market price and book value are not always the same.

7.1.8.2. Market Value Calculation

Typically, all you have to do is search for the common stock's current market price quote. You might occasionally need historical market prices, but they might not always be easily available. This can occur when you need to know how a stock's price has changed over time while conducting research on it. To estimate the historical market price, you can use the Price/Earnings (P/E) ratio. A popular metric is the price-to-earnings ratio (P/E ratio), which is computed by dividing the market price on a particular date by the earnings per share for the accounting period. Look up the P/E ratio and earnings per share for the accounting period in the company's annual report to get an idea of the market price on that date. Add the two figures together. For example, if the company reported EPS of $7.50 and the P/E ratio was 20, then the estimated market price would be $150 per share. Put another way, if all other things were equal, this is the price per share that you would anticipate paying.

7.1.8.3. Market Value Ratios

A variety of financial ratios make use of the market price per common stock share. These ratios are frequently used by investors to determine whether a stock is undervalued or overvalued, which could present a chance to purchase the stock at a discount. Here are two instances: The most popular market price ratio is the P/E ratio. It indicates the amount of money you need to invest in order to earn $1. When comparing businesses in the same industry, the P/E ratio works best. Tech companies, for instance, might promise rapid growth rates, which would drive up share prices for investors. In this instance, a high P/E ratio does not always signify an expensive stock. On the other hand, a utility might provide steady profits but constrained expansion. A business in this sector typically has a low P/E ratio. The ratio of price to book value indicates how much equity you get for every dollar you invest. The market price of common stock is divided by its book value to determine P/BV. A stock with a $100 share price and a $50 book value, for instance, has a P/BV of 2. A P/BV of less than one is interpreted by many investors as suggesting that the stock might be a good deal. Nevertheless, to ensure that the low price is actually a good deal and not a red flag that the company is having issues, you should pay close attention to other indicators, such as earnings per share.

7.2. FUNDAMENTAL ANALYSIS OF STOCKS

The process of analyzing an organization's fundamentals to ascertain whether a venture has proven to be a wise investment is known as fundamental analysis of stocks. In other words, fundamental analysis entails in-depth research with regard to financial statements like the balance sheet. Its goals are to provide answers to questions about business finance and capital investment, such as "what are the probabilities that this business investment is going to fail or become bankrupt" and "how sure can a portfolio manager be that the stock continues to pay dividends." It is regarded as a total opposite to stock technical analysis. The primary goal of fundamental analysis of stocks is to ascertain a security's intrinsic value by examining its financial, economic, and other quantitative and qualitative components. This method can also be applied to any type of security, including bonds and money, even though it is used to assess the value of a company's stock. Fundamental analysis, also referred to as quantitative analysis, entails examining a company's financial statements, such as the balance sheet, profit and loss accounts, and so forth., in order to examine various financial indicators such as revenues, earnings, costs, assets, and liabilities. Investors, brokers, and analysts are usually the ones who carry out this kind of research.

7.2.1. Stages of Fundamental Analysis

Gain is the investor's main goal when purchasing stock. It is speculative if he invests for a short time; however, if he holds it for a considerable amount of time, he expects to receive a return on his investment. A technique used by investors to determine the future price of a stock or share they want to purchase is called fundamental analysis of stocks. The process of fundamental stock analysis entails;.

1. **Company Analysis:** Company analysis is the study of the factors that have a qualitative and quantitative impact on a firm's future. It is a technique for evaluating a company's profitability and competitive standing, as well as its operational efficiency and financial standing in relation to shareholder earnings. The underlying premise of this analysis is that every share of a company has intrinsic value, which is determined by the financial performance, management caliber, and earnings and dividend history of the company. They think that eventually, the market price of a share will converge to its intrinsic value. A share is considered undervalued and should be bought if its market price is less than its intrinsic value, as determined by a fundamental analysis of stocks. On the other hand, if the share's current market price exceeds its intrinsic value, it should be sold, per the theory. The fundamental methodology is examined by

means of an organization's financial statements. The income statement, balance sheet, and statement of changes in financial position are the fundamental financial statements that are necessary for fundamental analysts to have as tools. These statements are helpful to creditors, investors, and internal management of a company. Based on these statements, investors in the company may decide how to proceed in the future.

While evaluating a company, its statement must be carefully judged to find out that they are:

i. Correct;
ii. Complete;
iii. Consistent; and
iv. Comparable.

2. **Industry Analysis:** The term "industry" refers to uniform groups of people engaged in comparable tasks or activities. In India, the published stock exchange list serves as the basis for the broad industry classification. In various forms, including engineering, banking and insurance, textiles, cement, steel mills and alloys, chemicals and pharmaceuticals, retail, sugar, information technology, automobiles and ancillary, telecommunications, FMCG, and miscellaneous, this provides a clear classification to industry to industry. A life cycle analysis or evaluation of the industry is also necessary. The industrial life cycle state can also be used to study the industry life cycle. An industry typically has three stages. These phases are known as the pioneering, expansion, and stagnation phases.

i. **The Pioneering Stage:** New inventions and technological advancements occur during the pioneering stage of the industrial life cycle. Investors will see a significant increase in the company's activity during this time. There will be a strong demand for the product relative to production, which will increase. Because the technology is still new, the profits are also very high at this point. Seeing the potential for profit, a lot of new businesses enter the same industry until it becomes competitive. With the entry of new companies, the pressures of market competition increase, prices continue to fall, and profits eventually decline. At this point, every company is in competition with one another, leaving only a small number of capable companies to manage the company while the majority of other companies are destroyed during the pioneering phase.

ii. **The Expansion Stage:** Now that they've entered the market, the efficient firms realize it's time to stabilize them. Even though there is competition, there are still a lot of businesses operating in the industry because fewer businesses existed during the pioneering stage. Now is the moment for everyone to demonstrate their superiority and competitive strength. It will become clear to the investor that now is the ideal time to invest. Selecting which of the many firms to invest in was challenging during the pioneering stage. However, by waiting for the stability period, a dynamic selection process has taken place, and only a small number of the large number of firms remain in the industry. This phase, which is also known as the firm's maturity period, is one of safety and security. This stage of a company's life spans 5 to 50 years, depending on its potential, productivity, and ability to adapt quickly to changing consumer habits and competitive market conditions.

iii. **Stagnation Stage:** Investors will discover that while an organization's sales are increasing during the stagnation stage, these increases are unrelated to the profits the business is making. Although the company is still making money, it is not growing as quickly as it did during the expansion phase. The industry discovers that it is losing strength and is unable to grow. At this point, the majority of businesses that have come to understand how competitive the market is start to alter their strategy and launch new ventures. Investors should continuously assess their investments. Investors should sell their holdings in companies where they have made money for a long time and have reached a stagnation stage in order to pursue better opportunities in companies where the expansion stage has begun, possibly in a different industry.

3. **Economic Analysis:** The economic factors that impact the performance of companies in which they want to invest by buying stock are of concern to investors. An understanding of the economic forces would help predict future corporate earnings as well as the amount of interest and dividends that investors will receive. The following are a few of the general forces that the investment factors function under:

   i. **Population:** A country's population can provide insight into the nature of its labor force. While population growth has slowed down in some countries, there has been an explosion in India and other third-world countries. An increase in population will drive up demand for a variety of businesses, including lodging, hotels, and service sectors like healthcare and automobiles. Similarly, since these sectors will likely yield higher rates of return in the future, investors ought to favor investing in those with a large labor force.

   ii. **Research and Technological Developments:** The economic factors influencing investments would depend on how much money the government invested in a given technological advancement that would have an impact on the future. Generally speaking, investors should put their money into sectors of the economy that receive a sizable portion of the funding for national development. For instance, automobile industries and space technology are currently receiving more attention in India. The investor might think about making investments in these areas.

   iii. **Capital Formation:** Investors

should also take into account the type of capital goods a company invests in as well as the money it spends on asset replacement and modernization. The location, value, and property position of an industry, the group to which it belongs, and the annual returns through corporate profits are examples of economic indicators that can be used to evaluate a specific industry or company that an investor may wish to invest in.

iv. **Natural Resources and Raw Materials:** Natural resources play a major role in the economic growth of a nation and the general improvement of the business growth environment. Technological advancements in India, such as material recycling, nuclear and solar energy, and new synthetic materials, should present investors with the chance to invest in as yet unexplored or recently discovered resources, thereby yielding higher returns on their capital.

7.2.2. Advantages of Fundamental Analysis

Fundamental analysis of stocks is beneficial for:

- Identification of the intrinsic value of a security
- Identification of long-term investment opportunities because it includes real time data
- Employing fundamental analysis for predicting future prices is based on the principle of "one thing causes another," and hence tries to recognize the causing factors. Therefore, with this concept, the approach of fundamental analysis is said to be intuitively appealing.
- Because relationships are examined by mathematical and statistical techniques, fundamental analysis is objective. Those relationships that fail are removed, whereas those that successfully pass are considered to be credible. Further, there is no room for personal opinion or bias. Many traders greatly depend on objectivity and hold little confidence in their ability to predict prices on pure discretion basis. Furthermore, future traders do not find it difficult to attempt to predict variables through the process of fundamental analysis. Organizations attempt to predict sales, government agencies attempt to predict unemployment and meteorology specialists attempt to predict the weather conditions. With all of these sectors trying to harness the power of fundamental analysis, one advantage of using fundamental analysis is the enhancement and refinement in the pool of techniques available for fundamental analysis. For instance, if an effective technique is developed for predicting the weather, it can be easily applied to future prices and help in obtaining satisfactory outcomes. And this is just how a specific form of fundamental analysis termed as the Chaos Theory, entered the realm of the future traders.

7.2.3. Disadvantages of Fundamental Analysis

However, fundamental analysis of stocks is equipped with the following drawbacks:

- It can be used only for analyzing long-term investments.
- Too many economic indicators together with widened macroeconomic data tends to produce confusion for new investors.
- Similar set of information regarding macroeconomic indicators may impose different effects on the same currencies at varied times.
- Fundamental analysis of stocks requires a significant amount of human labor, including time and effort. Furthermore, as methods have become more sophisticated recently, fewer people are turning to hiring professional economists who are adept at using the available technology to assist them. For instance, in order to create their internal prediction models, big banks typically employ teams of economists.
- A substantial amount of data is required for fundamental analysis of stocks in order to evaluate the significance of various variables. These kinds of data are frequently hard to obtain and, more significantly, are seldom offered for free. Additionally, there are noticeable errors in data that need to be found and fixed first.
- Even though time, energy, and data can be acquired, it is frequently difficult to define a relationship that is highly reliable and permits accurate price prediction. This could be partly because it gets harder to identify causal relationships because so many variables are interconnected and have different effects on one another. One could spend a great deal of time, effort, and money searching for causal relationships without ever finding one.

7.3. TECHNICAL ANALYSIS OF STOCKS

Technical analysis is the process of using historical trading data and stock price trends associated with a particular security and comparing those to the historical responses of other similar investments to similar patterns. Furthermore, once a pattern has been recognized, the investor can forecast that the target investment's pricing will probably react in the future in a way that is comparable to previous patterns. The underlying premise of technical analysis of stocks is that the current prices should accurately reflect all available market information. In addition to reflecting inherent truths, prices also convey human emotion, the prevailing mass psychology, and the current atmosphere. The ultimate driver of prices is supply and demand. But human emotions, such as fear, greed, panic, hysteria, euphoria, etc., change moment to moment, also have a significant impact on prices. It is possible for markets to fluctuate based on expectations rather than actual data. A market "technician" bases his trading decisions on chart formations, figuring that prices reflect both emotion and fact, an attempt to ignore the emotional aspect of trading.

The main goal of technical analysis is to predict future price movements by analyzing historical market data related to volume and price. Technical analysis also helps in projecting the possible price movement over time rather than being used for pure prediction. Technical analysis can be applied to commodities, futures, stocks, foreign exchange, forex, indices, or any other tradable asset whose price is determined by market trends in supply and demand. It is also utilized by short-term investors and day traders who engage in investment markets such as the stock and foreign exchange markets. Hedgers are frequent users of this type of analysis as well. To determine whether the current market is in a bull market or a bear market, analysts use their technical research. Technical analysis operates under the assumption that price takes into account all relevant market data and aspects individually. This kind of analysis is also motivated by the idea that price fluctuations are dependent on trends rather than being totally random. Technical analysis gives a trader the ability to identify a trend that is currently in motion, trade with it, and profit from it as it moves forward.

7.3.1. Stock Charts

A stock chart is a straightforward graph of price and time plotted on the two axes (X-Y). Every equity, market, and index that is listed on a public exchange has a chart that shows how its price changes over time. The closing price for each day can be used to create individual data plots for charts. The graph is made up of connections between the plots made in a single line. Additionally, the data plots can be created using a combination of the market session's opening, closing, high, and/or low prices. A price BAR is the term for this second category of data. Next, a detailed visual representation of stock movement is produced by overlaying individual price bars onto the graph. There are two ways to draw stock charts. Every price unit on an arithmetic chart is separated by the same vertical distance. A percentage growth chart is what a logarithmic chart is.

7.3.2. Trends

The current trend is determined using the stock chart. The average rate of change in a stock's price over time is reflected in a trend. All markets and all time periods have trends. Three categories exist for trends: range-bound, down, and upward. A stock will often rally in an uptrend, interspersed with periods of consolidation or movement in the opposite direction. On the stock chart, it creates a sequence of higher highs and higher lows by doing this. The rate of price change over time will be positive during an uptrend. A stock will typically decline in a downtrend, interspersed with periods of consolidation or movement in the opposite direction. It creates a sequence of lower highs and lower lows on the stock chart in doing so.

The rate of price change over time will be negative during a downtrend. Range-bound prices oscillate for extended periods of time between clearly visible upper and lower bounds. The stock chart's price movement has no discernible direction, and the rate of change in price will either be negligible or nonexistent. Trends typically endure over time. A stock in an uptrend will keep rising until a condition or a change in value takes place. Dropping stocks won't stop until there is a change in the situation or value. Readers of charts look for tops and bottoms, or the places where a rise or fall ends. It can be very profitable to enter a position close to a top or a bottom. Trendlines can be used to quantify trends. Frequently, a straight line can be drawn over pullbacks from declines or under three or more pullbacks from rallies. Price bars typically find support or resistance and bounce off the line in the opposite direction when they return to that trend line.

7.3.3. Volume

Volume gauges how engaged the audience is. Below the price pane on stock charts, separate histograms show volume. These frequently display red bars on bad days and green bars on good days. By keeping an eye on the number of consecutive up or down days and how their volume compares to days when the price moves in the opposite direction, traders and investors can gauge the interest in buying and selling. Under accumulation refers to stocks that are purchased with more interest than they are sold for. Under distribution occurs when more stocks are sold than are purchased. Prices fluctuate as a result of accumulation and distribution frequently.

Put differently, stocks that are being accumulated tend to increase in value after the buying phase starts. On the other hand, distribution stocks frequently decline after selling starts. A stock can rise with volume, but it can also fall on its own. The crowd must participate enthusiastically in rallies. A stock can fall quickly when there are no more participants in a rally. To determine whether participation is leading (ahead of) or lagging (behind) the price action, traders and investors use indicators like on balance volume.

The average volume of daily stock trades establishes the stock's liquidity. Traders find it very simple to buy and sell liquid stocks.

Buying or selling liquid stocks often entails extremely high spreads (transaction costs), and they are frequently difficult to remove from a portfolio quickly. On illiquid stocks, stock chart analysis is not very effective.

7.3.4. Patterns and Indicators

With the use of charts, traders and investors can make informed decisions and reasonable predictions by examining both historical and current price action. This medium is primarily visual. It is distinct from the chilly realm of value-based analysis by this one fact. The logic and creative faculties of the left and right brains are stimulated by the stock chart. It follows that two distinct forms of analysis that center on these lines of critical examination have emerged over the past century. Pattern analysis is the most traditional method of chart interpretation. Charles Dow's writings and Technical Analysis of Stock Trends, a seminal book on the subject published shortly after World War II, both contributed to the rise in popularity of this approach. Indicator analysis, a more recent method of interpretation, is a quantitative investigation in which price and volume are broken down into their most basic components and then subjected to a series of calculations to determine where the price will go next. The power of pattern analysis stems from charts' propensity to repeatedly display the same bar formations. Over time, these patterns have been classified as having a bullish or bearish bias. The HEAD and SHOULDERS, triangles, rectangles, double tops, double bottoms, and FLAGS are a few popular examples. Furthermore, it is stated that elements of the chart landscape like trendlines and gaps have a significant impact on how the price will move in the future. Indicator analysis compares the current price to previous price movements using mathematical computations. Almost all indicators fall into one of two categories: oscillators or trend-following. On balance volume, MACD, and moving averages are common trend-following indicators. RSI, rate of change, and stochastics are examples of common oscillators. Compared to oscillators, trend following indicators respond far more slowly. In order to find the future, they peep closely into the rearview mirror. Oscillators oscillate rapidly in response to brief price fluctuations, swinging between OVERBOUGHT and OVERSOLD levels. Indicators and patterns are both used to quantify market psychology. As prices rise and fall, the core group of traders and investors that make up the market every day often behave in unison. This "crowd" has a propensity to acquire recognizable traits that recur repeatedly. By interpreting charts with the help of these two crucial analytical tools, one can see how crowd stress is increasing, which should eventually cause prices to shift.

7.3.5. Moving Averages

The moving average is a widely used technical indicator in stock chart analysis. This adaptable tool has a wide range of crucial applications for traders and investors. Take the total of all past close prices and divide it by that same number. This establishes the stock's average price over that time frame. Plotting this result in the same graphic pane as the price bars allows you to see a moving average by recalculating it every day. Put differently, it will require a certain amount of time for the moving average to "catch up" if there is a sudden and significant change in the price. Plotting moving averages on stock charts shows how well the price is doing right now in comparison to its historical performance. The moving average line's strong relationship with the price bars accounts for part of its power. The current price will always be calculated with a moving average above or below it. Conditions are "bullish" when it is higher. Conditions below are considered "bearish." Moving averages will also gradually slope higher or lower. This gives a stock analysis another visual dimension. Trends in stocks are defined by moving averages. They are calculable over any time interval. When they offer advice on short-, intermediate-, and long-term trends, traders and investors find them to be of greatest use. This is why it is helpful to use multiple moving averages that represent these qualities when making crucial decisions. Moving averages of 20 days for the short term, 50 days for the intermediate term, and 200 days for the long term are commonly used settings for daily stock charts. In all of chart analysis, the moving average crossover is one of the most prevalent buy or sell signals. They arise when there are two moving averages, each representing a distinct trend. A sell signal is produced, for instance, when a short-term average crosses below a long-term average. A buy signal is produced, on the other hand, when the short term crosses above the long-term. By applying additional mathematical computations, moving averages can be "sped up." Simple mean averages, or SMAs, are common averages. These are typically very slow. A faster exponential or EMA moving average can be produced by weighting the recent price changes more heavily than those from many bars ago. The EMA is preferred by many technicians over the SMA. Fortunately, all popular stock charting software, both offline and online, plots price accurately while handling the challenging moving average computations.

7.3.6. Support and Resistance

Understanding and interpreting stock charts requires an understanding of support and resistance. Natural boundaries for rising and falling prices are defined by support and resistance, much like a ball bounces when it hits the floor or falls after being thrown to the ceiling. There is perpetual conflict between buyers and sellers. Support is the point at which buyers' strength prevents further price declines. The point at which sellers are too powerful to permit a price increase is known as resistance. In both up and down trends, support and resistance have distinct functions. A retreat from a rally should end at support in an uptrend. Resistance is the point at which a pullback from a decline should terminate in a downtrend. Price has memory, which creates support and resistance. When prices return to those levels, the mix of participants will typically be similar to what it was when large buyers or sellers entered the market in the past. Price establishes a new level of support when it breaks above resistance. Price turns a level into resistance when it drops below resistance. Price often surges ahead quickly when a level of support or resistance is broken because everyone rushes to buy or sell as soon as they see the BREAKOUT. If a level is broken but does not draw in large volumes of buyers or sellers, it frequently retreats back below the previous level of support or resistance. We call this kind of failure a FALSE BREAKOUT. There are many different types and intensities of support and resistance. The most common way they appear is as horizontal price tiers. However, trend lines at different angles also show resistance and support. The strength or weakness of a support or resistance level is determined by how long it has been in place. The amount of buying or selling interest needed to break the level depends on the strength or weakness. Additionally, a level will be stronger the more trading volume there is at that level. All markets and all time periods have support and resistance. Levels with longer durations have greater strength than those with shorter durations. Technical analysis of stocks today is based on the theories of Charles Dow, the first editor of the Wall Street Journal (The Dow Jones Theory on Stock Market Movements). The patterns of behavior he saw are relevant to global markets.

7.3.7. Advantages of Technical Analysis

- **Powerful Focus on Price Movement:** Technical analysis primarily concentrates on price movement. Stated differently, charts are utilized to illustrate how and when prices move, as well as the direction and intensity of those movements. In addition, oscillators, volume, and momentum provide a clearer picture of the state of the market. This is information that is easily gathered. Unlike fundamentalists, technicians do not use economic reports that look at the demand for a given currency.
- **Finding Patterns is Simple:** The ability of market action to self-regenerate in precise, well-defined patterns is one of its basic characteristics. A trader can identify patterns and predict price movements based on these patterns with the help of charts. Charts and patterns can be composite and complex, just like start constellations. Effective patterns that are followed by multiple currency prices include head-and-shoulder patterns, round tops and bottoms, descending and ascending triangles, and double and triple tops. As such, they have strong predictive abilities. Furthermore, they cannot be found without a chart.
- **Trends are Simple to Identify:** A cursory look at a moving averages line indicates whether a price is trending upward or downward within a range. A currency that shows a trend, whether it be up, down, or oblique, can be seen on a chart right away. Trends are essential to technicians because a currency will always move in the direction of a trend, and charts are a clear and accurate way to display these trends.
- **Charting is Quick and Inexpensive:** With most people no longer having to perform complex mathematical operations due to computer workstations, the Internet provides a wealth of different technical indicators that enable traders to make more profitable and dependable trades. These kinds of technical indicators are offered by a number of brokers as part of their package. In light of this, technical analysis is less expensive and time-consuming than fundamental analysis. In addition, it can be finished in a few countable minutes, and the services are typically provided for free or at a minimal cost.
- **Data is Abundantly Available on Charts:** Both indicators and charts have the capacity to provide enormous amounts of data. Trends are simple to identify, and levels of resistance and support are quickly located. It is quick and simple to access trading forms, momentum, and volatility. There are more than 50 different kinds of indicators, and each one provides important details on a range of topics related to the precise movement of a currency.

It is said that technicians need this knowledge to make wise and profitable trades.

Charts also show how a currency's personality and price movement are represented. In terms of the data distribution, this representation may be complex due to a variety of ups and downs. Moreover, charts are limited to offering basic details about a trend, resistance, and support. However, they get much more insightful when they start to reveal details about how strong a trend is, how momentum is building, and whether or not trading-friendly formations are starting to form.

7.3.8. Disadvantages of Technical Analysis

Because technical analysis is based on statistics and mathematics and produces results that give the impression of accuracy and predictability, it is popular among traders who trade stocks all over the world. Nonetheless, traders should be aware of the various shortcomings in technical analysis. The following are some of the limitations of technical stock analysis.

All technical indicators are fundamentally based on price, which is just a reflection of what has already happened in the market, regardless of how complex they may be. Technical analysis is therefore considered to be very reactive rather than genuinely predictive of future events. The markets of today are far more erratic and chaotic than they were in previous decades. Hedge funds and automated ultra-short term trading are to blame for this. More false signals and irregular patterns from technical analysis techniques follow as a result. Nearly every technical trader gives trend-following a shot. Although trend-following strategies have the potential to generate significant profits over time, they also have a high drawdown and a poor accuracy rate. The majority of trades are total losses, and it's not unusual to be down between 50 and 60% at any given time. This is a good example of this. Moreover, a number of traders experience psychological difficulties in managing this consequence, leading them to ignore trading signals and switch between systems. One significant shortcoming is that most technical traders still rely on indicators that were developed in the 1970s. Because of this tendency on the part of traders to overuse these indicators, the markets reduce their efficiency. Graphs of non-market-related actions, like temperature charts, can exhibit patterns found in traditional trading charts. Furthermore, the chart's scaling may cause certain patterns to emerge or vanish. And this strongly suggests that chart patterns have no predictive value and are just tricks of the eye.

7.3.9. Difference between Fundamental and Technical Analysis

There are two main types of analysis used in forex trading to examine price movement. Individuals who focus solely on price movement and disregard other factors tend to direct their efforts towards improving their technical analysis skills, while traders who prioritize analyzing the economic events driving market action primarily focus on their efforts towards fundamental analysis. The majority of traders want to combine the data from these two types of analysis to produce precise trading signals. Others concentrate on a single area of analysis and exclude the other type from the calculations; however, both strategies may be appropriate in certain situations. To put it simply, some traders have become well-known and wealthy by using fundamental analysis to guide their trading decisions. Though these two disagree on a number of issues, they would almost certainly concur that emotional and behavioral self-control—rather than analytical aptitude—are the most important components of a successful trading career. When the inevitable counter-trend action occurs, technical analysts can examine his charts, identify the extreme values associated with the indicators, and warn against pursuing a trend that could suffer from a sudden reversal. The fundamental analyst, on the other hand, will notice the excitement in the analyst community and news outlets, consider the different statements made by government figures and agencies, and broadcast the same cautionary message. Although these two types of people use different tools and indicators, their behaviors usually align with one another. Technical and fundamental analysis are not exactly the same; over the long term, at least, the predictive power of the fundamental studies is significantly higher. But these two kinds of analysis—at least in retrospect—are closely linked to two distinct languages that are employed to characterize the same phenomenon, and they present the same direction and reach the same conclusion.

To put it simply, technical analysts only make trades or investments based on the volume and price movements of securities. They trade on momentum, independent of the fundamentals, by utilizing charts and a number of other instruments. One of the fundamental ideas of technical analysis is that, as previously stated, the market discounts every entity, even though it is quite possible to combine the two analysis methods. Comparably, every piece of information about a company is priced into its stock; therefore, stock price movements can reveal more about the underlying, essential components of the company as a whole. On the other hand, proponents of the effective market hypothesis frequently disagree with both fundamental and technical analysis. In this particular context, the efficient market hypothesis posits that generating market-beating returns over the long term through technical or fundamental analysis is nearly impossible. The underlying premise of this debate is that, since the market prices all stocks on an ongoing basis, any legitimate opportunities for excess returns derived from technical or fundamental analysis would be promptly curtailed by market participants. This would prevent any trader from materially outperforming the market over an extended period of time. In a functional sense, traders and investors use both analysis techniques to choose investments whose prices will move in a profitable and productive direction for them; traders who wish to buy investments use the "up" technique, and traders who want to sell or reduce their investments use the "down" technique. By using fundamental analysis, an investor can discover an investment that is undervalued in the market compared to its true value, which is determined by the investor's analysis. By using technical analysis, an investor can find investments whose patterns coincide with previously observed patterns and, if followed, will cause the investment's price to move in the desired direction. Lastly, the market is viewed as a rational sector by fundamental analysis. It also presumes that the price of a security will eventually represent the investment's actual value. Technical analysis, on the other hand, believes that the market is simply repeating itself and its historical patterns, and that the price of a security will eventually move like the prices of other investments.

7.4. STOCK VALUATION

The ability to value stocks accurately is the most important ability that investors need to possess in order to assess whether a stock is currently overvalued or undervalued in relation to the performance and growth prospects of the company. The current market price, which is determined by supply and demand, may or may not correspond with the intrinsic value, which is determined by business fundamentals. Finding a share's fair price is aided by the application of stock valuation. Active investors use a number of metrics to calculate a stock's true value in order to compare it to the market price because they think that a stock's intrinsic value is distinct from its current price. The efficient market hypothesis, which holds that the market price is determined by all available information, is the foundation of the case made by a different group of investors known as passive investors. It is therefore the stock's true value. Investing in index funds or exchange-traded funds (ETFs) that track market returns is advised by the passive investing theory as an alternative to valuing stocks differently in an attempt to beat the market. An investor may find the complicated process of stock valuation to be too much to handle. As a result, investors ought to be able to concentrate on pertinent data while eliminating noise. Familiarity with fundamental valuation types and techniques is required.

7.4.1. Types of Stock Valuation

There are two primary types of stock valuation methods: Absolute and Relative.

- **Absolute:** The fundamental analysis of a company is the foundation of the absolute method of stock valuation. It uses a variety of financial data from financial statements, primarily from cash flow, dividends, and growth rate metrics, to determine valuation. The residual income model, asset-based model, discounted cash flow model (DCF), and dividend discount model (DDM) are all computed when determining a stock's value using the absolute method. As its name implies, the absolute method does not evaluate a company's performance against its competitors.
- **Relative:** In order to derive the same metrics for the company under focus, the relative valuation method compares important financial ratios of similar companies. Analyzing comparable companies is a popular method. The fundamental component of the relative valuation approach is calculating the P/E ratio. For example, the company's stocks are cheap if its P/E ratio is lower than that of its peer.

  Let's understand with an example. Company A reported diluted earnings per share for the fiscal ending in January 2021 as $6.76 and price at the time of calculation, $203. To obtain a P/E ratio, we will divide the share price by EPS.

  P/E = ($203/ 6.76) = $30.03.

One can easily obtain EPS value from a company's financial statements and price is the current value of its shares in the market.

7.4.2. Common Stock Valuation Methods

Let's now see what popular stock valuation methods you can apply.

- **Dividend Discount Model (DDM):** The dividend discount model is a recognized technique for figuring out a stock's absolute value. It determines the true cost by taking into account the dividends that the business gives to its owners. Analysts contend that since dividends are the real cash flow of the company to its owners, figuring out the present value of future dividend payments should accurately reflect the value of the stock. The best companies for DDM valuation are those with sizable dividend payments that occur on a consistent basis. Subsequently, investors employ the Golden Growth Model, or GGM, presuming a steady rate of dividend growth. It eliminates the complexities of variable dividend payout and is a simple method.
- **Discount Cash Flow Model (DCF):** Investors utilize a discounted cash flow model, which bases its computation on discounted future cash flow rather than dividend rate, when a company doesn't pay a dividend or has an irregular dividend model. The discounted cash flow model is applicable to a broad class of non-blue-chip companies, including those that have no dividend policy. There are multiple methods for calculating DCF. The most widely used DCF model, though, is the two-stage version, in which investors compute free cash flow estimates for a period of 5 to 10 years first, and then determine the terminal value of all cash flows that exceed the projections. Companies that want to use the DCF model for valuation must have steady and consistent free cash flow. Therefore, mature businesses that have passed the growth stage are thought to be the best candidates for DCF valuation.

7.4.3. The Comparable Analysis

To ascertain the true value of stocks, the comparable analysis compares several important financial ratios between companies. It involves contrasting figures such as the price-to-book ratio, EBITDA, and P/E ratio. Its foundation is the "law of one price" principle, which states that two comparable assets ought to be valued at the same amount; deviance from this rule indicates either undervaluation or overvaluation. One of the most straightforward approaches to stock valuation that anyone can use is a comparable analysis. The foundation of stock valuation is a comparison of the P/E ratio. The price of the company's stock divided by its most recent reported earnings per share (EPS) is known as the P/E ratio. An investor will find a stock appealing if it has a low P/E ratio.

7.4.4. Trading Valuation

Generally speaking, unless otherwise restricted, shareholders may transfer their shares of a company to other parties through a sale or other means. Such transfers are governed by laws and regulations in the majority of jurisdictions, especially if the issuer is a publicly traded company. The establishment of stock exchanges—organizations that offer markets for the trading of shares as well as other derivatives and financial products—was prompted by investors' desire to trade their shares. These days, a stockbroker who buys and sells shares of various companies on these exchanges typically represents stock traders. If a business complies with and upholds the listing standards of a specific stock exchange, it may list its shares on the exchange numerous sizable non-U.S. businesses decide to list on a U.S. exchange in addition to one back home to increase the size of their investor base. These businesses are required to keep a block of shares, usually equivalent to a predetermined portion of their capital, at a US bank. The holding bank creates American depositary shares based on this, and for each share a trader purchases, it issues an American depositary receipt (ADR). Similarly, a lot of big U.S. businesses to raise money overseas, list their shares on foreign exchanges. (Mrzygłod et al., 2013).

Small businesses that don't meet the requirements for listing on the major exchanges or don't qualify may trade over-the-counter (OTC) through an off-exchange mechanism where trading takes place directly between parties. The electronic quotation systems OTC Bulletin Board (OTCBB) and OTC Markets Group (formerly known as Pink OTC Markets Inc.) are the two main over-the-counter (OTC) markets in the United States.) where a brokerage firm also represents individual retail investors and the quotation service has low requirements for a company to be listed. These quotation services typically list shares of companies that are facing bankruptcy after the stock is removed from an exchange.

7.4.4.1. Buying

Purchasing and financing stocks can be done in a number of ways, the most popular being through a stockbroker. Brokerage firms facilitate the transfer of stock from a seller to a buyer, regardless of whether they are full-service or discount brokers. In reality, brokers who are registered with a stock exchange handle the majority of trades. One can select from a wide variety of brokerage firms, including full service and discount brokers. Discount brokers charge less for trades but offer little to no investment advice, whereas full service brokers typically charge more per trade but provide more personalized service or investment advice. A bank or credit union that has an agreement in place with a full-service or discount broker would be an example of another kind of broker. Purchasing stock does not always have to be done through a broker. One method is through the business directly. Most businesses permit the direct purchase of shares through their investor relations departments if at least one share is held. But the company's first share of stock will need to be acquired via a standard stock broker. Direct Public Offerings (DPOs), in which the company typically sells its own stock, are an additional means of purchasing company stock. An initial public offering (IPO) known as a "direct public offering" occurs when stock is bought straight from the company, typically without the assistance of brokers.

There are two options available for financing the purchase of stocks: using funds that the buyer already owns or buying stock on margin. Purchasing stocks on margin entails borrowing money to purchase stocks that are valued lower than other stocks in the same account. If the buyer is unable to repay the loan, the stockbroker has the right to sell the stocks, which serve as collateral, in order to cover the outstanding balance. If the share price falls to less than the required margin, he may sell for at least half of the account's total stock value. Purchasing on margin functions similarly to taking out a loan against the value of an automobile or home and using that asset as security. Furthermore, borrowing doesn't come without cost; the broker typically adds 8–10% interest.

7.4.4.2. Selling

Purchasing and selling stocks work in similar ways procedurally. Although there are a variety of circumstances that could lead an investor to sell at a loss, generally speaking, the investor wants to buy low and sell high, if not in that order (short selling). g. in order to stop more losses. Similar to purchasing stock, the broker's work in facilitating the transfer of stock from a seller to a buyer is compensated with a transaction fee. Depending on the type of brokerage handling the transaction—full service or discount—this fee may be high or low. The seller is then entitled to receive all of the money after the transaction has been completed. Monitoring the profits is a crucial aspect of selling. Crucially, in states where they apply, capital gains taxes on any additional proceeds—if any—above the cost basis must be paid upon selling the stock.

7.4.4.3. Short Selling

An investor who engages in short selling sells borrowed shares right away and then purchases them back at a lower price (a process known as covering). In essence, this type of investor is placing a wager that the shares will decline in value, allowing them to be repurchased at a reduced cost and subsequently paid back to the lender at a profit. Generally speaking, buying stock carries less risk than short selling it. This is due to the possibility of an infinite loss because the stock's value could increase forever.

7.4.4.4. Stock Price Fluctuations

The principle of supply and demand is the primary cause of a stock's price fluctuations. A stock's price is influenced by demand, just like the prices of all commodities on the market. Nonetheless, a variety of factors can affect how much demand there is for a specific stock. Both technical and fundamental analysis make an effort to forecast future price levels and comprehend the market dynamics that influence price fluctuations. According to a recent study, there is a significant correlation between a stock's market value and customer satisfaction as indicated by the American Customer Satisfaction Index (ACSI). Analysts' business projections for the company and outlooks for its overall market segment may have an impact on the stock price. Pump and dump scams can also cause significant fluctuations in stocks.

7.4.4.5. Share Price Determination

The price of an equity at any given time is solely determined by supply and demand. The quantity of shares offered for sale at any given time is known as the supply, also known as the float. The quantity of shares that investors want to purchase at that precise moment is known as the demand. The stock price fluctuates in an effort to establish and preserve equilibrium. The market capitalization of the company offering the equity at that particular moment is the result of multiplying this instantaneous price by the float. The price increases when there are more potential buyers than sellers. After a while, buyers and sellers reach equilibrium when sellers drawn by the high asking price enter the market and/or buyers depart. Prices decrease when there are more sellers than buyers. Eventually, sellers depart and/or buyers arrive, reestablishing equilibrium. As a result, every investor's vote, cast in cash, determines the share price of a company at any given time. A stock's price will increase if more buyers are willing to pay more for it. A stock's price will decrease if more investors are selling it and there aren't enough buyers (Mithas Sunil, 2006).

That doesn't explain how individuals determine the lowest price they will accept for a product or the highest price they will pay for one. Although this theory is debatable in academic and professional circles, the efficient market hypothesis (EMH) is still widely accepted in professional investment circles. In short, the Efficient Market Hypothesis (EMH) states that: (1) share prices of equities are priced efficiently, meaning that they accurately represent the expected value of the stock, as best it can be known at a given moment; (2) the price of a stock at any given moment represents a rational evaluation of the known information that might bear on the future value of the company; and (3) investing is generally (weighted by the standard deviation) rational. Stated differently, prices are the outcome of deducting anticipated future cash flows.

If accurate, the EMH model has at least two noteworthy ramifications. First, the return on equity should be slightly higher than that of non-equity investments because financial risk is assumed to require at least a small premium on expected value. If not, equity investors would likely move to these safer non-equity investments, which should yield a similar or higher return at a lower risk, based on the same rational calculations. Second, relative to the expected return curve, prices will typically follow a random walk as new information emerges (randomly) over time. This is because the price of a share at any given time is an efficient reflection of expected value. As a result, professional equity investors immerse themselves in the flow of fundamental information in an attempt to outsmart their rivals, who are primarily other professional investors, by better interpreting the news as it emerges. The process of determining equity prices does not appear to be fully described by the EMH model. Stock markets, for instance, are more erratic than the EMH would suggest. It is now widely acknowledged that share markets are not entirely efficient, possibly more so in developing nations or other markets where knowledgeable professional investors do not hold a disproportionate amount of influence. The study of behavioral finance has produced yet another theory regarding how share prices are determined. Behavioral finance holds that people frequently make irrational decisions based on fears and incorrect outcomes perceptions, especially when it comes to purchasing and selling securities. The prices of securities can frequently deviate from fundamental, rational price assessments due to irrational trading behavior. For example, due to the greater fool theory, technology companies were frequently bid beyond any rational fundamental value during the late 1990s technology bubble (which was followed by the dot-com bust of 2000–2002). According to the greater fool theory, one should choose securities that they think someone else will value at a higher level at some point in the future, regardless of the reasons behind that other party's willingness to pay a higher price, because selling them to another investor is the primary way to realize returns on equity. So even an investor who is rational can profit from the irrationality of others.

7.4.4.6. Arbitrage trading

There is a chance that the value of shares

on various exchanges will differ when businesses raise money by selling their stock on multiple exchanges. Knowing about these differences and being a shrewd investor, one can engage in arbitrage trading—making investments with the expectation that the discrepancies will eventually converge. According to the efficient-market hypothesis, electronic trading has increased price transparency. If there are price differences, they are transient and swiftly equilibrate.

7.4.5. P/E Ratio Forms the Basis of Stock Valuation Theory

The price-to-earnings ratio calculation is the most widely used method of stock valuation. A company's stock price is valued using the P/E ratio in relation to its most recent reported earnings per share (EPS). The P/E ratio is a metric used by investors to assess the stock value of a company. Higher P/E ratios are indicative of overvalued stock. On the other hand, low P/E suggests undervalued shares when compared to peers and the overall market. Value investors are always on the lookout for cheap stocks with room to grow. To ascertain whether the price per share appropriately reflects expected earnings per share, analysts look at the P/E ratio. P/E (TTM), which is the trailing 12-month earnings per share or the company's income over the previous 12-month period, is frequently the EPS used to calculate the P/E ratio.

7.4.5.1. Good P/E Ratio

A P/E ratio that makes sense for one investor might not for another. This is due to the fact that investors' perspectives on the P/E ratio vary based on whether they are value- or growth-oriented investors. When a low P/E ratio indicates that a company's shares are undervalued in relation to its competitors, value investors will always choose that company. On the other hand, growth investors will look at businesses with a high P/E because they believe there are more opportunities for growth. Growth investors compute two P/E ratios: the price-to-earning-to-growth (PEG) ratio and the forward-looking P/E ratio. Investors compute the forward-looking P/E ratio using a straightforward formula. They replace the trailing 12 months' EPS with the estimated EPS for the upcoming fiscal year. On the other hand, the PEG ratio, which is computed by dividing a company's P/E ratio by the rate of earnings growth, indicates the growth in earnings per share of the company. While calculating the PEG ratio for five years is the most popular method, it can be adjusted for any duration, which makes it flexible when determining stock price. Investors utilize the Price/Sales and Price/Book ratios in addition to the P/E ratio when valuing stocks.

7.4.6. Avoiding Value Trap

Value investors frequently take a chance when selecting equities with low P/E ratios due to inherent business conditions, such as deteriorating market conditions and weak fundamentals. If a company's P/E seems unusually low, investors should investigate its fundamentals to avoid falling victim to a value trap. Stock valuation assists investors in determining a stock's actual value. Stock valuation can be done in a number of ways, each with pros and cons of its own. Stock valuation can be divided into two main categories: absolute and relative. The Relative technique assesses a company's position in relation to peers and industry standards, while the Absolute method determines a stock's true value based on the financials and fundamentals of the business. Make sure the model you choose for valuation is suitable for the company. Investors frequently combine various valuation techniques to perform comparative valuation against rivals and larger markets in order to gain a comprehensive understanding. One important factor in determining fair value is stock valuation. It enables investors to learn through comparative analysis of stocks that have the potential to increase in value over time. There are various perspectives and interpretations of stock valuation, though. Thus, when determining a company's value, investors need to take both its strengths and weaknesses into account. Businesses with a large base benefit from network effects, but those with a distinct competitive advantage have a better chance of surviving in the face of growing competition.

7.4.7. Common Stock Valuation: The Two Approaches

Since corporations were first established as distinct legal entities, common stock has grown to be one of the most significant financial instruments in existence. Generally speaking, when people talk about the "market," they are talking about the stock market. To the layman, stocks are the same as investing. However, the general public is ignorant of the proper way to value stocks. This essay will clarify the differences between the theoretical model and the way the general public values stock prices.

7.4.7.1. The Theoretical Model

According to theories, shares truly stand for fractional ownership. As a result, if you own 1% of a company's shares, their value should equal 1% of the company's anticipated value. Now, when we talk about expected value, we have to realize that value will only start to accumulate later on as and when the business operates over time. There are currently beliefs and anticipations regarding the value in the future. To determine the company's future valuation, we must discount these fictitious future values using the appropriate discount rate. We can calculate the share value by extrapolating this future valuation once it has been determined. For example, if the total enterprise value is $100, then 1% of the company's stock should be worth $1. This serves as the scientific foundation for valuing shares at a share price. This method has the advantage of being far more objective than the others. This approach allows one to determine what they believe to be a company's fair market value. Then, they can determine if the current market price offers a good chance to purchase at a discount. This process is known as the discounted cash flow (DCF) method, and it is what we will be talking about from now on.

7.4.7.2. The Behavioral Model

Theoretically, the model is excellent. But frequently, it might not be used in real life. There is an easy explanation for this. DCF models need a great deal of data. Next, they make the assumption that the investor is knowledgeable enough to sort through all of this data, make sense of it, and determine the right price. However, that isn't the case. Typically, investors consider historical stock performance, peer performance data, and so forth. They make an effort to have a very vague notion of how the industry's future developments are anticipated to unfold and what each specific company stands to gain or lose from them. They make their decision about whether or not to purchase a share based on this extremely imprecise heuristic. This strategy has the drawback of encouraging bubbles. The share that is already increasing in value will seem appealing since there is no objective valuation, which will encourage more people to purchase it and drive up the price even higher. The same is true for falling prices as well, proving that this strategy is not firmly based in reality. It is not reasonable to expect the future to unfold as the past did. Therefore, over all guessing games, the DCF method is always preferred. The DCF approach to stock valuation, which is theoretically correct, will be covered in the remaining articles.

7.4.8. Choosing a Valuation Model

Now that we know that there are a variety of models available for use in valuing a company or asset, the next question that naturally arises is: which one should we use? How can we determine which valuation model is best suited for a particular company over the others? The truth is that we cannot say for sure. Since valuation is an art, our only options for choosing a particular valuation model are general guidelines.

- **Characteristics of the Company:** The qualities of the company that is being valued are the first and most crucial component. Think about how the quantity of assets under a company's control can be used to determine its value, such as in the case of Ford Motor Company. But we can't value a Google-like company using the same method. The majority of Google's assets are intangible and intellectual. They might not be useful to the acquirer if they are incomplete. Therefore, it is necessary to ascertain whether the company can be valued using its assets as the basis for its valuation as the first consideration. The asset valuation model needs to be disregarded if the company has assets that are primarily intangible or if only they can benefit from them. Next, we must take into account a company's dividend policy. For example, utility companies have consistently distributed dividends and are expected to continue doing so in the near future. Conversely, Microsoft and other corporations have not distributed dividends for a significant portion of their history. Because of this, businesses such as Microsoft cannot be valued similarly to utility companies, which are subject to discounted dividend valuation. Finally, the individual carrying out the valuation exercise needs to understand the analysis's goal. A long-term investment will have a different valuation than a short-term one. Because of this, businesses with a competitive advantage may be offered a higher premium in the near term if there is no threat from the competition.
- **Characteristics of the Investor:** Although it might not seem evident, the qualities of the investor also have a significant impact on the model that should be chosen for valuation. Take the situation of a retail investor, for example. It is true that the asset is owned by a retail investor. They are not in charge of the assets, though. They are therefore unable to forecast their cash flows in any other way and are at the whim of the company's dividend policy. Among other methods, a discounted dividend approach might be more appropriate in this situation. Let us now examine the situation of an institutional investor. With their vast financial resources, institutional investors can purchase a sizeable enough stake to persuade

management to alter the dividend payout schedule. The discounted dividend model might not be very useful in this situation. The amount of free cash flow that the business can produce is what counts instead. Because of this, discounted free cash flow models are more frequently used by institutional investors. Finally, in the event of a rival company acquisition, they will have the ability to affect not only the dividend payout policy but also the day-to-day operations of the company. Therefore, using the discounted residual income model will result in a more accurate valuation in this case.

- **Purpose of Investment:** Finally, a key factor in selecting a valuation model is the investment's goal. Take the scenario where a conglomerate company purchases a business that is unrelated, for example. In this case, the value that investors receive will be directly correlated with the asset's value. It's possible that the ideas of synergy and value growth don't apply there. However, if a rival company buys out a company, they can take advantage of the economies of scale and other synergies that come with doing so. Thus, the idea of synergy might also apply in this situation. Additionally, investors occasionally purchase private businesses with the intention of selling them later on by going public. In this scenario, the retail investor's assessment of the company's value will be the sole determinant of the valuation. Therefore, using a different valuation model might be necessary.
- **Multiple Models:** It is noteworthy that investors frequently employ multiple models, as opposed to just one, to determine a company's valuation. The analyst can confirm whether they are receiving comparable or identical value measures from each model by utilizing multiple models. Even in the event that the estimates do not match, they will still have a better idea of the underlying reason for the higher valuation and whether the extra premium is justified. Therefore, it is always preferable to use multiple valuation models rather than base a valuation solely on one.

7.4.9. Value Investing Demystified: How to Spot Undervalued Stocks

Finding opportunities that promise growth and value is a challenge that many investors face in the fast-paced world of financial markets. Value investing is one strategy that endures over time; it is based on patient patience and fundamental analysis. Even though there are many investment options available today, such as Altrix Sync, the age-old wisdom of spotting cheap stocks should not be disregarded. We'll demystify value investing in this piece and explain how to find those hidden treasures in the stock market. Value investing is a philosophy that transcends the exhilaration and fanfare that are frequently connected to stock markets. It focuses on identifying stocks that provide investors with a margin of safety by trading below their intrinsic value. Value investors have a longer term outlook than speculators, who chase market trends and quick profits. They look for businesses with solid fundamentals that the market has overlooked or undervalued. Even though there can be a strong allure to contemporary investment opportunities like crypto-currencies, it's important to remember the timeless value investing principles. Even though there are now many trading platforms available, including those that concentrate on digital assets, value investing in stocks is still a tried-and-true method that offers stability and the possibility of long-term growth. Having established the significance of value investing, let's examine the doable methods for identifying cheap stocks.

- **Fundamental Analysis:** Value investors start with a thorough analysis of a company's financial statements. Key indicators to focus on include earnings per share (EPS), price-to-earnings (P/E) ratio, and debt levels. By comparing these metrics to industry averages and historical data, investors can gauge whether a stock is undervalued.
- **Margin of Safety:** One of the core tenets of value investing is the concept of a "margin of safety." This means buying a stock at a price significantly lower than its intrinsic value to protect against unforeseen market downturns. By doing so, investors cushion themselves from potential losses.
- **Competitive Advantage:** Seek out companies with a sustainable competitive advantage, often referred to as a "moat." A strong competitive position can help a company maintain profitability and market share over the long term, making it a prime candidate for value investing.
- **Contrarian Thinking:** Value investors often go against the crowd. If a stock has fallen out of favor with the market due to short-term issues or negative sentiment, it may present an opportunity for a contrarian investor to buy at a discount.
- **Dividend Yield:** Companies that pay consistent dividends can be attractive to value investors. A healthy dividend yield can provide a steady income stream and signal a company's financial stability.
- **Price-to-Book (P/B) Ratio:** The P/B ratio compares a company's market value to its book value (assets minus liabilities). A low P/B ratio may indicate an undervalued stock, as investors can buy the company's assets for less than their book value.
- **Qualitative Analysis:** In addition to quantitative factors, value investors also consider qualitative aspects such as management quality, industry trends, and the company's growth potential. A well-managed company with a bright future can be a hidden gem.

Let's take a hypothetical example to illustrate the process of identifying undervalued stocks:

Let us consider XYZ Inc., a manufacturing company., which regularly produces positive cash flows and dividends. Nevertheless, because of a recent decline in the industry, XYZ Inc.'s stock price has drastically decreased, resulting in a low P/E ratio when compared to its historical average and peers in the industry. A value investor would study XYZ Inc. in great detail. 's financial statements, evaluate its position in the market, and take the long-term outlook for the industry into account. An investor may choose to buy shares of XYZ Inc. if they conclude that the company's fundamentals are still solid and that the stock has been unfairly undervalued by the market., ready for a possible correction in price.

7.4.10. Investment Diversification

The goal of diversification is to lower overall portfolio risk by combining various asset classes in an investment portfolio. Stated differently, the process of choosing an asset mix to lower the return uncertainty on an investment portfolio is known as investment diversification. Since different investments may rise and fall independently of one another, diversification helps to lower the risks associated with investing. Combining these assets will lessen risk by offsetting the effects of fluctuation. The majority of financial assets are held as components of portfolios rather than as individual items. Diversified portfolios are mandated for banks, mutual funds, insurance companies, pension funds, and other financial institutions. Even individual investors typically hold stock portfolios rather than the stock of a single company, at least those whose securities holdings account for a sizable portion of their overall wealth. One major explanation for this is the reduction of risk, or the possibility of receiving no return at all or a negative return on some assets. A single asset owner is heavily reliant on the issuer company, its performance, dividend policy, and the state of the market as a whole. Conversely, having a well-diversified portfolio shields an individual from issuer internal issues as well as market swings. A diversified portfolio contributes to consistent investment returns.

A portfolio can be made more diverse in a variety of ways. People are able to diversify within a single asset class, like stocks. Buying stock in the top businesses in numerous unrelated industries would be one way to achieve this. There exist numerous alternative strategies for investment diversification. Your investment portfolio can be diversified by allocation to different regions (such as a state, region, or country) or by a combination of asset classes (stocks, bonds, and real estate, for instance). There are thousands of choices. Fortunately, increasing returns while lowering risks is the ultimate objective of practically all successful investment diversification strategies. A fund manager may use the following strategies when deciding on the mode of investment diversification.

- **Diversify within an industry:** Since the returns of companies within an industry are typically highly correlated, investing in a variety of different stocks within the same industry does not result in a diversified portfolio. Still, this is preferable to buying just one stock.
- **Diversify across industry groups:** Compared to firms within an industry, there is probably less correlation between industries. To maximize the benefits of diversification, choose stocks from industries that either move in opposite directions or have very little correlation with one another. This is because some industries can have strong correlations with other industries.
- **Diversify across geographical regions:** Businesses that operate in the same geographic area are vulnerable to similar risks, such as changes in state or local taxes and natural disasters. These risks can be spread by making investments in businesses whose operations are not located in the same area.
- **Diversify across countries:** Stocks within a nation have a tendency to be more correlated than stocks among nations. This is due to the fact that numerous tax and

regulatory concerns are universal to all stocks within a given nation. One way to diversify these risks is through international diversification.

- **Diversify across asset classes:** Investing across asset classes such as stocks, bonds, and real property also produces diversification benefits. The returns of two stocks tend to be more highly correlated, on average, than the returns of a stock and a bond or a stock and an investment in real estate.

CASE STUDY

WARREN BUFFET'S INVESTMENT STYLE

Warren Buffett is the only billionaire in history to amass his fortune entirely through shrewd investing. He started investing with 10,000 dollars earned from a paper route and went on to become one of the wealthiest people in the world. Today his worth is staggering $30 billion.

Warren Buffett was born on August 30, 1930 in Omaha, Nebraska. Since his early childhood, he has been fond of reading various kinds of investment books and The Wall Street Journal. He bought his first stock at age 11. He regretted later as he made delay in purchasing his first stock. At the age of 15, he had saved enough money to buy a 40 acre land from his father at Nebraska. By the age of 20, his fortune was estimated $9800 and it was about $68000 in inflated dollars at the end of 1999.

Buffett completed his degree from University of Nebraska, Lincoln. In 1950, Buffett applied to Harvard Business School but was rejected in a 10 minute interview. Then Buffett joined to Columbia Business School and he graduated a year later with a master's degree in economics. During his tenure in Columbia University, Buffett came across Benjamin Graham whose lessons grounded on premise that stocks should reflect the inner worth of a company and that superior returns could be experienced by buying undervalued securities, coursed through Buffett like a lightning bolt. After Graduation, Buffett worked as a stock salesman for his father until 1954. After three years of pestering, Graham hired Buffett to work at his investment management company, Graham Newman. But Graham shuttered the company two years later and retired. Buffett returned to home with net worth estimated $140000.

Buffett started an investment pool with $100 of his own money and persuading family and friends to contribute $105000. Buffett found that he could buy a significant position in an undervalued company, demand a board sit, take a leading role in righting the company's financial problems and then assist management in selling the company for a higher price than Buffett paid. The most famous of these control investments was a textile mill called Berkshire Hathaway. From this point forward, Buffett's fortunes were inextricably linked to Berkshire but he could mostly control it. If he could continuously increase the intrinsic value of Berkshire, he could ultimately enhance his own net worth. Through Berkshire Hathaway, Buffet invested in many stocks and owned many companies which led to the tremendous growth in his fortune. The strategy through which Buffet picked the stocks and the way, Buffett analyzed the company and invested in them which in turn helped to make his fortune are discussed below:

Warren Buffett gives the tremendous importance to the power of compounding. No force exerts more influence on portfolio than time. Time takes a bigger toll on terminal wealth than do taxes, inflation and poor stock picking combined. The longer that money can compound, the larger the sum will be. The rate of return attained acts as a lever that magnifies or minimizes the ultimate wealth. Adding just a few percentage points a year to overall returns can have unfathomable consequence to the wealth. Choosing good companies at fair prices seldom has produced losses for investors willing to wait patiently for the stock price to track the growth of the company. The power of compounding begins working its magic as the year progresses and allows net worth to gather momentum and increase value by greater and greater amounts. Buffett has been occasionally criticized for not donating more of its wealth to his shareholders. But Buffett's reasoning is perfectly consistent with his investment philosophy. As long as he can continue to compound money at great rates, society would be better off if he didn't give away money now. He is behaving as any rational CEO would. If a company generates high return on its assets, it should withhold dividends to investors and plow as much money as it can each year back into business. Only when it can no longer generate a strong internal return should a company think about returning money to shareholders.

Investors should never accept average returns because that's the best they will ever attain. They should instead seek ways to magnify their yearly returns. Adding a few percentage points of gain each year compounds into huge amounts over time. The return will be much higher if the stocks are bought when market underpriced the company. An undervalued security must eventually rise in price and an overvalued security must fall. The immutable law of mathematics ultimately will bestow higher returns upon stocks more apt to rise than fall. In order to enhance return, stocks must be bought at the lowest possible price. The lower the price paid, the higher the expected returns. Warren Buffett is also insisting on price be linked to growth and quality. Investors tend to be irrational and forever willing to overpay for glamour stocks and follow the crowd when stocks crash. They also have psychological penchant for avoiding stocks that decline in value. Some investors also think that diversification is the best strategy to avoid losses when market is down. However, diversification is the bane of high returns. A properly diversified portfolio is one that eliminates non-systematic risks, the risk that a single stock can cause material disruptions to returns. A large portfolio merely reduces the probability of loss but it does not reduce systematic risk, the risk of an unforeseen event causing the entire stock market to drop.

The goal of every investment is to maximize the total return on investment. Every dollar spent by an enterprise on a capital project must generate the highest possible return. Every dollar spent on a single item is a dollar unavailable for other items. The dollar must provide a suitable return measured against what could have been earned on that dollar somewhere else.

Warren Buffett detests rapid trading. To him, it's a money wasting activity that usually leads to inferior returns for investors. Further, it causes wide disparities in pricing that may prompt management to take unnatural or irrational actions to stem investors' biases. Certainly many investors who casually buy and sell stocks online a few times a week may believe they are on the road to success but their success is due only to the extraordinary persistence of the bull market, not to their own acumen. Lured by fabulous success of internet stocks and by the advent of online trading, many have concluded that it's a breeze to amass a small fortune by hitting a few key strokes each day. But Buffett is so confident in his stock picking ability that he wants to continue holding an investment perpetually. Rather than lull himself into believing he can win by continually darting in and out of the market, Buffett believes he can earn and retain more money picking a few choice companies and letting them grow over time.

The game of investment is a game of probabilities. An investor needs to quantify risks, make mental calculation of potential return, stir up those assumptions in a pot and produce a stock picking strategy that works the majority of the time. Too much analysis, however, inevitably leads to trouble. There comes a point at which stock picking systems break down and prove futile because they are too complicated. Warren Buffett is keenly aware of the limitations of data and shuns most artifices routinely used by professional investors today. He has not hurt himself by shunning basic tools. His lack of resources has probably served him better than if he had operated Bloomberg Terminals, Quotrons or statistical software packages. The more components one adds to one's investing model, the more complicated one makes the stock picking system and the more often it will fail. Because the probability of errors multiplies as fast as one adds more layers of details to the analysis, he or she will learn to avoid relying on models that use numerous variables especially models based on future forecasts. This is the chief reason value investors such as Warren Buffett have little use for market forecasts or extravagant stock picking systems.

The stock market fires thousands of pitches a day, with each pitch representing a certain stock at a certain price. One should avoid situations where chances of success are even at the best. Instead, one should concentrate on investments where one has high confidence in earning a profit. Warren Buffett, like many other great investors, avoids the temptation of buying a stock that seems alluring at the moment simply because he has surplus cash in his hand. Any stock can be potentially be a value if the price is right, but Buffett does not allow himself to be fooled into buying stocks just because they are undervalued. Buffett avoids this trap by identifying all the stocks he wishes to own over the next several years and buys them one at a time, but only when they fall to an attractive price. If the stocks do not fall to his desired price immediately, he does not take any action. He knows that the odds favor a decline in price sooner or later. In the interim, he will devote his attention to other desirable companies whose price may already have fallen to appealing levels.

Every business possesses an intrinsic value that reflects both the long term earning power of the enterprise and the risks of holding the investment over time. Intrinsic value is dynamic and it changes with time. But a firm's value should be equal to what it can earn over its eternal lifetime and adjusting earnings for inflation and time value of money. For a cyclical company, future earnings can be determined by taking average earnings in the past year while for a steady growth company, future earnings will determined by estimating the growth rate and interpolating the growth rate in future. Appropriate risk free rate should be taken as discount rate while valuing a company. If the investment in a particular stock can't yield a return that can beat a bond's yield, it's better to invest in the bond.

Buffett's book value scorecard clearly ranks him among the top CEOs of the twentieth century. A company can grow its book value by simply issuing more shares, by acquiring other companies or by letting profits sit in the bank and drawing interest. These should be taken into account during calculation of a company's book value.

Return on Equity (ROE) plays an important role in analyzing companies and putting stock prices and valuation levels in proper context. Most investors tend to concentrate on company's past and projected earnings growth. However, a company's ability to produce high return on owners' capital is equally as crucial to long term growth. Buffett believes that companies that can generate and sustain high ROEs should be coveted because they are relatively rare. They should be purchased when their stocks trade at attractive levels relative to their earnings growth and ROEs because it is extremely difficult for companies to maintain high ROEs as they increase in size. Before Buffett buys shares of a company, he makes sure the stock is capable of returning at least 15% a year for him over a long period.

Warren Buffett craves consistency because it helps remove risk from a stock portfolio. Research has shown that a consistent track record of performance tends to result in consistent share price growth. A company with a long track record of stable performance is much more likely to have a stable stock price than a company whose growth streak is pockmarked with sharp gain and losses.

The essence of successful investing can be summarized by two rules:

1. Don't lose money.
2. Don't forget rule number (i).

CLASS ACTIVITY

STOCK VALUATION ANALYSIS

Objective: To understand and apply stock valuation techniques using the Price-to-Earnings (P/E) ratio.

Materials needed: Computers with internet access, financial statements, calculator, and worksheet etc.

Assessment: Divide the class into small groups of 3–4 students. Assign each group a different publicly traded company. Ensure a mix of companies from various sectors. Encourage groups to consider other factors that might affect valuation (e.g., market conditions, company performance, industry trends).

Extension: As a follow-up assignment, ask students to research another valuation method (e.g., Dividend Discount Model, Price-to-Book Ratio) and apply it to their assigned company, comparing results with the P/E ratio analysis.

SUMMARY

- A stock, also known as equity, is a security that represents the ownership of a fraction of the issuing corporation. Units of stock are called shares, which entitle the owner to a proportion of the corporation's assets and profits equal to how much stock they own.
- Corporate property is legally separated from the property of shareholders, which limits the liability of both the corporation and the shareholder. If the corporation goes bankrupt, a judge may order all of its assets sold, but a shareholder's assets are not at risk.
- Stock typically takes the form of shares of either common stock or preferred stock. As a unit of ownership, common stock typically carries voting rights that can be exercised in corporate decisions. Preferred stock differs from common stock in that it typically does not carry voting rights but is legally entitled to receive a certain level of dividend payments before any dividends can be issued to other shareholders.
- Beta coefficient is a comparative measure of how the stock performs relative to the market as a whole. It is determined by plotting the stock's and market's returns at discrete intervals over a period of time and fitting (regressing) a line through the resulting data points.

- It is a process of encompassing many activities of investment in assets and securities. The portfolio management includes the planning, supervision, timing, rationalism and conservatism in the selection of securities to meet investor's objectives.
- The portfolio management deals with the process of selection of securities from the number of opportunities available with different expected returns and carrying different levels of risk and the selection of securities is made with a view to provide the investors the maximum yield for a given level of risk or ensure minimize risk for a given level of return.
- A number of financial ratios use the market price per share of common stock. Investors often rely on these ratios to assess whether a stock is overvalued or if it is undervalued – and therefore may offer an opportunity to buy the stock at a bargain price.
- Technical analysis is the process of utilizing past trading information and stock price trends related to a specific security, and then equating those to how other likewise investments have responded throughout history to similar patterns.
- A stock chart is a simple two-axis (X-Y) plotted graph of price and time. Each individual equity, market and index listed on a public exchange has a chart that illustrates this movement of price over time. Individual data plots for charts can be made using the closing price for each day.
- The stock chart is used to identify the current trend. A trend reflects the average rate of change in a stock's price over time. Trends exist in all time frames and all markets. Trends can be classified in three ways: UP, down or range-bound.

REVIEW QUESTIONS

1. How do the different types of stock beta influence investment decisions?
2. What are the key factors that influence the investment choices of value investors versus growth investors?
3. What factors should be considered when determining the number of shares to issue for a new business?
4. What are the key metrics and tools used in fundamental analysis compared to technical analysis?
5. Why the P/E ratio is considered a fundamental metric in stock valuation theory?

REFERENCES

1. Hawk, B. (2015). *Law and Commerce in Pre-Industrial Societies*. Brill Publishers. ISBN 978-90-04-30622-6.
2. Irwin, D. A. (1991). Mercantilism as strategic trade policy: The Anglo-Dutch rivalry for the East India trade. *The Journal of Political Economy, 99*(6), 1296–1314. https://doi.org/10.1086/261801.

3. Jackson, T. (2001). *The Logic and Limits of Bankruptcy Law*. Oxford University Press. ISBN 1-58798-114-9.

4. Mithas, S. (2006). Increased customer satisfaction increases stock price. *Research@ Smith*. University of Maryland.

5. Mrzygłod, U., & Nowak, S. (2013). Stock exchanges go public: The case of Warsaw Stock Exchange. *Journal of International Studies, 6*(2), 111–123. https://doi.org/10.14254/2071-8330.2013/6-2/10.

6. Summers, D. (2007). *Longman Business English Dictionary*. Pearson Longman. ISBN 978-1-4058-5259-3.

7. Venkatesan, P. (2018). National stock exchange vs Bombay stock exchange: A comparative analysis. *International Journal of Trend in Scientific Research and Development, 3*(1), 659–661. https://doi.org/10.31142/ijtsrd19030.

CHAPTER 8

Risk and the Cost of Capital

LEARNING OBJECTIVES

After studying this chapter, you will be able to:

- Identify which types of securities have historically had the highest returns and which have been the most volatile
- Compute the average return and volatility of returns from a set of historical asset prices
- Understand the cost of capital
- Describe the components of cost of capital
- Discuss the weighted average cost of capital (WACC)
- Differentiate between cost of debt and cost of equity

KEY TERMS FROM THIS CHAPTER

Benchmark index
Capital gains
Cash flow
Exchange rate risk
Interest rate risk
Market performance
Penny stocks
Rate of return
Capital budgeting
Capital structure
Discount rate
Expected return
Investment
Market risk
Political risk
Realized return

INTRODUCTION

Businesses are all about making a profit, and in order to meet their daily financial needs, they must identify the appropriate sources of funding. This entails a meticulous evaluation of multiple sources where the cost of capital continues to be the lowest rate of return on investment in order to meet investor expectations for business revenue generation. Investors may choose to fund the company with term-specific loans, equity shares, debentures, or a combination of these. It continues to be crucial in determining the sensible capital structure of the business. As the finance manager, it is your responsibility to minimize shareholder wealth by giving top priority to the cost of capital and the financing vehicle or medium that will yield the highest expected rate of return.

The return needed to justify a company's capital investment project is referred to as the cost of capital. Equity and debt funding are included in the cost of capital. Market risk influences capital cost by raising the price of equity financing. Usually, the CAPM is used to examine cost of equity.

8.1. RISK AND RETURN

In 1925, your great-grandparents could have made over $15 million in profits if they had invested just $100 in a portfolio of small businesses. As we will see, though, this kind of decision would have been fraught with risk, and we can only know in hindsight that it would have been profitable.

We start our analysis of risk and return by showing how investor choices and returns are impacted by the risk premium. Assume that at the end of 1925, your great-grandparents had made a $100 investment on your behalf. They gave their broker instructions to reinvested any dividends or interest received in the account through the start of 2010. If the $100 had been invested in any of the following securities, how would it have increased in value?

1. **Standard & Poor's 500 (S&P 500):** A portfolio, constructed by Standard & Poor's, comprising 90 U.S. stocks up to 1957 and 500 U.S. stocks after that. The firms represented are leaders in their respective industries and are among the largest firms, in terms of market capitalization (share price times the number of shares in the hands of the shareholders), traded on U.S. markets.
2. **Small Stocks:** A portfolio of stocks of U.S. firms whose market values are in the bottom 10% of all stocks traded on the NYSE. (As stocks' market values change, this portfolio is updated so it always consists of the smallest 10% of stocks.)
3. **World Portfolio:** A portfolio of international stocks from all of the world's major stock markets in North America, Europe, and Asia.
4. **Corporate Bonds:** A portfolio of long-term, AAA-rated U.S. corporate bonds with maturities of approximately 20 years.
5. **Treasury Bills:** An investment in three-month U.S. Treasury bills (reinvested as the bills mature).

The outcome of investing $100 at the end of 1925 for each of these five distinct investment portfolios is displayed in Figure 8.1 through the end of 2009. The numbers are startling: if your grandparents had put $100 into the small-stock portfolio at the start of 2010, the investment would have been worth over $15 million! In contrast, if they had put their money into Treasury bills, the investment would have only been worth $2635.

In Figure 8.1, the bottom line, you can see how prices have changed based on the Consumer Price Index (CPI) over the same period. Small stocks in the US saw the highest long-term return from 1925 to 2009; these were followed by large stocks in the S&P 500, foreign stocks in the global portfolio, corporate bonds, and Treasury bills. Every investment increased more quickly than the CPI-measured inflation.

In Figure 8.1, a second pattern is visible. The portfolio with the fewest stocks did the best over the long term, but its value fluctuated the most. For instance, during the 1930s Depression, small-stock investors suffered the biggest losses. For example, let's say that in 1925 your great-grandparents invested $100 in a small-stock portfolio with the intention of using it for their own retirement in 1940, 15 years later. Investing in corporate bonds would have yielded $217, whereas they would have had only $175 to live on in retirement. Furthermore, their investment's value would have decreased to as little as $33 over the course of the 15-year period. However, if they had placed their money in Treasury bills, they would have made consistent, if modest, gains every year instead of suffering any losses during the Great Depression. The same order holds true when we order the investments based on the magnitude of their value increases and decreases: small stocks had the most volatile returns, followed by the world portfolio, corporate bonds, S&P 500, Treasury bills, and finally, small stocks.

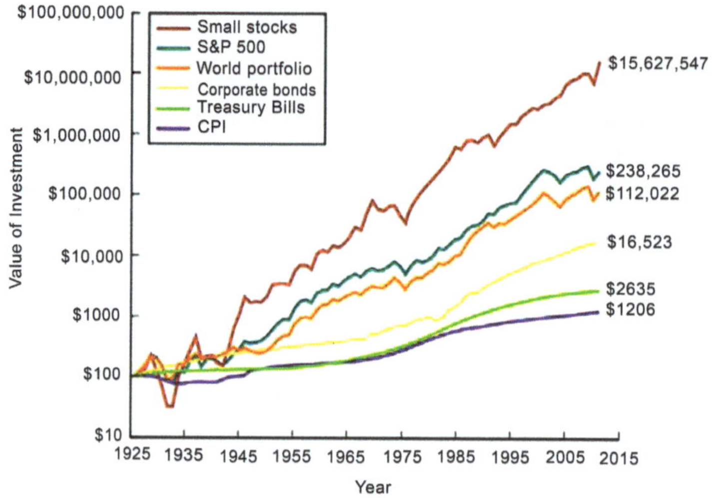

Figure 8.1. *Value of $100 invested at the end of 1925 in U.S. large stocks (S&P 500), Small Stocks, world stocks, corporate bonds, and treasury bills.*

Source: Jonathan Berk, Peter DeMarzo, and Jarrad Harford. Fundamentals of Corporate Finance, Second edition. Pearson Education. ISBN: 978-0-13-214823-8.

Because they are sensitive to changes in the value of their investments, investors require higher expected returns on riskier investments. More importantly, though, is that investors prefer not to have losses on their investments exacerbate their already dire circumstances. It's unlikely that you would have gotten the money back even if your great-grandparents had invested the $100 in a small-stock portfolio in 1925. More likely, your great-grandparents would have used their investments to augment their income during the worst of the Great Depression. The first 10 years of returns for several of the investments shown in Figure 8.1 are shown in Table 8.1. Red indicates negative returns, or losses. Take note of the small stock returns' lengthy, negative run from 1929 to 1932. Regretfully, during the Great Depression, your great-grandparents' modest stock portfolio would not have provided much assistance; in 1932, their initial $100 investment would have only been worth $33. In retrospect, the small-stock portfolio appears to have been a wise investment after 85 years, but in 1932, it would have appeared to be a grave error. It could be for this reason that your great-grandparents refrained from really investing your money in small stocks. The anguish of the investment failing right when funds were needed for other purposes is not nearly offset by the satisfaction of knowing that their great-grandchild might become a millionaire one day.

Table 8.1. Realized Returns, in Percent (%) for Small Stocks, the S&P 500, Corporate Bonds, and Treasury Bills, Year-End 1925–1935

Year	Small Stocks	S&P 500	Corp Bonds	Treasury Bills
1926	1.09	11.14	6.29	3.30
1927	31.37	37.13	6.55	3.15
1928	65.36	43.31	3.38	4.05
1929	−43.08	−8.91	4.32	4.47
1930	−44.70	−25.26	6.34	2.27
1931	−54.68	−43.86	−2.38	1.15
1932	−0.47	−8.85	12.20	0.88
1933	216.14	52.88	5.25	0.52
1934	57.20	−2.34	9.73	0.27
1935	69.11	47.22	6.86	0.17

Source: Jonathan Berk, Peter DeMarzo, and Jarrad Harford. Fundamentals of Corporate Finance, Second edition. Pearson Education. ISBN: 978–0-13–214823–8.

8.1.1. Risk and Return Definition

The potential financial gain or loss from investing in securities is discussed in the concepts of risk and return. A return on investment is the term used to describe an investor's profit. On the other hand, risk represents the likelihood that an investor will experience a loss of capital. The potential return is frequently low if an investor decides to put their money into an asset with little risk. On the other hand, there is a greater chance of greater profits from an investment containing a high level of risk (Horcher Karen, 2005).

A risk is the chance or odds that an investor is going to lose money.

A gain made by an investor is referred to as a return on their investment.

8.1.1.1. Risk

Risk can be defined in a multitude of ways. But when it comes to investing and financial management, it can be defined as the return volatility of an investment over a specific time period or as the likelihood of losing "X" amount of an investment.

An investor should be prepared to lose some or perhaps all of their money if they choose to make a very high-risk investment. For instance, an investor runs the risk of losing all of their money if they own stock (shares) in a high-risk business that files for bankruptcy.

Standard deviation is commonly used to characterize return volatility. This statistical measure, which is the square root of the variance, quantifies the dispersion of a dataset with respect to its mean.

To measure return volatility, the standard deviation is typically applied to the yearly return of an investment. Increased risk is implied by higher standard deviation, which also denotes increased investment volatility.

8.1.1.2. Return

A return is typically expressed as a percentage with respect to the initial investment over a specified time frame. It is also known as a financial return or an investment return. In financial management, there are two commonly utilized rates of return.

1. Nominal rates of return that include inflation
2. Real rates of return that exclude inflation

There are many different ways that an investment can yield a return, such as capital gains, interest, dividends, or, in the case of real estate, rental income. Once more, the typical presentation of these investment returns is as a percentage. Three variables can be used to calculate nominal investment returns in their most basic form:

1. The initial investment
2. The ending value of investment
3. The investment time period

Let's assume an initial investment of \$100 that grows to \$120 in one year. The investment return is calculated as follows:

$$\text{Nominal rate of return} = (\$120/\$100) - 1 = 0.2 \text{ or } 20\%$$

As mentioned above, this is the nominal rate of return. Let's now assume that the inflation rate during this one-year period was 3%. We calculate the real rate of return by taking the nominal rate of return and subtracting the inflation rate.

$$\text{Real rate of return} = 20\% - 3\% = 17\%$$

Real rates of return better reflect the purchasing power of investment returns.

8.1.2. Risk and Return Examples

Let's run through a few examples of risk and return.

- **Example 8.1:** Assume you wish to invest in Bond X and Bond Z, the two possible bonds. Assume further that Bond X has a 45% chance of failing (losing) and a 15% chance of non-payment. Given that Bond A gives you a better chance of keeping your money, you are naturally more inclined to choose it in the absence of any other information. Bond Z's success depends on raising interest rates until the benefit outweighs the risk of default. Then, even with its higher risk, Bond Z can lure you back.

  Higher profits from a riskier investment are necessary to offset the risks. Some investors are drawn in by the potential profits, while others are put off by the risk. Conversely, a less hazardous investment might yield relatively low rates of return because investors are more drawn to a less risky option than to the possibility of greater returns.

- **Example 8.2:** In order to have additional funds saved for retirement, a professor wishes to start investing. Option 1, Option 2, and Option 3 are the three options he is considering. Option 1 will be a complete loss because it will fail 100% of the time within the year. Option 2 will definitely make $100 by the end of the year, while Option 3 has a 50% chance of making $100 in profit and a 50% chance of losing everything.

Which option do you think the professor will choose? Let's break it down:

- Option 1 guarantees that the professor will lose all of his money so this is not the best option.
- Option 2 is equivalent to the professor already having the $100 in his account because there's a 100% chance of success.
- Option 3 is a toss-up: It's either worth $0 or $100 since the options are a total failure or total success. Therefore, to meet in the middle, this option is more than likely worth about $50 – calculated as the probability of success (50%) multiplied by the reward of success ($100). Many investors will be put off by the danger, whereas others will not want to lose out on the possible profit. Therefore, the price of option 3 is midway between option 1 and option 2.

8.1.3. Types of Risk and Return

There are several types of both risk and return.

8.1.3.1. Risks

There are several kinds of risks associated with saving and investing. However, risks are usually classified into two groups: systematic risks and unsystematic risks.

- **Systematic:** Systematic risks are those that have the potential to impact the whole economy or at least a sizable portion of it. These are the risks of asset loss resulting from different macroeconomic or political factors that affect the overall performance of the market. There are many types of systematic risks; a few of those are:
  - **Political Risk**: Political risk arises largely as a result of political insecurity in a nation or area. For example, if a country goes to war, the firms that operate there are deemed unsafe, and therefore risky.
  - **Market Risk** – Market risk is the byproduct of investors' overall inclination to follow the market. So it is essentially the inclination of security values to shift together.
  - **Exchange Rate Risk**: This type of risk arises from the unpredictability of currency value fluctuations. As a result, it impacts enterprises that conduct foreign exchange operations, such as export and import firms, or firms that do business in a foreign country.
  - **Interest Rate Risk**: A shift in the market's rate of interest causes this type of risk. It mostly affects fixed-income assets since bond costs are connected to interest rates, but it also affects the valuation of stocks.
- **Unsystematic:** Unsystematic risk is a kind of risk that exclusively affects one industry or one company. It is the risk of losing money on an

investment as a result of a risk unique to a company or industry. Unsystematic risk can take many different forms, such as a change in the company's leadership, a product safety recall, a law change that could affect sales, or the entry of a new competitor.

- **Systematic vs. Unsystematic:** In order to help you better understand, let's review a few of the main differences between systematic and unsystematic risks:
    - Systematic risks can't be controlled but unsystematic risks can be controlled.
    - Systematic risks are caused by external factors while unsystematic risks are caused by internal factors.
    - Systematic risks can cause chaos within an entire economy while unsystematic risks can only cause issues to a specific organization or sector.

8.1.3.2. Return

There are two types of return that are most focused on: realized return and expected return.

- **Realized**: Realized return is the actual return on an investment during a designated period of time. Realized returns are unchangeable, and this must be understood. It's essentially a post-fact number that cannot be changed. It merely gives investors information to aid in future financial decision-making.
- **Expected:** An investor's estimated potential profit or loss on an investment is known as the expected return. A measure used to determine whether an investment will, on average, have a positive or negative net outcome is called the expected return. Although it frequently sets reasonable expectations, the expected return is frequently based on historical data and cannot be guaranteed in the near future.

8.1.4. Risk and Return Concept

The amount of money people stand to lose on their initial investment serves as a proxy for the level of risk they are willing to take. Risk can take many forms, such as the possibility of a loss and the magnitude of that loss. Someone may imply that there is a significant chance that money will be lost or even a remote chance that all of a person's money could be lost when they label an investment as high-risk.

The term "return" refers to the amount of money you expect to get back from an investment over the initial amount. An investment has generated a return if it generates even a single cent more than you initially invested. However, if a return is stated negatively, it might also indicate how much money was lost. Returns are, in any event, frequently expressed as a percentage of the initial investment.

Risk and return should be closely correlated for an investment to be successful. The potential return on an investment increases with its level of risk. Conversely, a very safe (low-risk) investment should normally yield lower returns.

8.1.5. Risk and Return Relationship

The way the risk-return relationship

affects investment pricing is one of its most important aspects. The price of an asset in a profitable market reflects the balance between the asset's potential return and failure risk. Risk is calculated using the degree of volatility, or the difference between actual and expected returns. Standard deviation is the name given to this disparity. Compared to other investments, returns with a high standard deviation—the largest deviation from the mean—are more erratic and dangerous.

Essentially, risk and return are mutually exclusive concepts because investors aim for low risk but high returns. In a market that functions well, higher potential profits are correlated with larger risks. Concurrently, safer (lower risk) investments tend to yield smaller returns. These concepts describe how investors choose assets from the market and determine the values of those assets.

8.1.6. Risk-Return Tradeoff

According to the risk-return trade-off, potential return increases as risk increases. People use this principle to relate high levels of risk or uncertainty to high potential returns, and low levels of uncertainty to low potential returns.

The risk-return trade-off states that an investor can only make larger profits on their investment if they are willing to assume a greater chance of losing money.

The trading principle that connects high risk and high reward is known as the risk-return tradeoff. A number of variables, such as an investor's risk tolerance, the number of years until retirement, and the ability to replace lost funds, determine the proper risk-return trade-off. Determining a portfolio with the right amounts of risk and reward also requires a lot of time. For instance, an investor can potentially profit from bull markets and mitigate the risks associated with bear markets if they can invest in stocks for an extended period of time. Conversely, if an investor can only make short-term investments, the same stocks carry a higher risk.

The risk-return trade-off is a crucial factor that investors consider when making any investment decision and when evaluating their portfolios overall. Risk-return trade-offs at the portfolio level can involve evaluations of holdings' diversity or concentration, as well as whether the mix offers too much risk or a lower-than-desired potential for returns.

8.1.6.1. Uses of Risk-Return Tradeoff

1. **Measuring Singular Risk in Context:** An investor can apply the risk-return tradeoff to a vehicle both individually and in the context of the portfolio as a whole when evaluating high-risk, high-return investments. Investments with high risk and high return include leveraged exchange-traded funds (ETFs), penny stocks, and options. In general, the risks associated with individual investment positions are diminished by a diversified portfolio. If a penny stock position is the only one of its kind in a larger portfolio, for instance, the risk associated with holding the stock is negligible even though it may have a high risk when held alone.
2. **Risk-Return Tradeoff at the Portfolio Level:** There is a risk-return trade-off at the portfolio level as well. A portfolio made up entirely of stocks, for instance, has a higher potential return but also a higher risk. Risk and return can be raised

in an all-equity portfolio by focusing on certain industries or by taking on single positions that account for a sizable portion of holdings. Investors can determine whether a portfolio assumes enough risk to meet long-term return objectives or if the risk levels are too high given the current mix of holdings by evaluating the cumulative risk-return tradeoff of all positions.

8.1.6.2. Calculating Risk-Return

8.1.6.2.1. Alpha Ratio

The alpha ratio, which measures returns on investment above the benchmark return, can be used to calculate excess returns on investment. Put differently, it quantifies the excess returns obtained from the benchmark index.

"Alpha, often regarded as the active return on an investment, measures an investment's performance against a market index or benchmark that is thought to reflect the movement of the market overall," according to Investopedia."

A straightforward method of calculating alpha is to deduct an investment's total return from a benchmark that is similar to it in the same asset class. Utilizing the capital asset pricing model (CAPM) as the benchmark, Jensen's alpha is a method for calculating alpha that accounts for asset investments that are not exactly alike.

Here's an example of alpha:

- If a mutual fund has underperformed by 1% against its benchmark, it will have an alpha of -1.0.
- If a mutual fund has neither underperformed nor outperformed, it will have an alpha of zero because it will not have lost or gained value compared to the benchmark index.
- If a mutual fund has outperformed by 1%, it will have an alpha of +1.0.

8.1.6.2.2. Beta Ratio

A beta calculation shows how correlated the stock is vs. a benchmark, typically the Standard and Poor's 500 Index, or S&P 500, that serves as a gauge for the entire market. The S&P 500 is an index of 500 of the top publicly traded companies in the United States, weighted by market capitalization.

Divide the variance, or the market's movement in relation to its mean, by the covariance, or the return of a stock in relation to the market, to get the beta value.

Here's an example of beta:

- If a stock has a beta of 1%, it is highly correlated to the S&P 500.
- If a stock has a beta of zero, it is not very correlated to the S&P 500.
- If a stock has a beta of -1%, it is inversely correlated—in other words, it has a contrary relationship—to the S&P 500.

When investors conduct additional analysis and ask, "Is there a reason why a particular stock is underperforming or outperforming?" beta can help answer that question when assessing relative performance overall by potentially illuminating the reasons behind the stock's periodic outperformance or underperformance.

8.1.6.2.3. Sharpe Ratio

To evaluate if a risk is worthwhile, one can use the Sharpe ratio. When comparing peers or ETFs that hold comparable assets, it is employed.

The adjusted return divided by the degree of risk, or its standard deviation, is how the Sharpe ratio is calculated.

The difference over time between realized, or expected, returns and a benchmark—such as the risk-free rate of return or the performance of a specific investment category—is the numerator of the Sharpe ratio, according to Investopedia."

When comparing similar portfolios, a higher Sharpe ratio is generally preferable because it indicates an appealing risk-adjusted return—that is, the return after accounting for the level of risk assumed to achieve it.

8.2. HISTORICAL RISKS AND RETURNS OF STOCKS

This section explains how to use historical stock market data to calculate average returns and a risk measure, or volatility. Investors may find it helpful to estimate potential future returns by examining the distribution of previous returns. We begin by outlining the process for computing historical returns.

8.2.1. Computing Historical Returns

A financial asset's historical return, be it a bond, stock, security, fund, index, or otherwise, is the sum of its previous performance and rate of return. Financial analysis frequently uses historical data to project future returns or identify potential influencers and their relative importance in influencing future returns. Standard deviations can be predicted using past returns as a guide for upcoming data points.

An overview of how a financial asset or security has been responding to external or internal events that may have led to returns growing or declining can be obtained through the analysis of historical data and performance. These occurrences may be worldwide occurrences or they may be related to shifts in the economic cycle. Historical data does not predict actual future returns, but it can be used to project future returns and what investors can expect. It might not be the best idea to estimate returns using too-old data.

A financial asset's historical returns are typically tracked starting at the start of the year (i.e., from January 1st) until the year's conclusion (i.e., December 31st) in order to calculate the yearly return for that specific year. To display historical returns over a number of years, a compilation of prior annual returns is required. Analysts and investors can calculate the average historical returns of a financial asset by obtaining the historical returns data.

It is crucial to remember that average returns do not take potential return fluctuations into account. It's possible that returns increased significantly in some years while declining in others. An average return may not always accurately represent all the data required for forecasting because the high returns balance out the low or negative returns. Any financial asset, including stocks, mutual funds, commodities, stocks, real estate, portfolios, and indexes like the S&P 500, can have its historical returns estimated.

We start with realized returns for a portfolio and an individual investment. The total return that happens over a specific time period is known as the realized return.

8.2.1.1. Individual Investment Realized Return

Let's say a month ago you made a \$10 stock investment. It paid a \$0.50 dividend today, and you sold it for \$11. What was your return? The dividend and the price change accounted for both of your returns. Through the dividend, you received \$0.50 on your \$10 investment, yielding a return of \$0.50/\$10 = 5%, and the price increase yielded a return of \$1/\$10, or 10%. Your total return was 15%:

$$\text{Return} = \frac{\$0.50}{\$10} + \frac{(\$11 - \$10)}{\$10} = 5\% + 10\% = 15\%$$

In general, assume you buy a stock on date t for price P_t. If the stock pays a dividend, Div_{t+1}, on date t + 1, and you sell the stock at that time for price P_{t+1}, then the timeline of your cash flows for the stock looks like this:

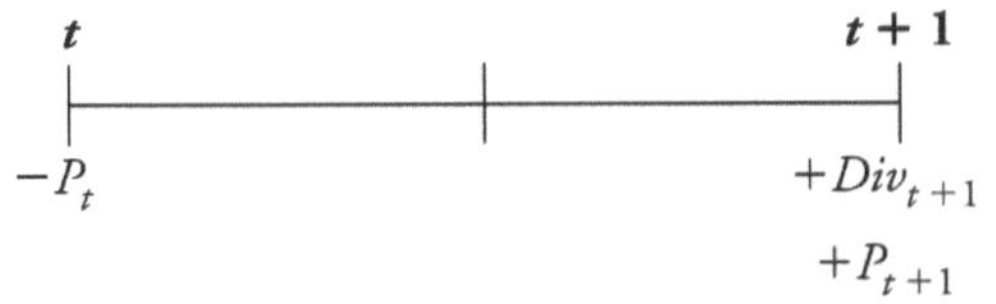

The realized return from your investment in the stock from t to t + 1 is:

$$\begin{aligned} R_{t+1} &= \frac{Div_{t+1} + P_{t+1} - P_t}{P_t} = \frac{Div_{t+1}}{P_t} + \frac{P_{t+1} - P_t}{P_t} \\ &= \text{Dividend Yield} + \text{Capital Gain Yield} \end{aligned} \qquad (1)$$

Alternatively known as the total return, your realized return for the time interval from t to t + 1 is the sum of the dividend yield and the capital gain expressed as a percentage of the initial price. You will have 1 + R_{t+1} at date t + 1 for every dollar invested at date t. In the same manner, we can calculate the total return for any security by substituting any cash flows paid by the security (for instance, coupon payments would replace dividends on a bond) for the dividend payments.

We need to know how you plan to invest any interim dividends you receive in order to calculate your return if you hold the stock after the first dividend date. We make the assumption that all dividends are instantly reinvested and used to buy more shares of the same stock or security in order to concentrate on the returns of a single security. In this instance, the return on a stock between dividend payments can be calculated using Eqn. 1, and the return over a longer time horizon can be calculated by compounding the returns from each dividend interval. If a stock pays dividends at the end of each quarter, with realized returns R_1,..., R_4 each quarter, then we show the four quarterly returns for this stock as:

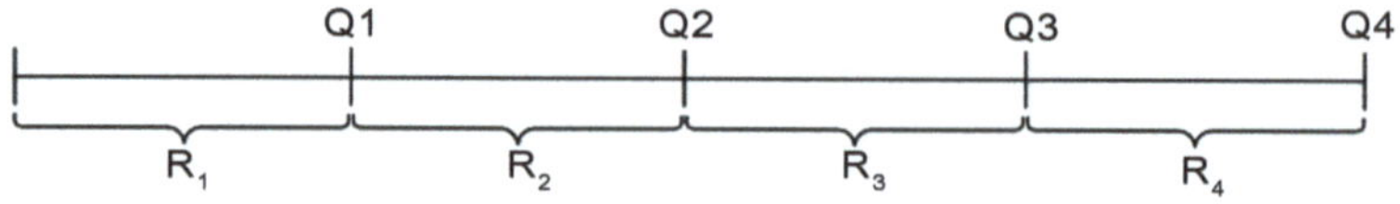

Its annual realized return, R_{annual}, is:

$$1 + R_{\text{annual}} = (1 + R_1)(1 + R_2)(1 + R_3)(1 + R_4) \quad (2)$$

We display a histogram of the annual returns for every US investment in Table 8.1 in Figure 8.2. The number of years that the annual returns fell within each range shown on the x-axis is represented by the height of each bar in this histogram. Take note of how much more erratic stock returns are in relation to Treasury bills.

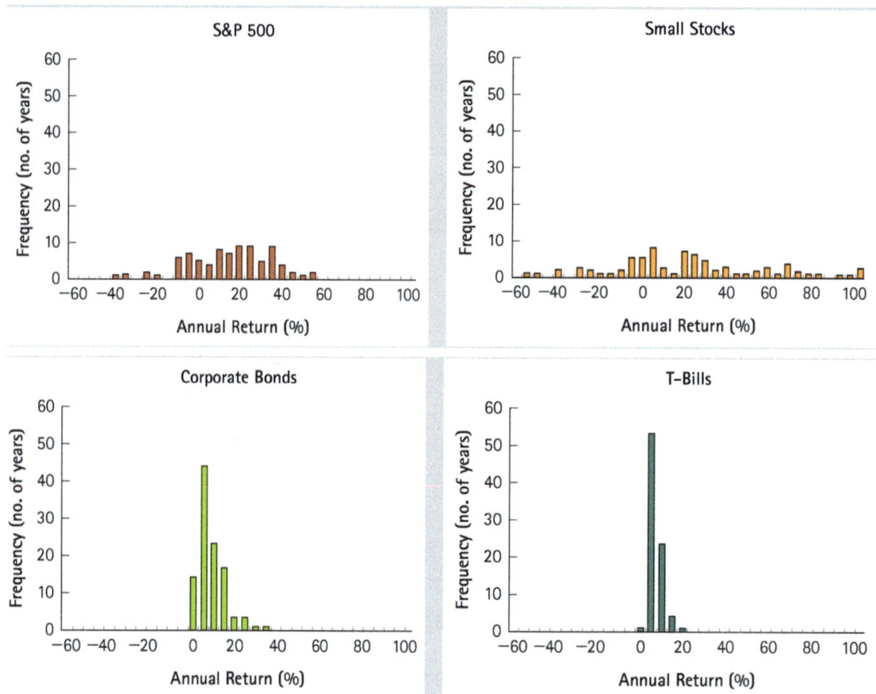

Figure 8.2. *The distribution of annual returns for U.S. large company stocks (S&P 500), small stocks, corporate bonds, and treasury bills, 1926–2009.*

Source: Jonathan Berk, Peter DeMarzo, and Jarrad Harford. Fundamentals of Corporate Finance, Second edition. Pearson Education. ISBN: 978-0-13-214823-8.

8.2.2. Average Annual Returns

We wish to determine the most likely return, indicated by the average, from the distribution of potential returns for each security shown in Figure 8.2. The mean yearly yield of an investment over a given historical period can be calculated by summing the annual realized returns for each year. That is to say, if is the realized return on an asset for every year t, then the average yearly return from 1 to T is:

Average Annual Return of a Security

$$\overline{R} = \frac{1}{T}(R_1 + R_2 + \cdots + R_T) \tag{3}$$

The average return gives us an idea of the expected return for any given year, assuming that the distribution of potential returns remains constant over time. This is not a return-specific concept. For instance, a manager at Starbucks can't predict with precision how many customers will visit today, but by examining historical averages, the manager can establish expectations for staffing and stocking levels.

We can use Eqn. 3 to calculate the average return for the S&P 500 for the years 2005–2009. The returns are:

2005	2006	2007	2008	2009
4.9%	15.8%	5.5%	–37.0%	26.5%

and the average return is:

$$\frac{1}{5}(4.9\% + 15.8\% + 5.5\% - 37.0\% + 26.5\%) = 3.1\%$$

Over the same time period, the average return on Treasury bills was 2.0%. As a result, during this time, holding the S&P 500 generated an average return of 1.1% (3.1% – 2.0%) more than investing in Treasury bills. This average is calculated using data spanning only five years. Naturally, the more data we use, the more accurate our estimate of the distribution's true average becomes. We display the average returns for different US investments from 1926–2009 in Figure 8.3.

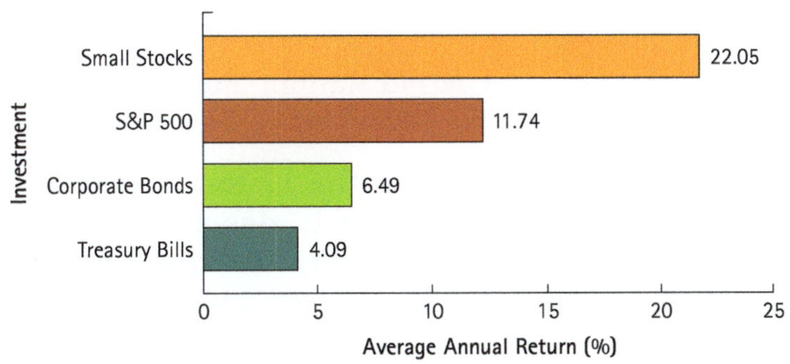

Figure 8.3. *Average annual returns in the U.S. for small stocks, large stocks (S&P 500), corporate bonds, and treasury bills, 1926–2009. Each bar represents an investment's average return.*

Source: Jonathan Berk, Peter DeMarzo, and Jarrad Harford. Fundamentals of Corporate Finance, Second edition. Pearson Education. ISBN: 978-0-13-214823-8.

8.2.3. The Variance and Volatility of Returns

As we can see from Figure 8.2, each investment has a very distinct return variability. If you had invested in small stocks, you would have lost more than 50% in some years and gained more than 100% in others! The returns on large company stocks in the SandP 500 are less variable than those on small company stocks, but they vary considerably more than those on corporate bonds or Treasury bills. Although the chart shows these variations in variability, we still need a formal method to measure them. We compute the standard deviation of the realized return distribution to ascertain the variability of returns. The variance of the realized return distribution squared is equal to the standard deviation. By squaring the differences between the returns and the average return, variance calculates the variability in returns. Since the unsquared differences from an average must, by definition, add up to zero, we must square the difference of each return from the average. The variance is expressed in "percent" or percent-squared units since the returns are squared. Since that is of little use to us, we calculate the standard deviation in percentage terms by taking the square root.

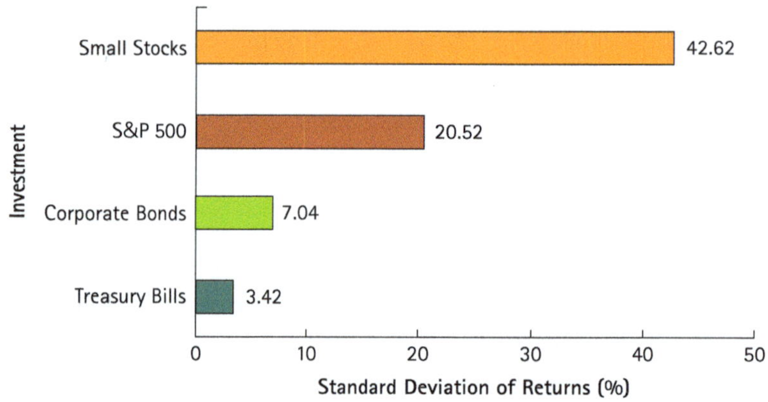

Figure 8.4. *Volatility (Standard Deviation) of U.S. Small Stocks, Large Stocks (S&P 500), Corporate Bonds, and Treasury Bills, 1926–2009. Each bar represents the standard deviation of the investment's returns.*

Source: Jonathan Berk, Peter DeMarzo, and Jarrad Harford. Fundamentals of Corporate Finance, Second edition. Pearson Education. ISBN: 978–0-13–214823–8.

Standard deviation just shows how much the historical returns deviate from their average and how much they tend to differ from it, despite the fact that this sounds a little abstract. Thus, the standard deviation effectively expresses our sense of risk: How often will we miss the mark and how far off will we be? To compute the variance, we use the following formula:

$$Var(R) = \frac{1}{T-1}[(R_1 - \overline{R})^2 + (R_2 - \overline{R})^2 + \cdots + (R_T - \overline{R})^2] \quad (4)$$

The standard deviation, which we will call the volatility, is the square root of the variance:

$$SD(R) = \sqrt{Var(R)} \quad (5)$$

To be able to measure the variation in the variability of the distributions that we saw in Figure 8.2, we started our review of statistics. This is now possible thanks to Table 8.1's standard deviation of US investment returns. Figure 8.4 presents these findings.

It is evident from comparing the standard deviations in Figure 8.4 that small and large companies have, respectively, had the most variable historical returns. Compared to stocks, corporate bonds and Treasury bills have substantially more stable returns; of all the investment classes, Treasury bills have the least volatility.

8.2.4. The Normal Distribution

There are more applications for the standard deviations we have calculated in Figure 8.4 than just sorting the investments by degree of risk. A normal distribution, as seen in Figure 8.5, is a symmetric probability distribution that is entirely described by its average and standard deviation. The standard deviation is also crucial in explaining this type of distribution. Approximately two-thirds of all possible outcomes fall within one standard deviation above or below the average, and approximately 95% of all possible outcomes fall within two standard deviations above or below the average. These figures are significant. These results are displayed for small company stocks in Figure 8.5.

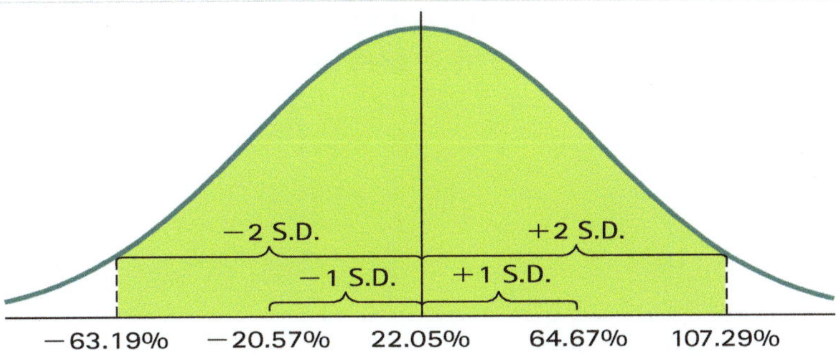

Figure 8.5. *Normal distribution. The height of the line reflects the likelihood of each return occurring. Using the data from Figures 8.3 and 8.4, if the returns of small companies are normally distributed, then two-thirds of all possible outcomes should lie within one standard deviation of the average return of 22.05% (given in Figure 8.3) and 95% should lie within two standard deviations. Figure 8.4 shows the standard deviation to be 42.62%, so that puts 95% of possible outcomes between and (the shaded area of the distribution).*

Source: Jonathan Berk, Peter DeMarzo, and Jarrad Harford. Fundamentals of Corporate Finance, Second edition. Pearson Education. ISBN: 978-0-13-214823-8.

Because the return for the following year will, approximately 95% of the time, be within two standard deviations of the average, the 95% prediction interval is defined as follows: [the average − 2 × standard deviation] to [the average + 2 × standard deviation]:

$$\text{Average} \pm (2 \times \text{standard deviation})$$
$$\bar{R} \pm (2 \times SD(R)) \tag{6}$$

Table 8.2 provides an overview of the key ideas and formulas we worked through in this section. The past performance of investments and their potential future performance can be determined by computing historical averages and volatilities. Predicting the future with historical data is undoubtedly a risky endeavor.

Table 8.2. Summary of Tools for Working with Historical Returns

Concept	Definition	Formula
Realized Returns	Total return earned over a particular period of time	$R_{t+1} = \frac{Div_{t+1} + P_{t+1} - P_t}{P_t}$
Average Annual Return	Average of realized returns for each year	$\bar{R} = \frac{1}{T}(R_1 + R_2 + \dots + R_T)$
Variance of Returns	A measure of the variability of returns	$Var(R) = \frac{1}{T-1}[(R_1 - \bar{R})^2 + (R_2 - \bar{R})^2 + \dots + (R_T - \bar{R})^2]$
Standard Deviation or Volatility of Returns	The square root of the variance (which puts it in the same units as the average—namely "%")	$SD(R) = \sqrt{Var(R)}$
95% Prediction Interval	The range of returns within which we are 95% confident that next period's return will lie	$\bar{R} \pm 2 \times SD(R)$

Source: Jonathan Berk, Peter DeMarzo, and Jarrad Harford. Fundamentals of Corporate Finance, Second edition. Pearson Education. ISBN: 978–0-13–214823–8.

8.3. UNDERSTANDING COST OF CAPITAL

The minimal return required to support starting a capital budgeting project, like constructing a new factory, is calculated as the cost of capital. It is an assessment of whether the projected decision's costs can be justified (Modigliani & Miller, 1958).

Many businesses finance their business expansion by combining debt and equity. For these businesses, the weighted average cost of all capital sources is used to calculate the overall cost of capital. This is referred to as the WACC, or weighted average cost of capital.

The most important piece of data for figuring out a project's hurdle rate is the cost of capital. Before starting a large project, a business needs to estimate how much money it will need to make in order to pay for the project's overhead and maintain profitability. The debt-levered cost of capital may be used by the business to calculate the capital cost. As an alternative, they could examine the projects debt-free—that is, unlevered. When evaluating the potential return on an investment, such as purchasing stock shares, investors view this as the cost of capital. There may be best- and worst-case scenarios included in this estimate To assess if the price of a stock is reasonable given its potential return, an investor may consider the financial results of the company and its volatility (beta).

8.3.1. Classification of Cost of Capital

Cost of Capital can be classified as follows:

1. **Explicit Cost and Implicit Cost**: The discount rate that compares the present value of the anticipated additional cash inflows to the present value of the incremental cash outflows is known as the explicit cost. It is therefore "the rat return of the financing opportunity's cash flows." The rate of return associated with the best investment opportunity for the company and its shareholders, on the other hand, that will be lost if the project the company is currently considering is approved is known as the implicit cost. To put it briefly, there are explicit costs associated with raising money and implicit costs associated with using money.
2. **Average Cost and Marginal Cost**: The weighted average of the costs of each fund component makes up the average cost. After ascertaining costs of each source of capital, appropriate weights are assigned to each component of capital. The weighted average cost of new funds raised by the company is known as the marginal cost of capital.

3. **Future Cost of Capital**: The term "future cost of capital" describes the anticipated costs associated with raising new capital, whereas "historical cost" refers to the costs associated with raising capital for the company in the past. When making financial decisions, the cost of capital in the future is comparatively more important.
4. **Specific Cost and Combined Cost**: Specific cost of capital refers to the expenses of each component of capital. Because it includes the cost of capital from all sources, the combined cost of capital is the average cost of capital. The combined cost of capital is used to determine whether to accept or reject investment proposals in capital budgeting decisions.

8.3.2. Importance of Cost of Capital

The cost of capital is a tool used by financial analysts and businesses to assess how well money is being invested. An investment will ultimately be a net benefit to the company's balance sheets if the return on it exceeds the cost of capital. On the other hand, it suggests that the money is not being spent prudently if the returns on an investment are either lower or equal to the cost of capital. One way to value a company is to look at its cost of capital. Investors are unlikely to find owning equity in a company with a high cost of capital valuable since such a company can anticipate lower long-term profits.

8.3.3. Cost of Capital by Industry

Each industry has a current average cost of capital that is unique to it. There is a large range in the numbers. For instance, a compilation from the Stern School of Business at New York University indicates that the retail grocery business has a significantly lower cost of capital—5.31%—than homebuilding, which has a relatively high cost of capital of 9.28%.

The Stern School of Business reports that Internet software companies, paper and forest companies, building supply retailers, and semiconductor companies have the highest cost of capital. These sectors frequently demand large capital expenditures. Rubber and tire companies, power companies, real estate developers, and financial services companies (non-bank and insurance) are among the industries with lower capital costs. These businesses might need less equipment or have extremely consistent cash flows.

8.3.4. How Does Market Risk Affect the Cost of Capital?

The return required for a business to invest in a significant project, such as constructing a factory or plant, is known as the cost of capital. A business will only make investments or increase operations in order to maximize profitability if the anticipated returns from a project outweigh the cost of capital, which includes both debt and equity.

Raising debt capital involves taking out loans or credit card financing, among other forms of borrowing money. Conversely, the process of selling shares of common or preferred stock is known as equity financing. Market risk primarily influences the cost of equity, which in turn influences the cost of capital. The money needed to pay interest on debt financing as well as dividends on equity funding is included in a company's total cost of capital. Estimating the average return on investment that could be anticipated based on returns produced by the larger market is how equity funding costs are calculated. Consequently, market risk influences the total cost of capital directly since it has a direct impact on the price of equity funding. The capital asset pricing model, or CAPM, is typically used to calculate the cost of equity funding. This formula calculates the rate of return that stockholders might reasonably expect given the perceived level of investment risk by using the beta value of the stock in question and the total average market return. The rate of return produced by a significant market index, such as the Dow Jones Industrial Average or the S&P 500, is used to estimate the average market return. The market risk premium and the risk-free rate are further divisions of the market return.

Since short-term Treasury bills have stable values and guaranteed returns backed by the US government, the rate of return on these securities is commonly used to estimate the risk-free rate of return. The market risk premium indicates the portion of investment return that can be attributable to stock market volatility and is calculated as the market return minus the risk-free rate. For instance, the market risk premium is equal to 12% minus 4%, or 8%, if the current average rate of return for investments in the S&P 500 is 12% and the guaranteed rate of return on short-term Treasury bonds is 4%.

8.3.5. Computing Cost of Capital with CAPM

The risk-free rate plus the market risk premium multiplied by the stock's beta value is the cost of equity capital as calculated by the Capital Asset Pricing Model (CAPM). A stock's beta is a measure of how volatile a particular stock is in comparison to the market as a whole.

A beta value of one signifies that the volatility of the stock in question is comparable to that of the broader market. For example, if the S&P 500 jumps 15%, the stock is predicted to gain 15% as well. A beta value of 0 to 1 indicates that the stock is less volatile than the market, whereas a value of 1 or higher indicates higher volatility.

Assume that the guaranteed rate of return on short-term Treasury bonds is 5.5%, the Nasdaq produces average returns of 10%, and a stock has a beta value of 1.2. The CAPM model can be used to calculate the rate of return that investors can reasonably expect:

$$\text{Return} = 5.5\% + 1.2 \times (10\% - 5.5\%) = 10.9\%$$

Businesses can minimize their overall cost of capital by identifying the most economical way to raise capital by using this method of estimating the cost of equity capital. From the investor's point of view, the outcomes can assist in determining whether the projected return, considering the possible risk, warrants investment.

Investopedia does not offer financial advice or services related to taxes or investments. The information may not be appropriate for all investors and is provided without taking into account the financial situation, risk tolerance, or investment objectives of any particular investor. Investing carries risk, which includes the potential for principal loss.

8.4. COMPONENTS OF COST OF CAPITAL

Cost of capital is the highest rate of return on investment that a business needs to achieve in order to maintain the market value of its equity shares. This aligns with the company's overarching goal of optimizing wealth. This is only feasible if the company generates a return on projects funded by equity shareholders' funds that is at least equal to the rate of return they anticipated. The market value of the company's shares would decline if it couldn't generate returns at the anticipated rate, which would lower the shareholders' total wealth. "The rate of return the firm requires from investment in order to increase the value of the firm in the market place" is the definition of a firm's cost of capital, then.

The three components of cost of capital are:

1. Cost of Debt;
2. Cost of Preference Capital; and
3. Cost of Equity Capital.

8.4.1. Cost of Debt

Debt can be issued at a premium, discount, or par value. It could be redeemable or perpetual. The method used to calculate the costs in each scenario has been described subsequently.

8.4.1.1. Debt Issued at Par

Calculating the cost of debt issued at par is a relatively simple process. It is the explicit interest rate that has been further adjusted for the company's tax liability. It may be computed according to the following formula:

$$Kd = (1-T)R$$

Where;

- Kd = Cost of debt;
- T = Marginal tax rate;
- R = Debenture interest rate.

Since interest is regarded as an expense when determining the firm's income for tax purposes, the tax is subtracted from the interest that is payable. But only in situations where the "earnings of the firm before interest and tax" (EBIT) equals or exceeds the interest should the tax adjusted rate of interest be applied. Prior to modifying the interest rate for taxes, the cost of debt should be determined if EBIT is negative.

8.4.1.2. Debt Issued at Premium or Discount

The cost of debt should be determined using the net proceeds received from the issuance of the bonds or debentures, if they are issued at a premium or discount. These expenses could be further modified in light of the company's applicable taxes. Cost of debt can be calculated according to the following formula:

$$Kd= I(1-T)/NP$$

Where;

- Kd = Cost of debt after tax.
- I = Annual interest payment.
- NP = Net proceeds of loans or debentures.
- T = Tax rate.

8.4.2. Cost of Preference Capital

The calculation of preference capital's cost, however, presents certain conceptual issues. There is a legal requirement for the company to pay interest at predetermined rates when it comes to borrowings, but not when it comes to preference shares. For this reason, some contend that dividends paid on the capital of preference shares are not considered a cost. However, this is not true.

This is due to the fact that, even though it is not required by law, preference share dividends are typically paid out whenever the business generates enough revenue. Equity shareholders may have reason for grave concern regarding the nonpayment of dividends. In the event that the company fails to pay preference shareholders their dividends, they may even lose control of the business as preference shareholders have the legal right to attend general meetings alongside equity shareholders under specific circumstances. Furthermore, the right of equity shareholders to receive dividends may be negatively impacted by the accumulation of preference dividend arrears. This is due to the fact that they are not eligible for a dividend unless the preference dividend arrears are settled. These factors lead to the cost of preference capital being calculated using the same methodology as debentures. The following equation represents the computation method:

$$Kp=Dp/Np$$

Where; Kp is the Cost of preference share capital; Dp is the Fixed preference dividend; Np is the Net proceeds of preference shares.

The cost of capital for redeemable preference shares is calculated by applying a discount rate that combines the present value of future dividend payments and principal repayments with the net proceeds from the sale of preference shares.

8.4.3. Cost of Equity Capital

Calculating equity capital costs is a challenging task. As was noted in the case of preference shares, some contend that there are no expenses associated with equity capital. They contend that the company is not required by law to distribute dividends to its equity shareholders. This strategy doesn't seem to be the best one because equity shareholders purchase shares in hopes of receiving dividend payments from the business. Additionally, the business never issues equity shares without planning to distribute dividends to investors. As a result, the expected return by the shareholders determines the market price of the equity shares.

The minimal rate of return that a company must achieve on the equity-financed portion of an investment in a project in order to maintain the market price of such shares is known as the conceptual cost of equity share capital.

It is implied that one must be able to ascertain what the shareholders as a class expect from their investment in equity shares in order to ascertain the cost of equity capital. Due to the unpredictable and elusive nature of shareholders as a class, this is a challenging proposition. Diverse authorities have communicated varying justifications and methodologies.

The cost of equity capital can be separated into two categories: new equity and existing equity. The cost of equity capital can be calculated using some of the appropriate criteria listed below:

8.4.3.1. Dividend Price (D/P) Approach

Using this method, the investor capitalizes the set of anticipated dividend payments to determine the market price of equity shares. Thus, "the discount rate that equates the present value of all expected future dividends per share with the net proceeds of the sale (or the current market price) of a share" is the definition of cost of equity capital. Stated differently, the rate of anticipated dividends that sustains the current market value of equity shares will be the cost of equity capital.

This strategy correctly highlights the significance of dividends, but it fails to take into account the fact that retained earnings also affect the market price of equity shares. As a result, the strategy doesn't seem very sensible.

The cost of new equity can be determined according to the following formula:

$$Ke = D/NP$$

Where;

- Ke= Cost of equity capital;
- D= Dividend per equity share;
- NP = Net proceeds of an equity share.

When determining the cost of equity for existing equity shares, the market price of the company's shares should be used. It can be computed in the current instance using the formula below:

$$Ke = D/MP$$

Where;

- Ke= Cost of equity capital;
- D= Dividend per equity share;
- MP = Market price of an equity share.

8.4.3.2. Dividend Price Plus Growth (D/P + g) Approach

The cost of equity capital is ascertained using this method by adding the predicted dividend rate to the dividend growth rate. Based on the amount of dividends paid by the company over the previous few years, the rate of growth in dividends is calculated. With this method, the cost of capital can be calculated using the following formula:

$$Ke = (D/NP) + g$$

Where;

- Ke = Cost of equity capital;
- D= Expected dividend per share;
- NP = Net proceeds of per share;
- g= Growth in expected dividend.

It should be mentioned that the aforementioned formula can also be used to calculate the cost of equity capital in the case of existing equity shares. Nevertheless, the net proceeds (NP) of the shares as stated above should be substituted with the market price (MP).

8.4.3.3. Earning Price (E/P) Approach

This method states that the market price of the shares is determined by the earnings per share. This is predicated on the idea that, in assessing their share holdings, the shareholders capitalize a stream of future earnings (as opposed to dividends). Therefore, in order to maintain a constant market price for equity shares, the cost of capital should be correlated with that earnings percentage. Consequently, this method accounts for both retained earnings and dividends. Regarding the application of both earnings and market price data, proponents of this strategy disagree. Some people calculate the cost of capital by simply using the current earning rate and the share price of the company at the market. Some suggest calculating the average market price of equity shares based on the market price over the previous few years, while others suggest calculating the average rate of earnings based on the earnings of the previous few years.

The formula for calculating the cost of capital according to the approach is as follows:

$$Ke = E/NP$$

Where;

Ke is the Cost of equity capital; D is the Earnings per share; and NP is the Net proceeds of an equity share.

On the other hand, market price (MP) should be used for calculating the cost of capital rather than net proceeds (NP) in the case of existing equity shares.

8.4.3.4. Realized Yield Approach

This method states that the returns that investors in a company actually receive on their equity shares should be used to calculate the cost of equity capital. Therefore, in order to calculate the cost of equity capital, this approach takes into account historical dividend records for a given period as well as actual capital appreciation in the value of the shareholders' equity shares.

For businesses with a track record of consistent dividend payments and growth, this strategy yields reasonably good results. When it comes to these companies, it can be reasonably assumed that their past behavior will continue into the future.

8.5. WEIGHTED AVERAGE COST OF CAPITAL (WACC)

The average after-tax cost of capital for a business coming from all sources—bonds, preferred stock, common stock, and other debt—is represented by the weighted average cost of capital, or WACC. WACC is, therefore, the average interest rate that a business anticipates paying on its debt. WACC is a popular method for calculating required rate of return (RRR) because it sums up the return that investors and bondholders require in exchange for their capital being provided to the business. If a company's debt is viewed as risky or its stock is relatively volatile, investors will likely demand higher returns, which will raise the WACC of the company (Frank Murray& Shen Tao, 2012).

8.5.1. Definition of WACC

The weighted average cost of capital (WACC) of a company is the total cost of capital from all sources combined, including debt, preferred shares, and common shares. Each capital type's cost is divided into equal parts according to its percentage of total capital, and the total cost is then added.

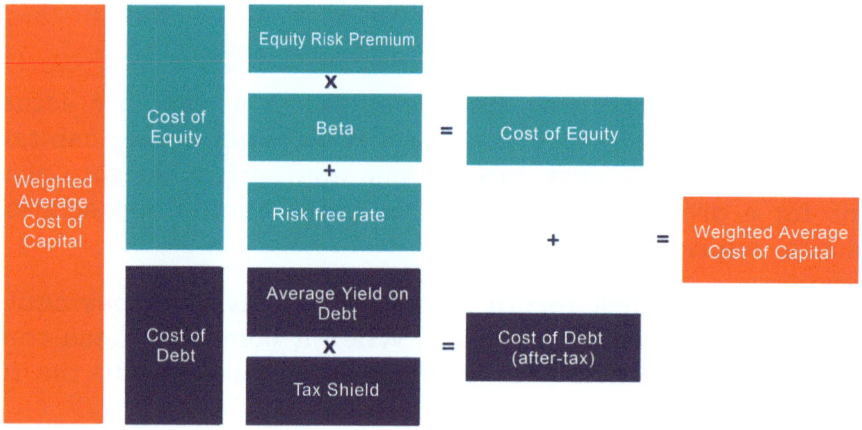

Figure 8.6. *Weighted average cost of capital.*

Source: https://corporatefinanceinstitute.com/resources/valuation/what-is-wacc-formula/.

WACC is the discount rate used in financial modeling to determine a company's net present value. To be more precise, WACC is the discount rate applied in the unlevered free cash flow approach to business or project valuation. WACC can also be understood as the required rate that an investor must meet in order to contemplate making an investment in the company (Hargrave Marshall, 2022).

8.5.2. WACC Formula

As shown below, the WACC formula is:

$$WACC = (E/V \times Re) + ((D/V \times Rd) \times (1 - T))$$

Where; E is the market value of the firm's equity (market cap); D is the market value of the firm's debt; V is the total value of capital (equity plus debt); E/V is the percentage of capital that is equity; D/V is the percentage of capital that is debt; Re is the cost of equity (required rate of return); Rd is the cost of debt (yield to maturity on existing debt); and T is the tax rate.

An extended version of the WACC formula is shown below, which includes the cost of preferred stock (for companies that have preferred stock).

WACC

WACC = Cost of Equity * %Equity + Cost of Debt * %Debt* (1-Tax Rate)
+ Cost of Perferrd Stock* %Preferred Stock

WACC is used to calculate the cost of each component of a company's capital structure according to the percentage of equity, debt, and preferred stock that the company possesses. The business incurs costs for each component. The business typically pays a fixed dividend on its preferred stock and a fixed rate of interest on its debt. A company may not pay a set rate of return on its common equity, but it frequently distributes cash dividends.

Understanding the weighted average cost of capital is crucial for finance professionals, particularly those in investment banking, equity research, and corporate development roles, as it is a fundamental component of a DCF valuation model. We will go over each step of the WACC calculation in this article.

8.5.3. WACC Part 1 – Cost of Equity

The cost of equity is calculated using the Capital Asset Pricing Model (CAPM) which equates rates of return to volatility (risk vs reward). Below is the formula for the cost of equity:

$$Re = Rf + \beta \times (Rm - Rf)$$

Where; Rf is the risk-free rate (typically the 10-year U.S. Treasury bond yield); β is the equity beta (also known as the levered beta); and Rm is the annual return of the stock market.

An implicit cost, also known as an opportunity cost of capital, is the price of equity. It's the rate of return needed by an investor to offset the risk associated with stock investments. The volatility of a stock's returns in relation to the overall stock market is measured by its beta, which is typically represented by a sizable stock index such as the S&P 500 index.

- **Risk-Free Rate:** The return that can be obtained by investing in a risk-free security is known as the risk-free rate, e.g., U.S. Treasury bonds. The risk-free rate is typically calculated using the yield on the U.S. Treasury's 10-year note. Although there is no default risk, there are still other risks, such as interest rate risk, which is why it is called risk free.
- **Equity Risk Premium (ERP):** The extra yield that can be obtained by investing in the stock market above the risk-free rate is known as the equity risk premium (ERP). Subtracting the risk-free return from the market return is a straightforward method of estimating ERP. For the majority of basic financial analyzes, this information is typically sufficient. In actuality, though, estimating the ERP can require far more in-depth work. Banks typically obtain the ERP from Morningstar or Kroll publications (formerly known as Duff and Phelps).
- **Levered Beta:** The volatility or riskiness of a stock in relation to all other stocks in the market is referred to as its beta. There are two methods for calculating a stock's beta. Regression analysis is used to determine the company's historical beta, which is the first and easiest method. As an alternative, a number of financial data providers make betas available to businesses.

Using comparables from public companies to estimate a company's beta again is the second, and more comprehensive, method. Using this method, one of the financial data services provides the beta of similar companies. Next, each company's unlevered beta is determined using the following formula:

Unlevered Beta = Levered Beta/((1 + (1 − Tax Rate) * (Debt/Equity))

Leveraged beta takes into account both business risk and the risk associated with taking on debt. But since every company is different in terms of its capital structure, the unlevered beta, or asset beta, is a measure of pure business risk that takes extra risk out of debt. Next, based on the capital structure of the business being valued, the average of the unlevered betas is computed and re-levered:

Levered Beta = Unlevered Beta * ((1 + (1 − Tax Rate) * (Debt/Equity))

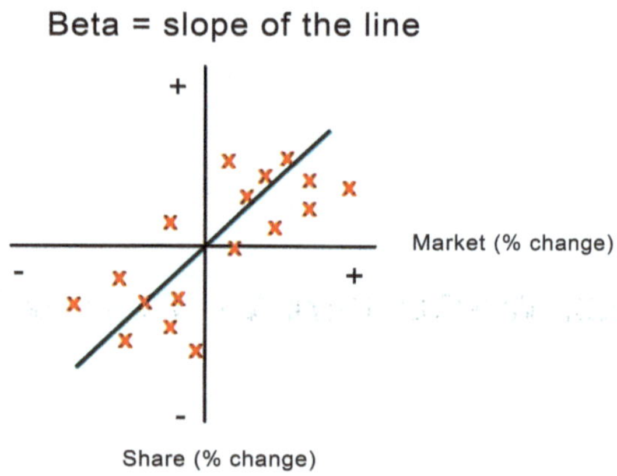

Figure 8.7. *Beta.*

Source: https://corporatefinanceinstitute.com/resources/valuation/what-is-wacc-formula/.

When beta is re-levered, the firm's existing capital structure is typically utilized. However, beta would be re-levered using the firm's target capital structure if there was information indicating that the capital structure of the company might change in the future. After calculating the risk-free rate, equity risk premium, and levered beta, the cost of equity = risk-free rate + equity risk premium * levered beta (Figure 8.7).

8.5.4. WACC Part 2 – Cost of Debt and Preferred Stock

The WACC calculation's easiest part to figure out is probably the cost of debt and preferred stock. The yield on the firm's debt at maturity is known as the cost of debt. The dividend yield on the company's preferred stock is equivalent to the cost of preferred stock. Just multiply the percentage of debt and preferred stock in a company's capital structure by the cost of debt and the yield on preferred stock, respectively.

The cost of debt must be multiplied by (1 – tax rate), also known as the value of the tax shield, because interest payments are tax deductible. Preferred stock is exempt from this since preferred dividends are paid from after-tax profits.

The after-tax cost of debt to be used in the WACC formula is calculated by taking the weighted average current yield to maturity of all outstanding debt, multiplying it by one, and then deducting the tax rate.

8.5.5. What Is WACC Used For?

The discount rate used to determine a business's value is the Weighted Average Cost of Capital. Since WACC is thought to represent the firm's opportunity cost of capital, it is also used to assess investment opportunities. For this reason, businesses use it as a hurdle rate. WACC is frequently used by a business as the hurdle rate for financial modeling of internal investments and for assessing mergers and acquisitions (M&A). An investment opportunity should not be made if its Internal Rate of Return (IRR) is less than its Weighted Average Cost of Capital (WACC). Instead, it should buy back its own shares or distribute dividends to shareholders.

8.5.6. Nominal vs. Real Weighted Average Cost of Capital

Real free cash flows (which do not include inflation) should be discounted by a real weighted average cost of capital, while nominal free cash flows (which do include inflation) should be discounted by a nominal WACC. In actuality, nominal is more prevalent, but it's crucial to understand the distinction.

8.5.7. Use in Valuation

When performing a valuation using the unlevered free cash flow (UFCF) approach, WACC is used as the discount rate. An implied enterprise value for a company is obtained by discounting UFCF by WACC. After deducting net debt from enterprise value, equity value can be calculated. Divide the equity value by the total number of outstanding fully diluted shares to get equity value per share.

8.5.8. Limitations of WACC

Despite its prevalence in corporate finance, WACC does have several limitations:

1. **Difficult to Measure in Practice**: Even with the above explanation, there are still some WACC inputs

that are challenging to measure in real-world scenarios and call for analyst judgment. For instance, in order to determine a company's levered beta, an analyst needs to compile a reasonable list of comparable businesses.

2. **Difficult to Apply to a Specific Project**: WACC is typically computed using the target capital structure and the company's cost of equity at the corporate level. The risk-and-return characteristics of individual investments that a company is considering may or may not match those of the parent company when calculating the weighted average cost of capital (WACC). One way around this is for a business to adjust its corporate-level WACC by a margin of error to reflect the possible increased risk associated with the individual investments.
3. **Use of Historical Data**: Although a lot of the inputs to WACC are based on historical data, valuation is looking forward-looking. For instance, both beta and the equity risk premium are nearly invariably dependent on historical data. Consequently, WACC makes the implicit assumption that the past will persist into the future, which is obviously untrue in many cases.
4. **Private Companies**: WACC calculations are feasible for private businesses, but they are more challenging, particularly when it comes to cost of equity. By calculating beta using the comparable company method, this can be lessened. Furthermore, the cost of debt of a privately held company can be approximated by comparing it to the cost of debt of similarly rated companies.

8.6. COST OF DEBT AND COST OF EQUITY

An expert should identify the strategies that propel the business forward, whether in terms of benefits or profits or goodwill and reputation. If we use the terms benefit or profit, we are implying the creation of income or revenue. Businesses search for investments that go toward equity rather than debt. There is extraordinary agreement between these two terms. In the event that the business is entirely financed by equity, the rate of return that should be allowed for the investors' investment is known as the expense or cost of capital. This is referred to as the equity cost or expense. Since debt typically supports or funds a portion of capital as well, debt holders should be able to afford the cost of debt.

8.6.1. Cost of Debt

The return a business gives to its creditors and debt holders is known as the cost of debt. For taking on any risk when lending money to a business, these capital providers must be paid. The cost of debt is comparatively easier to calculate than the cost of equity because observable interest rates play a significant role in this calculation. The cost of debt not only indicates a company's default risk but also the market's interest rate environment. Furthermore, it is a crucial component in figuring out the Weighted Average Cost of Capital, or WACC, for a business.

- **Meaning of Cost of Debt:** Capital costs, or expenses, are related to equity and debt. Debt costs include taxes on resources, borrowings, and other expenses. The loan fee, interest rate, or other amount of interest that management or a company pays on its current debts is, if we are to understand it, the expense of debt. An organization needs to know the entire amount of interest that is planned to be paid on all of its debts for the year in order to calculate the worth or value. It divides that figure by the total amount of its debt at that point. The cost of debt is the answer that one will hear. A significant role is assumed by discernible loan fees or observable interest rates in decomposing the cost or expense of debt. It is primarily intended for the estimation of debt costs as opposed to equity costs. Not only does the cost of debt indicate a company's default risk, but it also reflects the extent of loan costs that are currently being considered. It is a crucial component in determining the weighted average cost of capital (WACC) of an association.

8.6.2. Estimating the Cost of Debt: YTM

The cost of debt can be calculated in two common ways. The first method is to examine the debt of a company's current yield to maturity, or YTM. A publicly traded company may have visible debt on the market. A straight bond that pays interest on a regular basis and returns the principal at maturity would be one example.

This method is frequently applied in situations where the company under study has a straightforward capital structure and does not have several debt tranches, such as senior or subordinated debt, each of which has a noticeably different interest rate.

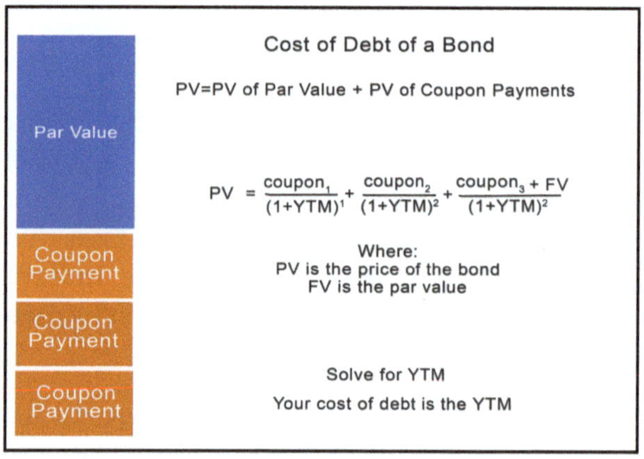

Figure 8.8. *Cost of debt.*

Source: https://corporatefinanceinstitute.com/resources/valuation/cost-of-debt/.

8.6.2.1. Matrix Pricing – Debt Ratings

An alternative strategy is to examine the company's credit rating from credit rating agencies like Moody's, Fitch, and S&P. Based on the given rating, one can calculate a yield spread over US treasuries. The cost of the company's debt can then be calculated by adding that yield spread to the risk-free rate. This strategy is especially helpful for private businesses without a market-based cost of debt that can be directly observed.

To put it simply, in order to estimate its cost of debt, a company lacking current market data will need to consider its implied or current credit rating as well as comparable debts. The company's capital structure ought to be comparable to that of its competitors.

The analyst can estimate a company's rating if both the debt-rating method and the YTM approach prove ineffective. This occurs in cases where the company has multiple ratings or neither a bond nor a credit rating. We would examine the company's leverage ratios, paying special attention to the interest coverage ratio. A borrower who has a higher ratio is considered safer. From that rating, one can then estimate the yield spread.

8.6.2.2. Debt as a Relatively Cheaper Form of Finance

Issuing debt is typically thought to be a less expensive option for raising capital from outside sources than issuing equity. One explanation is that fixed interest payments are a feature of debt, like corporate bonds. However, there are claims on earnings in equity financing. A shareholder's participation in the potential upside of the company's earnings increases with the size of their ownership stake. The tax advantages of interest expense are another justification. Because the interest on debt is subtracted from taxable income, a business's income tax payment will be reduced. In contrast, dividends paid to equity holders are not tax deductible. The after-tax rate is computed using the marginal tax rate.

The true cost of debt is expressed by the formula:

After-Tax Cost of Debt = Cost of Debt x (1 – Tax Rate)

8.6.3. Cost of Equity

The rate of return a business gives equity investors is known as the "cost of equity." Cost of equity is a tool used by businesses to evaluate the relative merits of investments, including both internal initiatives and outside acquisition prospects. Businesses usually combine debt and equity financing, with equity capital being the more costly option (Figure 8.9).

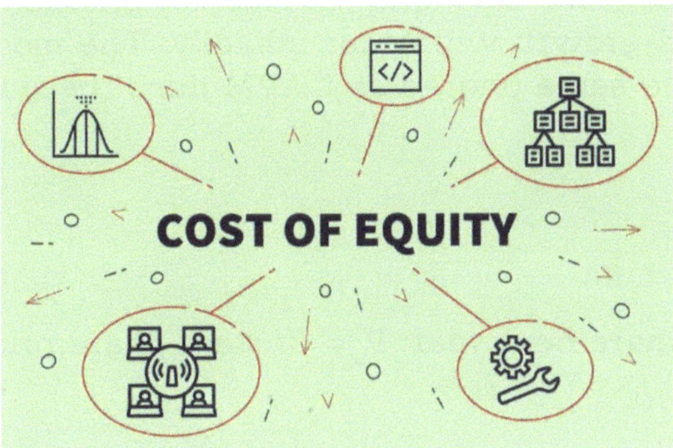

Figure 8.9. *Cost of equity.*

Source: https://corporatefinanceinstitute.com/resources/valuation/cost-of-equity-guide/.

8.6.3.1. Meaning of Cost of Equity

In the end, what matters are the profits made. It's something that is necessary and elevates motivation and willpower. The process of creating income is also central to the cost of value, or cost of equity. It suggests management or organizational profits, or it is supposed to determine whether a venture satisfies the requirements for capital returns. To put it simply, it's the portion that an organization receives from its investors.

The value or equity expenditure of an organization covers the services, administrations, or important items that the markets or business sectors require in exchange for securing resources and taking on the risk of ownership. While there are other models available for determining value, the dividend capitalization model and the capital resources estimating model (CAPM) are the most superior ones.

The formula takes into account the following year's profit per share, the stock's current market value, and the rate at which profits or dividends are growing. It alludes to the party or the lender in question changing two distinct ideas.

8.6.4. How to Calculate Cost of Equity

The Dividend Capitalization Model (for companies that pay dividends) or the Capital Asset Pricing Model (CAPM) can be used to determine the cost of equity.

8.6.4.1. CAPM (Capital Asset Pricing Model)

The riskiness of an investment in relation to the market is taken into consideration by CAPM. Because the model uses historical data and estimates were made during calculation, it is less accurate.

CAPM Formula:

$$E(R_i) = R_f + \beta_i * [E(R_m) - R_f]$$

Where; $E(R_i)$ = Expected return on asset I; R_f = Risk-free rate of return; β_i = Beta of asset I; and $E(R_m)$ = Expected market return

- **Risk-Free Rate of Return:** The anticipated yield on a risk-free investment (the 10-year Treasury note could be used to calculate the expected return for a US company).
- **Beta:** The asset's volatility, or measure of systematic risk, in

relation to the market. One can find beta online or compute it through regression, which involves dividing the variance of the market by the covariance of the asset and market returns.

β_i < 1: Asset i is less volatile (relative to the market)

β_i = 1: Asset i's volatility is the same rate as the market

β_i > 1: Asset i is more volatile (relative to the market)

- **Expected Market Return:** This is usually the average return over a given time period (5 to 10 years is an appropriate range) of the market, of which the underlying security is a part.

8.6.4.2. Dividend Capitalization Model

Only dividend-paying companies are covered by the Dividend Capitalization Model, which also makes the assumption that dividend growth will occur steadily. The model does not take investment risk into account to the same degree as CAPM does (because CAPM requires beta).

Dividend Capitalization Formula:

$$R_e = (D_1/P_0) + g$$

Where; R_e = Cost of Equity; D_1 = Dividends/share next year; P_0 = Current share price; and g = Dividend growth rate

- **Dividends/Share Next Year:** Dividends are typically announced by companies well in advance of the distribution. Press releases or company filings (annual and quarterly reports) contain the information. If the data is not found, an assumption can be made (i.e., whether the dividend for the following year will be similar based on historical data).
- **Current Share Price:** One way to find a company's share price is to use a reliable search engine or look up the company name or ticker on the exchange where the stock is traded.
- **Dividend Growth Rate:** The dividend growth rate of the company can be found by averaging the past dividend growth rates, which are calculated annually.

The growth rate for each year can be found by using the following equation:

$$\text{Dividend Growth} = (D_t/D_{t-1}) - 1$$

Where; D_t is the Dividend payment of year t; and D_{t-1} = Dividend payment of year t-1 (one year before year t)

- Example

Below are the dividend amounts paid every year by a company that has been operating for five years.

	Year 1	Year 2	Year 3	Year 4	Year 5
Dividend:	$1.00	$1.02	$1.04	$1.07	$1.10
Dividend Growth Rate:	N/A	=($1.02/ $1.00)-1	=($1.04/ $1.02)-1	=($1.07/ $1.04)-1	=($1.10/ $1.07)-1
Dividend Growth Rate:	N/A	2.00%	1.96%	2.88%	2.80%

Average:
=(2.00%+1.96%+2.88%+2.80)/4
2.41%

The average of the growth rates is 2.41%.

8.6.5. Dividend Capitalization Model Example

In addition to recently announcing a dividend of $0.50 per share to be distributed the following year, XYZ Co. is currently trading at $5 per share. Based on past data, an analyst calculated XYZ Co.'s dividend growth rate to be 2%. What does equity cost?

- D_1 = $0.50
- P_0 = $5
- g = 2%

R_e = ($0.50/$5) + 2%

R_e = 12%

The cost of equity for XYZ Co. is 12%.

8.6.6. Cost of Equity vs. Cost of Debt

Generally speaking, the cost of equity is higher than the cost of debt. Because equity is riskier than debt, investors in equity receive higher compensation because of the following

- Debt holders are paid before equity investors (absolute priority rule).
- Debt holders are guaranteed payments, while equity investors are not.
- Debt is often secured by specific assets of the firm, while equity is not.
- In exchange for taking less risk, debt holders have a lower expected rate of return.

8.6.7. Cost of Equity vs. WACC

In contrast to the Weighted Average Cost of Capital (WACC), which takes both debt and equity investments into consideration, the cost of equity only applies to equity investments.

In the event that the company is debt-free, the cost of equity can be utilized to calculate the relative cost of an investment (i.e., the company doesn't raise funds other than by selling stock).

For a company with debt, the WACC is utilized instead. Since it uses a weighted average of the interest rates for debt and equity (and debt financing is cheaper), the value will always be lower.

8.6.8. Cost of Equity in Financial Modeling

WACC is commonly applied to unlevered free cash flow (FCFF) as a discount rate. The value of WACC, which takes into account the cost of debt and equity, can be used to discount the firm's total free cash flow (FCFF). It is crucial to apply a discount rate equal to the cost of financing (WACC). If you utilize levered free cash flow (FCFE), you can use the cost of equity as a discount rate. Since FCFE is the cash available to equity investors, the cost of equity is the appropriate rate to discount FCFE by. The cost of equity represents the cost to raise capital from equity investors.

8.6.9. Difference between Cost of Debt and Cost of Equity

A company's capital structure includes both the cost of debt and the cost of equity, which have an impact on its investment and financial planning decisions. The interest rate a business pays on borrowed money is known as the cost of debt, whereas the rate of return shareholders anticipate on their investment is known as the cost of equity.

Table 8.3. Difference Between Cost of Debt and Cost of Equity

Cost of Debt	Cost of Equity
Meaning	
The expense of debt is essentially how much interest an organization pays on its borrowings or the debt held by debt holders of an organization.	The expense of value or equity is the expected rate of return by value investors or shareholders, or we can say the values or equities, and securities that are held by investors.
Basis of the Model	
The expense of debt doesn't have anything to do with models since it's with regards to taxes.	The expense of equity is determined through a model proposed, and that is CAPM.
The Basis on Interest	
Since the services or resources are acquired, then, at that point, interest is intended to be paid.	There's no paying of interest whenever.

The Basis on the Rate of Return	
The expense of debt is the pace or rate of return expected by the debt holders or bondholders for their ventures and investments.	COE is fundamentally a return rate requested from the investors from an organization.
Formula	
COD = r(D)* (1-t) where r(D) is the pre-tax rate, (1-t) is tax adjustment.	The formula for calculating the cost of equity is $r(a) = r(f) + \beta(a) [r(m) - r(f)]$ Where r(f) is risk-free rate, ß(a) is beta of the security, r(m) – r(f) is equity market risk premium.

Source: https://corporatefinanceinstitute.com/resources/valuation/cost-of-equity-guide/.

ROLE MODEL

FRANCO MODIGLIANI

Franco Modigliani (18 June 1918 – 25 September 2003) was an Italian-American economist and the recipient of the 1985 Nobel Memorial Prize in Economics. He was a professor at University of Illinois at Urbana–Champaign, Carnegie Mellon University, and MIT Sloan School of Management.

Early Life and Education

Modigliani was born on 18 June 1918 in Rome to the Jewish family of a pediatrician father and a voluntary social worker mother.

He entered university at the age of seventeen, enrolling in the faculty of Law at the Sapienza University of Rome. In his second year at Sapienza, his submission to a nationwide contest in economics sponsored by the official student organization of the state, won first prize and Modigliani received an award from the hand of Benito Mussolini. He wrote several essays for the fascist magazine *Lo Stato* where he showed an inclination for the fascist ideological currents critical of liberalism.

Among his early works in Fascist Italy was an article about the organization and management of production in a socialist economy, written in Italian and arguing the case for socialism along lines laid out by earlier market socialists like Abba Lerner and Oskar Lange.

But, that early enthusiasm evaporated soon after the passage of racial laws in Italy. In 1938, Modigliani left Italy for Paris together with his then-girlfriend, Serena Calabi, to join her parents there. After briefly returning to Rome to discuss his *laurea* thesis at the city's university, he obtained his diploma on 22 July 1939, and returned to Paris.

The same year, they all immigrated to the United States and he enrolled at the Graduate Faculty of the New School for Social Research. His Ph.D. dissertation, an elaboration and extension of John Hicks' IS–LM model, was written under the supervision of Jacob Marschak and Abba Lerner, in 1944, and is considered "ground breaking."

Career

From 1942 to 1944, Modigliani taught at Columbia University and Bard College as an instructor in economics and statistics. In 1946, he became a naturalized citizen of the United States. In 1948, he joined the University of Illinois at Urbana–Champaign faculty. From 1952 to 1962, he was a member of the Carnegie Mellon University faculty. In 1962, he joined the faculty of MIT, as an Institute Professor.

Contributions to Economic Theory

Modigliani, beginning in the 1950s, was an originator of the life-cycle hypothesis, which attempts to explain the level of saving in the economy. The hypothesis that consumers aim for a stable level of consumption throughout their lifetime (e.g., by saving during their working years and then spending during their retirement).

The rational expectations hypothesis is considered by economists to originate in the paper written by Modigliani and Emile Grunberg in 1954.

When he was a member of the Carnegie Mellon University faculty, he formulated in 1958, along with Merton Miller, the Modigliani–Miller theorem for corporate finance. The theorem posits that, under certain assumptions, the value of a firm is not affected by whether it is financed by equity (selling shares) or by debt (borrowing money), meaning that the debt-to-equity ratio is unimportant for private firms.

In the early 1960s, his response, co-authored with Albert Ando, to the 1963 paper of Milton Friedman and David I. Meiselman, initiated the so-called "monetary/fiscal policy debate" among economists, which went on for more than 60 years.

In 1975, Modigliani, in a paper whose co-author was his former student Lucas Papademos, introduced the concept of the "NIRU," the non-inflationary rate of unemployment, ostensibly an improvement over the "natural rate of unemployment" concept. The terms refer to a level of unemployment below which inflation rises.

In 1997, Modigliani and his granddaughter, Leah Modigliani, developed what is now called the "Modigliani Risk-Adjusted Performance," a measure of the risk-adjusted returns of an investment portfolio that was derived from the Sharpe ratio, adjusted for the risk of the portfolio relative to that of a benchmark, e.g., the "market."

Appointments and Awards

In October 1985, Modigliani was awarded the Nobel prize in Economics "for his pioneering analyzes of saving and of financial markets."

In 1985, Modigliani received MIT's James R. Killian Faculty Achievement Award. In 1997, he received an *honoris causa* degree in Management Engineering from the University of Naples Federico II in 1997.

Late in his life, Modigliani became a trustee of the Economists for Peace and Security organization, formerly "Economists Allied for Arms Reduction" and was considered an "influential adviser": in the late 1960s, on a contract with the Federal Reserve, he designed the "MIT-Pennsylvania-Social Science Research Council" model, a tool that "guided monetary policy in Washington for many decades."

A collection of Modigliani's papers is housed at Duke University's Rubenstein Library.

Criticism

Modigliani's work on fiscal policy came under criticism from followers of Post-Keynesian economics, who disputed the "Keynesianism" of his viewpoints, pointing out his contribution to the NAIRU concept, as well as his general stance on fiscal deficits. The Modigliani-Miller theorem implies that, for a closed economy, state borrowing is merely deferred taxation, since state spending can be financed only by "printing money," taxation, or borrowing, and therefore monetary financing of state spending implies the subsequent imposition of a so-called "inflation tax," which ostensibly has the same effect on permanent income as explicit taxation.

Nonetheless, they acknowledged his dissenting voice on the issue of unemployment, in which Modigliani concurred early on with heterodox economists that Europe-wide unemployment in the late 20th century was caused by the lack of demand induced by austerity policies.

Personal Life

In 1939, while they were in Paris, Modigliani married Serena Calabi. They had two children, Andre and Sergio Modigliani.

Modigliani died in Cambridge, Massachusetts, in 2003, while still working at MIT, and teaching until the last months of his life. He was 85. Serena Modigliani-Calabi, active to the end in progressive politics, most notably with the League of Women Voters, and an outspoken believer in participatory democracy, died in 2008.

CLASS ACTIVITY

Consider two local banks. Bank A has 100 loans outstanding, each for $1 million that it expects will be repaid today. Each loan has a 5% probability of default, in which case the bank is not repaid anything. The chance of default is independent across all the loans. Bank B has only one loan of $100 million outstanding that it also expects will be repaid today. It also has a 5% probability of not being repaid. Explain the difference between the types of risk each bank faces. Assuming you are averse to risk, which bank would you prefer to own?

SUMMARY

- The concept of risk and return makes reference to the possible economic loss or gain from investing in securities. A gain made by an investor is referred to as a return on their investment. Conversely, the risk signifies the chance or odds that the investor is going to lose money. In the case that an investor chooses to invest in an asset with minimal risk, the possible return then is often modest. In contrast, an investment with a high-risk component has a higher probability of generating larger profits
- Risks that can influence a complete economic market or at minimum a significant portion of it are known as systematic risks. They are the dangers of losing assets as a result of various macroeconomic or political risks which impact the general market performance.
- Unsystematic risk is a type of risk that impacts only one sector or one business. It is the danger of losing money on an investment because of a business or sector-specific hazard. A shift in leadership, a safety recall on a good, a legislative reform that might reduce firm sales, or a new rival in the market are all examples of unsystematic risk.
- Realized return refers to the actual return on an investment over a specific time frame. It is critical to recognize that nothing can alter a realized return. It's really a post-fact number that no action can alter. It merely provides information to investors to help them make wiser financial choices in the future.
- An expected return is the estimate of profits or losses that an investor may expect from an investment. The expected return is a metric used to estimate if an investment will have a positive or negative net outcome on average. The expected return is often founded on previous data and so cannot be guaranteed in the foreseeable future; yet, it frequently establishes acceptable expectations.
- Risk-return tradeoff states that the potential return rises with an increase in risk. Using this principle, individuals associate low levels of uncertainty with low potential returns, and high levels of uncertainty or risk with high potential returns.
- The historical return of a financial asset, such as a bond, stock, security, index, or fund, is its past rate of return and performance. The historical data is commonly used in financial analysis to project future returns or determine what variables may impact future returns and the extent to which the variables may influence returns. Concerning standard deviations, historical returns can be used to predict future data points.
- Cost of capital is a calculation of the minimum return that would be necessary in order to justify undertaking a capital budgeting project, such as building a new factory. It is an evaluation of whether a projected decision can be justified by its cost.
- Explicit cost is the discount rate that equate the present value of the expected incremental cash inflows with the present value of its incremental cash out flows. Thus, it is 'the rat return of the cash flows of financing opportunity.' In

contrast, implicit cost is the rate of return associated with the best investment opportunity for the firm and its shareholders that will be foregone if the project presently under consideration by the firm were accepted. In a nutshell, explicit costs relate to raising of funds while implicit costs relate to usage of funds.

- The average cost is the weighted average of the costs of each components of funds. After ascertaining costs of each source of capital, appropriate weights are assigned to each component of capital. Marginal cost of capital is the weighted average cost of new funds raised by the firm.
- Future cost of capital refers to the expected cost to be incurred in raising new funds while historical cost represents cost of capital incurred in the past in procuring funds for the firms. In financial decision making future cost of capital is relatively more relevant.
- The costs of individual components of capital are specific cost of capital. The combined cost of capital is the average cost of capital as it is inclusive of cost of capital from all sources. In capital budgeting decisions, combined cost of capital is used for accepting/rejecting the investment proposals.
- Weighted average cost of capital (WACC) represents a company's average after-tax cost of capital from all sources, including common stock, preferred stock, bonds, and other forms of debt. As such, WACC is the average rate that a company expects to pay to finance its business.
- The cost of debt is the return that a company provides to its debt holders and creditors. These capital providers need to be compensated for any risk exposure that comes with lending to a company.
- Cost of Equity is the rate of return a company pays out to equity investors. A firm uses cost of equity to assess the relative attractiveness of investments, including both internal projects and external acquisition opportunities. Companies typically use a combination of equity and debt financing, with equity capital being more expensive.

REVIEW QUESTIONS

1. What is risk and return?
2. Why do investors demand a higher return when investing in riskier securities?
3. What is risk-return tradeoff?
4. What are the components of a stock's realized return?
5. What is the intuition behind using the average annual return as a measure of expected return?
6. What is cost of capital?
7. Why Is Cost of Capital Important?
8. Name the three components of cost of capital.
9. What are the difference between cost of debt and cost of equity?
10. What is weighted average cost of capital?

REFERENCES

1. Brealey, R. A., & Myers, S. C. (2008). *Principles of Corporate Finance* (9th ed.). McGraw-Hill/Irwin. ISBN 978-0-07-340510-0.

2. Francis, J., Lafond, R., Olsson, P. M., & Schipper, K. (2004). Costs of equity and earnings attributes. *The Accounting Review, 79*(4), 967–1010. https://doi.org/10.2308/accr.2004.79.4.967.

3. Frank, M., & Shen, T. (2012). Investment, Q, and the weighted average cost of capital. *Social Science Research Network, 119*(2), 300–315. SSRN 2014367.

4. Gebhardt, W., Lee, C., & Swaminathan, B. (2001). Toward an implied cost of capital. *Journal of Accounting Research, 39*(1), 135–176. https://doi.org/10.1111/1475-679X.00007.

5. Horcher, K. A. (2005). *Essentials of Financial Risk Management*. John Wiley & Sons. ISBN 978-0-471-70616-8.

6. Modigliani, F., & Miller, M. (1958). The cost of capital, corporation finance and the theory of investment. *American Economic Review, 48*(3), 261–297. https://www.jstor.org/stable/1809766 (accessed on 16 July 2024).

7. Rosenbaum, J., & Pearl, J. (2009). *Investment Banking: Valuation, Leveraged Buyouts, and Mergers & Acquisitions*. John Wiley & Sons. ISBN 978-0-470-44220-3.

8. Titman, S. (2002). The Modigliani and Miller theorem and the integration of financial markets. *Financial Management, 31*(1), 101–115. https://doi.org/10.2307/3666323.

9. Yee, K. K. (2005). Aggregation, dividend irrelevancy, and earnings-value relations. *Contemporary Accounting Research, 22*(2), 453–480. https://doi.org/10.1506/GEH4-WNJR-G58F-UM0U.

CHAPTER 9

Corporate Capital Structure

LEARNING OBJECTIVES

After studying this chapter, you will be able to:

- Understand the concept of capital structure
- Examine how capital structures vary across industries and companies
- Understand why investment decisions, rather than financing decisions, fundamentally determine the value and cost of capital of the firm
- Describe how leverage increases the risk of the firm's equity
- Demonstrate how debt can affect a firm's value through taxes and bankruptcy costs
- Show how the optimal mix of debt and equity trades off the costs (including financial distress costs) and benefits (including the tax advantage) of debt
- Describe the additional consequences of leverage: agency costs and information

KEY TERMS FROM THIS CHAPTER

Agency costs	Assets
Balance sheet	Capital structure
Cost of capital	Debt-to-equity
Financial distress	Financial leverage
Homemade leverage	Leverage ratio
Levered equity	Long-term debt
Optimal capital structure	Preferred stock
Tradeoff theory	Unlevered equity

INTRODUCTION

Any kind of business needs finance as a necessary component for both working capital and long-term investments. The total amount of money used by a business comes from a number of sources. The owners contribute a portion of the funds, and the remaining amount is borrowed from institutions and other people. All of these funds together make up the firm's overall financial structure. Some are retained in the business permanently, like share capital and reserves (owned funds); others are held for an extended length of time, like long-term borrowings or debentures; still other funds are borrowed for a short time. You are aware that short-term investments fluctuate frequently. Therefore, it's possible that the ratio of different sources of short-term funding cannot be strictly established. The company must adopt a flexible strategy. When it comes to the capital structure—the arrangement of long-term funds—more precise guidelines are frequently established. The policy's dividend decision and debt-to-equity ratio are its two most important components. The latter has an impact on retained earnings accumulation, which is a crucial part of long-term owned funds. The phrase "financial structure" is frequently used to refer to the capital structure of the company since permanent or long-term funds frequently make up a sizable share of total funds and involve long-term policy decisions.

Corporate entities can typically obtain long-term funding from a few different sources. The principal funding sources are long-term debt, including debentures (funds of creditors) and share capital (owners' funds). The owners' funds, or profits from operations, can either be reinvested in the company or given as dividends to the owners, or shareholders. The owners' money is reinvested in the business as a portion of the profits. As a result, it provides long-term funding as well. The primary components of the business's capital, or capital structure, are all these sources combined.

9.1. CONCEPT OF CAPITAL STRUCTURE

The combination of different types of outside funding, or capital, that is utilized to finance a business is referred to as its capital structure. It is shown in the balance sheet of the business and is made up of preferred stock, debt (borrowed money), and shareholders' equity. A company is said to have more financial leverage (also known as gearing in the UK) the more debt it has relative to its other sources of capital. An excessive amount of debt can make a company riskier and less flexible financially, which eventually worries investors and raises the cost of capital. Establishing a capital structure for the company that keeps the cost of capital as low as feasible while maximizing the use of financial leverage is the responsibility of company management (Groppelli, et al., 2000; Harris Milton et al., 1991).

In the US, capital structure plays a significant role in determining the rates that regulated utilities charge their consumers. Although regulators determine the appropriate capital structure and cost of capital for ratemaking purposes, the utility company is free to choose any capital structure it sees fit (Louiselle Bruce & Heilman Jane, 1982).

Financial analysts keep a close eye on various leverage or gearing ratios to determine how much debt is present in a company's capital structure (Melicher Ronald & Welshans Merle, 1988). According to the Miller and Modigliani theorem, a firm's market value remains unchanged when its capital structure changes. This school of thought is typically seen as a purely theoretical result because it makes the assumption that there is a perfect market and ignores potential variables like fluctuations and uncertain situations when financing a business. The debate and relaxation of Miller and Modigliani's assumptions to explain why a firm's capital structure matters to its real-world value have received a lot of attention in the academic community.

9.1.1. Dynamics of Debt and Equity

The balance sheet shows both equity and debt. Debt or equity are used to buy company assets, which are also shown on the balance sheet. A company's long-term debt, short-term debt, common stock, and preferred stock can all be a part of its capital structure. When examining a company's capital structure, the ratio of short-term to long-term debt is taken into account.

Analysts typically refer to a company's debt-to-equity (D/E) ratio when discussing capital structure because it gives an indication of how risky the company's borrowing practices are. A business that relies largely on debt typically has a more aggressive capital structure, which increases investor risk. However, this risk might be the main driver of the company's expansion.

One of a company's two primary avenues for capital raising on the capital markets is debt. Businesses benefit from debt because of its tax advantages; interest paid on loans may be deductible from taxes. Unlike equity, debt enables a company or business to maintain ownership. In addition, debt is widely available and accessible during periods of low interest rates.

Equity enables external investors to acquire a portion of the business. Debt is less expensive than equity, particularly during a period of low interest rates. Equity, however, is not repaid, in contrast to debt. In the event that earnings decline, this will help the business. Equity, on the other hand, is the owner's claim to the company's future profits.

9.1.2. Optimal Capital Structure

Businesses with an aggressive capital structure and a high leverage ratio finance their assets and operations primarily through debt rather than equity. A business with a conservative capital structure and a low leverage ratio is one that pays for assets with more equity than debt. Nevertheless, while a conservative capital structure can result in lower growth rates, a high leverage ratio and an aggressive capital structure can also lead to higher growth rates. The D/E ratio is used by analysts to compare capital structures. By dividing total liabilities by total equity, it is computed. Astute businesses have figured out how to balance equity and debt in their business plans. However, businesses can occasionally rely too much on outside financing, especially debt. By tracking the D/E ratio and contrasting it with the company's peers in the industry, investors can keep an eye on a company's capital structure. The optimal capital structure, or the right balance of debt and equity, is what business management looks for when determining how to finance operations (Melicher Ronald & Welshans Merle, 1988).

9.1.3. Capital Structure Planning

The arrangement of different long-term funding sources within the overall capitalization of the business is known as the capital structure. Ownership and creditor ship securities are the two primary sources. Most large industrial companies use both kinds of securities and long-term loans from financial institutions.

Any business should prioritize capital structure planning from the beginning because it has a significant impact on profitability. A poor first choice in this regard could end up costing the business a lot of money.

The choice a company makes regarding its capital structure is crucial because it can affect its solvency and profitability. Small businesses frequently don't prepare their capital structure. The capital structure is not formally planned; it is allowed to evolve. These businesses might succeed in the near term, but eventually they will run into serious problems. The company is unable to use its funds economically due to the unplanned capital structure. As a result, a business should design its capital structure to maximize its benefits and facilitate easier adaptation to shifting market conditions. Rather than employing a methodical approach to determine the ideal ratio of various forms of capital that will minimize capital costs and optimize market value, an organization may choose to adopt a capital structure that is similar to that of other similar businesses or seek guidance from an institutional lender. Theoretically, a business should design its ideal capital structure to maximize the market value of its stock. When each source of funding has the same marginal real cost, the value will be maximized. The debate over the ideal capital structure is typically very theoretical. Finding the ideal capital structure in practice is a difficult task that requires more than just theory. This could be the reason for the notable differences in capital structure between industries and between companies in the same industry. A company's choice of capital structure is influenced by several factors. The judgment of the individual or group deciding on the capital structure is very important. If the decision makers at two similar companies have different opinions about how important different factors are, then the two companies may have different capital structures. These variables are qualitative, complex, and highly psychological; they also don't always follow the conventional wisdom. Because capital markets are not flawless, decisions must be made with incomplete information and associated risk. You may now be curious to know which significant variables actually affect how the capital structure is planned in practice.

9.1.4. Features of an Appropriate Capital Structure

Ordinary shareholders' interests are typically taken into consideration when planning a capital structure. Since they are the company's ultimate owners, common shareholders are able to choose the directors. The financial manager ought to prioritize optimizing the equity shares' long-term market price when formulating a suitable capital structure for the company. In actuality, most businesses within an industry would have a range of suitable capital structures with relatively little variation in share market values. In this case, it is possible to determine a capital structure empirically. A business might operate, for instance, in an industry where the average debt to total capital ratio is 60%. Based on empirical data, it can be concluded that shareholders generally don't mind if the business operates within a 15% range of the average capital structure for the industry. Therefore, a debt to total capital ratio of between 45% and 75% represents the proper capital structure for the business. Subject to additional requirements like flexibility, solvency, etc., the company's management should aim to find the capital structure near the top of this range in order to maximize the use of favorable leverage.

A sound appropriate capital structure should have the following features:

- **Profitability**: The capital structure of the company should be most advantageous, within the constraints. Maximum use of leverage at a minimum cost should be made.
- **Solvency**: The use of excessive debt threatens the solvency of the company. Debt should be used judiciously.
- **Flexibility**: The capital structure should be flexible to meet the changing conditions. It should be possible for a company to adapt its capital structure with minimum cost and delay if warranted by a changed situation. It should also be possible for the company to provide funds whenever needed to finance its profitable activities.

Put another way, we must approach capital structuring with appropriate conservation when considering solvency. It is not advisable to go over the company's debt limit, which is based on its potential to produce future cash flows. It should have sufficient funds to cover the principal amount upon maturity as well as regular fixed charges to creditors. The general characteristics of a suitable capital structure are listed above. Certain additional specific features may be reflected in a company's unique characteristics. Furthermore, each of these features may be prioritized differently by different companies. For instance, one company might value flexibility more than control, despite the fact that control may be another desired feature. On the other hand, another company might prioritize solvency over all other requirements. Furthermore, as circumstances alter, so too might the relative significance of these requirements.

9.1.5. Determinants of Capital Structure

A company's capital structure must be decided upon when it is promoted. The initial capital structure needs to be meticulously planned. A target capital structure should be established by the company's management, and any further financing decisions should be made with that target capital structure in mind. The financial manager must then handle the current capital structure once the company has been formed and operating for a while. The business might require money to continuously finance its operations. The financial manager considers the advantages and disadvantages of different financing sources each time funds are needed, selecting the most beneficial sources while keeping the target capital structure in mind. As a result, the decision regarding the capital structure is ongoing and must be made each time a company requires additional funding.

When choosing a capital structure, one should generally take into account the following factors: (i) Leverage or Trading on Equity; (ii) Cost of Capital; (iii) Cash flow; (iv) Control; (v) Flexibility; (vi) Size of the Company; (vii) Marketability; and (viii) Floatation costs. Let's discuss these factors in brief.

9.1.5.1. Leverage or Trading on Equity

Financial leverage or trading on equity refers to the use of fixed-cost financing sources, such as debt and preference share capital, to finance the company's assets. Earnings per share will rise without an increase in the owners' investment if the debt-financed assets produce a return higher than the cost of the debt. Similarly, if preference share capital is utilized to purchase assets, earnings per share will also rise. However, the impact of leverage is greater when debt is involved because (i) debt typically has lower capital costs than preference share capital, and (ii) interest paid on debt is deductible from profits when determining taxable income, but dividends on preference shares are not.

When planning a company's capital structure, financial leverage is a crucial factor to take into account due to its impact on earnings per share. High leverage ratios can be profitably used by companies with high Earnings before Interest and Taxes (EBIT) to boost return on shareholders' equity. Analyzing the relationship between Earnings per Share (BPS) at various EBIT levels under alternative financing methods is a popular way to look at the impact of leverage. One crucial tool in the financial manager's toolbox for understanding the company's capital structure management is the EBIT-EPS analysis. He can think about potential EBIT swings and assess how they would affect EPS under various financing scenarios.

The company's shares will be in high demand and command a premium price in the market. Sometimes, business managers purposefully aim to make equity shares extremely desirable and valuable assets. They can accomplish this by engaging in equity trading. The key to financial leverage's advantage is that, while the total return (before taxes) on capital used is 25%, the returns on debt and preference shares are only 12% and 10%, respectively. The management is able to increase the return on equity shares thanks to the savings that arise from this discrepancy.

Leverage can raise shareholders' financial risk even though it boosts EPS in favorable circumstances. The use of debt raises financial risk due to two factors: (a) the possibility of insolvency and (b) the increased volatility in shareholder earnings. If a company's capital structure excludes debt, it can completely eliminate financial risk. However, the benefit of increases in EPS resulting from financial leverage will not be available to the shareholders if there is no debt used in the capital structure. Thus, a company should use debt only to the extent that the benefit of higher profits per share (EPS) is greater than the perceived financial risk in the eyes of the shareholders.

9.1.5.2. Cost of Capital

Assessing the expenses of different funding sources is a complicated topic that requires its own discussion. It goes without saying that lowering the cost of capital is preferable. Therefore, given all other factors being equal, it is better to use less expensive sources.

The lowest return that a source of funding's suppliers will accept is known as the source's cost. The level of risk that investors take on determines the expected return. Compared to debt holders, shareholders bear a greater amount of risk. Regardless of whether the business is profitable or not, it is legally required to pay interest to debt holders at a fixed rate. The dividend rate is not set for shareholders, and even in cases where the company has made profits, the Board of Directors is not required by law to distribute dividends to shareholders. Debt holders' loans are reimbursed within a set time frame, but shareholders' capital isn't refunded until the business is closed. This suggests that debt is a more affordable funding option than equity. The cost of debt is further decreased by interest charges being tax deductible. While preference share capital is less expensive than equity capital, it is still more expensive than debt. Therefore, a business should use a lot of debt in order to reduce the total cost of capital.

It should be understood, though, that a business cannot continue to use debt to reduce its overall cost of capital. There comes a point at which debt becomes more costly due to the elevated risk of excessive debt to shareholders and creditors. The risk to creditors rises in tandem with the amount of leverage. When the company's debt reaches a certain amount, they might demand a higher interest rate or stop lending money altogether. Furthermore, the position of the shareholders is extremely risky due to the excessive debt. The result is an increase in the cost of equity. Thus, using debt reduces the overall cost of capital up to a certain point. However, after that, the cost of capital would start to rise, making further use of debt unfavorable. Therefore, a mix of debt and equity is used to maximize market value per share while minimizing the average cost of capital for that company.

The price of retained earnings and the cost of issuing new shares are included in the cost of equity. Debt is less expensive than either of these two equity funding sources. Retained earnings is less expensive when compared to the cost of new issues. Retained earnings are less expensive than new issues because the company does not have to pay personal taxes that shareholders must pay on distributed earnings and because, in contrast to new issues, there are no floatation costs associated with retained earnings. Therefore, retained earnings are the better of the two sources.

Taking into account the leverage and cost of capital factors, it makes sense for a company to use a lot of debt as long as its earnings don't fluctuate too much. Indeed, debt can be utilized up to the point where it has the lowest average cost of capital. The maximum amount of debt that can be used is determined by combining these two factors. To ascertain a company's ideal capital structure, additional considerations must be made. In theory, a business should have a debt to equity ratio that minimizes its total cost of capital.

9.1.5.3. Cash Flow

Conservation is one of the characteristics of a sound capital structure. Utilizing little or no debt is not the same as conservation. Conservatism pertains to evaluating the fixed charge liability resulting from the capital structure's use of debt or preference capital, taking into account the company's capacity to generate cash flow to cover these fixed charges. A company's fixed charges consist of principal, interest, and preference dividend payments. If the business uses a lot of debt or preference capital, the fixed charges will be high. Anytime a business considers taking on more debt, it should assess how it will pay for the fixed expenses in the future. Interest must be paid, and the principal amount owed must be returned. A business may have to declare financial insolvency if it cannot make enough money to pay its fixed obligations. Businesses that anticipate significant and consistent cash inflows are able to use a high debt load in their capital structure. Using fixed-fee sources of capital for businesses with erratic or unpredictable cash inflows carries some risk.

9.1.5.4. Control

Sometimes the current management's desire to maintain control over the company influences how the capital structure is designed. In addition to wanting to be elected to the Board of Directors, the current management group may also want to run the business independently of outside influence.

Ordinary shareholders are legally entitled to choose the company's directors. The company runs the risk of losing control if it issues new shares. When considering a widely held company, this is not a crucial factor to take into account. Such a company's shares are dispersed widely. The majority of shareholders have no desire to be actively involved in the management of the company. They don't feel driven or have the time to attend the meetings. All that matters to them is the growth in share prices and dividends. It is nearly impossible to lose control over shares if they are distributed widely and in small lots.

But in the case of a closely held business, maintaining control might be a big concern. The company could be taken over by a shareholder or group of shareholders if they buy all or most of the new shares. Closely held businesses frequently put off going public out of fear of having to cede control and potential outside interference. The companies may raise debt capital or issue preference shares in order to mitigate the risk of losing control. Since debt holders are not entitled to vote, it is frequently recommended that a business use debt in order to prevent losing control. However, in order to safeguard their interests, debt holders place numerous restrictions on a company that uses a lot of debt. The management's ability to manage the company is restricted by these rules. Bankruptcy, which denotes total loss of control, can also result from having too much debt.

9.1.5.5. Flexibility

The term "flexibility" refers to the capacity of the company to modify its capital structure in response to evolving circumstances. If a company can easily change its sources of funding or capitalization, its capital structure is flexible. The business should be able to raise money whenever it's needed, without incurring unnecessary costs or delays, to finance its profitable ventures. Additionally, if future circumstances warrant it, the company should be able to redeem its debt or preference capital. The company's financial plan should allow for the modification of the capital structure's composition. To minimize the amount of money used, it should be able to switch from one type of financing to another.

9.1.5.6. Size of the Company

A company's size has a big impact on the money that is available from various sources. It can be challenging for a small business to obtain long-term financing. If it is able to secure a long-term loan, it will be offered on unfavorable terms and at a high interest rate. Small business loan agreements contain extremely restrictive covenants that render their capital structure quite rigid. As a result, management cannot conduct business as usual. For their long-term funding, small businesses must therefore rely on owned capital and retained earnings. A large business can design its capital structure with more flexibility. It is able to issue debentures, preference shares, and common shares to the public in addition to obtaining loans on favorable terms. A business should plan its capital structure to take full advantage of its size.

9.1.5.7. Marketability

In this context, "marketability" refers to the company's capacity to offer or promote a specific kind of security within a given time frame, which is contingent upon investors' willingness to purchase that security. Although marketability may not have a significant impact on the initial capital structure, it is a crucial factor to take into account when determining when to issue securities. The market may accept ordinary share issues readily at one point in time and favor debenture issues at another. The company must determine whether to raise money through debt or common shares due to shifting market sentiments. In the event of a down market for shares, the company should consider issuing debt instead of common stock and hold off on issuing common stock until the market recovers. In the event of a share market boom, the company might find it difficult to successfully issue debentures. As a result, it should refrain from using its debt capacity and instead issue common stock to raise money.

9.1.5.8. Floatation Costs

When the money is raised, flotation expenses are incurred. Generally speaking, floating a debt issue is less expensive than floating an equity one. This could incite a business to issue debt instead of common stock. There are no floatation costs if the owner retains the earnings, increasing their capital. With the exception of small businesses, flotation cost typically has little bearing on a company's capital structure.

9.2. CAPITAL STRUCTURE CHOICES

A company's capital structure is made up of the various amounts of outstanding debt, equity, and other securities. Companies must decide what kind of capital structure to have and what kind of security to issue when they raise money from outside investors. The two most popular options are debt and equity combined financing and equity financing only. What aspects should a financial manager take into account when selecting a financing option, and how do businesses determine their capital structures?

First and foremost, in return for the money raised today, different financing options will guarantee varying future amounts to each security holder.

Beyond that, though, the company might also have to think about whether the securities it issues will be priced fairly in the market, whether they will have tax ramifications, whether they will involve transaction costs, or even if they will alter its options for future investments. Determining whether to repurchase shares, pay dividends, pay off debt, or accumulate cash also has an impact on a company's capital structure. We contextualize these financing decisions within real-world firm practices before delving into the theory that guides this analysis.

9.2.1. Capital Structure Choices across Industries

The average debt-to-value ratios for US stocks across industries are displayed in Figure 9.1. The percentage of a company's total value that is attributed to debt is known as the debt-to-value ratio, or D/(E + D). You'll notice that different industries choose different debt levels from financial managers. Software firms like Microsoft, for instance, are far less leveraged than automakers like Ford Motor Company (having less debt in relation to equity).

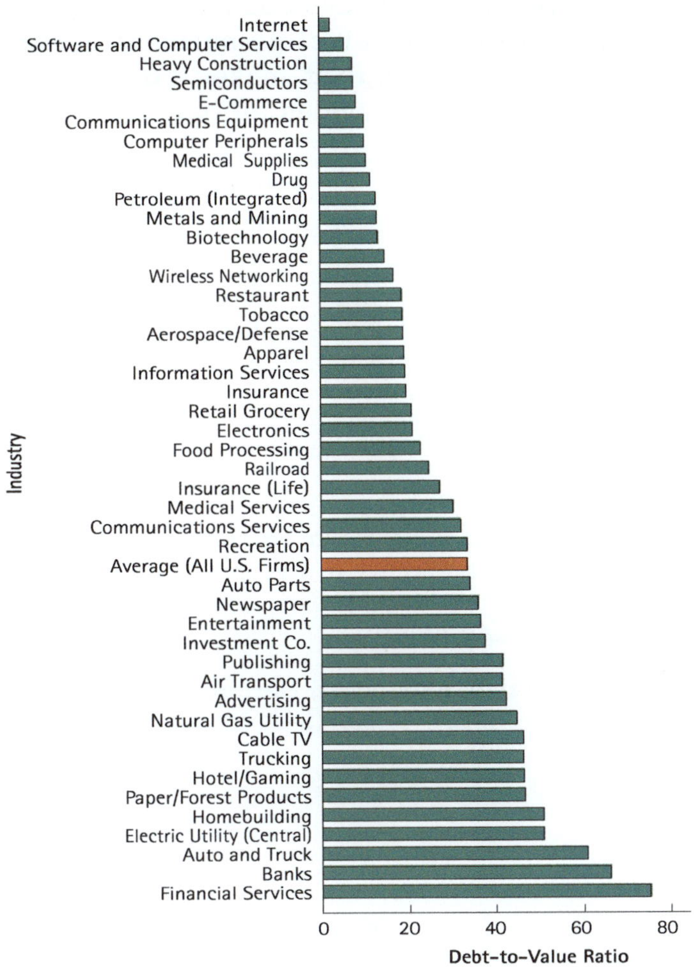

Figure 9.1. *Debt-to-value ratio [D/(E + D)] for select industries. The bars represent debt-to-value ratios across a wide variety of industries. Debt levels are determined by book values, and equity by market values. The average debt financing for all U.S. stocks was about 33%, but note the large differences by industry.*

Source: Jonathan Berk, Peter DeMarzo, and Jarrad Harford. Fundamentals of Corporate Finance, Second edition. Pearson Education. ISBN: 978-0-13-214823-8.

9.2.2. Capital Structure Choices within Industries

There are notable variations in capital structures amongst industries. However, two rival companies may decide to set their debt-to-value ratios differently even within the same industry. For instance, as shown in panels (a) and (b) of Figure 9.2, two companies in the book retailing sector, Amazon.com and Barnes and Noble, have radically different capital structures. Panel (a) illustrates that Barnes & Noble has 33% debt and 67% equity, while panel (b) shows that Amazon has almost no debt! Despite being direct competitors, Amazon.com and Barnes & Noble have very different assets and histories.

For the most part, Barnes & Noble has always been a company that sells books through "brick and mortar" stores. Amazon does all of its business online via shipping and has never kept a physical storefront. Although it makes up a very minor portion of their overall business, Barnes & Noble also provides an online/mail service.

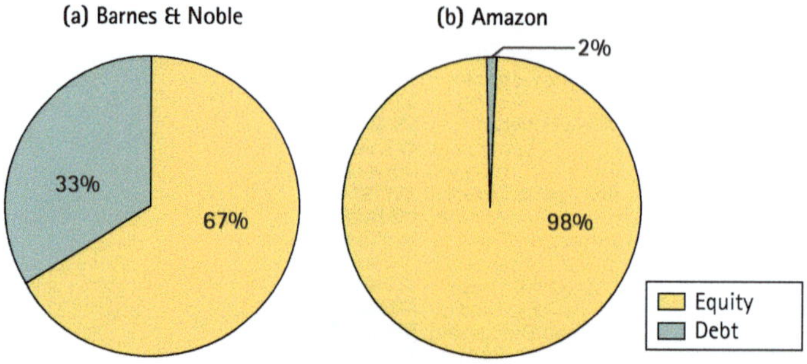

Figure 9.2. *Capital structures of Amazon.com and Barnes & Noble. The pie charts in panels (a) and (b) show the split between debt and equity in two competing firms, Amazon.com and Barnes & Noble. Both are part of the book retailing industry. Even within an industry, two companies can choose a different mix of debt and equity.*

Source: Jonathan Berk, Peter DeMarzo, and Jarrad Harford. Fundamentals of Corporate Finance, Second edition. Pearson Education. ISBN: 978-0-13-214823-8.

9.3. CAPITAL STRUCTURE IN PERFECT CAPITAL MARKETS

A company's decision to issue debt, equity, or other securities in order to finance a new investment could have a number of unintended consequences. Whether or not a particular decision will impact the firm's value and, consequently, the amount of capital it can raise is by far the most crucial question for a financial manager. We start by thinking about this query in a straightforward setting: an ideal capital market. A perfect capital market is a market in which:

1. Securities are fairly priced. Investors and firms can trade the same set of securities at competitive market prices equal to the present value of their future cash flows.
2. There are no tax consequences or transactions costs. There are no tax consequences, transactions costs, or other issuance costs associated with financing decisions or security trading.
3. Investment cash flows are independent of financing choices. A firm's financing decisions do not change the cash flows generated by its investments, nor do they reveal new information about those cash flows.

The notion of flawless capital markets could appear constrained and impractical. However, we will see that by beginning with them, we will obtain crucial understanding of the actual costs and advantages of leverage.

9.3.1. Application: Financing a New Business

Let's start with an illustration of a potential financing choice made in an ideal capital market. Let's say you have one more year of college left and would like to get a little extra cash before you graduate. An opportunity to manage the coffee shop in the lobby of a nearby office building has been presented to you. Prior to a significant renovation, the building's owner is willing to give you this privilege for a period of one year.

Based on your research, it looks like you'll need to start the business with a $24,000 upfront investment. At the end of the year, you hope to have $34,500 in cash flow after paying your overhead, which includes paying yourself a respectable salary. As of right now, the risk-free interest rate is 5%. However, you think that your profits will be somewhat volatile and contingent on the general market (which will impact building activity and demand for your business). As a result, you think a 10% risk premium is reasonable, for a total discount rate of 15% (5% + 10%). As a result, you determine the NPV of this coffee shop investment as follows:

$$NPV = -\$24{,}000 + \frac{\$34{,}500}{1.15} = -\$24{,}000 + \$30{,}000 = \$6000$$

The investment's NPV is therefore positive.

You must raise the funds for the initial investment even though the investment appears appealing. What is the estimated amount that can be raised, and how should the funds be raised?

9.3.1.1. Equity Financing

Initially, you might think about selling your friends and family only stock in the company in order to raise money. Remember that a security's value is equal to the present value of its future cash flows, so let's see how much they would be willing to pay for those shares based on the cash flow estimates. In this scenario, the $34,500 payout that equity holders in your company will anticipate at the end of the year carries the same level of risk as the cash flows produced by the coffee shop. Consequently, the equity cost of capital for your company will be 15%, and the equity's current value will be:

$$PV\,(\text{equity cash flows}) = \frac{\$34{,}500}{1.15} = \$30{,}000$$

Remember that having no debt equates to having no financial leverage. Unlevered equity is the term used to describe equity in a company that has no debt. Seling all of the unlevered equity in your company will allow you to raise $30,000 because the present value of the equity cash flows is $30,000. By doing this, you can pay the $24,000 investment cost and retain the $6000 net present value as profit. To put it another way, the project's net present value (NPV) is the value the project creates for the company's original owner, in this case you, the entrepreneur.

9.3.1.2. Levered Financing

Alternatively, you might think about taking out a loan for a portion of the required investment funds. Assume that the company will always generate at least $16,000 in cash flow. Then, at the current risk-free interest rate of 5%, you can borrow $15,000. There is no chance of default when you pay the debt of $15,000 × 0.5 = $15,750 at the end of the year.

Leveraged equity is the term for equity in a company that also has outstanding debt. How much can you raise by selling equity in your company right now? Equity holders will receive $34,500 – $15,750 = $18,750 after the debt is paid off. What expected return will investors demand? What discount rate should we use to value leveraged equity?

It is tempting to stick with the previous equity cost of capital of 15%. In that scenario, you could raise $18,750/1.15 = $16,304 by selling leveraged equity. Should this outcome hold true, employing leverage would enable you to raise a total of $15,000 + $16,304 = $31,304, or $1304 more than in the scenario without leverage, including the debt.

Therefore, it would appear that a project's value can be increased by merely using leverage to finance it. It's true that if something seems too good to be true. Our analysis was based on the assumption that, even with leverage, your company's equity cost of capital would stay at 15%. That won't be the case, though, as we'll see in a moment, as leverage raises the firm's equity cost of capital and increases equity risk. To find out why, as well as to comprehend what will truly transpire, we consult the seminal research of researchers Merton Miller and Franco Modigliani.

9.3.2. Leverage and Firm Value

Researchers Modigliani and Miller (abbreviated MM) examined if leverage would raise the firm's overall value in a significant thesis. At the time, researchers and practitioners were taken aback by their response to this query. They maintained that a firm's total value shouldn't be based on its capital structure in a perfect capital market. Their reasoning is that, as Figure 9.3 illustrates, your company's total cash flows—that is, the cash flows paid to debt and equity holders—remain equal to the cash flows of the coffee shop, with the same expected value of $34,500 and the same overall risk.

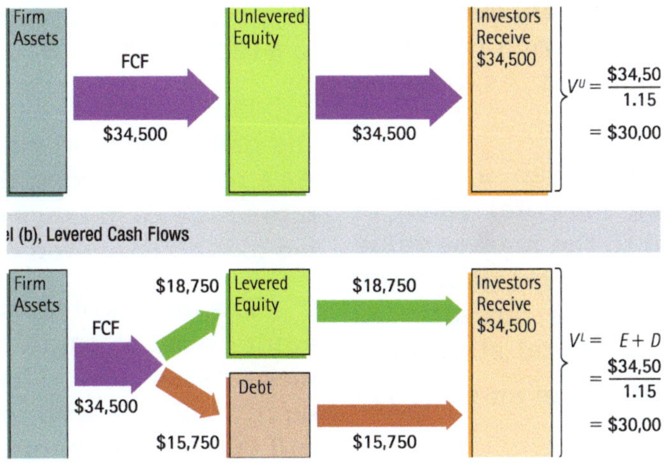

Figure 9.3. *Unlevered versus levered cash flows with perfect capital markets. When the firm has no debt, as shown in panel (a), the cash flows paid to equity holders correspond to the free cash flows generated by the firm's assets. When the firm has the debt, shown in panel (b), these cash flows are divided between debt and equity holders. However, with perfect capital markets, the total amount paid to all investors still corresponds to the free cash flows generated by the firm's assets. Therefore, the value of the unlevered firm, V^U, must equal the total value of the levered firm, V^L, which is the combined value of its debt D and levered equity E.*

Source: Jonathan Berk, Peter DeMarzo, and Jarrad Harford. Fundamentals of Corporate Finance, Second edition. Pearson Education. ISBN: 978-0-13-214823-8.

The Valuation Principle states that since the combined cash flows from debt and equity equal the cash flows from the unlevered firm, their market values must also equal. Specifically, we calculated earlier that the value of the unlevered firm, V^U, is:

$$V^U = \$34{,}500/1.15 = \$30{,}000$$

Thus, the total value of the levered firm, V^L, which is the combined value of its debt, D, and levered equity, E, must be the same:

$$V^L = D + E = \$30{,}000$$

Consequently, the initial market value of the levered equity must be E = \$30,000 – \$15,000 = \$15,000. This is because the initial market value of the debt is D = \$15,000 (the amount borrowed).

Therefore, in a perfect capital market, Modigliani and Miller contended, leverage only modifies how cash flows are distributed between debt and equity, leaving the firm's overall cash flows unchanged. As a result, they concluded that:

- **MM Proposition I**: In a perfect capital market, the total value of a firm is equal to the market value of the free cash flows generated by its assets and is not affected by its choice of capital structure.

We can write this result in an equation as follows:

$$V^L = E + D = V^U \quad (1)$$

According to this equation, the firm's total value remains constant whether leverage is used or not.

In our example, take note that the price at which levered equity sells (\$15,000 versus \$30,000) is less than that of unlevered equity due to the smaller cash flows of the former. But, this does not imply that you are in worse shape because the leveraged equity is worth less. Just as you did with unlevered equity alone, you will still raise a total of \$30,000 by issuing debt and leveraged equity, and you will keep the \$6000 profit that results from the difference between the \$30,000 you raise and your \$24,000 cost. You will therefore have no preference between these two options for the capital structure of the company.

9.3.3. The Effect of Leverage on Risk and Return

The common belief that leverage would impact a firm's value even in the presence of perfect capital markets was refuted by Modigliani and Miller's conclusion. Specifically, it was believed that the leveraged equity's value should be greater than \$15,000 because, as we previously computed, the present value of the equity's expected cash flow at a 15% discount rate is \$18,750/1.15 = \$16,304.

This is untrue because leverage raises the risk associated with a company's equity. As a result, applying the same 15% discount rate to the cash flows of leveraged equity as we did for unlevered equity is inappropriate.

The impact of leverage on the company's equity cost of capital will be examined in more detail now. The expected return for equity holders who are only willing to pay \$15,000 for the leveraged equity, given the estimated payoff of \$18,750, is as follows:

$$\text{Expected return of levered equity} = \$18{,}750/\$15{,}000 - 1 = 25\%$$

Investors may find this return attractive, but keep in mind that the cash flows from the coffee shop are not guaranteed. Table 9.1 compares the security payoffs and returns with unlevered equity to the scenario in which you borrow \$15,000 and raise an additional $15,000 using levered equity, taking into account the various demand and free cash flows that the coffee shop may generate. Keep in mind that the returns with and without leverage differ significantly. Unlevered equity has an expected return of 15% and can yield returns ranging from -10% to 40% when there is no debt. In contrast to the much more volatile returns of leveraged equity, which can range from -25% to 75%, debt holders who use leverage receive a risk-free return of 5%. Leveraged equity holders receive a higher expected return of 25% in order to offset this increased risk.

Table 9.1. Returns to Equity in Different Scenarios with and Without Leverage

Coffee Shop		Security Cash Flows			Security Returns		
Demand	Free Cash Flows	Unlevered Equity	Debt	Levered Equity	Unlevered Equity	Debt	Levered Equity
Weak	$27,000	$27,000	$15,750	$11,250	−10%	5%	−25%
Expected	**$34,500**	**$34,500**	**$15,750**	**$18,750**	**15%**	**5%**	**25%**
Strong	$42,000	$42,000	$15,750	$26,250	40%	5%	75%

Source: Jonathan Berk, Peter DeMarzo, and Jarrad Harford. Fundamentals of Corporate Finance, Second edition. Pearson Education. ISBN: 978–0-13–214823–8.

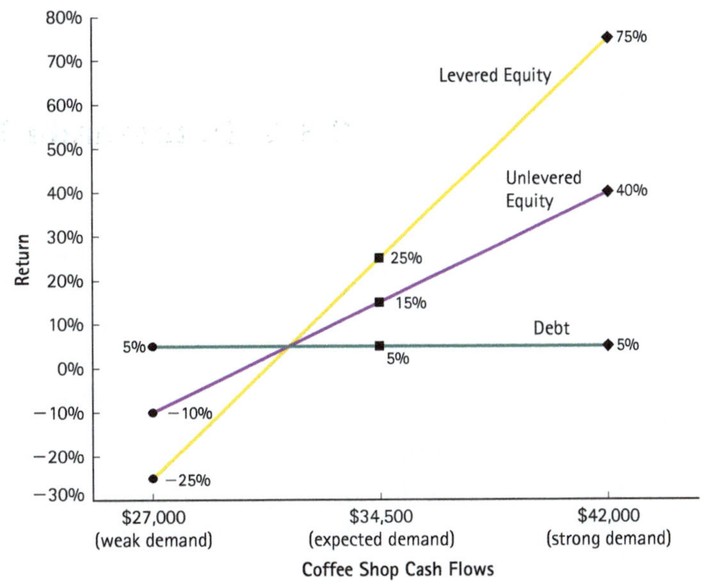

Figure 9.4. *Unlevered versus levered returns with perfect capital markets. Leverage splits the firm's return between low-risk debt and high-risk levered equity compared to the equity of an unlevered firm. In this example, the returns of levered equity are twice as sensitive to the firm's cash flows as the returns of unlevered equity. This doubling of risk implies a doubling of the risk premium from 10% to 20%.*

Source: Jonathan Berk, Peter DeMarzo, and Jarrad Harford. Fundamentals of Corporate Finance, Second edition. Pearson Education. ISBN: 978–0-13–214823–8.

In Figure 9.4, we further demonstrate how leverage affects returns. Leverage effectively "splits" the returns of the unlevered firm between low-risk debt and much higher-risk leveraged equity. Keep in mind that if the coffee shop's cash flows decline, the returns on leveraged equity will decline twice as quickly as those on unlevered equity. The risk premium, which is 25% – 5% = 20% for leveraged equity and 15% – 5% = 10% for unlevered equity, should also double in proportion to the doubling of risk. Leverage raises the risk of equity even in situations where there is no chance that the company will default, as this example demonstrates.

Example 9.1. The Risk and Return of Levered Equity

- **Problem:** Suppose you borrow only $6000 when financing your coffee shop. According to Modigliani and Miller, what should the value of the equity be? What is the expected return?
- Solution
  - **Plan:** The value of the firm's total cash flows does not change: It is still $30,000. Thus, if you borrow $6000, your firm's equity will be worth $24,000. To determine the equity's expected return, we will compute the cash flows to equity under the two scenarios. The cash flows to equity are the cash flows of the firm net of the cash flows to debt (repayment of principal plus interest).
  - **Execute:** The firm will owe debt holders $6,000 × 1.05 = $6,300 in one year. Thus, the expected payoff to equity holders is $34,500 – $6,300 = $28,200, for a return of $28,200/$24,000 – 1 = 17.5%.
  - **Evaluate:** While the total value of the firm is unchanged, the firm's equity in this case is more risky than it would be without debt, but less risky than if the firm borrowed $15,000. To illustrate, note that if demand is weak, the equity holders will receive $27,000 – $6,300 = $20,700 for a return of $20,700/$24,000 – 1 = -13.75%. Compare this return to -10% without leverage and -25% if the firm borrowed $15,000. As a result, the expected return of the levered equity is higher in this case than for unlevered equity (17.5% versus 15%), but not as high as in the previous example (17.5% versus 25%).

9.3.4. Homemade Leverage

MM demonstrated that the firm's capital structure decision has no bearing on its value. Let's say, however, that investors would rather have a different capital structure than the one the company has selected. MM proved that investors can accomplish the same goal in this situation by lending or borrowing on their own. For instance, an investor can borrow additional leverage for their portfolio if they desire it beyond what the firm has selected. This kind of leverage addition will reduce the security's out-of-pocket expense while raising the portfolio's risk. We refer to an investor's use of homemade leverage when they use leverage in their own portfolios to modify the firm's leverage selection. Homemade leverage is an ideal replacement for the firm's use of leverage, provided that investors are able to lend or borrow at the same interest rate as the firm, which is the case in perfect capital markets. Therefore, different capital structure decisions have no effect on the firm's value because they do not benefit investors in perfect capital markets.

9.3.5. Leverage and the Cost of Capital

Modigliani and Miller's insight can help us comprehend how leverage affects a company's cost of capital. Remember from Figure 9.3 and Eqn. 1 that the value and cash flows of a levered firm's debt and equity portfolio are equal when viewed as a combined entity. As a result, the portfolio's expected return should match the unlevered firm's expected return. The weighted average of the expected returns of each security is the expected return of the debt and equity in the portfolio. Thus, with r_E representing the expected return of levered equity, r_D the expected return of debt, and r_U the expected return of the unlevered equity, we have:

Weighted Average Cost of Capital (Pretax)

$$\underbrace{r_E \frac{E}{E + D} + r_D \frac{D}{E + D}}_{\text{Pretax WACC}} = r_U \tag{2}$$

The amounts $\frac{E}{E + D}$ and $\frac{D}{E + D}$ represent the fraction of the firm's value financed by equity and debt, respectively. The weighted average cost of capital (WACC) of the company is therefore found on the left side of Eqn. 2. Please take note that since we are assuming "perfect capital markets" and are therefore ignoring taxes, the cost of debt is not adjusted for them. The term "firm's pretax WACC" refers to the weighted average cost of capital (WACC) that is computed without taxes. Eqn. 9.2 says that the firm's pretax WACC stays the same and equals the firm's unlevered cost of capital regardless of the capital structure option chosen.

Let's examine this outcome using our coffee shop example. The firm's debt cost of capital was $r_D = 5\%$ and its equity cost of capital increased to $r_E = 25\%$ when leverage was applied. Regarding the portfolio weights, in this instance the company issued equity valued at E = 15,000 and borrowed D = 15,000, for a total value $V^L = E + D = 30{,}000$. Therefore, its pretax WACC is:

$$r_E \frac{E}{E + D} + r_D \frac{D}{E + D} = 25\%\left(\frac{15{,}000}{30{,}000}\right) + 5\%\left(\frac{15{,}000}{30{,}000}\right) = 15\%$$

As a result, $r_U = 15\%$, the firm's unlevered cost of capital, is equal to the pretax WACC.

There are two offsetting effects of leverage: we finance a larger portion of the firm with debt, which has a lower cost of capital, but at the same time adding leverage raises the firm's equity cost of capital. How come the weighted average cost of capital for the firm remains the same even after adding leverage? These two effects should precisely cancel out, leaving the firm's WACC unchanged, because the total risk of the company has not changed—it has simply been divided between these two securities. To be more precise, we can use Eqn. 2 to ascertain how leverage affects the firm's equity cost of capital. Solving the equation for r_E, we have:

MM Proposition II: The Cost of Capital of Levered Equity

$$r_E = r_U + \frac{D}{E}(r_U - r_D) \quad (3)$$

Or, in words:

- **MM Proposition II**: The cost of capital of levered equity is equal to the cost of capital of unlevered equity plus a premium that is proportional to the debt-equity ratio (measured using market values).

Let's check MM Proposition II for the coffee shop example. In this case:

$$r_E = r_U + \frac{D}{E}(r_U - r_D) = 15\% + \frac{15{,}000}{15{,}000}(15\% - 5\%) = 25\%$$

This outcome is consistent with the expected return on leveraged equity that we determined in Table 9.1.

The impact of increasing leverage in a company's capital structure on its debt cost of capital, equity cost of capital, and WACC is depicted in Figure 9.5. We calculate the firm's leverage in the figure using the debt-to-value ratio, or D/(E + D).

The WACC is the same as the unlevered equity cost of capital in the absence of debt. Eqn. 3 shows that the firm's equity cost of capital increases as it borrows money at the low cost of capital for debt. In the end, the firm's WACC remains unaltered. Naturally, when a company has more debt, there is a greater chance that it will default, making the debt riskier and raising the debt cost of capital.

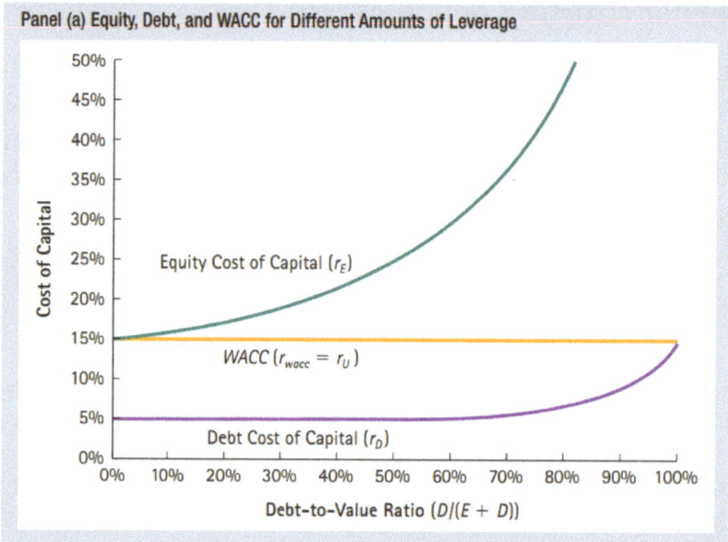

Panel (b) WACC Data for Alternative Capital Structures

E	D	r_E	r_D	$r_E \frac{E}{E+D} + r_D \frac{D}{E+D}$	$= r_{wacc}$
30,000	0	15.0%	5.0%	15.0% × 1.0 + 5.0% × 0.0	= 15%
24,000	6,000	17.5%	5.0%	17.5% × 0.8 + 5.0% × 0.2	= 15%
15,000	15,000	25.0%	5.0%	25.0% × 0.5 + 5.0% × 0.5	= 15%
3,000	27,000	75.0%	8.3%	75.0% × 0.1 + 8.3% × 0.9	= 15%

Figure 9.5. *WACC and leverage with perfect capital markets. Panel (a) represents the data in panel (b) for the coffee shop example. As the fraction of the firm financed with debt increases, both the equity and the debt become riskier and their cost of capital rises. Yet because more weight is put on the lower-cost debt, the weighted average cost of capital, r_{wacc}, remains constant.*

Source: Jonathan Berk, Peter DeMarzo, and Jarrad Harford. Fundamentals of Corporate Finance, Second edition. Pearson Education. ISBN: 978–0-13–214823–8.

Nearly all of the debt would be nearly as risky as the assets themselves (much like unlevered equity). However, because more of the company is financed with debt, which has lower costs than equity, the WACC stays constant even though both the debt and equity costs of capital rise when leverage is high.

Example 9.2. Computing the Equity Cost of Capital

- **Problem:** Suppose you borrow only $6,000 when financing your coffee shop. According to MM Proposition II, what will your firm's equity cost of capital be?
- Solution
  - **Plan**: Because your firm's assets have a market value of $30,000, according to MM Proposition I the equity will have a market value of $24,000 = $30,000 – $6,000. We can use Eqn. 3 to compute the cost of equity. We know the unlevered cost of equity is r_u = 15%. We also know that r_D is 5%.
  - Execute

$$r_E = 15\% + \frac{6000}{24{,}000}(15\% - 5\%) = 17.5\%$$

  - **Evaluate:** This result matches the expected return calculated in Example 9.1 where we also assumed debt of $6,000. The equity cost of capital should be the expected return of the equity holders.

9.4. DEBT AND TAXES

Thus far, we have employed the ideal capital markets environment to highlight the essential idea that the firm's overall cost of capital is primarily determined by the projects and investments it chooses, which also determines its value and risk. However, imperfect markets exist in the real world, and these imperfections may require a firm's capital structure. In this section, we highlight corporate taxes as a significant source of market friction and demonstrate how a firm's capital structure decision can impact the taxes it must pay and, consequently, the value it offers investors.

9.4.1. Debt

The amount of money owed by one person to another is referred to as debt. Credit card debt and loans, with or without mortgages, are the most common types of debt. Debt can be lent by one individual to another at a fixed or variable interest rate. Therefore, over the course of the loan repayment period, the borrower will repay both the principal and interest amount. The word "debt" originates from the old French word "Dette," which denotes a duty.

Credit card debt, income taxes, auto loans, and mortgages are common debt categories held by families and individuals. For an individual, debt is a means of using projected income plus future purchasing power before making the same amount of money.

Corporates, on the other hand, have a wide range of debt options. Debts may be either long-term or short-term. Debt can be used by businesses for working capital or daily operations. As an alternative, they might examine the capital structure and include bonds or term loans as debt. Other forms of financing options include guarantees and letters of credit. The Reserve Bank of India (RBI) regulates banks, which are crucial in facilitating loans and serving as lenders.

9.4.2. Advantages of Debt

To understand the significance of debt, one must be familiar with the terms "good debt" and "bad debt." The amount of debt that a business or individual can afford to take on is determined by their financial situation or the ratio of assets to liabilities. A "Good Debt" is one that is repayable without resulting in a default. If sales decline, a company with significant debt may not be able to make interest payments. As a result, it will be risking the company's bankruptcy. In the end, it might be a "Bad Debt." Conversely, a company that does not use debt may pass up chances to grow its operations.

Therefore, having debt is essential to maintaining a current credit score. Debt typically comes with a lower cost than equity raising. Furthermore, compared to equity, financing debt carries less risk. When considering insolvency and bankruptcy from the perspective of the investor, a company has a greater obligation to repay debts owed to investors than to shareholders.

9.4.3. The Interest Tax Deduction and Firm Value

Interest costs are deductible by corporations from their taxable income. Because of the deduction, they pay less in taxes, which frees up more money to pay investors. The corporation's value rises as a result of the interest tax deduction. Let's examine how interest costs affect Safeway, Inc.'s tax payments as an example. a chain of grocery stores. Safeway reported $1.85 billion in earnings before interest and taxes in 2008, along with $350 million in interest expenses. Table 9.2 allows us to compare Safeway's actual net income to its debt-free equivalent at a corporate tax rate of 35%.

Table 9.2. Safeway's Income with and without Leverage, 2008 ($ Millions)

	With Leverage	Without Leverage
EBIT	$1850	$1850
Interest expense	-350	0
Income before tax	1500	1850
Taxes (35%)	–525	–648
Net income	$975	$1202

Source: Jonathan Berk, Peter DeMarzo, and Jarrad Harford. Fundamentals of Corporate Finance, Second edition. Pearson Education. ISBN: 978–0-13–214823z-8.

Table 9.2 shows that Safeway's net income in 2008 was less when using leverage than it would have been in the absence of leverage. As a result, Safeway's debt obligations decreased the equity's value. More importantly, though, leverage increased the total amount available to all investors:

	With Leverage	Without Leverage
Interest paid to debt holders	350	0
Income available to equity holders	975	1202
Total available to all investors	$1325	$1202

By using leverage, Safeway was able to pay out $1.325 billion to its investors overall, as opposed to just $1.202 billion without it, which is a $123 million increase.

It may seem strange that a company with lower earnings could benefit more from leverage. A company's worth is the total sum of money it can raise from all sources of investors—not just equity holders who get to keep the profits. Therefore, the company will be able to raise more total capital at first if it can pay out more money overall by using leverage.

Table 9.2 shows us that this gain is equal to the leveraged tax reduction of $648 million – $525 million = $123 million. What is the source of the additional $123 million?

Safeway is exempt from corporate tax on the $350 million in pretax earnings it used to pay interest since it does not owe taxes on that amount. This results in tax savings of 35% × $350 million = $123 million. The interest tax shield is the general term for the benefit that investors receive from interest payments being deductible from their taxes. The extra money a company can give investors by avoiding paying taxes it would have otherwise had to pay in the absence of leverage is known as the interest tax shield. We can calculate the amount of the interest tax shield each year as follows:

Interest Tax Shield = Corporate Tax Rate × Interest Payments (4)

Example 9.3. Computing the Interest Tax Shield

- **Problem:** Shown below is the income statement for E. C. Builders (ECB). Given its marginal corporate tax rate of 35%, what is the amount of the interest tax shield for ECB in years 2007 through 2010?

1	**ECB Income Statement ($ million)**	**2007**	**2008**	**2009**	**2010**
2	Total sales	$3,369	$3,706	$4,077	$4,432
3	Cost of sales	−2,359	−2,584	−2,867	−3,116
4	Selling, general, and administrative expense	−226	−248	−276	−299
5	Depreciation	−22	−25	−27	−29
6	**Operating income**	762	849	907	988
7	Other income	7	8	10	12
9	**EBIT**	769	857	917	1,000
10	Interest expense	−50	−80	−100	−100
11	**Income before tax**	719	777	817	900
12	Taxes (35%)	−252	−272	−286	−315
13	**Net income**	$467	$505	$531	$585

- Solution
  - **Plan**

    From Eqn. 4, the interest tax shield is the tax rate of 35% multiplied by the interest payments in each year.
  - **Execute**

1	**($ million)**	**2007**	**2008**	**2009**	**2010**
2	Interest expense	50	80	100	100
3	**Interest tax shield (35% × interest expense)**	**17.5**	**28**	**35**	**35**

  - **Evaluate:** By using debt, ECB is able to reduce its taxable income and therefore decrease its total tax payments by $115.5 million over the four-year period. Thus, the total amount of cash flows available to all investors (debt holders and equity holders) is $115.5 million higher over the four-year period.

9.4.4. Value of the Interest Tax Shield

Every year, a corporation benefits from the interest tax shield when it uses debt. We must calculate the present value of the stream of future interest tax shields the company will receive in order to assess the benefit of leverage for the firm's value. As we saw with Safeway and in Example 9.3, each year a firm makes interest payments, the cash flows it pays to investors will be higher than they would be without leverage by the amount of the interest tax shield:

$$\begin{pmatrix}\text{Cash Flows to Investors}\\ \text{with Leverage}\end{pmatrix} = \begin{pmatrix}\text{Cash Flows to Investors}\\ \text{without Leverage}\end{pmatrix} + (\text{Interest Tax Shield})$$

This relationship is illustrated in Figure 9.6. Take note of the distribution of each pretax cash flow dollar. The company pays investors the remaining amount after using a portion to cover taxes. The amount of pretax cash flows that must be paid as taxes is reduced by raising the amount paid to debt holders through interest payments. The interest tax shield is the increase in total cash flows to investors.

The Valuation Principle states that since the cash flows of the leveraged firm equal the total of the cash flows from the unlevered firm plus the interest tax shield, the present values of these cash flows must also equal these amounts. With the following modification to MM Proposition I in the presence of taxes, we can let V^L and V^U stand for the firm's value with and without leverage, respectively.

The total value of the levered firm exceeds the value of the firm without leverage due to the present value of the tax savings from debt:

$$V^L = V^U + PV\text{ (Interest Tax Shield)} \quad (9.5)$$

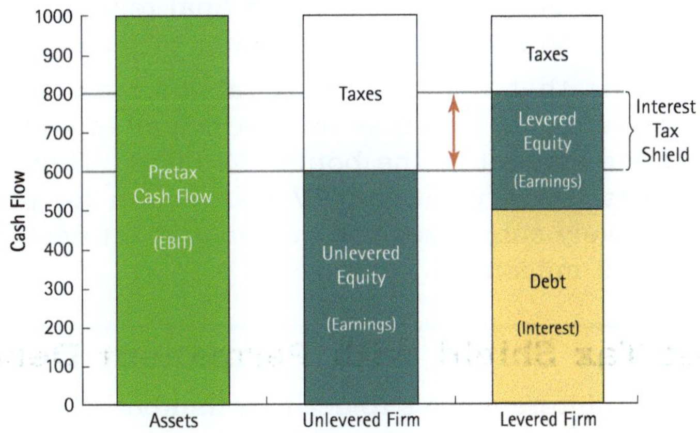

Figure 9.6. *The cash flows of the unlevered and levered firm. By increasing the cash flows paid to debt holders through interest payments, a firm reduces the amount paid in taxes. The increase in total cash flows paid to investors is the interest tax shield. (The figure assumes a 40% marginal corporate tax rate).*

Source: Jonathan Berk, Peter DeMarzo, and Jarrad Harford. Fundamentals of Corporate Finance, Second edition. Pearson Education. ISBN: 978-0-13-214823-8.

There is undoubtedly a significant tax benefit to using debt financing. To calculate the increase in the firm's total value associated with the interest tax shield, however, we must project how a firm's debt—and consequently, its interest payments—will change over time. The question is, how big is this tax benefit? We can calculate the interest tax shield and its present value by discounting the future interest payments at a rate commensurate with their risk, given a forecast of future interest payments.

Example 9.4. Valuing the Interest Tax Shield.

- **Problem:** Suppose ECB from Example 9.3 borrows $2 billion by issuing 10-year bonds. ECB's cost of debt is 6%, so it will need to pay $120 million in interest each year for the next 10 years, and then repay the principal of $2 billion in year 10. ECB's marginal tax rate will remain 35% throughout this period. By how much does the interest tax shield increase the value of ECB?
- **Solution**

  o **Plan:** In this case, the interest tax shield lasts for 10 years, so we can value it as a 10-year annuity. Because the tax savings are as risky as the debt that creates them, we can discount them at ECB's cost of debt: 6%.

  o **Execute:** The interest tax shield each year is 35% × $120 million = $42 million. Valued as a 10-year annuity with a discount rate of 0.06, we have:

$$PV(\text{Interest Tax Shield}) = \$42 \text{ million} \times \frac{1}{0.06}\left(1 - \frac{1}{1.06^{10}}\right)$$
$$= \$309 \text{ million}$$

Because only interest is tax deductible, the final repayment of principal in year 10 is not deductible, so it does not contribute to the tax shield.

  o **Evaluate:** We know that in perfect capital markets, financing transactions have an NPV of zero—the interest and principal repayment have a present value of exactly the amount of the bonds: $2 billion. However, the interest tax deductibility makes this a positive-NPV transaction for the firm. Because the government effectively subsidizes the payment of interest, issuing these bonds has an NPV of $309 million.

9.4.5. The Interest Tax Shield with Permanent Debt

The future tax savings from interest are subject to a number of variables. The following factors usually affect how much interest is paid in the future:

- Changes the firm makes in the amount of debt outstanding;
- Changes in the interest rate on that debt;
- Changes in the firm's marginal tax rate; and
- The risk that the firm may default and fail to make an interest payment.

Instead of trying to cover every scenario here, we will look at the unique situation where the company issues debt with the intention of never changing the debt's total amount.

The company could, for instance, issue a perpetual consol bond and never repay the principal—just interest. Let's assume, more practically, that the company issues short-term debt, like a bond with a five-year coupon. The company issues new debt to raise the funds required to pay the principal when it becomes due. By refinancing the principal when it becomes due, the company avoids ever having to pay it off. The debt is essentially irreversible in this case.

A lot of big businesses have a policy of keeping a specific level of debt on their balance sheets. They initiate new loans and issue new bonds as existing bonds and loans mature. Take note that, as opposed to using a figure that varies depending on the size of the company, we are evaluating the interest tax shield's value using a fixed dollar amount of outstanding debt.

If the debt is fairly priced, the Valuation Principle implies that the market value of the debt today must equal the present value of the future interest payments:

$$\text{Market Value of Debt} = D = PV\ (\text{Future Interest Payments}) \qquad (6)$$

If the firm's marginal tax rate (T_c) is constant, then we have the following general formula:

Value of the Interest Tax Shield of Permanent Debt

$$\begin{aligned} PV\,(\text{Interest Tax Shield}) &= PV(T_c \times \text{Future Interest Payments}) \\ &= T_c \times PV\,(\text{Future Interest Payments}) \\ &= T_c \times D \end{aligned} \qquad (7)$$

The interest tax shield's magnitude is displayed by this formula. It means that, at a corporate tax rate of 35%, the firm's value rises by $0.35 for every $1 in new permanent debt that the company issues.

9.4.6. Leverage and the WACC with Taxes

We can also take advantage of the firm's future interest tax shield in another way. The majority of companies do not have preferred stock, so for them, the WACC with taxes is as follows:

Weighted Average Cost of Capital with Taxes

$$r_{wacc} = r_E \frac{E}{E+D} + r_D(1 - T_C)\frac{D}{E+D} \qquad (8)$$

By modifying the cost of debt to the firm, we are able to incorporate the interest tax shield benefit in Eqn. 8. The effective after-tax cost of debt is lowered to when the firm pays interest on its debt because it receives a tax shield. This is demonstrated by comparing the pretax WACC Eqns. (2) and (8), which show that corporate taxes lower the effective cost of debt financing and thereby lower the weighted average cost of capital. Actually, Eqn. 8 suggests:

$$r_{wacc} = \underbrace{r_E \frac{E}{E+D} + r_D \frac{D}{E+D}}_{\text{Pretax WACC}} - \underbrace{r_D T_C \frac{D}{E+D}}_{\substack{\text{Reduction Due}\\ \text{to Interest Tax Shield}}} \quad (9)$$

As a result, as debt financing increases, so does the WACC reduction. The tax benefit of debt is more fully utilized and the firm's WACC is lowered the more leverage it has. Figure 9.7 shows how the WACC decreases with leverage. The pretax WACC is also displayed in the figure, as it is in Figure 9.5.

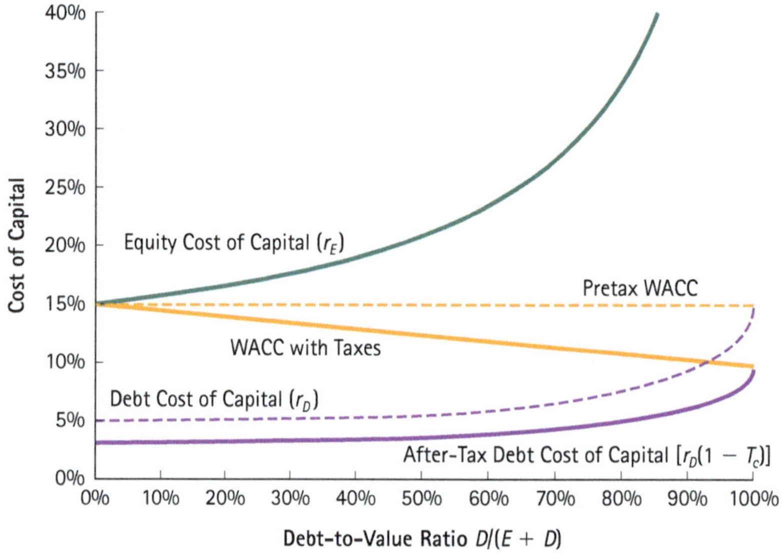

Figure 9.7. *The WACC with and without Corporate Taxes. We compute the WACC as a function of leverage using Eq. 9.9. Whereas the pretax WACC remains constant, with taxes the WACC declines as the firm increases its reliance on debt financing and the benefit of the interest tax deduction grows. The figure assumes a marginal corporate income tax rate of 35%.*

Source: Jonathan Berk, Peter DeMarzo, and Jarrad Harford. Fundamentals of Corporate Finance, Second edition. Pearson Education. ISBN: 978-0-13-214823-8.

9.4.7. Debt and Taxes: The Bottom Line

As we've seen in this section, debt financing benefits from the interest expenses being deductible from corporate taxes. There are two methods by which we can determine the benefit to the company's value. Initially, we can estimate and calculate the present value of the company's future interest tax shields. This method is particularly easy to apply when the debt is fixed, in which case $T_C \times D$ represents the tax shield's value.

Using the WACC to include the interest tax shield in the company's cost of capital is an additional method of calculating its benefit. Because of the interest tax shield, the WACC with taxes decreases with leverage in contrast to the pretax WACC. The present value of the company's or an investment's free cash flow will be higher by a certain amount if we apply this lower discount rate, which represents the benefit of the future interest tax shields. This strategy works best when the company modifies its debt in order to maintain a consistent debt-to-value ratio over time. In summary, the interest tax shield can be taken into account when determining the worth of a business or investment using one of these techniques:

1. Discounting its free cash flow using the pretax WACC, and adding the present value of expected future interest tax shields, or
2. Discounting its free cash flow using the WACC (with taxes).

We will discover that the firm's value will rise with leverage using either of these approaches. Therefore, capital structure is important, unlike in a situation with perfect capital markets. However, we now have a new conundrum: Why don't businesses use debt financing nearly exclusively given the tax benefit?

9.5. THE COSTS OF BANKRUPTCY AND FINANCIAL DISTRESS

Increased debt increases the likelihood that the company won't be able to pay its interest and will miss payments on its debt. A company is in financial distress if it finds it difficult to pay its debts. The assumption of perfect capital markets ignores the long and complex process of bankruptcy, which has a negative impact on the company and its investors in both direct and indirect ways.

9.5.1. Direct Costs of Bankruptcy

Every nation has a bankruptcy code that describes how to handle a company that has fallen behind on its debts. The goal of the bankruptcy code is to establish a systematic method for paying off a company's debts. The procedure is still expensive, time-consuming, and complex, though. Outside experts, such as consultants, appraisers, auctioneers, legal and accounting specialists, and others with experience selling distressed assets, are typically hired when a corporation experiences financial distress. A possible financial restructuring may also benefit from the assistance of investment bankers. The creditors may have expenses during the bankruptcy process in addition to the money the firm spends. When it comes to reorganization, creditors frequently have to wait a number of years to be paid after a plan is approved. Creditors may seek independent legal counsel and professional advice to make sure that their rights and interests are upheld and to help value their claims in a proposed reorganization. Pre-bankruptcy market value of all assets is usually equivalent to 3–4% of the average direct costs of bankruptcy, according to studies. Due to the possibility of greater difficulty in reaching a consensus among numerous creditors regarding the ultimate disposition of the firm's assets, the costs are estimated to be higher for businesses with more intricate business operations and for businesses with a higher number of creditors. Smaller firms generally incur higher costs, expressed in percentage terms, during the bankruptcy process because many aspects are unaffected by the firm's size.

9.5.2. Indirect Costs of Financial Distress

Financial distress is linked to numerous indirect costs in addition to the direct legal and administrative costs of bankruptcy (whether or not the firm has formally filed for bankruptcy). These expenses are often far higher than the direct costs of bankruptcy, despite the fact that they are hard to quantify.

When a company experiences financial difficulties, it may break both explicit and implicit agreements, which results in indirect bankruptcy costs. For instance, a software company that goes bankrupt does not have to provide support for one of its products. Customers who depend on this kind of assistance may decide to purchase software from businesses with lower leverage, or those with a lower likelihood of going bankrupt. Crucially, a lot of these indirect expenses might be incurred even in the event that the company does not currently experience financial difficulties but rather faces a high risk of going bankrupt in the future. Consider the following examples:

- **Loss of Customers**: Customers may be reluctant to buy products whose value depends on continued support or services from the company if bankruptcy allows the business to escape future obligations to them.
- **Loss of Suppliers**: If suppliers believe they won't be paid, they might be reluctant to give a company inventory. For instance, Swiss Air had to close its doors in 2001 as a result of its suppliers refusing to fuel its aircraft due to financial difficulties.
- **Cost to Employees**: Financial distress to employees is a significant expense that is frequently extensively covered by the media. The majority of businesses provide long-term employment contracts to their staff members explicitly or implicitly guarantee job security. Nevertheless, these agreements and commitments are frequently disregarded during bankruptcy, and a sizable number of workers may be let go. Employees will demand higher compensation in anticipation of this, as they will be less willing to work for companies that carry a significant risk of bankruptcy. Therefore, for a company with significant leverage, hiring and keeping key personnel may be expensive. For example, Pacific Gas and Electric Corporation launched a retention program that cost more than $80 million in order to keep 17 key employees during its 2003 bankruptcy.
- **Fire Sales of Assets**: In order to raise money, a struggling business might be forced to sell assets quickly and might have to settle for less money than the assets are truly worth to the company. When creditors attempt to force liquidation even at low prices because they are more pessimistic than management about the value of the assets, this cost is likely to be significant.

Financial distress can have significant indirect costs overall. Gregor Andrade and Steven Kaplan estimated that a financial distress could cost a company between 10 and 20% of its value in their study of highly leveraged companies. Crucially, a great deal of these indirect costs might be incurred even in the unlikely event that the company experiences financial difficulties in the future rather than just now.

9.6. OPTIMAL CAPITAL STRUCTURE: THE TRADEOFF THEORY

Now, we can use the costs of financial distress and the advantages of leverage from the interest tax shield to calculate how much debt a company should issue in order to maximize its value. This section's analysis, which compares the costs of financial distress associated with leverage with the benefits of debt resulting from shielding cash flows from taxes, is known as the tradeoff theory. The static tradeoff theory is another name for this theory that is occasionally used.

The tradeoff theory states that the total value of a leveraged firm is equal to the present value of the tax savings from debt less the present value of the costs associated with financial distress, plus the value of the firm without leverage.

$$V^L = V^U + PV\text{ (Interest Tax Shield)} - PV\text{ (Financial Distress Costs)} \qquad (10)$$

Leverage comes with costs as well as benefits, as demonstrated by Eqn. 10. Businesses are compelled to take on more debt in order to take advantage of the tax advantages. However, they run the greater risk of default and financial distress expenses when they have too much debt.

9.6.1. Differences Across Firms

While figuring out the interest tax shield's benefits is clear in the section above, it is exceedingly challenging, if not impossible, to determine the exact present value of financial distress expenses. (1) The likelihood of financial distress and (2) The amount of direct and indirect costs associated with financial distress that the company will bear are the two primary qualitative factors that determine the present value of financial distress costs.

The amount of financial distress costs will depend on the relative importance of the sources of these costs and will probably differ by industry. What determines each of these factors?

Technology companies, for instance, are more likely to experience significant financial distress costs because of the possibility of losing important employees and customers as well as the absence of readily liquidable tangible assets. Companies that produce forest products, on the other hand, are probably less likely to experience financial difficulties because a large portion of their value comes from real assets (mills and timber land) that can be sold if needed. It should come as no surprise that Figure 9.1 illustrates how differently leverage policies apply to these two industries: technology companies typically have very low debt levels, while forest products companies typically have high leverage levels. In a similar vein, Figure 9.2 showed that Amazon has almost no debt and Barnes and Noble has a significant amount. To pay off creditors, Barnes & Noble may be able to sell its properties and retail locations. Apart from its inventory of books, Amazon does not have many other assets that could be sold to satisfy creditors' demands.

The possibility that a company won't be able to pay its debts in full and will eventually default determines the likelihood of financial distress. The likelihood rises as a company's liabilities (in proportion to its assets) increase. It also rises in tandem with the cash flow and asset value volatility of a company. As a result, businesses with consistent, reliable cash flows, like utility companies, can use large debt loads with very little chance of default. Companies with highly volatile values and cash flows, like semiconductor companies, need to have significantly lower debt levels in order to reduce the risk of default.

9.6.2. Optimal Leverage

According to Eqn. 10, Figure 9.8 illustrates how a levered firm's value, V^L, fluctuates with the amount of permanent debt, D. When there is no debt, the company is worth V^U. The interest tax shield, which has a present value T_CD as indicated by Eqn. 7, increases as leverage rises, but the risk of default stays low for low debt levels. The value would rise at this rate in the absence of financial distress costs until the tax shield is depleted and the interest on the debt surpasses the company's earnings before interest and taxes.

The value of the leveraged company, V^L, is decreased by the costs of financial distress. According to the tradeoff theory, businesses should increase their leverage until it reaches the level D* for which V^L is maximized. The amount of the reduction increases with the probability of default, which in turn increases with the level of the debt D. At this point, the increased likelihood of experiencing the costs of financial distress simply outweighs the tax savings that come with increasing leverage.

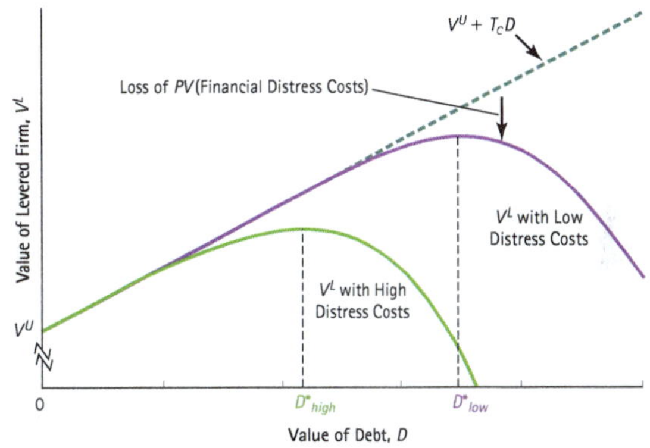

Figure 9.8. *Optimal leverage with taxes and financial distress costs. As the level of debt increases, the tax benefits of debt increase until the interest expense exceeds the firm's EBIT. However, the probability of default, and hence the present value of financial distress costs, also increases. The optimal level of debt, D*, occurs when these effects balance out and the value of the levered firm is maximized. D* will be lower for firms with higher costs of financial distress.*

Source: Jonathan Berk, Peter DeMarzo, and Jarrad Harford. Fundamentals of Corporate Finance, Second edition. Pearson Education. ISBN: 978-0-13-214823-8.

Additionally, Figure 9.8 shows the best debt options for two different kinds of businesses. The best debt option for a company with low financial distress costs is shown by D^*_{low}, and the best debt option for a company with high financial distress costs is shown by D^*_{high}. It should come as no surprise that when a company has higher financial distress costs, it is best to select less leverage.

The tradeoff theory helps to resolve two important facts about leverage:

1. The presence of financial distress costs can explain why firms choose debt levels that are too low to fully exploit the interest tax shield.
2. Differences in the magnitude of financial distress costs and the volatility of cash flows can explain the differences in the use of leverage across industries.

9.7. ADDITIONAL CONSEQUENCES OF LEVERAGE: AGENCY COSTS AND INFORMATION

In reality, there are other capital market imperfections besides taxes and financial distress costs. We continue to dispense with the notion of perfect capital markets in this section to examine additional ways that capital structure may impact a firm's valuation. We start off by talking about how managers' incentives are impacted by leverage and how this affects their investment choices. Next, we tackle the intricacies arising from disparate information held by stakeholders within the organization.

9.7.1. Agency Costs

An internal business expense known as an "agency cost" results from an agent's activities on behalf of a principal. When there are fundamental inefficiencies, discontents, and disturbances—like conflicts of interest between shareholders and management—agency costs usually follow.

When there are conflicts of interest amongst stakeholders, agency costs result. The agency problem—which occurs when managers prioritize their own interests over those of the shareholders—was briefly discussed. We talk about how debt can help with this issue here. It might, however, also skew equity holders' preferences for the kinds of projects the company pursues.

9.7.1.1. Managerial Entrenchment

Even though they frequently do own company stock, managers typically own a relatively tiny portion of the outstanding shares in large corporations. The board of directors, on behalf of the shareholders, has the authority to remove managers. In actuality, they hardly ever do this unless the company performs dreadfully.

Because there is less chance that managers will be fired and replaced, they are free to operate the company in their own best interests. This ownership and control separation raises the possibility of management entrenchment. Managers might therefore decide in a way that benefits them at the expense of investors. In an attempt to increase the size of the company (and their pay) at the expense of shareholder value, managers may work less hard, spend excessively on perks like corporate jets, or engage in wasteful projects known as "empire building." These choices are an agency cost if they have a negative net present value (NPV) for the company.

These agency costs are most likely to occur when the firm has a lot of cash on hand for managers to spend on unnecessary projects and when equity ownership is highly diluted, making it impossible for any individual shareholder to monitor management closely. Thus, debt can be beneficial in two ways. First, ownership of the company may remain more concentrated by borrowing money rather than issuing shares, which would enhance management oversight. Second, debt limits the amount of money available to management because it forces the company to make cash payments for principal and interest. Managers need to have the money to invest in order to make unnecessary investments. Managers won't be driven to operate the company as efficiently as possible unless finances are tight. Leverage, then, can offer managers incentives to manage the company profitably and successfully. These advantages give users even more motivation to choose debt financing over equity financing.

9.7.1.2. Equity-Debt Holder Conflicts

A conflict of interest arises when an investment decision affects the value of debt differently than the value of equity in a leveraged firm. When there is a high likelihood of financial distress, conflicts like these are more likely to arise. Managers may occasionally act in a way that benefits shareholders at the expense of the company's creditors and reduces the firm's overall value.

To understand this, imagine yourself in the position of the shareholders of a struggling business that is about to miss payments on its debt. If things carry on as usual, the bondholders will probably gain control over the company and the value of your shares.

Alternatively, you could:

1. Roll the dice and take on a risky project that could save the firm, even though its expected outcome is so poor that you normally would not take it on.
2. Conserve funds rather than invest in new, promising projects.
3. Cash out by distributing as much of the firm's capital as possible to the shareholders before the bondholders take over.

Even if the project fails, you are not worse off because you were going to default anyway, so why would you roll the dice? If it is successful, you will stay out of default and keep ownership of the business. This incentive breeds excessive risk-taking, which is what happens when a business is on the verge of bankruptcy and investors are enticed to put money into high-risk, negative-NPV ventures that will devalue the company as a whole and the debt holders in particular. In anticipation of this conduct, holders of securities will initially pay less for the company. For businesses that can readily raise the risk of their investments, this expense is probably going to be the highest. However, in cases where default is highly probable, a company may decide not to pursue a promising project before default because bondholders will benefit in part or entirely (by lowering the risk or extent of default). For instance, the project has a positive net present value (NPV) of $30 + $90 – $100 = $20 if a company can invest $100 in it, increasing the value of its debt by $30 and its equity by $90. Equity investors won't want to contribute because their profit ($90) is less than the project's $100 cost. Underinvestment occurs when shareholders decide against funding a positive net present value (NPV) project due to the company's financial difficulties and the fact that bondholders will benefit more from the investment than they will. Due to the NPV of the lost opportunities, this inaction is expensive for the firm's debt holders as well as its overall value. For businesses that are most likely to have lucrative future growth opportunities requiring significant investments, the cost is highest.

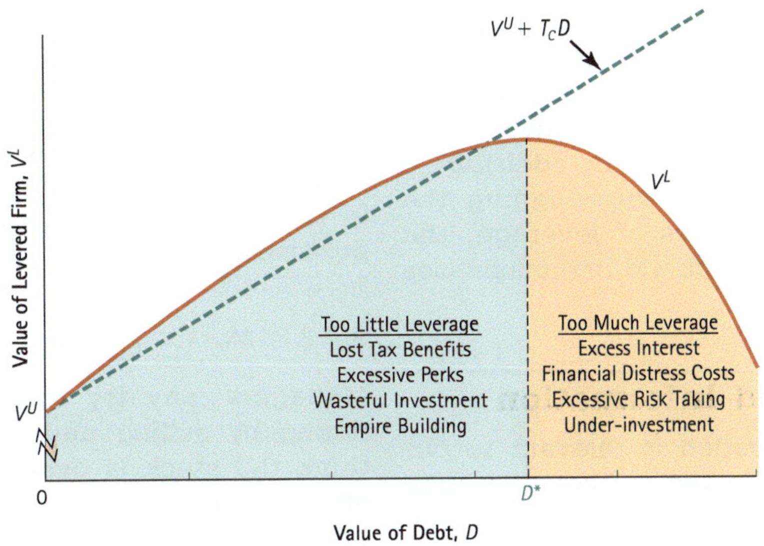

Figure 9.9. *Optimal leverage with taxes, financial distress, and agency costs. As the level of debt increases, the value of the firm increases from the interest tax shield ($T_C D$) as well as improvements in managerial incentives. If leverage is too high, however, the present value of financial distress costs, as well as the agency costs from debt holder–equity holder conflicts, dominates and reduces firm value. The optimal level of debt, D^*, balances these benefits and costs of leverage.*

Source: Jonathan Berk, Peter DeMarzo, and Jarrad Harford. Fundamentals of Corporate Finance, Second edition. Pearson Education. ISBN: 978–0-13–214823–8.

Cashing out represents the pinnacle of underinvestment. Assuming that the bondholders will eventually acquire the company, shareholders are motivated to extract as much capital as possible from the company prior to its bankruptcy and transfer to the debt holders. Seling off all of the company's assets and giving the money raised as a special dividend to the shareholders would be an extreme example of this. The business would then file for bankruptcy, leaving it a worthless shell. Bondholders are aware of this issue and frequently demand limitations on the amount of dividends paid out and the source of funding for those payments.

Based on our discussion, we can build a more comprehensive capital structure tradeoff model that includes agency costs and benefits of debt in addition to tax benefits and costs associated with financial distress. Figure 9.9 shows this tradeoff model that represents the ideal leverage.

When a company's debt level is too low, increasing leverage boosts its worth by offering tax advantages and encouraging managers to run the company more profitably (by avoiding unnecessary investments). However, if the company has too much debt, it will suffer from underinvestment and excessive risk taking in addition to financial distress costs. By weighing the benefits and drawbacks of leverage, the ideal debt level (D*) is found that maximizes firm value.

9.7.2. Debt and Information

The role of information is relevant to our final imperfection in the market. We have assumed that managers, stockholders, and creditors have access to the same information throughout this chapter. Additionally, we believe that the prices of securities are reasonable because the debt and shares of the company are valued at their actual underlying value. In real life, these presumptions might not always hold true. Managers' knowledge of the company and its future cash flows is probably better than outside investors' because of asymmetric information. This asymmetric information could spur managers to change the capital structure of their company.

9.7.2.1. Leverage as a Credible Signal

A company may agree to make sizable future debt payments in order to persuade the stock market that it has excellent projects. If the projects are successful, the company will have no issues paying off its debt. However, the company will face financial difficulties and difficulties making payments to its creditors if it continues to make false claims and does not expand. The company will suffer financial losses as a result of this turmoil, and the managers will probably lose their jobs as well. Therefore, even if the managers are unable to offer concrete information about the sources of growth, they can still use leverage to persuade investors that they do have knowledge of the company's potential for growth. The increased leverage will be seen by investors as a reliable indication of the managers' assurance. The signaling theory of debt is the application of leverage to convey positive information to investors.

9.7.2.2. Market Timing

Managers may try to engage in market timing by selling new shares when they think the stock is overvalued and relying on debt and retained earnings (and possibly repurchasing shares) if they believe the stock is undervalued. This occurs when managers have better knowledge than outside investors regarding the value of the company. Long-term shareholders gain from managers who effectively time the market by trading the company's shares whenever they are undervalued. In an effort to time the market, the managers would issue new equity, reducing the leverage, or new debt, increasing the leverage, changing the firm's capital structure. As a result, depending on management's perception of the share price in relation to its true value, the firm's capital structure may diverge above or below the optimal level indicated by the tradeoff theory.

9.7.2.3. Adverse Selection and the Pecking Order Hypothesis

Assume for the moment that managers attempt to issue equity at a price that exceeds its actual value. Knowing this, how would investors respond? They would reduce the price they are willing to pay for the stock, fearing they are being sold a "lemon."

The capital structure issue is impacted by the adverse selection problem. If managers must lower the price of equity in order to find buyers, they will not want to sell it. As a result, they might look for different sources of funding. Adverse selection may also be a factor in debt problems. The discount required to entice buyers will be lower for debt than for equity since the value of low-risk debt is mostly driven by interest rates and is less susceptible to managers' personal knowledge of the company. Naturally, if a company can finance an investment with cash (retained earnings), it can completely avoid underpricing. According to the pecking order hypothesis, managers will prefer to use retained earnings to fund investments, followed by debt, and will only issue equity as a last resort in order to avoid this "lemons cost."

This theory affects the capital structure of businesses. Businesses that are profitable and make enough money to finance their investments will only use their retained earnings rather than issuing debt or equity. High-profit businesses will therefore have a low level of debt in their capital structure. Only businesses that require outside funding sources will have substantial debt financing. The pecking order hypothesis states that companies should hardly ever issue equity. The capital structure of the company will actually probably be shaped by a number of factors, and firms will issue equity when the costs of debt, whether from agency fees or financial distress, become too high.

Example 9.5. The Pecking Order of Financing Alternatives

- **Problem:** Axon Industries needs to raise $9.5 million for a new investment project. If the firm issues one-year debt, it may have to pay an interest rate of 8%, although Axon's managers believe that 6% would be a fair rate given the level of risk. However, if the firm issues equity, the managers believe the equity may be underpriced by 5%. What is the cost to current shareholders of financing the project out of retained earnings, debt, and equity?
- **Solution:**
    - **Plan:** We can evaluate the financing alternatives by comparing what the firm would have to pay to get the financing versus what its managers believe it should pay if the market had the same information they do.
    - **Execute:** If the firm spends $9.5 million out of retained earnings, rather than paying that money out to shareholders as a dividend, the cost of financing the project is $9.5 million.

      Using one-year debt costs the firm $\$9.5 \times (1.08) = \$10.26$ million in one year, which has a present value based on management's view of the firm's risk of $\$10.26 \div (1.06) = \$9.68$ million.

If equity is underpriced by 5%, then to raise $9.5 million the firm will need to issue shares that are actually worth $10 million. (e.g., if the firm's shares are each worth $50, but it sells them for 0.95 × $50 = $47.50 per share, it will need to sell $9.5 million ÷ $47.50/share = 200,000 shares. These shares have a true value of 200,000 shares × $50/share = $10 million.) Thus, the cost of financing the project with equity will be $10 million.

- **Evaluate:** Comparing the three options, retained earnings are the cheapest source of funds, followed by debt, and finally by equity. The ranking reflects the effect of differences in information between managers and investors that result in a lemons problem when they issue new securities, and particularly when they issue new equity.

ROLE MODEL

MERTON MILLER

Merton Howard Miller (May 16, 1923 – June 3, 2000) was an American economist, and the co-author of the Modigliani–Miller theorem (1958), which proposed the irrelevance of debt-equity structure. He shared the Nobel Memorial Prize in Economic Sciences in 1990, along with Harry Markowitz and William F. Sharpe. Miller spent most of his academic career at the University of Chicago's Booth School of Business.

- **Early Years:** Miller was born in Boston, Massachusetts to Jewish parents Sylvia and Joel Miller, a housewife and attorney. He attended Harvard University as an undergraduate student. He worked during World War II as an economist in the division of tax research of the Treasury Department, and received a Ph.D. in economics from Johns Hopkins University, 1952. His first academic appointment after receiving his doctorate was Visiting Assistant Lecturer at the London School of Economics.
- **Career:** In 1958, at Carnegie Institute of Technology (now Carnegie Mellon University), he collaborated with his colleague Franco Modigliani on the paper *The Cost of Capital, Corporate Finance and the Theory of Investment*. This paper urged a fundamental objection to the traditional view of corporate finance, according to which a corporation can reduce its cost of capital by finding the right debt-to-equity ratio. According to the Modigliani–Miller theorem, on the other hand, there is no right ratio, so corporate managers should seek to minimize tax liability and maximize corporate net wealth, letting the debt ratio chips fall where they will.

The way in which they arrived at this conclusion made use of the "no arbitrage" argument, i.e., the premise that any state of affairs that will allow traders of any market instrument to create a riskless money machine will almost immediately disappear. They set the pattern for many arguments based on that premise in subsequent years.

Miller wrote or co-authored eight books. He became a fellow of the Econometric Society in 1975 and was president of the American Finance Association in 1976. He was on the faculty of the University of Chicago's Booth School of Business from 1961 until his retirement in 1993, although he continued teaching at the school for several more years.

His works formed the basis of the "Modigliani-Miller Financial Theory."

He served as a public director on the Chicago Board of Trade 1983–85 and the Chicago Mercantile Exchange from 1990 until his death in Chicago on June 3, 2000. In 1993, Miller waded into the controversy surrounding $2 billion in trading losses by what was characterized as a rogue futures trader at a subsidiary of Metallgesellschaft, arguing in the *Wall Street Journal* that management of the subsidiary was to blame for panicking and liquidating the position too early. In 1995, Miller was engaged by Nasdaq to rebut allegations of price fixing.

Personal Life: Miller was married to Eleanor Miller, who died in 1969. He was survived by his second wife, Katherine Miller, and by three children from his first marriage: Pamela (1952), Margot (1955), and Louise (1958), and two grandsons.

CLASS ACTIVITY

You have just read about several factors that affect the determination of capital structure in a company. In this context, meet the finance manager of a large company and ascertain which of these factors had bearing on their capital structure and to what extent.

SUMMARY

- Capital structure refers to the mix of various forms of external funds, known as capital, used to finance a business. It consists of shareholders' equity, debt (borrowed funds), and preferred stock, and is detailed in the company's balance sheet.
- Both debt and equity can be found on the balance sheet. Company assets, also listed on the balance sheet, are purchased with debt or equity. Capital structure can be a mixture of a company's long-term debt, short-term debt, common stock, and preferred stock. A company's proportion of short-term debt versus long-term debt is considered when analyzing its capital structure.
- Companies that use more debt than equity to finance their assets and fund operating activities have a high leverage ratio and an aggressive capital structure. A company that pays for assets with more equity than debt has a low leverage ratio and a conservative capital structure. That said, a high leverage ratio and an aggressive capital structure can also lead to higher growth rates, whereas a conservative capital structure can lead to lower growth rates.
- Capital structure is the composition of various sources of long-term finance in the total capitalization of the company. The two main sources are ownership and creditor ship securities. Both types of securities as well as the long-term loans from financial institutions are used by most of the large industrial companies.
- Capital structure planning, initially and on continuing basis, is of great importance to any company as it has a considerable bearing on its profitability. A wrong initial decision in this respect may prove quite costly for the company.
- Capital structure is usually planned keeping in view the interests of the ordinary shareholders. The ordinary shareholders are the ultimate owners of the company and have the right to elect the directors. While developing an appropriate capital structure for his company, the financial manager should aim at maximizing the long-term market price of equity shares.
- The use of sources of finance with a fixed cost, such as debt and preference share capital, to finance the assets of the company is known as financial leverage or trading on equity. If the assets financed by debt yield a return greater than the cost of the debt, the earnings per share will increase without an increase in the owners' investment.
- The cost of a source of finance is the minimum return expected by its suppliers. The expected return depends on the degree of risk assumed by investors. A high degree of risk is assumed by shareholders than debt-holders.
- Flexibility means the firm's ability to adapt its capital structure to the needs of the changing conditions. The capital structure of a firm is flexible if it has no difficulty in changing its capitalization or sources of funds.
- Floatation costs are incurred when the funds are raised. Generally, the cost of floating a debt is less than the cost of floating an equity issue. This may encourage a company to use debt rather than issue ordinary shares.

- Debt refers to sum of money owed by one person and due to another person. Most popular kinds of debt are loans with or without mortgages and credit card debt. One person can lend debt to another at a fixed or a floating interest income.
- Corporations can deduct interest expenses from their taxable income. The deduction reduces the taxes they pay and thereby increases the amount available to pay investors. In doing so, the interest tax deduction increases the value of the corporation.
- Bankruptcy is a long and complicated process that imposes both direct and indirect costs on the firm and its investors that the assumption of perfect capital markets ignores.
- The bankruptcy code is designed to provide an orderly process for settling a firm's debts. However, the process is still complex, time-consuming, and costly. When a corporation becomes financially distressed, outside professionals, such as legal and accounting experts, consultants, appraisers, auctioneers, and others with experience selling distressed assets, are generally hired. Investment bankers may also assist with a potential financial restructuring.
- Indirect bankruptcy costs often occur because the firm may renege on both implicit and explicit commitments and contracts when in financial distress.

REVIEW QUESTIONS

1. What is capital structure?
2. Explain the importance of capital structure and planning?
3. What are the features of an appropriate capital structure?
4. What are the determinants of capital structure? Explain briefly.
5. What constitutes a firm's capital structure?
6. What are some factors a manager must consider when making a financing decision?
7. How does leverage affect the risk and cost of equity for the firm?
8. What is Debt?
9. How does the interest tax deduction affect firm value?
10. Why are the indirect costs of financial distress likely to be more important than the direct costs of bankruptcy?

REFERENCES

1. Brealey, R., Myers, S., & Allen, F. (2019). *Principles of Corporate Finance*. New Delhi: McGraw Hill.
2. Brigham, E. F., & Huston, J. F. (2018). *Fundamental of Financial Management*. New Delhi: Cengage Learning India.

3. Chandra, P. (2019). *Financial Management: Theory and Practice*. New Delhi: McGraw-Hill.
4. Fama, E. F., & Miller, M. H. (1972). *The Theory of Finance*. New York: Holt, Rinehart & Winston.
5. Gitman, L. J. (1985). *Principles of Managerial Finance*. New York: Harper & Row.
6. Groppelli, A. A., & Nikbakht, E. (2000). *Finance* (4th ed.). Hauppauge, NY: Barron's Educational Services, Inc.
7. Harris, M., & Raviv, A. (1991). The theory of capital structure. *The Journal of Finance, 46*(1), 297–355. https://doi.org/10.1111/j.1540-6261.1991.tb03753.x.
8. Kessel, R. A., Coase, R. H., & Miller, M. H. (1980). *Essays in Applied Price Theory*. Chicago: University of Chicago Press.
9. Khan, M. Y., & Jain, P. K. (2002). *Cost Accounting and Financial Management*. New Delhi: Tata McGraw Hill.
10. Khan, M. Y., & Jain, P. K. (2018). *Financial Management*. New Delhi: McGraw Hill Education.
11. Louiselle, B. M., & Heilman, J. E. (1982). The case for the use of an appropriate capital structure in utility ratemaking: The general rule versus Minnesota. *William Mitchell Law Review, 8*(2), 426.
12. Melicher, R. W., & Welshans, M. T. (1988). *Finance: Introduction to Markets, Institutions and Management* (7th ed.). Cincinnati, OH: South-Western Publishing Co.
13. Miller, M. H. (1991). *Financial Innovations and Market Volatility*. Cambridge, MA: Blackwell Publishing.
14. Miller, M. H., & Upton, C. W. (1986). *Macroeconomics: A Neoclassical Introduction*. Chicago: University of Chicago Press.
15. Pandey, I. M. (2021). *Financial Management*. New Delhi: Pearson Education India.
16. Titman, S., Keown, A. J., & Martin, J. D. (2019). *Financial Management: Principles and Applications*. New Delhi: Pearson Education India.
17. Van Horne, J. C., & Wachowicz, J. M. (1985). *Fundamentals of Financial Management*. New Delhi: Prentice-Hall of India.

CHAPTER

10 Risk Management

LEARNING OBJECTIVES

After studying this chapter, you will be able to:

- Define insurance
- Explain about commodity price risk
- Discuss about exchange rate risk
- Describe interest rate risk

KEY TERMS FROM THIS CHAPTER

Actuarially fair	Business interruption insurance
Business liability insurance	Currency timeline
Daily settlement	Deductible
Duration-neutral portfolio	Floating rate
Forward exchange rate	Immunized portfolio
Insurance premium	Interest rate swap
Liquidity risk	Margin
Moral hazard	Natural hedge
Property insurance	Purchase property insurance
Spot exchange rate	Vertical integration

INTRODUCTION

Risk management is a critical component of corporate finance, playing a pivotal role in ensuring a company's long-term viability and success. At its core, risk management involves identifying, assessing, and mitigating financial risks that could negatively impact a company's assets, earnings, or overall financial stability. These risks can be broadly categorized into market risk, credit risk, liquidity risk, and operational risk, each presenting unique challenges and requiring specific strategies for effective management.

Market risk arises from fluctuations in market prices, including interest rates, foreign exchange rates, and commodity prices. For instance, a sudden rise in interest rates can increase the cost of borrowing, while currency volatility can affect the profitability of international operations. To manage market risk, companies often employ hedging techniques such as derivatives (options, futures, and swaps), which allow them to lock in prices and rates, thus reducing uncertainty.

Credit risk pertains to the possibility of a counterparty failing to fulfill its financial obligations, leading to potential losses for the company. This is particularly relevant for companies that extend credit to customers or rely on loans and investments. Effective credit risk management includes conducting thorough credit assessments, setting credit limits, and diversifying the credit portfolio to minimize exposure to any single entity.

Liquidity risk involves the risk of a company being unable to meet its short-term financial obligations due to insufficient cash flow. To mitigate this risk, companies maintain liquidity reserves, establish lines of credit, and manage cash flows meticulously to ensure they can cover operational costs and debt repayments even in times of financial stress.

Operational risk encompasses risks arising from internal processes, systems, or external events that could disrupt operations, such as fraud, cyber-attacks, or natural disasters. Companies manage operational risk through internal controls, regular audits, and by implementing robust business continuity and disaster recovery plans.

Effective risk management in corporate finance not only protects the company from potential financial losses but also enhances its reputation, supports strategic decision-making, and ensures regulatory compliance. By proactively managing risks, companies can achieve greater financial stability, foster investor confidence, and create long-term value for stakeholders.

10.1. INSURANCE

Businesses most frequently utilize insurance as a means of lowering risk. To protect their assets from risks like fire, storm damage, vandalism, earthquakes, and other natural and environmental disasters, many businesses buy property insurance. Other common types of insurance include:

- Business liability insurance, which covers the costs that result if some aspect of the business causes harm to a third party or someone else's property
- Business interruption insurance, which protects the firm against the loss of earnings if the business is interrupted due to fire, accident, or some other insured peril
- Key personnel insurance, which compensates for the loss or unavoidable absence of crucial employees in the firm

We illustrate the role of insurance in reducing risk and examine its pricing and potential benefits and costs for a firm.

10.1.1. The Role of Insurance: An Example

To comprehend the function of insurance in mitigating risk, let us examine an oil refinery that has a 1-in-5000, or 0.02%, probability of being destroyed by fire within the upcoming year. The company calculates that the cost of rebuilding and lost revenue would come to $150 million if it is destroyed. We can summarize the risk from fire with a probability distribution:

Event	Probability	Loss (in $ million)
No fire	99.98%	0
Fire	0.02%	150

Given this probability distribution, the firm's expected loss from fire each year is

$$99.98\% * (\$0) + 0.02\% * (\$150 \text{ million}) = \$30{,}000$$

The company is exposed to a significant negative risk in the event of a fire, even though the expected loss is minimal. The company would make an investment that would have a positive net present value (NPV) if it could totally eliminate the risk of fire for less than the annual present value of $30,000. However, with current technology, preventing any possibility of a fire is probably not possible (or at least would cost far more than $30,000 per year). As a result, the company can control the risk by getting insurance to replace its $150 million loss. In return, the business will give the insurance company an annual payment known as an insurance premium. Insurance enables the business to do this by exchanging a predetermined upfront cost for a random future loss.

10.1.2. Insurance Pricing in a Perfect Market

A company transfers the risk of a loss to an insurance company when it purchases insurance. To assume that risk, the insurance company demands an up-front premium. In a perfect market, how much will the insurance company be willing to pay to cover the risk?

Insurance companies should compete until they are only making a fair return and the net present value (NPV) from selling insurance is zero in a perfect market with no other frictions. If the cost of insurance is equal to the present value of the anticipated payment, the NPV is zero; in this scenario, the price is deemed actuarially fair. The actuarially fair premium can be computed as follows if rL represents the proper cost of capital given the risk of loss:

$$\text{Insurance Premium} = \frac{\Pr(\text{Loss}) \times E[\text{Payment in the Event of Loss}]}{1 + r_L} \quad (1)$$

where Pr(loss) is the probability that the loss will occur, $E[\cdot]$ is the expected payment if the loss occurs, and r_L is the appropriate cost of capital.

The capital cost, r_L, as employed in Eq. 1 Depending on the risk that is insured. Think about the oil refinery once more. There is no doubt that the risk of fire has nothing to do with how the economy or stock market are doing. Rather, this risk is unique to this company and can be diversified across a wide range of assets. Insurance companies can create very-low-risk portfolios with relatively predictable annual claims by combining the risks from multiple policies. Stated differently, since the beta of fire risk is zero, it will not attract a risk premium. Here, the risk-free interest rate, $r_L = r_f$, applies.

Not every risk that can be insured has a beta of zero. Certain risks, like earthquakes and hurricanes, can result in losses amounting to tens of billions of dollars and may be challenging to fully diversify. Different kinds of losses could be related amongst businesses. Health insurance and liability insurance claims are more likely to arise for all businesses due to rising health care costs and stricter environmental regulations. Lastly, certain risks can have a direct impact on the stock market. For example, the terrorist attacks of September 11, 2001, not only caused a $34 billion loss to insurers but also caused the SandP 500 to drop by 12% in the first week of trading after the attacks.

A risk premium will be included in the cost of capital rL for risks that are not fully diversified. Because it pays off in bad times, insurance for non-diversifiable hazards is typically a negative beta asset. This means that when total losses are high and the market portfolio is low, the insurance payment to the company is typically higher. Because of this, the risk-adjusted rate (r_L) for losses is higher in Eqn. 1 than the risk-free rate (r_f). Insurance purchases by businesses result in a return on investment of $r_L < r_f$, but the transaction has no net present value (NPV) due to the negative beta of the insurance payout.

10.1.3. The Value of Insurance

Insurance will be priced in a perfect capital market such that the net present value (NPV) for both the insurer and the insured is zero. However, what advantage does buying insurance have for the company if its net present value is zero?

The answer to this question has already been given to us by Modigliani and Miller: in a perfect capital market, the firm gains nothing from any financial transaction, including insurance. A zero-NPV transaction that has no impact on value is insurance. While insurance enables the company to allocate its risk in a novel manner (e.g., insurers bear the risk of fire instead of debt and equity holders), so the firm's overall risk and, consequently, its value, stay the same.

Therefore, the value of insurance must come from lowering the cost of market imperfections on the firm, just like a firm's capital structure does. Now let's look at the possible advantages of insurance in relation to the flaws in the market that we discussed in Part 5.

10.1.3.1. Bankruptcy and Financial Distress Costs

Borrowing makes a company more likely to run into financial trouble. We observed that the company may incur large direct and indirect costs as a result of financial distress, including agency costs like excessive risk-taking and underinvestment. The company can lower the possibility that it will have to pay these expenses by purchasing insurance against risks that could cause trouble. Financial distress could arise for an airline with significant leverage if one of its planes is involved in an accident and losses are incurred. The costs associated with the distress could amount to an extra $40 million, even though the incident may have actually cost $150 million. By acquiring insurance that will cover the $150 million loss, the airline can avoid these distress costs. The $150 million that the insurer paid in this instance is worth $190 million to the company.

10.1.3.2. Issuance Costs

A company may need to issue securities in order to raise capital from outside investors when it experiences losses. Issuing securities is a costly undertaking. Underwriting fees, transaction costs, costs resulting from underpricing due to adverse selection, and possible agency costs resulting from decreased ownership concentration are all included. Insurance can lower a company's requirement for outside funding and, consequently, the cost of issuing because it gives the company cash to cover losses.

10.1.3.3. Tax Rate Fluctuations

If a company is in a higher tax bracket when it pays the premium than when it receives the insurance payment in the event of a loss, insurance can result in a tax savings when the company is subject to graduated income tax rates.

Consider an almond grower with a 10% chance of a weather-related crop failure. If the risk of crop failure has a beta of zero and the risk-free rate is 4%, the actuarially fair premium per $100,000 of insurance is:

$$\frac{1}{1.04} \times 10\% \times \$100{,}000 = \$9615$$

Suppose the grower's current tax rate is 35%. In the event of a crop failure, however, the grower expects to earn much less income and face a lower 15% tax rate. Then, the grower's NPV from purchasing insurance is positive:

$$NPV = -\$9615 \times (1 - 0.35) + \underbrace{\frac{1}{1.04} \times 10\% \times \$100{,}000}_{= \$9615} \times (1 - 0.15)$$
$$= \$1923$$

The grower gains this advantage because it can move income from a time when its tax rate is high to a time when it is low. If the possible losses are large enough to significantly affect the firm's marginal tax rate, then insurance may provide a sizable tax benefit.

10.1.3.4. Debt Capacity

Companies reduce their leverage to minimize the costs of financial distress. Insurance can ease this trade-off and permit the company to use more debt financing because it lowers the risk of financial distress. We discovered that debt financing offers the company a number of significant benefits, such as reduced agency costs (by reducing excess cash flow and increasing equity ownership concentration), lower issuance costs, and lower corporate tax payments because of the interest tax shield.

10.1.3.5. Managerial Incentives

Insurance reduces volatility caused by risks outside of management's control, making the company's profits and stock price useful tools for assessing management effectiveness. As a result, the company can depend more on these metrics for performance-based pay plans without putting managers at needless risk. Furthermore, insurance can promote concentrated ownership by an outside director or investor who will keep an eye on the company and its management by reducing stock volatility.

10.1.3.6. Risk Assessment

Risk assessment is their area of expertise. They frequently have more knowledge than the company's managers regarding the severity of specific risks the company faces. The company stands to gain from this information by making better investment choices. For example, requiring the company to get fire insurance suggests that when selecting a warehouse, the company will take into account variations in fire safety and how they affect the insurance premium. If not, the managers might ignore these distinctions. Insurance companies can also offer value-adding safety recommendations and conduct routine monitoring of the companies they cover.

10.1.4. The Costs of Insurance

Using insurance to manage the firm's risk can lower expenses and lead to better investment choices when insurance premiums are actuarially fair. However, in practice, there are flaws in the market that can cause insurance premiums to exceed actuarially fair levels and partially offset these benefits.

10.1.4.1. Insurance Market Imperfections

There are three primary areas where the company and its insurance could clash. First, there are overhead and administrative costs associated with assigning the risk to an insurance company. The insurance company needs to hire salespeople to find customers, underwriters to evaluate the risks associated with a specific piece of real estate, appraisers and adjusters to evaluate the damages in the event of a loss, and attorneys to settle any disputes that may arise regarding the claims. These costs will be factored in by insurance companies when determining premiums. Over 29% of premiums collected in 2011 went toward industry expenses for property and liability insurance.

Adverse selection is a second factor that drives up insurance costs. A company's desire to purchase insurance may indicate that it carries higher risk than average, much as a manager's desire to sell equity may indicate that the manager knows the company is likely to perform poorly. Higher premiums are required from insurance companies to make up for this adverse selection if businesses possess confidential information about their level of risk.

The third element that affects insurance pricing is agency costs. Insurance lowers the company's motivation to stay out of danger. For instance, a business may choose to reduce expenses on fire prevention after acquiring fire insurance. We call this behavioral shift brought about by insurance coverage "moral hazard." Insurance fraud is the most extreme instance of moral hazard, wherein insured parties purposefully cause losses or fabricate information in order to obtain insurance money. According to estimates from property and liability insurance providers, moral hazard expenses make up over 11% of premiums.

10.1.4.2. Addressing Market Imperfections

Insurance firms employ a variety of strategies to reduce the costs associated with moral hazard and adverse selection. They accurately assess the risk of each applicant through screening in order to prevent adverse selection. Large commercial insurance policies require plant inspections and reviews of safety procedures, just as medical exams are frequently needed for those seeking life insurance. Insurance companies regularly examine losses to search for proof of fraud or intentional intent in an effort to discourage moral hazard.

Additionally, insurance companies design their policies to cut these expenses. For instance, the majority of policies have both policy limits, which set a maximum amount of loss that is covered by insurance regardless of the degree of damage, and a deductible, which is the initial amount of loss that is not covered by insurance. Because of these clauses, even after the loss is insured, a portion of the risk remains with the company. By doing this, moral hazard is decreased because the company still has an incentive to prevent the loss. Additionally, insurance companies can use the firm's policy selection to help determine its risk and lessen adverse selection, as riskier businesses will typically choose higher limits and lower deductibles due to their increased likelihood of suffering a loss.

10.1.5. The Insurance Decision

In an ideal capital market, an organization's value is not increased by acquiring insurance. In the event of market imperfections, it can provide value; however, market imperfections also have the potential to increase insurance premiums. Insurance needs to benefit the company more than the extra premium the insurer charges in order to be appealing.

These factors make insurance more appealing to businesses that are currently solvent, do not require outside funding, and have high current tax rates. They stand to gain the most from covering risks that could result in cash shortages or other financial difficulties, which insurers can precisely evaluate and keep an eye on to avoid moral hazard.

Risks involving businesses that are highly susceptible to moral hazard or about which a lot of private information is known are unlikely to make full insurance appealing. Additionally, companies that are already facing financial difficulties have a strong incentive not to buy insurance because they need the money now and are willing to take a risk because their debt holders will probably have to pay for any losses in the future.

10.2. COMMODITY PRICE RISK

Businesses utilize insurance to guard against the improbable scenario that risks like fires, hurricanes, accidents, and other calamities that occur outside of their regular business operations cause damage to or destroy their real assets. However, a lot of the risks that businesses encounter come from inherent business operations. The biggest risk to a company's profitability for a lot of them may come from shifts in the market prices of the products and raw materials they use. For instance, jet fuel is the second-biggest expense in the airline industry after labor. Most significant carriers found it difficult to turn a profit as oil prices rose from a low of $17 per barrel in 2001 to almost $150 per barrel in the middle of 2008. According to industry analysts, the industry's annual jet fuel expenses increase by $425 million for every $1 increase in the price of oil per barrel. In 2011, United Airlines alone spent over $12 billion on fuel—more than 30% of its total yearly revenue. Variations in oil prices are undoubtedly a significant source of risk for an airline.

We go over strategies businesses can use to hedge, or lessen, their exposure to changes in commodity prices. Similar to insurance, hedging entails agreements or deals that give the company cash flows to counteract its price-related losses.

10.2.1. Hedging with Vertical Integration and Storage

By actually investing in assets that have an offset risk, businesses can reduce their risk. The two most popular tactics are storage and vertical integration.

The merging of a company with its supplier (or a company with its customer) is known as vertical integration. These companies can reduce their risks by joining together because rising commodity prices increase both the supplier's and the firm's expenses. For instance, in an effort to reduce expenses, the Japanese tire manufacturer Bridgestone bought a sizable rubber plantation in Indonesia in 2005. The rubber plantation's profits will rise in tandem with the price of rubber, offsetting the increased tire manufacturing costs. In a similar vein, airlines could combine with an oil company to reduce their exposure to oil price risk.

Vertical integration doesn't always result in more value, even though it can lower risk. Remember the main takeaway from Modigliani and Miller: Companies don't add value by performing tasks that investors can complete on their own. Buying shares of the company and its supplier can help investors who are worried about commodity price risk diversify their holdings by "vertically integrating" their portfolios. The shareholders of the acquiring firm would typically find it less expensive to diversify on their own because the acquiring firm frequently pays a sizable premium over the current share price of the firm being acquired.

If integrating the companies creates significant synergies, vertical integration may be beneficial. For instance, Boeing ultimately made the decision to buy several of the suppliers it had used for the 787 "Dreamliner" in order to enhance coordination and quality control and shorten production delays. However, in many cases, the more likely result of vertical integration would be diseconomies because the combined company wouldn't have a strategic focus (e.g., carriers and petroleum companies). Last but not least, vertical integration is not a perfect hedge because a company's supplier faces a variety of risks in addition to commodity prices. Vertical integration reduces one risk while introducing new ones for the company.

Long-term inventory storage is a related tactic. An airline worried about growing fuel prices could buy a lot of fuel now and keep it in storage until it's needed. By doing this, the company locks in its fuel costs at the current rate plus storage expenses. However, the cost of storage for a lot of commodities makes this approach unappealing. Such a plan also necessitates a large initial financial investment. The company would have to raise outside funding if it lacked the necessary funds, which would result in issuance and adverse selection expenses. Last but not least, keeping a lot of inventory would significantly raise the company's need for working capital.

10.2.2. Hedging with Long-Term Contracts

A long-term supply contract is an alternative to storage or vertical integration. Businesses frequently lock into long-term real estate lease agreements, determining the cost of their office space many years in advance. Similar to how steelmakers sign long-term contracts with mining companies for iron ore, utility companies sign long-term supply contracts with power generators. Both parties can obtain price stability for their input or product through these contracts.

Southwest Airlines provides a good example. CEO Gary Kelly devised a plan to shield the airline from an increase in oil costs in the early months of 2,000, when the price of a barrel was almost $20. Upon the airline industry's financial collapse later that year due to oil prices surpassing $30 per barrel, Southwest had already secured contracts guaranteeing a price for its fuel equal to $23 per barrel.

Figure 10.1 illustrates how the savings from its fuel hedge accounted for nearly half of Southwest's profits in that year. Kelly went on to become CEO of Southwest, and the company has kept up this cost-hedging approach for fuel. 83% of Southwest's profits between 1998 and 2008 came from savings the company made on jet fuel—$35,5 billion more than it would have paid if it had paid the industry average.

Naturally, commodity hedging doesn't always increase a company's profits—just like insurance does. If oil prices had dropped below $23 per barrel in the fall of 2000, Southwest's hedging strategy would have forced the company to pay $23 per barrel for its oil, which would have decreased earnings and possibly prevented Kelly from becoming CEO. Southwest presumably believed that, even in the event that oil prices dropped, it could still afford to pay $23 per barrel. As a matter of fact, declining oil prices caused Southwest and a number of other airlines to report significant hedging losses in 2011 and 2012. Notwithstanding changes in oil prices, Southwest's earnings were consistently stabilized at a respectable level thanks to the long-term contracts. The way in which hedging stabilizes earnings is shown in Figure 10.1.

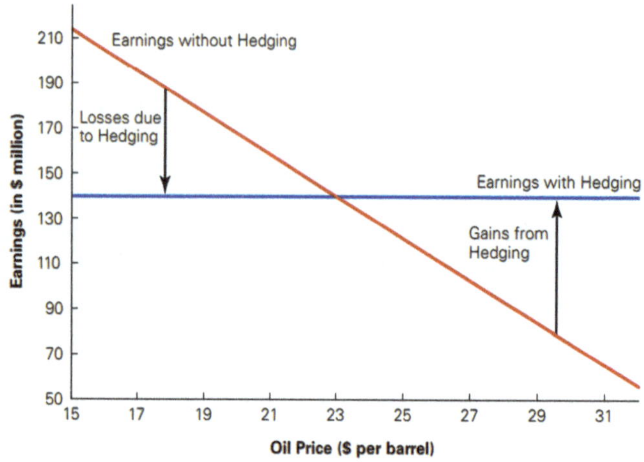

Figure 10.1. *Commodity hedging smoothes earnings by locking in its fuel costs through longterm supply contracts, Southwest Airlines has kept its earnings stable in the face of fluctuating fuel prices. With a long-term contract at a price of $23 per barrel, Southwest would gain by buying at this price if oil prices go above $23 per barrel. If oil prices fall below $23 per barrel, Southwest would lose from its commitment to buy at a higher price.*

Source. https://vk.com/doc399904795_480298778?hash=sLEzOoz8DP50Y9wyqDdcmJvt0O71bxw1T7jHQuy2Q8T.

Long-term supply agreements are frequently bilateral agreements negotiated by a seller and a buyer. These contracts may have a number of drawbacks. They first put each party at risk of the other party defaulting and not upholding their end of the bargain. As a result, they expose the companies to credit risk even though they shield them from commodity price risk. Second, since the buyer and seller are aware of each other's identities, such contracts cannot be signed in secret. The absence of anonymity could have unfavorable strategic effects. Finally, it might be challenging to track gains and losses and difficult or impossible to cancel the contract if necessary due to the uncertainty surrounding the market value of the agreement at any given time.

10.2.3. Hedging with Futures Contracts

One kind of long-term contract meant to circumvent the aforementioned drawbacks is a commodity futures contract. An agreement to trade an asset at a fixed price today at a future date is known as a futures contract. Futures contracts are typically very liquid and are traded anonymously on an exchange at a price that is visible to the public. By selling it to a third party at the going rate, either the seller or the buyer may terminate the agreement at any time. Finally, futures contracts are made to completely eliminate credit risk through a mechanism that we will discuss in a moment.

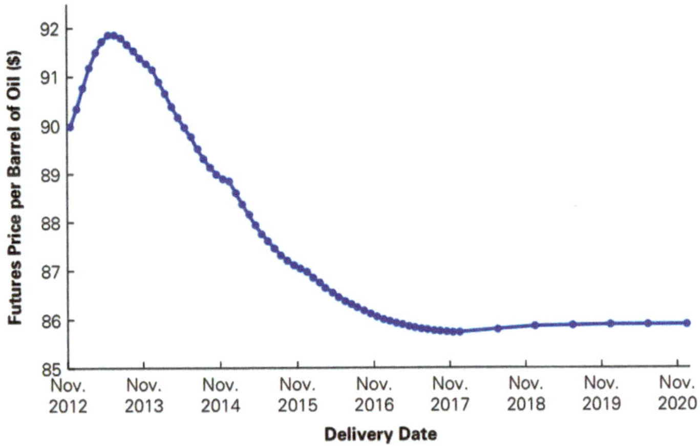

Figure 10.2. *Futures prices for light, sweet crude oil, September 2012 Each point represents the futures price per barrel that was available in September 2012 for the delivery of oil in the month indicated. While the spot price of oil was $90 per barrel, the futures contract price for delivery in November 2015 was $87.*

Source. https://vk.com/doc399904795_480298778?hash=sLEzOoz8DP50Y9wyqDdcmJvt0O71bxw1T7jHQuy2Q8T.

The prices of September 2012 futures contracts for light, sweet crude oil traded on the New York Mercantile Exchange (NYMEX) are displayed in Figure 10.2. Every contract is an agreement to exchange 1000 barrels of oil on the delivery date at the futures price. For instance, in September 2012, buyers and sellers agreed to trade 1000 barrels of oil in November 2015 at a price of $87 per barrel through the November 2015 contract. They were able to fix the price they will pay or receive for oil more than three years ahead of time by doing this.

Prices that are paid today are not the futures prices displayed in Figure 10.2. Instead, they are future-paying prices that were agreed upon today. The market sets the futures prices for each delivery date based on supply and demand. They are based on projected oil prices for the future, modified by a suitable risk premium.

10.2.3.1. Eliminating Credit Risk

How can the seller ensure that a buyer who promises to buy crude oil in November 2015 at $87 per barrel will actually fulfill that commitment? If the real price of oil in November 2015 is only $50 per barrel, the buyer will have a strong incentive to back out of the deal. In a similar vein, in November 2015, if the real price of oil exceeds $87, the seller will be incentivized to default.

Two methods are employed by futures exchanges to stop sellers or buyers from defaulting. Initially, when purchasing or selling commodities through futures contracts, traders must post collateral, also known as margin. This collateral acts as a pledge from traders to fulfill their commitments. Additionally, there is daily settlement of all profits and losses through a process known as marking to market, as opposed to waiting until the end of the contract. In other words, daily calculations and exchanges of gains and losses are made in response to fluctuations in the futures contract's price.

10.2.3.2. Marking to Market: An Example

Assume for the purposes of this analysis that during the 800 trading days that remain between September 2012 and the delivery date in November 2015, the price of the November 2015 futures contract fluctuates as indicated in Table 10.1. A buyer agrees to pay the futures price of $87 per barrel of oil when they sign the contract on date 0. The buyer's position loses $2 per barrel if the next day's futures price is only $85 per barrel. The buyer's margin account is immediately credited with $2 to cover this loss. The buyer's margin account gains $1 if the price rises to $86 per barrel on day 2. The daily profits and losses are displayed throughout this process, which lasts until the contract delivery date. The total of these daily amounts represents the buyer's cumulative loss, which is always equal to the difference between the current contract price and the original contract price of $87 per barrel.

Table 10.1. Example of Marking to Market and Daily Settlement for the November 2015 Light, Sweet Crude Oil Futures Contract ($/bbl)

	September 2012								November 2015
Trading Day	0	1	2	3	4	...	798	799	800
Futures price	87	85	86	84	83	...	62	64	65
Daily marked to market profit/loss		−2	1	−2	−1	...	...	2	1
Cumulative profit/loss		−2	−1	−3	−4	...	−25	−23	−22

Source. https://vk.com/doc399904795_480298778?hash=sLEzOoz8DP50Y9wyqDdcmJvt0O71bxw1T7jHQuy2Q8T.

Delivery occurs in November 2015 at the final futures price, which is the same as the going rate for oil at that point in time. The buyer in Table 10.1's example pays $65 per barrel for oil, but her margin account has lost $22 per barrel. She initially committed to purchasing oil at a price of $87 per barrel, so her total cost is $65 + $22 = $87 per barrel. Instead of waiting until the final delivery date, buyers and sellers pay for any losses as they happen thanks to this daily marking to market. Thus, this mechanism eliminates the risk of default as long as the margin balance is adequate to cover the daily variation in price.

With a fixed price of $87 per barrel of oil, the November 2015 futures contract is essentially the same as a long-term supply agreement. In contrast to a bilateral contract, however, both the buyer and the seller have the flexibility to terminate their positions at any moment (and accept the cumulative gains or losses in their margin accounts). In that case, the contract will be redistributed to a new buyer or seller at the going rate. Commodity futures contracts are the main way that many businesses hedge oil price risk due to their liquidity and lack of credit risk. Many other commodities, such as coal, natural gas, electricity, silver, gold, aluminum, soybeans, corn, wheat, rice, cattle, pork belly, cocoa, sugar, carbon dioxide emissions, and even frozen orange juice, are also covered by comparable futures contracts.

10.2.4. Deciding to Hedge Commodity Price Risk

Commodity supply contracts and futures contracts have zero net present value (NPV) and do not alter the firm's value in an ideal market. However, the company can gain from commodity price hedging by lowering the cost of other frictions. Similar to insurance, there could be tax savings, better managerial incentives and risk assessment, less financial distress and issuance costs, and increased debt capacity. In particular, commodity producers and users can obtain important information from commodity futures markets. For instance, before investing millions of dollars in drilling a new well, an oil company can lock in the price of oil for the future. When choosing how much to plant, a farmer who is uncertain about crop prices in the future can lock in the price of wheat. Although purchasing insurance has comparable potential benefits to hedging commodity price risk, the costs are different. The commodity markets are less susceptible to the issues of moral hazard and adverse selection than the hazard insurance market. Businesses typically cannot control the risk of future fluctuations in commodity prices through their actions, nor do they have access to better information than outside investors about such risks. Furthermore, futures contracts have low administrative costs and high liquidity.

But there are other expenses associated with trading these contracts. First, hedging can sometimes result in financial loss for the company, as Figure 10.1 shows. The company needs to make sure it can withstand the losses until it realizes the offsetting gains, even though these losses will be offset by other gains or savings. Because of this, the company needs to have access to funds that it can pledge as collateral up until the final delivery date. Second, by signing deals that don't balance out the risks it really faces, the company might speculate. Rather than lowering the firm's risk, speculation raises it. Speculation becomes possible when a company allows managers to trade contracts for hedging. Through suitable governance processes, the company must protect itself from the risk of speculation.

10.3. EXCHANGE RATE RISK

Exchange rate fluctuations are a risk for multinational corporations. In this section, we'll look at two methods used by businesses to hedge this risk: currency options and forward contracts.

10.3.1. Exchange Rate Fluctuations

The market price at which one currency can be exchanged for another is known as the exchange rate. Think about the connection between the U. S. the euro and the dollar. The euro's (€) value against the US dollar peaked in April 2008 at a rate of 0.625 euros to the dollar, or comparable.

$$\frac{1}{€0.625/\$} = \$1.60 \textit{ per euro}$$

Similar to the majority of foreign exchange rates, the dollar/euro rate is subject to constant fluctuations based on the supply and demand for each currency in the market. The supply and demand for each currency is driven by three factors:

- **Firms Trading Goods:** A U.S. dealer exchanges dollars for euros to buy cars from a German automaker.
- **Investors Trading Securities:** A Japanese investor exchanges yen for dollars to purchase U.S. bonds.
- **The Actions of Central Banks in Each Country:** The British central bank may exchange pounds for euros to attempt to keep down the value of the pound.

Exchange rates are unstable because the supply and demand for currencies fluctuate with changes in the world economy. The dollar value of euros from January 1999 to mid-2012 is displayed in Figure 10.3. Observe that over intervals as short as a few months, the price of the euro frequently fluctuates by as much as 20%. The euro almost doubled in value in relation to the dollar from its low in 2000 to the summer of 2008, but in the aftermath of the financial crisis, it fell by nearly 20% between August and October.

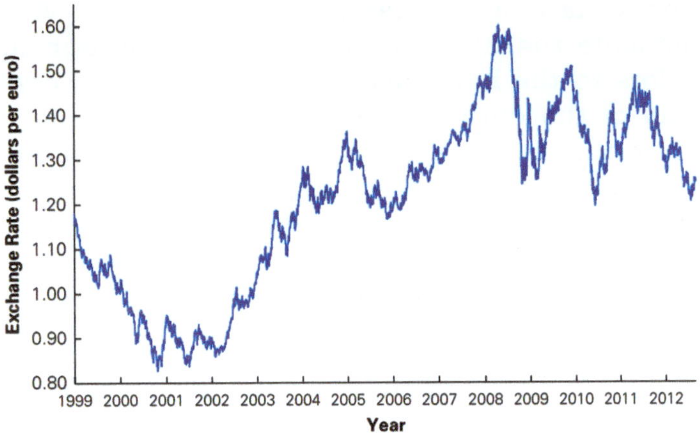

Figure 10.3. *Dollars per Euro ($/€), 1999–2012 Note the dramatic changes in the exchange rate over short periods.*

Source. https://vk.com/doc399904795_480298778?hash=sLEzOoz8DP50Y9wyqDdcmJvt0O71bxw1T7jHQuy2Q8T.

Businesses operating in foreign markets face an issue known as the importer-exporter dilemma as a result of fluctuating exchange rates. To give an example, think about the issue Manzini Cyclery, a tiny U S, is facing. creator of bicycle customs. Manzini must import parts from Campagnolo, an Italian supplier. Manzini runs the risk of the dollar depreciating, increasing the cost of euros and, consequently, the parts, if Campagnolo sets the price of its parts in euros. Campagnolo runs the risk of losing money if it sets its prices in dollars since it will get less money in euros for the parts it sells to the United States producer.

Any import-export relationship faces the general issue of exchange rate risk. Negotiating the transaction might be challenging or impossible if neither company is willing to take on the exchange rate risk.

10.3.2. Hedging with Forward Contracts

When two parties engage in a transaction using different currencies, exchange rate risk inevitably develops. If exchange rates change, one of the parties could be at risk. Hedging the transaction with currency forward contracts is the most popular strategy used by businesses to lower the risk associated with fluctuations in exchange rates.

A contract in which the exchange rate is predetermined is known as a currency forward contract. It fixes a currency exchange rate for a transaction that will take place at a later time and is typically written between a company and a bank. A currency forward contract outlines three key elements: (1) the exchange rate, (2) the amount of currency to be exchanged, and (3) the delivery date for the exchange. Because it pertains to an exchange that will take place in the future, the exchange rate specified in the contract is known as the forward exchange rate. A company can lessen or completely eliminate its exposure to changes in the value of a currency by entering into a currency forward contract, which locks in an exchange rate in advance. Where does the risk go if the importer can eliminate the risk of a stronger euro through the forward contract? The risk initially transfers to the bank that wrote the forward contract. The bank will lose money if the value of the euro rises since it has agreed to exchange dollars for euros at a set rate. First off, the bank can absorb the risk without running the risk of going bankrupt because it is typically much bigger and has more capital than a small importer. More significantly, the bank won't even assume the risk in most situations. The bank will instead look for a different party who is prepared to exchange euros for dollars. A second forward contract with offsetting risk would allow the bank to completely eliminate its risk.

Figure 10.4 shows an illustration of this scenario. An U. S. The importer buys euros from the bank through a forward contract with a forward exchange rate of $0.987 per euro in order to pay for the goods. The importer's cost is locked in at $493,500 with this transaction. In the same way, a U. S. Exporter uses a forward contract to sell the euros to the bank, locking in the exporter's revenue at $493,500. The exporter will be paid in euros. The first forward contract, which exchanges dollars for euros, and the second, which exchanges euros for dollars, are both held by the bank. The bank receives fees from both the importer and the exporter while taking on no exchange rate risk.

10.3.3. Cash-and-Carry and the Pricing of Currency Forwards

An alternative approach that allows a company or bank to remove exchange rate risk is the cash-and-carry strategy. We can use the Law of One Price to determine the forward exchange rate because this strategy offers the same cash flows as the forward contract. Let's start by talking about the various ways that investors can convert foreign currencies into US dollars at a later date.

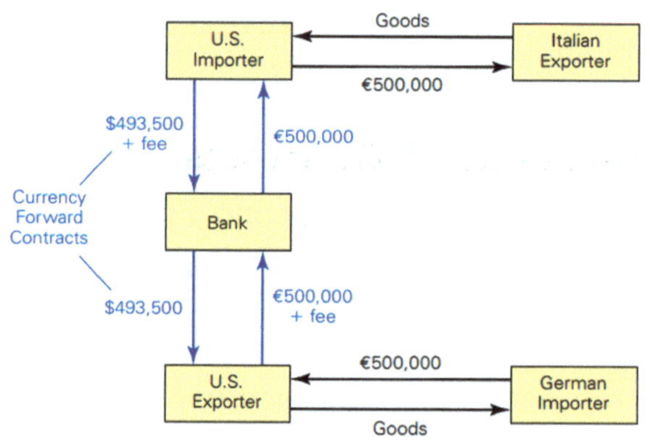

Figure 10.4. *The use of currency forwards to eliminate exchange rate risk in this example, the U.S. importer and the U.S. exporter both hedge their exchange rate risk by using currency-forward contracts (shown in blue). By writing offsetting contracts, the bank bears no exchange rate risk and earns a fee from each transaction.*

Source. https://vk.com/doc399904795_480298778?hash=sLEzOoz8DP50Y9wyqDdcmJvt0O71bxw1T7jHQuy2Q8T.

10.3.3.1. The Law of One Price and the Forward Exchange Rate

Through currency forward contracts, investors can swap foreign currencies at the forward exchange rate for dollars at a later date. We show an example of this kind of exchange in Figure 10.5, where time is represented horizontally by dates (just like in a conventional timeline) and vertically by currencies (dollars and euros). As a result, the timeline's upper-right point is represented by "dollars in a year" and its lower-right point by "euros in a year." We must convert cash flows between points at the proper rate in order to convert them. The rate at which we can use a forward contract to exchange euros for dollars in a year is known as the forward exchange rate, or F$/€.

Other transactions that we can use to switch between dates or currencies in the timeline are also shown in Figure 10.5. At the current exchange rate, S$/€, also known as the spot exchange rate, we can convert euros to dollars today. We can convert dollars today into dollars in a year by lending or borrowing at the dollar interest rate, r$. In conclusion, we can exchange euros today for euros in a year at the rate of interest in euros (r€), which is the amount that banks are willing to lend or borrow against accounts denominated in euros.

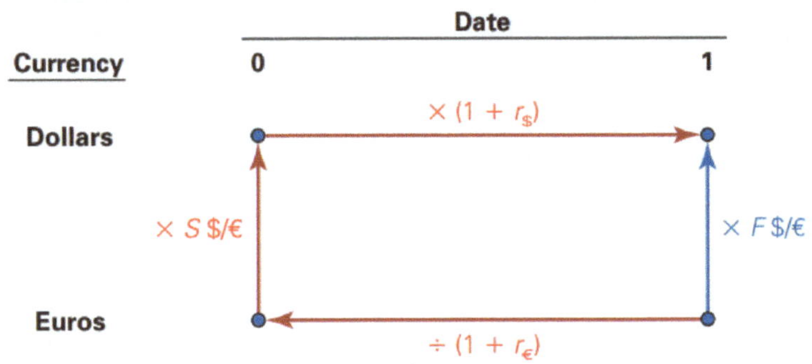

Figure 10.5. *Currency timeline showing forward contract and cash-and-carry strategy the cash-and-carry strategy (three transactions in red) replicates the forward contract (in blue) by borrowing in one currency, converting to the other currency at the spot exchange rate, and investing in the new currency.*

Source. https://vk.com/doc399904795_480298778?hash=sLEzOoz8DP50Y9wyqDdcmJvt0O71bxw1T7jHQuy2Q8T.

As Figure 10.5 shows, combining these other transactions provides an alternative way to convert euros to dollars in one year. The cash-and-carry strategy consists of the following three simultaneous trades:

1. Borrow euros today using a one-year loan with the interest rate $r_{€}$.
2. Exchange the euros for dollars today at the spot exchange rate S$/€.
3. Invest the dollars today for one year at the interest rate $r_{\$}$.

We will receive dollars (from the investment in transaction and owe euros (from the loan in transaction in a year. That is, similarly to the forward contract, we have converted euros to dollars in a year. The reason this approach is known as a cash-and-carry strategy is that we borrow money that we will later carry forward and invest.

Because the forward contract and the cash-and-carry strategy accomplish the same conversion, by the Law of One Price they must do so at the same rate. Combining the rates used in the cash-and-carry strategy leads to the following no-arbitrage formula for the forward exchange rate:

$$\underbrace{F}_{\frac{\$\text{ in one year}}{€\text{ in one year}}} = \underbrace{S}_{\frac{\$\text{ today}}{€\text{ today}}} \times \underbrace{\frac{1+r_{\$}}{1+r_{€}}}_{\frac{\$\text{ in one year}/\$\text{ today}}{€\text{ in one year}/€\text{ today}}} \quad (2)$$

The forward exchange rate is expressed in terms of the interest rates in each currency as well as the spot exchange rate in Eqn. 2. Keep in mind that the ultimate units on both sides of the equation are $/€ in a year.

Let's evaluate Eqn. 2 in an example. In December 2002, the spot exchange rate was $1/€, while one-year interest rates were 1.66% for dollars and 3% for euros. From Eqn. 2, the no-arbitrage forward exchange rate in December 2002 for an exchange to take place one year later was;

$$F = S \times \frac{1+r_{\$}}{1+r_{€}} = (\$1/€) \times \frac{1.0166}{1.0300} = \$0.987/€$$

Eqn. 2, sometimes known as the covered interest parity equation, asserts that there exists a relationship between the interest rate differential between the currencies and the variation in the forward and spot exchange rates. Investors are incentivized to borrow in the low-interest currency and invest in the high-interest currency when interest rates vary between nations.

Naturally, there is always a chance that the currency with the high interest rate will lose value while the investment is being held. If you attempt to mitigate this risk by using a forward contract to lock in the future exchange rate, Eqn. 2 suggests that any advantage from the higher interest rate will be exactly offset by the forward exchange rate, removing any chance for arbitrage.

10.3.3.2. Advantages of Forward Contracts

First off, the forward contract might have fewer transaction fees because it is less complicated and only requires one transaction as opposed to three. Second, many businesses find it difficult to borrow money in foreign currencies, and if their credit is bad, they might have to pay a higher interest rate. Large banks typically employ cash-and-carry strategies because they can borrow money the easiest and incur the least amount of transaction costs. Banks employ this tactic to manage the currency risks associated with forward contract commitments.

Eqn. 2 easily generalizes to a forward contract longer than one year. Using the same logic, but investing or borrowing for T years rather than one year, the no-arbitrage forward rate for an exchange that will occur T years in the future is:

$$F_T = S \times \frac{(1 + r_{\$})^T}{(1 + r_{€})^T} \quad (3)$$

where the spot and forward rates are in units of $/€ and the interest rates are the current risk-free T-year rates from the yield curve for each currency.

10.3.4. Hedging with Options

Another common strategy used by businesses to manage exchange rate risk is the use of currency options. Similar to stock options, currency options grant the holder the option—but not the duty—to exchange currencies at a specific exchange rate. Currency options enable businesses to protect themselves against the exchange rate rising above a specific threshold, while currency forward contracts let businesses lock in a future exchange rate.

Table 10.2. Cost of Euros ($/€) When Hedging with a Currency Option with a Strike Price of $1.20/€ and an Initial Premium of $0.05/€

Dec. 2006 Spot Exchange Rate	Exercise Option?	Exchange Rate Taken	+	Cost of Option	=	Total Cost
1.00	No	1.00		0.05		1.05
1.15	No	1.15		0.05		1.20
1.30	Yes	1.20		0.05		1.25
1.45	Yes	1.20		0.05		1.25

Source. https://vk.com/doc399904795_480298778?hash=sLEzOoz8DP50Y9wyqDdcmJvt0O71bxw1T7jHQuy2Q8T.

Let's look at a particular scenario to illustrate the distinction between hedging with options and forward contracts. The one-year forward exchange rate stood at $1.20 per euro in December 2005. A company that will require euros in a year can purchase a call option on the euro, which gives it the right to purchase euros at a maximum price, as an alternative to locking in this exchange rate with a forward contract. Assume that a euro one-year European call option with a strike price of $1.20 trades for $0.05 per euro. In other words, the company can purchase the right—but not the responsibility—to buy euros for $1.20 per euro in a year for a price of $0.05 per euro. By doing this, the company hedges against a significant rise in the euro's value while still reaping the rewards in the event of a fall.

Table 10.2 illustrates the result of using a call option for hedging in the event that the real exchange rate in a year falls into one of the values indicated in the first column. The company will not exercise the option and will instead convert dollars to euros at the spot exchange rate if the spot exchange rate is lower than the option's $1.20 per euro strike price. The company will exercise the option and convert dollars to euros at the rate of $1.20 per euro if the spot exchange rate is greater than that amount (see the second and third columns). The total dollar cost per euro that the company paid is then calculated by adding the option's initial cost (fourth column) (fifth column).

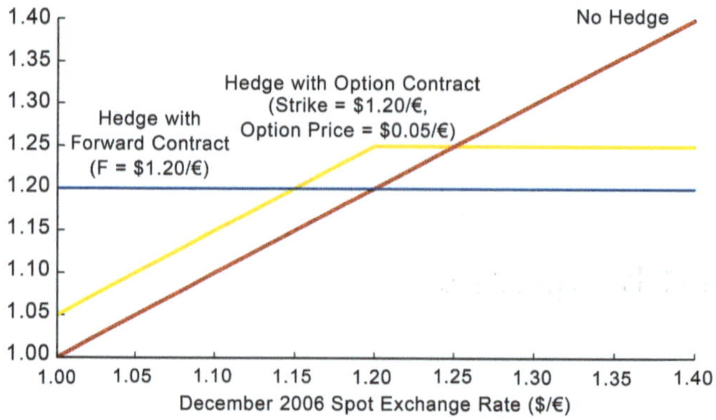

Figure 10.6. *Comparison of hedging the exchange rate using a forward contract, an option, or no hedge the forward hedge locks in an exchange rate and thus eliminates all risk. Not hedging leaves the firm fully exposed. Hedging with an option allows the firm to benefit if the exchange rate falls and protects the firm from a very large increase.*

Source. https://vk.com/doc399904795_480298778?hash=sLEzOoz8DP50Y9wyqDdcmJvt0O71bxw1T7jHQuy2Q8T.

The data from Table 10.2 is plotted in Figure 10.6, where we contrast using options for hedging with using a forward contract or doing nothing at all. The spot exchange rate is the firm's cost for euros if it chooses not to hedge. When a company uses a forward contract to hedge, its costs are fixed and the cost of euros is locked in at the forward exchange rate. Hedging with options is a middle-ground strategy, as Figure 10.6 illustrates. The firm caps its potential costs and stands to gain if the euro depreciates in value. In this instance, the actual exchange rate in December 2006 was $1.30/€, resulting in a $1.25 total cost).

10.3.4.1. Options Versus Forward Contracts

Rather than being forced to pay an above-market rate, many managers would prefer the company to gain if the exchange rate moves in their favor. If a company believes that the transaction they are hedging won't happen, they also prefer options to forward contracts. In this instance, an option gives them the flexibility to back out of the exchange, but a forward contract might obligate them to make an exchange for currency they do not require at a disadvantageous rate.

10.3.4.2. Currency Option Pricing

We assumed in the previous example that ICTV could buy a currency option for $0.05/£. However, how is the price of a currency option calculated? The same way that the forward exchange rate is calculated, it is based on how well banks can replicate a forward contract using a cash-and-carry strategy. Similarly, the prices of currency options are calculated by figuring out how well banks can replicate them using dynamic trading strategies similar to those used for stock options. The Black-Scholes formula and the binomial model are two pricing approaches that are actually applicable to currency options. We use the spot exchange rate instead of the stock price in this instance because the currency is the underlying asset. The dividend yield on a stock is comparable to the foreign interest rate you receive while holding the currency.

Recall that to price a European option on a dividend-paying stock, you simply replace the stock price, S, in the Black-Scholes formula with S^x, the current value of the stock excluding any dividends paid during the life of the option. In the case of a currency option, we exclude the foreign interest earned, so that if r; is the foreign interest rate, $S^x = S/(1 + r;)^T$. Thus, the price of a European call option on the euro that expires in T years with a strike price of K dollars per euro is:

$$C = \frac{S}{(1 + r_{€})^T} N(d_1) - \frac{K}{(1 + r_{\$})^T} N(d_2) \tag{4}$$

where N() is the normal distribution function and d_1 and d_2 are calculated using the fact that $S^x/PV(K) = F_T/K$, where F_T is the forward exchange rate from Eqn. 3:

$$d_1 = \frac{\ln(F_T/K)}{\sigma\sqrt{T}} + \frac{\sigma\sqrt{T}}{2} \quad \text{and} \quad d_2 = d_1 - \sigma\sqrt{T} \tag{5}$$

We can also use option pricing techniques to estimate the implied volatility of the exchange rate.

10.4. INTEREST RATE RISK

Businesses that take on debt have to pay interest on it. A rise in interest rates can lower a company's profitability by increasing their borrowing costs. Furthermore, a lot of businesses have fixed long-term obligations, like capital leases or pension fund liabilities. A decline in interest rates can reduce the firm's value by increasing the present value of these liabilities. Thus, interest rate risk is a concern for many firms during periods of volatility in interest rates.

We've looked at a few strategies businesses employ to control interest rate risk. But businesses need to be able to measure it before they can manage it. Therefore, we start out by talking about duration, which is the main tool used to measure interest rate risk. Next, we'll look at how businesses can reduce their interest rate risk by using duration-hedging.

10.4.1. Interest Rate Risk Measurement: Duration

We introduced the idea of a duration bond as a gauge of how sensitive it is to changes in interest rates informally. There, we observed that as zero-coupon bonds mature, so does their interest rate sensitivity. For instance, a one percentage point increase in the yield to maturity from 5 to 6% results in a decrease in the bond price per $100 face value for a 10-year zero-coupon bond.

$$\frac{100}{1.05^{10}} = \$61.39 \text{ } to \text{ } \frac{100}{1.06^{10}} = \$55.84$$

or a price change of (55.84 – 61.39)/61.39 = -9%. The price of a five-year bond drops only 4.6% for the same yield change. The interest rate sensitivity of a single cash flow is roughly proportional to its maturity. The farther away the cash flow is, the larger the effect of interest rate changes on its present value.

Now picture a bond or a portfolio that has different cash flows. The return of a portfolio is the value-weighted average of the returns of its constituent parts; in other words, how will its value change if interest rates rise? Since the maturity of a cash flow determines its interest rate sensitivity, the value-weighted maturity of a security with multiple cash flows determines its interest rate sensitivity.

Thus, we formally define a security's duration as follows:

$$\text{Duration} = \sum_t \frac{PV(C_t)}{P} \times t \qquad (6)$$

where C_t is the cash flow on date t, $PV(C_t)$ is its present value (evaluated at the bond's yield), and $P = \sum_t PV(C_t)$ is the total present value of the cash flows, which is equal to the bond's current price. Therefore, the duration weights each maturity t by the percentage contribution of its cash flow to the total present value, $PV(C_t)/P$.

Table 10.3. Computing the Duration of a Coupon Bond

t(years)	C_t	$PV(C_t)$	$PV(C_t)/P$	$[PV(C_t)/P] \times t$
1	10	9.09	9.09%	0.09
2	10	8.26	8.26%	0.17
3	10	7.51	7.51%	0.23
4	10	6.83	6.83%	0.27
5	10	6.21	6.21%	0.31
6	10	5.64	5.64%	0.34
7	10	5.13	5.13%	0.36
8	10	4.67	4.67%	0.37
9	10	4.24	4.24%	0.38
10	110	42.41	42.41%	4.24
		Bond price = 100.00	100.00%	Duration = 6.76 yrs

Source. https://vk.com/doc399904795_480298778?hash=sLEzOoz8DP50Y9wyqDdcmJvt0O71bxw1T7jHQuy2Q8T.

As demonstrated by the following result, the interest rate sensitivity of a stream of cash flows increases with duration, just as the interest rate sensitivity of a single cash flow increases with maturity.

10.4.1.1. Duration and Interest Rate Sensitivity

If r, the APR used to discount a stream of cash flows, increases to r + ε, where ε is a small change, then the present value of the cash flows changes by approximately

$$\text{Percent Change in Value} \approx -\text{Duration} \times \frac{\varepsilon}{1 + r/k} \qquad (7)$$

where k is the number of compounding periods per year of the APR.

As we can see, duration can be used to gauge a security's or portfolio's interest rate sensitivity. Now, we'll look at how businesses can mitigate this risk.

10.4.2. Duration-Based Hedging

The difference between the market values of an organization's assets and liabilities is what determines the market capitalization of that company. Interest rate changes will have an impact on these figures, which will impact the equity value of the company. By calculating the length of a company's balance sheet, we can determine how sensitive the company is to interest rates. Furthermore, we can insure the company against interest rate risk by reorganizing the balance sheet to shorten its duration.

10.4.2.1. Savings and Loans: An Example

Think about a standard savings and loan (SandL). These financial institutions maintain certificates of deposit in addition to checking and savings accounts for short-term deposits. Long-term loans like mortgages for homes and cars are also made by them. The majority of S&Ls encounter an issue since the length of the loans they make typically exceeds the length of their deposits. A firm has a duration mismatch when its liabilities and assets have substantially different durations. If interest rates drastically fluctuate, the S&L could be at danger due to this mismatch.

The market value and duration of each asset and liability are listed in Table 10.4, which shows the market-value balance sheet for Acorn Savings and Loan as an example. The duration of an investment portfolio is the value-weighted average of the durations of each investment in the portfolio. What is the total duration of Acorn's liabilities and assets? That is, a portfolio of securities with market values A and B and durations DA and DB, respectively, has the following duration:

$$D_{A+B} = \frac{A}{A+B} D_A + \frac{B}{A+B} D_B \quad (8)$$

Therefore, the duration of Acorn's assets is

$$D_A = \frac{10}{300} \times 0 + \frac{120}{300} \times 2 + \frac{170}{300} \times 8 = 5.33 \text{ years}$$

Similarly, the duration of Acorn's liabilities is

$$D_L = \frac{120}{285} \times 0 + \frac{90}{285} \times 1 + \frac{75}{285} \times 12 = 3.47 \text{ years}$$

Take note of the disparity between Acorn's liabilities and assets. Acorn's assets will depreciate far more quickly than its liabilities due to their extended duration. Consequently, an increase in interest rates may cause a large decline in the value of equity, which is the difference between assets and liabilities.

In fact, we can calculate the duration of Acorn's equity by expressing it as a portfolio that is long the assets and short the liabilities:

Equity = Assets − Liabilities

We can then apply Eq. 8 to compute the duration of equity:

$$D_E = D_{A-L} = \frac{A}{A-L} D_A - \frac{L}{A-L} D_L$$
$$= \frac{300}{15} \times 5.33 - \frac{285}{15} \times 3.47 = 40.67 \text{ years} \quad (9)$$

Table 10.4. Market-Value Balance Sheet for Acorn Savings and Loan

	Market Value (in $ million)	Duration (years)
Assets		
Cash Reserves	10	0
Auto Loans	120	2
Mortgages	170	8
Total Assets	300	
Liabilities		
Checking and Savings	120	0
Certificates of Deposit	90	1
Long-Term Financing	75	12
Total Liabilities	285	
Owner's Equity	15	
Total Liabilities and Equity	300	

Source. https://vk.com/doc399904795_480298778?hash=sLEzOoz8DP50Y9wyqDdcmJvt0O71bxw1T7jHQuy2Q8T.

Thus, Acorn's equity will lose roughly 40% of its value if interest rates increase by 1%. The value of Acorn's assets will decline by roughly 5.33% * 300 = $16 million, while the value of its liabilities will only decrease by 3.47% * 285 = $9.9 million, resulting in this decline in the value of equity. This results in a roughly 16 – 9.9 = $6.1 million or (6.1/15) = 40.67% decrease in Acorn's market value of equity.

Acorn requires an equity duration of zero in order to fully protect its equity from an overall increase or decrease in the level of interest rates. A duration-neutral or immune portfolio is one that has no duration, meaning that the value of the equity should not change even in the event of slight changes in interest rates.

Acorn needs to either lengthen the duration of its liabilities or shorten the duration of its assets in order to achieve equity duration neutrality. The company can sell some of its mortgages for cash in order to shorten the term of its assets.

We compute the amount to sell from the following formula:

$$\text{Amount to Exchange} = \frac{\text{Change in Portfolio Duration} \times \text{Portfolio Value}}{\text{Change in Asset Duration}} \qquad (10)$$

To reduce its risk from interest rate fluctuations, Acorn would like to reduce the duration of its equity from 40.7 to 0. Because the duration of the mortgages will change from 8 to 0 if the S&L sells the mortgages for cash, Eqn..10 implies that Acorn must sell (40.7 – 0) * 15/(8 – 0) = $76.3 million worth of mortgages. If it does so, the duration of its assets will decline to;

$$\overbrace{\frac{10+76.3}{300}}^{\text{Increased cash balance}} \times 0 + \frac{120}{300} \times 2 + \overbrace{\frac{170-76.3}{300}}^{\text{Decreased mortgage holdings}} \times 8 = 3.30 \text{ years}$$

Thus, its equity duration will fall to $\frac{300}{15} \times 3.30 - \frac{285}{15} \times 3.47 = 0$, as desired.

A portfolio can be made duration neutral by making adjustments, a process known as immunizing the portfolio—a term that suggests the portfolio is shielded from changes in interest rates. Acorn's market-value balance sheet following immunization is displayed in Table 10.5. Observe that there is no longer any equity duration.

10.4.2.2. A Cautionary Note

Although duration matching is a helpful strategy for managing interest rate risk, there are some significant drawbacks. First, the current interest rate affects how long a portfolio lasts.

The market values of the securities and cash flows in the portfolio fluctuate along with interest rates, which in turn modifies the weights that are utilized to calculate the duration as the value-weighted average maturity. As a result, it will be necessary to continuously adjust a duration-neutral portfolio when interest rates fluctuate.

Table 10.5. Market-Value Balance Sheet for Acorn Savings and Loan After Immunization

	Market Value (in $ million)	Duration (years)
Assets		
Cash Reserves	86.3	0
Auto Loans	120	2
Mortgages	93.7	8
Total Assets	300	3.30
Liabilities		
Checking and Savings	120	0
Certificates of Deposit	90	1
Long-Term Financing	75	12
Total Liabilities	285	3.47
Owner's Equity	15	0
Total Liabilities and Equity	300	3.30

Source. https://vk.com/doc399904795_480298778?hash=sLEzOoz8DP50Y9wyqDdcmJvt0O71bxw1T7jHQuy2Q8T.

The second significant drawback is that a duration-neutral portfolio is only hedged against changes in interest rates that have an equal impact on all yields. Stated differently, it provides protection against parallel upward or downward movements in the yield curve. Despite having a shorter duration, short-term securities would lose value in comparison to long-term securities if short-term interest rates increased while long-term rates stayed unchanged. To mitigate the risk of such shifts in the yield curve's slope, more techniques—which are outside the purview of this article—are needed.

Lastly, duration-based hedging will not shield against changes in the relative credit spreads of the assets, even if they have comparable maturities and distinct credit risks. For instance, Treasury interest rates dropped sharply during the fall 2008 financial crisis, but the yields on corporate bonds with comparable maturities rose concurrently.

10.4.3. Swap-Based Hedging

Through asset sales, Acorn Savings and Loan was able to lower its interest rate sensitivity. Since most companies need their assets to carry out their regular business operations, selling them is not usually a desirable option. An alternative way to change the firm's exposure to interest rate risk without purchasing or selling assets is through interest rate swaps. Similar to a forward contract, an interest rate swap is an agreement between a bank and a company to swap the coupons from two different kinds of loans. This section explains interest rate swaps and looks at some of the ways interest rate risk can be managed with them.

In a typical interest rate swap, coupons based on the current market interest rate for each coupon period are given to one party in exchange for a fixed interest rate payment. A floating rate is an interest rate that changes based on the state of the market. This swap is also known as a "fixed-for-floating interest rate swap" since the parties exchange a fixed-rate coupon for a floating-rate coupon. ."

Table 10.6. Cash Flows (in $ million) for a $100 Million Fixed-for-Floating Interest Rate Swap

Year	Six-Month LIBOR	Fixed Coupon	Floating-Rate Coupon	Swap Cash Flow: Fixed–Floating
0.0	6.8%			0.0
0.5	7.2%	3.9	3.4	0.5
1.0	8.0%	3.9	3.6	0.3
1.5	7.4%	3.9	4.0	−0.1
2.0	7.8%	3.9	3.7	0.2
2.5	8.6%	3.9	3.9	0.0
3.0	9.0%	3.9	4.3	−0.4
3.5	9.2%	3.9	4.5	−0.6
4.0	8.4%	3.9	4.6	−0.7
4.5	7.6%	3.9	4.2	−0.3
5.0		3.9	3.8	0.1

Source. https://vk.com/doc399904795_480298778?hash=sLEzOoz8DP50Y9wyqDdcmJvt0O71bxw1T7jHQuy2Q8T.

Consider a five-year, $100 million interest rate swap with a fixed rate of 7.8% to illustrate how an interest swap operates. Because semiannual coupons are used for standard swaps, the fixed coupon amounts every six months would be 1/2 (7.8% * $100 million) = $3.9 million. The six-month market interest rate, such as the six-month London Interbank Offered Rate (LIBOR) or the six-month Treasury bill rate, is usually the basis for the floating-rate coupons.

Over the course of the contract, this rate fluctuates. The interest rate that was in effect in the market six months before the coupon payment date is used to calculate each coupon. The cash flows of the swap are calculated over its life in Table 10.6 for a hypothetical set of LIBOR rates. For instance, at the first coupon date in six months, the floating-rate coupon is equal to 1/2 (6.8% * $10 million) = $3.4 million, while the fixed coupon is $3.9 million. This results in a net payment of $0.5 million from the fixed-rate payer to the floating-rate payer.

The amount of the difference between the fixed- and floating-rate coupons is what each swap payment is equal to. Different from a regular loan, there isn't a principal payment. The $100 million swap amount is known as the notional principal of the swap since it is only used to compute the coupons and is never paid for. Finally, there is no cash flow related to the swap at first. In other words, the swap contract is usually designed as a "zero-cost" security, just like forward and futures contracts. In order to ensure that the swap is a fair deal, the swap contract's fixed rate is set based on the state of the market has a zero net present value on both sides.

10.4.3.1. Combining Swaps with Standard Loans

Interest rate swaps are a common tool used by corporations to reduce their exposure to interest rate fluctuations. There are two reasons why an organization's loan interest rate might change. First, there could be changes to the market's risk-free interest rate. Second, the spread the company has to pay over the risk-free interest rate is determined by its credit quality, which can change over time. Firms can decide which of these sources of interest rate risk they will eliminate and which they will tolerate by combining loans and swaps. Let's look at a common illustration.

The machine tool manufacturer Alloy Cutting Corporation (ACC) is currently growing its business. To finance this expansion, $10 million in loans are required. The 10-year interest rate is currently 6%, while the six-month interest rate (LIBOR) is currently 4%; however, these rates are only available to AA-rated companies. The bank will charge the company a spread of 1% above these rates due to ACC's current low credit rating.

The managers of ACC are debating whether or not to take out a long-term, 10-year loan, or whether to borrow money on a short-term basis and refinance it every six months. If they take out a short-term loan, they are concerned that ACC may experience financial difficulties due to the higher interest rates they will have to pay when they refinance the debt if interest rates rise significantly. By locking in the interest rate for 10 years and taking out a long-term loan, they can minimize this risk. Yet there's a drawback to long-term borrowing as well. The managers of ACC anticipate that as the expansion brings in more money over the coming years, their company's credit rating will rise. If they take out a 10-year loan, ACC will have to pay a spread determined by the state of its credit at that time.

These trade-offs are highlighted in Table 10.7. Long-term borrowing has the benefit of interest rate locking, but it also has the drawback of preventing ACC from benefiting from its rising credit quality. While ACC can profit from short-term borrowing as its credit quality rises, there is a chance that interest rates will rise.

In this situation, ACC can use an interest rate swap to combine the best of both strategies. First, ACC can borrow the $10 million it needs for expansion using a short-term loan that is rolled over every six months. The interest rate on each loan will be $\tilde{r}_t + \delta_t$, where $\tilde{r}_t$ is the new (LIBOR) market rate and δ_t is the spread ACC must pay based on its credit rating at the time. Given ACC's belief that its credit quality will improve over time, δ_t should decline from its current 1% level.

Table 10.7. Trade-Offs of Long-Term Versus Short-Term Borrowing for ACC

Strategy	Pro	Con
Borrow long term at 6% + 1% = 7% fixed rate	Lock in current low interest rates at 6%	Lock in current high spread of 1% given low initial credit rating
Borrow short-term at $\tilde{r}_t + \delta_t$	Get benefit of spread δ_t falling below 1% as credit rating improves	Risk of an increase in interest rates $\tilde{r}_t$ above 6%

Note: $\tilde{r}_t$ is the six-month interest rate (LIBOR) on date t. δ_t is the spread ACC must pay based on its credit rating on date t.

Source. https://vk.com/doc399904795_480298778?hash=sLEzOoz8DP50Y9wyqDdcmJvt0O71bxw1T7jHQuy2Q8T.

Next, to eliminate the risk of an increase in the interest rate it will pay in the future, $\tilde{r}_t$, ACC can enter into a 10-year interest rate swap in which it agrees to pay a fixed rate of 6% per year in exchange for receiving the floating rate $\tilde{r}_t$. Combining the cash flows from the swap with ACC's short-term borrowing, we can compute ACC's net borrowing cost as follows:

Short-Term Loan Rate		Fixed Rate Due on Swap		Floating Rate Received from Swap		Net Borrowing Cost
$\tilde{r}_t + \delta_t$	+	6%	−	$\tilde{r}_t$	=	$6\% + \delta_t$

That is, ACC will have an initial net borrowing cost of 7% (given its current credit spread of 1%), but this cost will decline in the future as its credit rating improves and the spread δ_t declines. At the same time, this strategy protects ACC from an increase in interest rates.

10.4.3.2. Using a Swap to Change Duration

Interest rate swaps with duration-hedging techniques are also available to businesses. A swap's initial value of zero will change over time in response to changes in interest rates. The value of the swap will decrease for the party receiving the fixed rate and increase for the party paying the fixed rate in response to an increase in interest rates.

We can compute the interest rate sensitivity of a swap for the party receiving the fixed rate by considering it as a portfolio consisting of long-term bonds and short-term bonds, each with a face value equivalent to the notional principal. Consequently, a portfolio consisting of a 10-year, $10 million bond with a 6% coupon rate and a 6-month, $10 million bond at the current short-term rate is equal to a 10-year, $10 million interest swap with a 6% fixed rate. Similarly, the party making the fixed rate payment is long a six-month bond and short a 10-year bond.

As a result, a swap contract will adjust a portfolio's duration based on the variance between the corresponding long- and short-term bond durations. We can utilize Eq. 10 to find the notional principal needed to make a specific duration change. When used in this manner, swaps provide a practical means of adjusting a portfolio's duration without having to purchase or sell any assets.

CASE STUDY

THE CASE OF ABC MANUFACTURING INC.

Background

ABC Manufacturing Inc. is a mid-sized company in the industrial equipment sector, known for its high-quality machinery and robust market presence. The company operates globally, with significant revenue streams from North America, Europe, and Asia. Despite its strong market position, ABC faced considerable financial risks due to economic uncertainties, currency fluctuations, and volatile commodity prices, which could potentially impact its profitability and financial stability.

Identified Risks

1. **Market Risk**: ABC was exposed to significant fluctuations in raw material costs, particularly steel and aluminum, which are crucial for its manufacturing processes. These commodities experienced price volatility due to global supply chain disruptions and geopolitical tensions.
2. **Currency Risk**: With substantial revenue generated from international markets, ABC faced currency risk, especially against the euro and the Japanese yen. Fluctuations in exchange rates could lead to unpredictable profit margins and affect the overall financial performance.
3. **Interest Rate Risk**: ABC had significant long-term debt with variable interest rates. Changes in interest rates could affect the company's debt servicing costs, impacting its financial health.
4. **Operational Risk**: ABC's complex supply chain and dependence on just-in-time inventory systems made it vulnerable to disruptions, which could lead to production delays and increased costs.

Risk Management Strategies

To mitigate these risks, ABC implemented a comprehensive risk management plan, focusing on the following strategies:

1. **Commodity Hedging**: ABC entered into futures contracts for steel and aluminum to lock in prices and reduce the impact of price fluctuations. By doing so, the company could stabilize its production costs and maintain consistent profit margins.
2. **Currency Hedging**: To manage currency risk, ABC used forward contracts and options to hedge against unfavorable exchange rate movements. For instance,

it hedged its euro-denominated revenues by entering into forward contracts that locked in favorable exchange rates for future dates.

3. **Interest Rate Swaps**: ABC employed interest rate swaps to convert a portion of its variable-rate debt into fixed-rate debt. This strategy helped stabilize interest expenses and reduce the risk of increased debt servicing costs due to rising interest rates.
4. **Supply Chain Diversification**: ABC diversified its supplier base and invested in alternative logistics routes to mitigate operational risks. It also increased its inventory buffer for critical components to ensure continuity in production during supply chain disruptions.

Outcome and Lessons Learned

The implementation of these risk management strategies proved effective for ABC Manufacturing Inc. The company successfully mitigated the adverse effects of raw material price volatility, currency fluctuations, and interest rate changes. As a result, ABC maintained stable profit margins and enhanced its financial resilience.

Key lessons from ABC's experience include the importance of proactive risk identification and the need for a diversified approach to risk management. By using a combination of financial instruments and operational strategies, ABC was able to safeguard its financial health and continue its growth trajectory despite a challenging economic environment.

This case underscores the critical role of risk management in corporate finance, highlighting how strategic planning and the use of appropriate financial tools can help companies navigate uncertainties and maintain financial stability.

CLASS ACTIVITY

Assign a task where students analyze a current financial news article involving a corporate risk and propose a risk management strategy for the company involved. A multinational corporation experiences frequent cyber-attacks threatening its data security. What measures should it adopt to safeguard against these risks?

SUMMARY

- Insurance is the most common method firms use to reduce risk. Many firms purchase property insurance to insure their assets against hazards such as fire, storm damage, vandalism, earthquakes, and other natural and environmental risks.
- In a perfect market without other frictions, insurance companies should compete until they are just earning a fair return and the NPV from selling insurance is zero.
- Firms use insurance to protect against the unlikely event that their real assets are damaged or destroyed by hazards such as fires, hurricanes, accidents, and other catastrophes that are outside their normal course of business.
- Firms can hedge risk by making real investments in assets with offsetting risk. The most common strategies are vertical integration and storage.
- In a perfect market, commodity supply contracts and futures contracts are zero-NPV investments that do not change the value of the firm.
- An exchange rate is the market rate at which one currency can be exchanged for another currency.
- Exchange rate risk naturally arises whenever transacting parties use different currencies: One of the parties will be at risk if exchange rates fluctuate.
- Currency forward contracts allow investors to exchange a foreign currency in the future for dollars in the future at the forward exchange rate.
- Firms that borrow must pay interest on their debt. An increase in interest rates raises firms' borrowing costs and can reduce their profitability.
- A portfolio with a zero duration is called a duration-neutral portfolio or an immunized portfolio, which means that for small interest rate fluctuations, the value of equity should remain unchanged.

REVIEW QUESTIONS

1. Discuss the insurance pricing in a perfect market.
2. What do you understand by commodity price risk?
3. Write short note on exchange rate risk.
4. What is the duration of Acorn's equity?
5. What is swap-based hedging?

REFERENCES

1. Black, F., & Scholes, M. (1973). The pricing of options and corporate liabilities. *Journal of Political Economy, 81*(3), 637–654.
2. Brealey, R. A., Myers, S. C., & Allen, F. (2019). *Principles of Corporate Finance* (13th ed.). McGraw-Hill Education.
3. Chance, D. M., & Brooks, R. (2015). *An Introduction to Derivatives and Risk Management* (10th ed.). Cengage Learning.
4. Crouhy, M., Galai, D., & Mark, R. (2001). *Risk Management.* McGraw-Hill.
5. Culp, C. L. (2001). *The Risk Management Process: Business Strategy and Tactics.* Wiley.
6. Damodaran, A. (2007). *Strategic Risk Taking: A Framework for Risk Management.* Pearson Prentice Hall.
7. Froot, K. A., Scharfstein, D. S., & Stein, J. C. (1993). Risk management: Coordinating corporate investment and financing policies. *The Journal of Finance, 48*(5), 1629–1658.
8. Hull, J. C. (2018). *Risk Management and Financial Institutions* (5th ed.). Wiley.
9. Jensen, M. C., & Meckling, W. H. (1976). Theory of the firm: Managerial behavior, agency costs and ownership structure. *Journal of Financial Economics, 3*(4), 305–360.
10. Jorion, P. (2007). *Value At Risk: The New Benchmark for Managing Financial Risk* (3rd ed.). McGraw-Hill.
11. Merton, R. C. (1974). On the pricing of corporate debt: The risk structure of interest rates. *The Journal of Finance, 29*(2), 449–470.
12. Modigliani, F., & Miller, M. H. (1958). The cost of capital, corporation finance and the theory of investment. *The American Economic Review, 48*(3), 261–297.
13. Moles, P. (2016). *Financial Risk Management: Sources of Risk.* Wiley.
14. Roll, R. (1977). A critique of the asset pricing theory's test's part I: On past and potential testability of the theory. *Journal of Financial Economics, 4*(2), 129–176.
15. Ross, S. A. (1973). The economic theory of agency: The principal's problem. *The American Economic Review, 63*(2), 134–139.
16. Shapiro, A. C., & Titman, S. (1986). An integrated approach to corporate risk management. *The Journal of Financial and Quantitative Analysis, 21*(3), 251–270.
17. Sharpe, W. F. (1964). Capital asset prices: A theory of market equilibrium under conditions of risk. *The Journal of Finance, 19*(3), 425–442.
18. Smith, C. W., & Stulz, R. M. (1985). The determinants of firms' hedging policies. *Financial Management, 20*(4), 391–405.
19. Smith, C. W., & Stulz, R. M. (1985). The determinants of firms' hedging policies. *The Journal of Financial and Quantitative Analysis, 20*(4), 391–405.
20. Stulz, R. M. (2003). *Risk Management and Derivatives.* Southwestern.

Index

I

J

L

M

N

T

U

V

W

Y